MAGGIE SMITH

Also by Michael Coveney

The Citz: 21 Years of the Glasgow Citizens Theatre (1990)

The Aisle is Full of Noises (1994)

The World According to Mike Leigh (1996)

Knight Errant: Memoirs of a Vagabond Actor
(with Robert Stephens) (1996)

Cats on a Chandelier: The Andrew Lloyd Webber Story (1999)

Ken Campbell: The Great Caper (2011)

MICHAEL COVENEY

MAGGIE SMITH

A Biography

WEIDENFELD & NICOLSON

First published in Great Britain in 2015
by Weidenfeld & Nicolson

1 3 5 7 9 10 8 6 4 2

A CIP catalogue record for this book is
available from the British Library.

ISBN 978 1 474 60023 1 (HB)
ISBN 978 1 474 60114 6 (TPB)

Typeset at The Spartan Press Ltd,
Lymington, Hants

Printed and bound by CPI Group (UK) Ltd,
Croydon, CR0 4YY

The Orion Publishing Group's policy is to use papers that
are natural, renewable and recyclable and made from wood
grown in sustainable forests. The logging and manufacturing
processes are expected to conform to environmental
regulations of the country of origin.

Weidenfeld & Nicolson
The Orion Publishing Group Ltd
Carmelite House
50 Victoria Embankment
London EC4Y 0DZ

An Hachette UK Company
www.orionbooks.co.uk

CONTENTS

LIST OF ILLUSTRATIONS

SECTION ONE

Margaret, aged three

With her mother and brothers at Sandringham, 1938

Aged ten

Her parents, Meg and Nat Smith, 1965

At the Oxford High School for Girls, 1951

As Viola in *Twelfth Night*, 1952

With Kenneth Williams and members of the cast of *Share My Lettuce*, 1957 (David Sim / ArenaPal)

With George Nader in *Nowhere to Go*, 1958 (BFI / Studiocanal Films Ltd)

In *Strip the Willow*, 1960 (Mirrorpix)

Backstage preparing for *Mary, Mary*, 1963 (Mirrorpix)

With Laurence Olivier in *Othello*, 1965 (REX Shutterstock)

With Robert Stephens in *Much Ado About Nothing*, 1965 (Zoë Dominic)

With Peter Ustinov in *Hot Millions*, 1968 (ClassicStock / Alamy)

In *The Prime of Miss Jean Brodie*, 1969 (Silver Screen Collection / Getty Images)

Tigbourne Court

With newborn Toby, 1969 (Ian Showell / Keystone / Hulton Archive / Getty)

Celebrating her Oscar victory, 1970 (Peter Stone / Mirrorpix)

As Hedda Gabler, 1970 (Zoë Dominic)

SECTION TWO

Backstage with Robert Stephens, 1971 (John Olson / The LIFE Picture Collection / Getty)

With Robert in Malibu (John Olson / The LIFE Picture Collection / Getty)

With Robert and their sons, 1972 (Daily Mail / REX)

On the set of *Travels with My Aunt* with George Cukor, 1972 (akg-images / Album / MGM)

As Portia in *The Merchant of Venice*, 1972 (BBC Photo Library)

As Epifania in *The Millionairess*, 1972 (BBC Photo Library)

With Robert Stephens in *Private Lives*, 1972 (Zoë Dominic)

With Timothy Bottoms in *Love and Pain and the Whole Damn Thing*, 1973 (Columbia Pictures / Getty)

The Stratford Festival Theatre, Ontario (Zoë Dominic)

With Jeremy Brett in *The Way of the World*, 1976 (Zoë Dominic)

As Cleopatra in *Antony and Cleopatra*, 1976 (Zoë Dominic)

As Rosalind in *As You Like It*, 1977 (Zoë Dominic)

With David Niven in *Murder by Death*, 1976 (AF Archive / Alamy)

In *Death on the Nile*, 1978 (Moviestore Collection / REX)

With Diana Rigg in *Evil Under the Sun*, 1982 (Moviestore Collection / REX)

With Michael Caine in *California Suite*, 1978 (Moviestore Collection / Alamy)

With Laurence Olivier and members of the cast of *Clash of the Titans*, 1981 (AF Archive / Alamy)

With Michael Palin in *A Private Function*, 1984 (Island / Everett / REX)

With Beverley Cross and her sons, 1986 (Ian Cook)

At home with Beverley, 1986 (Ian Cook)

SECTION THREE

With Joan Plowright in *The Way of the World*, 1984 (Photostage)

As Jocasta in *The Infernal Machine*, 1986 (Donald Cooper / Photostage)

With Margaret Tyzack in *Lettice and Lovage*, 1987 (Zoë Dominic)

In *The Lonely Passion of Judith Hearne*, 1987 (akg-images / Album)

As Lady Bracknell with members of the cast of *The Importance of Being Earnest*, 1993 (Photostage)

As Miss Shepherd in *The Lady in the Van*, 1999 (John Haynes / Lebrecht Music & Arts)

'Of those whose business it is to imitate humanity in general and who do it sometimes admirably, sometimes abominably, some record is due to the world; but the player's art is one that perishes with him, and leaves no traces of itself but in the faint descriptions of the pen.'

William Hazlitt

'You have to have been desperately unhappy before you can play comedy, so that nothing can frighten you any more. And you can't do tragedy before you know absolute happiness, because having known that you are safe.'

Edith Evans

In the Company of a Secret Star

'I saw that Mary Smith in *Maggie, Maggie* . . .' The play was really called *Mary, Mary*, and Maggie Smith liked the chance, overheard remark because it jumbled up her identity with that of a character who never existed. Actors use and subsume their personalities in the identities of figments. They want both to hide behind someone else and to show off. By moulding imaginary characters to their own physical reality, they unwittingly reveal themselves, or a small part of themselves. And yet, with Maggie Smith, the mystery remains. She is, for starters, very funny. But, like the greatest of vaudevillians, she believes that she only properly exists in the spotlight. What she thinks of the world – ghastly and depressing, on the whole – she believes is of no interest to anyone else. She is brilliant, and she can be demanding. But she is not grand, and she is not boring. At work, she is obsessive. She looks at all people, all vanities and all enterprises, with a mocking sense of disquiet and disbelief. Her fear and astonishment at the world, allied to her instinctive technical talent, and her innate intelligence, have made her a great stage actress in both comedy and tragedy, and an international film star.

She has gone from revue to West End stardom, from the Old Vic before the advent of the National Theatre, to distinction as a founder member of Sir Laurence Olivier's first National Theatre company. She has won two Academy Awards, five *Evening Standard* best actress awards and, in recent years, achieved phenomenal worldwide success in the Harry Potter films and *Downton Abbey*. She was married for eight years to the vagabond actor Robert Stephens and had two sons with him. She disappeared from Britain for five years to lead the classical company at Stratford, Ontario, and to make films in Los Angeles. Her background is ordinary, her talent exceptional. Maggie Smith, even to those who know her best, is not only a mystery, but also an enigma.

'A star is someone with that little bit extra,' said Noël Coward, but the definition crumbles when you try to define 'bit extra'. An audience knows a star when it sees one. On screen, the cliché is that the camera loves a star. In the theatre, certain basic qualities of stardom are quantifiable: total audibility, eye contact throughout the house, animal magnetism, the precise ability to convey the process of thought, and physical allure, even with the back turned on the audience. In Maggie's case, the very pronunciation of her name stirs expectation and raises the spirits. As the journalist Bernard Levin once said, 'There's a glow around her, on stage and off, and everybody knows about that glow. It's real.' And yet, of all palpable stars, she is the last to place a boorish insistence on her status. Some big stars, such as Vanessa Redgrave and Helen Mirren, are perfectly charming and approachable people, but even in those two cases, the portcullis will descend at moments of crisis: they become elevated and remote. Maggie is unusual in that she behaves at all times as if she has no power or status whatsoever. On the night of her second son Toby's professional stage début in *Tartuffe* in 1991 at the Playhouse in Charing Cross, she stood unostentatiously in the foyer sipping a glass of champagne with screenwriter Beverley Cross, her second husband, impervious to the first-night throng and totally unrecognised. At the same time, Maggie-watchers knew that the 'Do Not Disturb' signs were up.

Paradoxically for a show-off, Maggie Smith chisels away at her work with the monastic dedication of the instinctive recluse. In a golden age of British acting, she is distinctly quiet and 'invisible', even compared to such leading peers as Vanessa Redgrave, who is three years younger, and Judi Dench, who is just three weeks (nineteen days) older. She rarely appears on television as 'herself', gives very infrequent, guarded interviews to the press, lends her name to no causes (well, very few: the Oxford Playhouse, her 'alma mater' is one), her signature to no petitions, her prestige to no boards of directors. Life is difficult enough without the hassle of good works and deeds. And the pettiness of the theatre, the rapacity of the film companies and the vanity of acting, you feel, are phenomena Maggie just lives with as the price she pays for the demon within.

The stage director Peter Wood, who has known her all her working life, says that 'psychological shingles is what she's got, an inflammation of the personality ends'. The Oscar-winning costume designer Anthony Powell is reminded of 'flayed anatomy, with those missing layers of skin, stripped away to show the formature of muscles and bones. She is more scared of being touched and hurt than anyone I know.' The stage offers security in spite of all its dangers. In the theatre, Maggie forfeits her individuality in a curious distillation of her personality, and at last knows who she is, what she should wear and to whom she must speak. Off stage, she is beset with confusion and indifference on all these points.

Or at least, that is the appearance. 'Dealing with her gift' is the spine of her life, according to the actor Brian Bedford, one of her favourite leading men, and nothing much else interferes with that task. She worries endlessly at a text, like a dog at a bone, not to find a new laugh, nor to perfect a new trick, but to make a line, a passage and then the whole play, come alive again. She is renowned for never ceasing to dig and delve in her texts. In rehearsals, she will habitually withdraw from the company coffee break and be found poring over the script at the back of the room. Even on the last night of a run she will sit in her dressing room transfixed over her script, puzzling out what else it might contain. The director William Gaskill, who worked with her in the early days at the National, and is one of her most trusted colleagues, says that Laurence Olivier would arrive at rehearsal with his performance intact, deliver it like a gift and adjust it thereafter if necessary. 'Maggie never has anything finished before she starts,' he says, 'which is why rehearsing with her is so exciting.' And unlike many actors half her age, she still practises her scales and arpeggios. 'Red lorry, yellow lorry' is a drama student's articulation exercise (repeated, fast, ad infinitum) she has never stopped using, like a trusty old toothbrush. She is fanatical about not putting on weight. She trains like a dancer.

Any attempt to 'place' Maggie in the annals of British acting is bound to consider her alongside Judi Dench and Vanessa Redgrave. These two were left to contest the crown of Peggy Ashcroft when

Glenda Jackson departed the scene to pursue a life in politics as a Labour MP. Dench and Redgrave are, in a way, the Gladys Cooper and Sybil Thorndike of our day, while Maggie is certainly the Edith Evans. She has had notable success in many of Edith Evans's roles – Millamant, Mrs Sullen, Rosalind, Cleopatra, Judith Bliss – and is the nearest we come to the idea of the chastely intelligent Anne Bracegirdle, for whom Congreve wrote his most famous female roles. Dame Edith's background, like Maggie's, had not a whiff of theatrical tradition; she was the only child of a minor civil servant in the Post Office and her mother, in Bryan Forbes's phrase, 'set great store by the proprieties', as did Maggie's. Her talent was instinctive, imaginative and untrained, and she had a way of finding words such as 'basin' inherently funny. Like Maggie, she never had to brazen it out in the provinces: 'God was very good to me,' she once said. 'He never let me go on tour.'

Evans knew Bernard Shaw – she was his Lady Utterword in *Heartbreak House*, his Serpent in *Back to Methuselah*, his Orinthia in *The Apple Cart* and, after a protracted scuffle, his Epifania Fitzfassenden in *The Millionairess*, a role Maggie played so deliciously on television – but was not all that devoted: 'He kissed me once. But I derived no benefit from it.' Nothing was allowed to interfere with her theatre work, which amounted to sixty glorious, uninterrupted years after she had been discovered as Cressida in Streatham Town Hall by William Poel. She had no children and was loyally supported by a self-sacrificing husband whom she knew from her teens, and whom she married in 1925 and hardly ever saw, as he worked abroad for British Controlled Oilfields. Like Maggie, Edith Evans was intensely private off stage. She had no real interest in the material world and no ambition in conventional show business terms. And she first went to the Old Vic as a West End star. Unlike Maggie, she wasn't innately funny or clownish, she did hardly any revue, made few films until much later in life ('I don't think I have a film face; it moves about too much,' she once told reporters) and wrote quite a lot of letters.

Maggie could wrest Millamant and Mrs Sullen from Edith Evans because the performances were a fading memory among critics and audiences. But Evans's Lady Bracknell in *The Importance of Being Earnest*, with its almost self-parodying haughtiness and deadly swoop on 'a hand-bag', bedevils any actress, thanks to its notoriety from the

1952 Anthony Asquith movie. Maggie herself used to do impressions of these intonations in her revue days. When Judi Dench played Lady Bracknell at the National Theatre in 1982, she brilliantly side-stepped all comparisons by portraying the tension and melancholy of a much younger dowager, non-stentorian and with the bloom still on, whose husband, dining alone with his meals on trays, was a considerable brake on her social and indeed sexual potential. Her success in the role did not obliterate Edith Evans; nor, to be fair, did Maggie herself when she finally delivered her surprisingly girlish and touchingly vulnerable Lady Bracknell in Nicholas Hytner's revival of the play at the Aldwych in 1993, the start of their significant collaboration together.

But both performances were pretty good swipes at reclaiming the role from old-fashioned, gorgonesque eccentricity. And Dench has also had her mould-breaking Royal Shakespeare Company triumphs as Hermione/Perdita in *The Winter's Tale*, and as Viola, Portia, the Duchess of Malfi, Beatrice, Lady Macbeth and Imogen in *Cymbeline*. She followed her Lady Bracknell at the NT with an equally unexpected, and equally memorable, Cleopatra. Any competition Maggie mustered at that time was confined to Canada, so that the impression, in Britain at least, was that Judi Dench had become our leading tragedienne. The release of feeling, a sort of glorious shiver with an instantly recognisable crack in her voice, characterises all these Dench performances. The renewed monstrosity of Bracknell she left to Maggie to accomplish when she got round to her second Aunt Augusta in *Travels with My Aunt* (Lady Bracknell's Christian name was adopted by Graham Greene for his nomadic gorgon); you could say that she ducked the challenge. Dench generously concedes, though, that it is Maggie's extraordinary way of looking at the world that marks her out, her delightful sense of the absurd: 'She does things in such a daring way that she leaves me standing. She also leaves me laughing.'

Everyone loves Judi Dench, just as everyone loved Ellen Terry. But her drive is of a different calibre to Maggie's, less gnawing, less obsessive. John Moffatt, who was in that first Old Vic company with both 'Jude and Mags' said that Maggie, like Paul Scofield, is possessed by a demanding and driving genius, but that she also skirmishes in the realms of camp by inhabiting a world that is peculiarly her own, rather as the revue star Beatrice Lillie did. Maggie loves a line of Bea

Lillie's, said of a hopeless case leaving the stage: 'She'll never find the kitchen, she's that moody.' And, as Maggie's performances are often a series of elaborately contrived masks that proceed to disintegrate, she further arouses interest in what she might really be like under the skin. As the director Peter Hall says, 'When the public sees Maggie Smith in a play, the public becomes voraciously interested in what kind of person Maggie Smith is.' There are various points of similarity between Maggie and Judi Dench, but that is not one of them. Judi Dench is known to be a cosy, comfy creature with good manners, good breeding and a pronounced liability to burst into giggles and gales of laughter. Everything is more dangerous, acidulous and beadily observed with Maggie.

This is not a value judgement on their respective talents. But Maggie, especially in comedy, presents the role, while Dench puts herself in its centre and works outwards, negotiating the limits of her own characterisation at the same time as she meets the rest of the actors and the surrounding production. This method leads, not all that surprisingly, to the occasional aberration in the costume and wig departments, where Dench is often reprehensibly careless. Maggie never makes such mistakes. With Vanessa Redgrave, the contrast is even greater, and has been well made by Simon Callow. 'To work with Maggie and then with Vanessa,' says Callow, speaking from experience, 'is to go from alpha to omega. They are the Gielgud and the Olivier in the sense that they represent absolute opposites. Vanessa inhabits poetic states and becomes infused with them; but what they are, and where they come from, is entirely mysterious. Maggie, on the other hand, is interested in a particular truth at every moment, and she goes at it like a forensic scientist. She never stops. Vanessa is so much more intuitive, and random; she throws a casual light over something, and because nobody's ever had such a strong beam before, you see all kinds of things reflected.'

Callow believes that Maggie, like Olivier, finds a kind of sanity only in technical craft: 'They are both tremendously needful personalities who don't go into "acting" at all, and must externalise what they do. But if it were only that, you wouldn't be interested in them. Maggie plucks at the script and says, "What am I supposed to do – I mean – I mean, you say – I mean, it's supposed to be funny." Then you say, "It's supposed to be funny," and she will press a button and go into comic mode, and what you have written or translated becomes like Congreve. For Vanessa, you have to create a whole imaginative framework, which takes about five hours to get across. You can't just say, "This woman hates men." Once Vanessa finally takes such an idea into her imaginative world, she takes it on completely. But one idea, put simply to Maggie, can instantly go through her whole performance. She is ecstatic at such moments and becomes the most beautiful, physical and most alive woman you have ever seen in your life.'

The hands, the gestures, what the director Robin Phillips, with whom she spent those seasons at the Stratford, Ontario, festival in Canada, once called 'those witty, witty elbows', the quizzical tilt of head, all are part of a technical mechanism whose inner working remains a mystery. Her friend and fellow actor Alec McCowen says that with most actors he can see how the wheels go round. With Maggie, he can't. Others have puzzled for years over her way of making a line, or a word, sit up and bop an audience on the nose. She once complimented the Irish actor Joseph Maher for 'never answering last night's question,' by which she meant that he played off exactly what came to him from the other actors. Maher confessed that he thought that was what actors were supposed to do. 'You find me five people who can,' Maggie snapped back. Maher also notes the insertion of an intake of breath, even a tiny 'd'you know', as a missing beat in a line that might not otherwise stand up and be funny. This is a good example of a purely instinctive technical gift, and only used very sparingly. Nicholas Pennell, who acted in Canada with Maggie, also thought long and hard about this trick, and reckons it is a way of ensuring that the line sounds as if it is being spoken for the very first time. Little repetitions come into it, too, sometimes almost imperceptibly. Pennell has heard a particular phrase repeated, very quickly, not to reiterate meaning, but to cancel it, so that attention is engaged by starting on an entirely different tack.

The American film critic Pauline Kael said of Diane Keaton in Woody Allen's *Annie Hall* that she raised anxiety to an art form. The phrase has often been reapplied to Maggie Smith as a way of dealing with that peculiar tetchiness and angularity, as well as the speed of thought and motion, which is her ineradicable trademark.

Because of her concentration and intellect, the fluffiness of her acting never curdles, though detractors sometimes complain of emotion that is entirely self-generated or mannerisms that are over-familiar. Maggie's reaction is to shrug sympathetically and mutter that she can't help being lumbered with her own deficiencies, as she adopts yet another gloomy view of the perennially hostile world. She uses her moods of depression to reactivate her determination to work out the best way of doing the next line, the next scene, the next play, the next film. Another profound aspect of her mystery is the fact that so much is buried and bottled up inside. As Angela Fox, mother of Edward, James and Robert, once said, 'You couldn't act like Maggie unless you'd known deep personal emotion. Vanessa's the same.'

Few actors come wittier than Maggie Smith. It is not so much that she deals in polished, highly quotable aphorisms, as did Mrs Patrick Campbell, say, or Coral Browne. With Maggie, it is her slightly jaundiced and highly critical way of looking at the world that both makes her funny and characterises her acting. She cannot help being funny. Harold Clurman once said she thinks funny. She enjoys nothing more, when in the mood, than a good calumniating gossip. 'Laying people out to filth,' she used to call it when opening the file on friends and foes with her sons' nanny Christine Miller. The waspishness of her nicknames for colleagues is invariably tinged with a precise germ of observation. Thus, Michael Blakemore is either 'the wily Aussie' or 'Crocodile Blakemore'; Vanessa Redgrave 'the red snapper'; Patrick Mower, who played opposite her in London in Tom Stoppard's *Night and Day*, 'the lawn-mower', with a drawling emphasis on the 'lawn'; Peter Shaffer, 'Ruby'; Brian Bedford simply 'the Duchess', as in the Duchess of Bedford; and Michael Palin, with whom no fault can be found, even more simply, 'the saint'.

Like John Gielgud, Maggie is widely imitated in other people's conversations, but remains entirely inimitable. Gielgud impersonations always suggest that the actor was ever so grand, which is the one thing he was not. No one, of course, is a better mimic of everyone else than Maggie herself. And like the late Coral Browne, and indeed another demon perfectionist with a devoted cult following, Patience Collier, Maggie thrives in the company of homosexuals. This may have something to do with the elimination of sexual tension in the relationship or the fact that theatrical gays are often funnier and more fun to be with than their straight counterparts. But she has always needed close and confidential gay friends. Kenneth Williams was Maggie's closest friend in her early days. He recounted how, when they were going round Fortnum's together, Maggie was aghast at the prices in the lingerie department. 'Seven guineas for a bra?' she exploded. 'Cheaper to have your tits off!'

Another Williams story has survived many reworkings. When Williams was cast as the young boy in Robert Bolt's *Gentle Jack*, Edith Evans was outraged. In her most extravagantly baroque and fluting of voices, she complained to the management, 'But you can't have him, he's got such a peculiar voice.' This pot-and-kettle story was recirculated when Maggie was said to have expostulated in a similar manner on hearing that Geraldine McEwan, another husky specialist in the loaded coloration of vowel sounds, was to succeed her in the London cast of Peter Shaffer's *Lettice and Lovage*.

When Maggie went to New York with *Lettice*, an all-dancing, all-singing black entertainment about Mahalia Jackson, performed by Queen Esther Marrow and her Harlem Gospel Singers, moved briefly into the Longacre, the theatre which backed on to her own. She was furious at having her backstage peace and calm shattered by the frantic and ecstatic singing going on next door. Executives of the Shubert Organization, who owned both theatres, were summoned to a matinée performance. After much rubbing of hands and beating of chests, they came up with what they hoped would be a satisfactory solution. Apologising for not having thought of it before, they said that they had some wonderful thick black velours which they could string around the inside back wall of both theatres, thus insulating Maggie and her fellow actors against the invasive gospel singing of Queen Esther and her exultant congregation. Maggie went off for a break and returned to the theatre for the evening performance. The company manager met her with the good news: 'I think you'll be very pleased, Dame Maggie. We've hung all the blacks.' Maggie threw him a severe riposte: 'Well, I don't think there was any need to go that far.'

There are two versions of a jovial altercation with Ronald Harwood, author of *Interpreters*, in which Maggie appeared with Edward Fox, and the second of her movies to be called *Quartet*. Even her closest friends have to judge very carefully as to when is the right moment to pay a backstage visit. Harwood was impervious to such niceties and was always popping into the dressing rooms of the Queen's to jolly along the actors in a play that had not been a resounding success. In addition, Fox and Maggie, not the most compatible of co-stars, were hardly speaking to each other. Eventually, Maggie had had enough and when Harwood put his head round her door yet again he promptly had it bitten off. 'Hello, Ronnie,' enquired Maggie coldly, 'and what are you up to now?' 'Struggling with a new play, darling,' Harwood replied. Maggie paused and inspected her nails, 'So are we, dear.' (The other, apocryphal version suggests that Harwood replied to Maggie's question with 'Trying to finish a new play, darling.' To which Maggie impatiently snapped, 'Try finishing this one first.')

The hasty three-week filming of the National Theatre's *Othello* with Olivier at Shepperton Studios in 1965 entailed a lot of rushing about for Maggie (as Desdemona), who was appearing at the time in *Miss Julie* and *Black Comedy* at Chichester. She was flown by helicopter between the theatre and the studios and was met on the first day of this arrangement by the director, Stuart Burge, who had gone out to give her some rehearsal notes. As Maggie emerged in a tangle from beneath the whirring blades, she exclaimed to Burge: 'Christ, I never thought I'd look down between my legs and see Guildford.'

Sister Act was a 1992 riff on Billy Wilder's masterpiece *Some Like It Hot* in which Maggie played a Mother Superior and Whoopi Goldberg a nightclub singer who has witnessed a murder and is taking refuge in the convent disguised as an inmate. She's a nun on the run. On location in Reno, the actors experienced some difficulty with the narrative logic, or lack of it, in the script. The Pope was supposed to have sent a message to his subordinates, but it was not clear how the plot line could have accommodated his intervention with any plausibility. How could His Holiness have contacted the underlings? 'By fax vobiscum, I presume,' offered Maggie from the sidelines.

Whenever Maggie bumps into Alec McCowen, she makes him do his 'turtle routine', for reasons which are now lost in the mists of time but have something to do with the fact that McCowen has an old joke in his repertoire in which he impersonates a turtle. 'Hello, turtle,' Maggie says, and off he goes, doing his turtle business, bubbling his cheeks and clawing the air in doggy-paddle-cum-breast-stroke movements. Does this palaver dignify, you may ask, one of our most eminent senior actors, a CBE and, what is more, a native of Tunbridge Wells? 'Oh, Alec's always been about twelve,' Maggie chortles. Her long-serving dresser, Christopher Downes, was a great collector of Maggie's barbs and asides and immodestly recounted one involving himself at a busy party. Downes was deep in conversation with another guest who was asking, 'Yes, Christopher, but what do you actually do?' At that precise moment, Maggie was wafting past with a tray and threw her voice back over her shoulder: 'He saves people's lives.'

This airiness, this waspishness, is displayed to great effect in many of her movie performances, and also as the Dowager Countess of Grantham in *Downton Abbey*. In the series so far, Maggie's dowager has duelled memorably with Shirley MacLaine, visiting Downton as her daughter-in-law Lady Cora's flamboyant mother; Isobel Crawley (Penelope Wilton) in every scene they share; even a tall new recruit to the downstairs staff: 'Are you really that tall? I thought you might be walking on stilts.' Each line is coloured with either mockery or disbelief, even if it doesn't always rise to the standard of Oscar Wilde or indeed Julian Fellowes himself at his best. She and Fellowes first collaborated on Robert Altman's *Gosford Park* (Fellowes won an Oscar for his screenplay), an upstairs/downstairs murder mystery movie set in 1932, eight years after the end of the fifth series of *Downton*. Maggie played Lady Constance Trentham, a visiting aristocrat at another grand country house for a weekend shooting party where the guests include the composer Ivor Novello (played by Jeremy Northam) shortly after he's made an unsuccessful movie. 'What was it?' asks Maggie, searching for the title, 'The Dodger?' '*The Lodger*,' replies the composer, through half-gritted teeth. (The 1927 Alfred Hitchcock silent movie was not really a flop, and is now rightly considered a cult classic.) 'It must be so disappointing when something ... flops ... like that,' she coos, unhelpfully, with a slight twist of her wrists, inviting a slap that no one would dare administer.

Just before the first airing of *Downton Abbey*, Fellowes and Maggie worked for a second time together on a film called *From Time to Time*, he as writer and director, she as the middle-class incumbent of a country estate whose grandson, during the Second World War, is sent to stay after his father goes missing, presumed dead, in action. There's an extraordinary moment when she stops at a doorway as it seems she has at last reached a sort of rapprochement with her sceptical young grandson, and says simply, starkly and unflinchingly, that she loves him more than anyone else in the world, apart from her own son. Most actresses would garnish this line with an emotional hiccup, or teary sniffle. Not her. She's adamantine stern, and all the more moving.

It occurred to me watching this movie that Maggie has become increasingly adept, indeed expert, in working with children over the past twenty years – in *The Secret Garden*, the Harry Potter movies (she said that her performance was, basically, Miss Jean Brodie in a wizard's hat, and was her pension for life; and that was nine years before *Downton Abbey* started!), *My House in Umbria*, Emma Thompson's second *Nanny McPhee* film – and I imagine that's palpably to do with the fact that she seems to treat them as adults in her acting. She's also an enthusiastic grandmother to the five children of her now middle-aged actor sons, Chris Larkin and Toby Stephens. Their favourite granny highlight is the moment in *Nanny McPhee* when she sits in a cowpat.

Golden times belong, by definition, to the past. But the past fifty years of Maggie's continuous career might soon qualify, not least because of her stage work in Alan Bennett, Edward Albee, Restoration comedy and Shakespeare (more of that in Canada than in England, alas), but also because of the way her screen acting has refined itself from comic extravagance to the raw, naked business of emotional exposition and truth-telling. Twenty years ago, it seemed to me that Maggie sustained within herself this battle between an unrivalled technical expertise and stark emotional revelation. But that expertise has been channelled, almost brutally, in the service of the latter function, and her performances, both on screen and stage, have acquired a severity that softens, rather than a flippancy which stiffens, so that even Lady Violet in *Downton Abbey* is someone you don't mess with before you realise there's a twinkle and a vaguely malicious humour round the edges.

Before *Downton*, her last television drama was Stephen Poliakoff's *Capturing Mary*, in which she gave a remarkable performance of both collapse and reminiscence as a woman stripped of her own talent by a vile intellectual seducer. Half the film, as far as her part in it was concerned, was in voice-over, but it is typical of her forensic methodology that she learned the entire script, off-stage cues and all, and recorded those voice-overs 'live' in character, costume, and on the set. This encapsulated her habit of both performing a role and standing outside of it, a unique ability long ago noted by Tom Stoppard, lending an air of spontaneity and critical wisdom to every role she plays.

— 1 —

The Flight from Ilford

Maggie Smith was born in Clayhall, a residential district in Ilford, Essex, on 28 December 1934. She moved with her family to Oxford in 1939, attended the Oxford High School for Girls from 1947 to 1951, spent two years as a student with the Oxford Playhouse Drama School, took part in countless University productions and made her London début in October 1954 at the New Watergate Theatre Club. In 1956 she went to New York and appeared on Broadway in Leonard Sillman's *New Faces* revue of 1956 at the Ethel Barrymore Theatre where, over thirty years later, she appeared in *Lettice and Lovage*. 'One went to school, one wanted to act, one started to act and one's still acting.' That is how Dame Maggie Smith sums up her life. There's a little more to it than that.

Ilford, a bustling, featureless urban sprawl which is part of the great East London overspill, is not a place bursting with show business connotations. Will Kempe, Shakespeare's clown, is said to have danced through Ilford in 1599 en route from London to Norwich in East Anglia. He stopped only long enough to refresh himself from 'the Great Spoon'. Not a lot happened after that, give or take the odd murder behind a privet hedge, until Ilford was granted borough status in 1926. The great housing development programmes gathered steam. The process had started before the First World War, with the new professional classes occupying the creeping network of solid Edwardian villas which began slowly to displace the Essex fields and meadows beyond Whitechapel and Shoreditch. The population intensified with the coming of the railway and the access it gave to the City of London.

Ilford and environs were solidly lower-middle-class. The idea of aspiration was reflected in the naming of some roads as 'Gardens', to lend an air of gentrification. As a schoolboy there myself in the 1950s,

I have a dim memory of an incongruous nightclub called the Room at the Top, on the top floor of the department store, Harrison Gibson. David Frost, Tommy Cooper, Barry Humphries and many other big, but mostly smaller, names appeared there quite regularly during the 1960s.

You could hardly imagine a less likely cradle for a stylish actress. But Ilford did not produce only Maggie Smith. Ian Holm, the incisive film and Shakespearean actor, and the late Ken Campbell, a remarkable stage raconteur and dabbler in alternative culture, are two of the best-known sons of Ilford. Dudley Moore, the composer and film star who made his name in the revue *Beyond the Fringe*, was born in Dagenham. And, skipping backwards, an actress whose transatlantic theatre fame equalled, and in some ways anticipated, Maggie Smith's, Lynn Fontanne, later Mrs Alfred Lunt, was born in 1887 in Woodford Bridge, an altogether leafier and more exclusive district than Clayhall, but hardly a bus stop or two away.

Margaret Natalie Smith, the third child of Nathaniel, or Nat, Smith, and his wife, Meg, was born in 68 Northwood Gardens. Margaret – she became 'Maggie' only in 1956 before going to America – was a pretty and mischievous little girl who was not particularly welcomed by her two elder brothers. Alistair and Ian, identical twins, had been born six years earlier on 8 December 1928, and were quite content with each other's company. The curious product of this Nat/Meg tree was a bundle of genealogical roots of ordinary working-class provenance but unusual vivacity. By the age of ten, Alistair and Ian had decided to become architects. Margaret cannot remember not wanting to be an actress. All three children did as they chose. But there was very little in their background to encourage them.

That background is essential to any attempt to understand Maggie Smith's personality. Her father, a medical laboratory technician, was a Geordie, from Newcastle. Her mother was a cold and dour Glaswegian. Both parents, like many working-class people, harboured ambitions for their children. They were strict, they were thrifty, they were sticklers for good manners and proper conduct, and they were church-goers. Nat was a devout Anglican, mainstream Church of England, Meg a Scottish Presbyterian.

In Ilford, and later in Oxford, Maggie lived in comfortable, but cramped, surroundings. She is renowned today for the stifled aside, the muttered barb, the malicious crack. You can see why. From an early age she developed two characteristics that are stamped through her professional life like the lettering in a stick of seaside rock: a keen sense of irreverence and a sharp instinct for privacy. She was a lonely child, at odds with her parents, with her school, with her brothers and even with herself. But her instinct was not to rebel; it was to mock tartly from the sidelines and to retain, by stealth, her own spirit and independence. A quiet life in a semi-detached house in Cowley, the Oxford suburb to which the family moved in 1939, was not for her. Cowley, like Ilford, was sleepy, respectable and slightly dull. The front box-bedroom she was obliged to inhabit through her teenage years and early adulthood measured scarcely twenty square feet.

Maggie's parents, too, had made telling adjustments to family expectations. Her father, born in 1902, was the seventh of nine children. Of just about average height and slim build, he was a delicate, chirpy fellow, rather bird-like, with surprisingly elegant wrists and fingers. Maggie's wrist work and elegantly tapering digits are two of her hallmarks. Nat had bright orange hair as a youngster and was nicknamed 'Carrot-head'. His father, a keen gambler and a hardened drinker, was a minor Post Office official who travelled for years on business between Newcastle and Birmingham. Ian, Maggie's surviving brother, still going strong and living with his wife in retirement in France (Alistair died suddenly of a heart attack in 1981), remembers the occasional family holiday in Scotland; but neither Nat nor his young family ever went back to Newcastle. Nat had been glad to get away.

Nat's family was religious, in spite of his father's faults, and young Nat was a dedicated church-goer and choirboy. Though their domestic circumstances were penurious, Jesmond, the Newcastle suburb where they lived, had a touch of class. Nat particularly liked the ecclesiastical garb of surplices and cassocks which was provided by a rich ship-owner in the parish church; underneath, he wore his ordinary clothes, unlike the other boys, who all wore Eton suits. In later life, Nat could preach and he could lecture and he always enjoyed the ceremonies of the church. A performing instinct of some kind was in his genes. He had, in fact, been named after an actor, his uncle Nathaniel Gregory, who had joined the army as an entertainer during the Boer War at the turn of the century. This dramatic relation figured only once in Nat's memory. As a boy of twelve or thirteen, he remembers a middle-aged Uncle Nat paying a call, appearing over the brow of a Jesmond slope in a tight black coat with an astrakhan collar, wielding a malacca cane with a silver knob. There was no question, said Nat, of him not being an actor. 'He was pedantic of speech and quoted Shakespeare all the time, which staggered the household.' Shortly afterwards, Uncle Nat, who was appearing at the Newcastle Hippodrome, cycled to Whitley Bay to visit Doris Rogers, the girl he was planning to marry. He suffered a heart attack, fell off his bike and died on the spot.

A year or so later, in 1918, young Nat left school and began menial work in the local medical college. He took a diploma as a laboratory technician and learned so much about morbid pathology that he was lecturing in the subject three years later, at the age of nineteen. One of the Newcastle laboratory demonstrators was appointed to a children's hospital in the East End of London. He wanted a technician and offered Nat the job; thus Nat moved south and started work in the Princess Elizabeth Hospital next to the Meredith and Drew biscuit factory in Shadwell.

Meg, whom Nat had met in Newcastle, where she had lived for a while in digs, had already moved to London. Six years older than Nat, she was living in Russell Square and working as head cashier for the London office of Maxwell Hart in Victoria Street. The company designed and built municipal parks, tennis courts, bowling greens and golf courses. Meg had originally worked for them in Glasgow. She married Nat at the Presbyterian Church in Regent Square, Grays Inn Road, on 2 January 1928. She continued working, but not for long: Ian and Alistair were born at the end of the year. Meg – christened Margaret Little Hutton – was of mixed Celtic extraction. Her grandmother was born in Newry, Northern Ireland. Her father was an illiterate Glaswegian shipyard worker who could do no more than make his mark on Meg's birth certificate. Meg left school in 1911 or 1912 to work in a laundry where, says Ian, 'the hard and degrading work instilled in her a lifelong horror of such soul-destroying employment'. She must have acquired secretarial skills at night school, because she subsequently worked in the offices of the Gleniffer Motor Company in Glasgow (and in Fraserburgh on the east coast of Scotland) which made marine engines. She then joined Maxwell Hart in 1918 or 1919. She was obviously highly valued by the company, and was appointed to the London office at some time in the early 1920s. Meg had a natural flair for figures. Nat said she could add up three columns of pounds, shillings and pence simultaneously. She counted money carefully all her life. But Ian also recalls her flair for drawing, which both he and Alistair inherited. She was practical and resourceful, and made all of Margaret's clothes when she was growing up.

Once married, Nat and Meg found a house in Barkingside, Ilford. Over the ten years they spent in Ilford, they owned three houses, never selling one when they bought the next, but renting it out. Meg supervised the rent collection and all the family's finances. The boys were born in the second house, in Martley Drive, very near Northwood Gardens. Young Margaret never got on particularly well with her mother; Ian recalls that Meg was not a woman capable of showing her children much affection, although she was fiercely protective of them. Her daughter would later draw almost callously upon this icy temperament and brusque organisational manner in her Oscar-winning performance in *The Prime of Miss Jean Brodie*. Ironically, it was only at that advanced point in Maggie's career that her mother stopped trying to convince her that she should do something sensible, such as a secretarial course, as an insurance against the vagaries of the theatre. She wanted the best for her children, and she believed in hard work. It was indicative of Meg's dominance on important household matters that, after she and Nat were married, they joined the Presbyterian, not the Anglican, congregation in Ilford. Ian remembers his father giving sermons as a lay Presbyterian preacher.

The house in Northwood Gardens was one of eighteen houses constructed in 1934 by the one builder. The neighbourhood was developed in batches as the farmland was sold off and the council gave approval. Ian remembers the 'terrible housing estates' going up around them. He found Ilford dreary beyond measure. One consolation was Clayhall Park, at the top of Northwood Gardens, a little oasis of flower beds and greenery where perambulators could be pushed and fresh air taken. And, a little further towards the centre of Ilford, on the other side of the London arterial road, there was Valentines Park, a sanctuary in olden times, which still exudes something of a holiday atmosphere with its pleasant walks, decrepit wishing-well, artificial lakes, cricket club, cedars and rhododendron dells. There is no bard of Ilford, but the poet Kathleen Raine, who was born there in 1908, evocatively described the provisional exile she experienced before being saved by her vocation and geographical removal to Northumberland. Maggie and her family carried the suburban blight of Ilford with them to Cowley, and although she could never articulate her resentment, it is clear that Maggie channelled her spiritual rebellion into an ambition to enter the theatre.

Ian and Alistair attended the Gearies primary school in Barkingside. In March 1939, they took the written examination, later called the eleven-plus, and won scholarships to Ilford County High School, for many years one of the best grammar schools in Essex. Significantly, Nat told me that his sons had also won places (not taken up) at Bancroft's School, a minor public school in Woodford Green. I suspect that Meg put her foot down on the cost involved. This reveals the extent to which reality and hard choices outstripped Nat's aspiration; his professional life, worthy though it was, smacked a little of disappointment. He was a lab technician whose only bar to professional distinction was his lack of qualifications, rather like the tramp in the Dudley Moore and Peter Cook sketch who shakes his head and says he could have been a High Court judge, 'but I didn't have the Latin'. And yet Nat's career was more than honourable. He took immense pride in his forensic medicine, and his complete absorption in it, as well as his dedication and ceaseless scavenging for detail, is surely reflected in his daughter's obsessive approach to her work.

The work in Shadwell was incessant. Nat remembered how he would arrive home on a Friday night, exhausted, 'and the phone would ring at four in the morning. There was a case of meningitis, say, needing a lumbar puncture, and I would have to get dressed and back to the hospital. I nearly went bonkers. On one occasion, when I'd had no sleep for two or three days, I broke down. And yet I loved every second of it.' In 1938, Nat volunteered, in the event of war, for 'work of national importance'. When Neville Chamberlain returned to England with his little piece of white paper and the Munich Agreement, Ian recalls that the family spent the period of the crisis at a vicarage in Norfolk. Nat and a neighbour in Northwood Gardens had concluded that, if hostilities broke out, there would be an immediate holocaust in London. So the children were dispatched to Hawkeden, near Bury St Edmunds, where young Margaret gave her ever-watchful mother cause for yet more distress by wandering blithely through a field full of beehives.

The minute war was declared on Germany in September 1939, Nat was posted to Oxford and the Dunn School of Pathology in South Parks Road. Thanks to neighbours in Ilford, he found digs in nearby Museum Road. At the end of the month, Meg and the children received the call from Nat to join him. They all stayed for a short while in Museum Road until a new family home was found. This was about two miles south-east of the centre of Oxford, along the Iffley Road in Cowley. As Europe went to war, the Smith family began a new life in 55 Church Hill Road. The house was very much like the one in Northwood Gardens, but with the advantage of being semi-detached. Nat's work became even more complex and interesting. The twins secured places at the City of Oxford High School. And little Margaret, nearly five, was enrolled at the nearby church school, St James's. She later moved to Greycotes, a fee-paying kindergarten and preparatory school on the Banbury Road. Thanks to Adolf Hitler, the escape from Ilford was complete. Nat's collection of second-hand books, which he kept at Shadwell, was lost in a bombing attack. Meg sold all three Ilford houses, and the income, though not exorbitant, would help pay for the fees at Greycotes preparatory school and a new set of boys' school uniforms. Only the best, as far as Nat and Meg could afford it, would do.

2

Schooling in Oxford Accents

The making of an actor is an odd, mostly incalculable, business. But Oxford definitely made Margaret Smith an actress. Her thespian development was part circumstantial, part temperamental. Although she has remained ambiguous on the subject of Oxford all her subsequent life, young Margaret found more room to manoeuvre and thrive than she would ever have done in Ilford. The family became, in a quiet way, an integral part of the medical and intellectual life of the city. Cowley may have been on the suburban fringe, but Nat, as a technician at the Dunn School, was involved in a body of work on penicillin therapy that was, in the words of the *Encyclopaedia of Oxford*, 'among the most valuable undertaken in the whole history of medicine'. The work was led by Howard Walter Florey, later Lord Florey of Adelaide, who in 1945 shared the Nobel Prize for medicine with Sir Ernst Boris Chain and Sir Alexander Fleming, who had discovered penicillin in 1928.

The new house was built between the wars on an estate next to the vicarage of St James's Church, a High Anglican establishment where Margaret attended the infants' school and her brothers painted theatrical scenery for the social club. There was a modest garden, nearby fields and a cemetery where ghoulish games were played. Margaret claims to have been compelled by her brothers to eat deadly nightshade, though Ian had no memory of this. Inevitably, 'the boys', as they were known to everyone, grew further apart from Margaret. Their back bedroom, cluttered with set squares, drawing equipment and two large elephant boards, was out of bounds to the little girl, who was nonetheless adept at making a nuisance of herself by stealing their pencils. There were hardly any toys in the house. It was a spartan, though certainly not deprived, childhood. Years later, Alistair's widow, Shân Smith, recalled a striking detail: at Christmas, the children were never given presents, but ten shillings each, and were told to go and buy what they wanted. Shân, who came from a stable middle-class Welsh background, maintains that all three Smith children, partly because of a repressive childhood, suffered from black depressions and a sense of failure that would haunt them all their lives. Today, Maggie does not, on the whole, look on the bright side of life. Gaiety and good cheer tend to be reserved for her performances, or at least some of them.

The next-door neighbours, the Jenkins family at Number 53, were considered a slightly 'rackety' crowd. Margaret was allowed to be friends with Shirley Jenkins under some degree of sufferance from Meg. Shirley herself, just four months older than Margaret, married an American airman at the age of eighteen and left Oxford for the United States. She remembers Nat doing little magic tricks at children's tea-parties. Shirley used to play the piano loudly in order to gain Margaret's attention, and Margaret would bang on the wall with a poker to let Shirley know that she could hear the music. Meg used the same poker to bang on the wall as a signal to Margaret that it was time to come home.

'During the summers,' Shirley recalls, 'we would, along with other neighbourhood children, do "concerts" in our back gardens. Dancing and singing and dressing up. We did all the usual childhood things – hide and seek, hopscotch, skipping, rolling hoops, whips and tops, frozen statues . . . In the spring we would ride our bikes to Radley Woods and pick armfuls of bluebells.'

The apparent normality of this childhood was a mask for an unusually strict atmosphere in the home. Ian does not remember Margaret being naughty, but there was a marked antagonism between her and Meg: 'It never erupted into the open; it just sort of simmered.' But she was certainly the apple of Nat's eye. The boys were allowed neither bikes nor roller-skates, and Meg forbade them to play rugby at school. If one of the children was scratched or bruised, bandages were efficiently applied, but the underlying parental attitude was, 'What did you do that for?' as though, Ian says, one had done it deliberately. Holidays were a rarity. And relatives were hardly ever made welcome. There was very little money – Nat was never well paid – and Meg watched every single penny. She had a job as an accounts secretary at the local Morris Motors car-manufacturing plant and was out every day. Margaret, cast as Cinderella from a very early age, did most of the ironing and cleaning around the house. She cannot recall her mother *not* going out to work.

Money was found for some things. While the boys settled into their new school and started on the long haul to fulfilling their ambition to become architects, Margaret moved from the little church school to Greycotes. One of her friends there was the novelist Graham Greene's daughter, Lucy, who was one year older but shared the same birthday. There was a piano in the house for a time, and Margaret went across the road for lessons with Mrs Loxton. Margaret was no new Moura Lympany. Her skills were rudimentary, but useful in later life when she was obliged to act at the keyboard, as in *The Guardsman* on stage and *A Private Function* on film. She also took ballet classes at the Vera Legge School of Dancing in a studio on the top floor of Taphouse's in Magdalen Street, equidistant by about fifty yards from both the Playhouse and the New Theatre.

No Oxford pantomime was complete in those days without a pirouetting band of Vera's prepubescent chorines, who were billed as 'Vera Legge's Juveniles'. There are photographs of the nine-year-old Margaret in her red satin blouse (with the initials 'VL' on the left breast), white pleated skirt and red ballet pumps, posing unpromisingly in the Church Hill Road back garden. Ian remembered his sister tap-dancing on the top of the Morrison shelter, the big steel table which families jammed into their dining rooms during the war in case of a bomb attack: 'She certainly gave a performance. I think she was pretty good. I was impressed.' Though Margaret did not herself appear at the New Theatre in pantomime, the possibilities of performance as an escape from suffocating home life must have loomed invitingly, if not necessarily more powerfully, than for any girl of Margaret's age. She first 'went public', according to Nat, after one of her ballet lessons. Still attired in blouse, skirt and pumps, she was taken shopping by her mother. While Meg went inside to join a queue, Margaret stayed outside on the pavement to regale a small crowd with one of Arthur Askey's popular ditties: 'I'm a little fairy flower, growing wilder by the hour.'

There were few outings to theatre or cinema, though Maggie does remember seeing *The Shop at Sly Corner*, a popular thriller, at the Playhouse in the late 1940s and being so impressed by John Moffatt's performance that she asked for his autograph. She worked many times with Moffatt in later life. His was the only autograph she remembers ever collecting. She saw her first movie, *The Jolson Story*, in 1946. She didn't think much of it, and thought even less when Nat beat her for going to the cinema in the first place. Otherwise, life was unexceptional after the war. Margaret continued at Greycotes through the freezing cold winter of 1946/47. Port Meadow froze over, and Maggie recalls Lucy Greene's father materialising before them like a great tall bear in a huge grey coat. Nat says that Margaret was a delightful, happy creature through early adolescence, but Ian speaks of 'a very rigid, inflexible upbringing and a humourless childhood. That Maggie managed to break out of it as she did is all the more remarkable.'

The children were beaten for any minor transgression. Bottoms were bared and Nat would do his duty with a leather belt. This was nothing unusual in working- and lower-middle-class families of the period. Neighbours, however, only saw an almost perfect small family, industrious and well-mannered, with two clever boys and a sweet little girl. A correspondent in the Cowley *Chronicle* of May 1970, Michael Clifford, painted a bright picture of Margaret aged twelve or thirteen:

> She could have been the inspiration for a Ronald Searle cartoon schoolgirl. Her red hair hung in a pair of long plaits, she had a freckled face and her teeth were rather agonisingly corrected from a Bugs Bunny aspect by a fierce metal brace which she parked on every possible occasion when her mother was not around. She was also as thin as a cocktail stick... Yet attractive she was even then. Her eyes were glorious and her delightful character sparkled through them. She was a born comedian and the actress showed in her brilliant recapitulation of things which had happened to her. Both my mother and I can remember our convulsions of mirth when Maggie recounted her efforts at making a white sauce in domestic science – a sauce which even the sink rejected as unpalatable.

A charming little school essay at about this time, 1946, gives a clue to future obsessions. It concerns the 'Jimbies', no doubt an afterthought to Edward Lear's Jumblies, in a 'nonsensical essay and a deal of truth'. These Jimbies, of no special shape, are like gremlins who get into the mechanics of a theatre and mess things up. Having isolated the problem, the young essayist outlines the steps to be taken: 'The only way to rid your theatre of them is to spray it regularly with DDT and spirit gum – and to drink as much tonic water and black coffee as possible.'

In the summer term of 1947, she went on an assisted place to Oxford High School for Girls, one of the best schools in Britain. Its list of old girls includes the former headmistress and moral scientist Dame Mary Warnock, the writer Rose Macaulay, the poet Elizabeth Jennings, the academic Helen Darbishire, the entrepreneur Martha Lane Fox, the actress Miriam Margolyes and the conductor – the first woman ever to wave the baton in the pit of the Royal Opera House, Covent Garden, and music director of English National Opera in the 1990s – Sian Edwards. During her four years there, in spite of being remembered for the imagination she brought to English composition, Margaret made little academic impression and hardly any at all as an actress. Nonetheless, her school years had a considerable, if negative, influence in determining her future on the stage.

The boys went from strength to strength. On arrival from Ilford, Ian and Alistair had gone for interviews at the City of Oxford High School, just across the road from the New Theatre in George Street. Ian remembers that both he and Alistair had been struck by the story of Lawrence of Arabia, a fact that emerged in the course of the interview. The master said that T. E. Lawrence had been at the school at the turn of the century, and that therefore the twins had better be enrolled in Lawrence House. The new world of physics and mathematics excited the boys, but they were even more impressed by their new surroundings. The school had been designed in the late 1870s, in the Early English Renaissance style, and they came to this architecturally meritorious haven after attending a primary school in Ilford of no architectural distinction whatsoever.

It was taken for granted that Ian and Alistair would become architects. They were precociously good draughtsmen and would go into the city at every spare moment to draw. When it came to the School Certificate, the teachers balked at allowing them to take the architecture paper, chiefly because the school didn't teach it. But after pressing their case, they were allowed to sit the exam. At the age of fourteen, both gained distinctions. Alistair, who was counted the brighter of two very bright boys, took his Higher Schools Certificate two years later in 1944, but Ian had already left, impatient to start studying at the School of Architecture within the Schools of Technology, Art and Commerce, later the Polytechnic in Headington, and later still one of the campuses of Oxford Brookes University.

When Alistair joined Ian at the School, he caught up with him on the five-year course, compressing his studies into four, and both took the final examinations in 1949, aged twenty. The minimum age for election to the Royal Institute of British Architects was twenty-one. Ian and Alistair kicked their heels for a time before leaving Church Hill Road, and Oxford, for good in 1950. They went to London and shared a flat in Peel Street, Kensington.

Margaret had no intention of competing with this sort of academic distinction. In the summer of 1951, she was in the first batch of British girls to take the new General Certificate of Education at Ordinary Level. She managed to scrape four unimpressive passes, in English Language, English Literature (her best result: 54/100), French (by one mark) and art; she failed, quite badly, in history, geography and biology. She had not fitted in. One month before he died, Nat waxed more maudlin than usual on this subject:

> Even as a child, Margaret lived in a world where she was conscious of failure. She was a gorgeously happy child but one couldn't help but recognise that, beneath it all, there was a private world that Mother or Dad had no access to . . . She was very open as a girl, but I don't think she was entirely happy at the High School. The teacher in English was part of the cause, the one who stopped her acting in the play . . .

That obstructive, later philosophically semi-repentant, teacher was Dorothy Bartholomew, and the play was *Twelfth Night*, in which Margaret was cast as a page when she had set her heart on Viola or Feste. Ian saw this production: 'Her part was to come on between the acts and announce the scene changes by holding up a big piece of cardboard. She would then bow, and go off. There was no sign at all of this being the first step in an illustrious career!' In a curious way, however, it was. The whole fairly unhappy experience of the Oxford High School had the effect of concentrating Margaret's ambition elsewhere.

The school, founded in 1875, was the eighth of the great Girls' Public Day Schools Company. Its first prospectus declared its aim of receiving girls from all walks of life and of providing them with 'an education as thorough if not as extensive as that which their brothers are receiving at the public schools'. Its first home was the Judges' Lodgings in St Giles, but a new building was erected on the Banbury Road in 1880. Charles Dodgson, the mathematician of Christ Church better known as Lewis Carroll, the author of *Alice's Adventures in Wonderland*, delivered some lectures in logic at the school in 1887. The library still has several dedicated copies, in both English and German, of Carroll's most celebrated book.

Daughters of the University's intellectual élite, not surprisingly, dominated the school. In Margaret Smith's time there, one of the school's star pupils was Paquita Florey, daughter of the Professor of Pathology for whom Nat worked. There were 240 girls on the school roll in 1888; by 1951, when Margaret left, there were 468, and the school's activities and dormitories (the school always had a proportion of boarders) spilled over into other more modest addresses in the vicinity. She must have thought at times that she was exchanging one cramped environment at home for another at school. Other girls remember her walking into a classroom, bumping into a desk and raising a laugh. Much of Maggie Smith's physical comedy derives from her limbs seeming to extract themselves gracefully from tricky situations. It is tempting to suggest that her gesticulatory repertoire derives in part from being cribb'd, cabin'd and confined wherever she lived, and wherever she turned, in her childhood.

The school was renowned for its interest in acting. Apart from that early dynasty of Smith girls, there were also the Power sisters, one of whom, Elizabeth, became an eminent economic historian. Beryl Power was deemed magnificent as Flavius 'with a beard and a whip and a naturally powerful voice'. The plays were usually Shakespeare or Greek-in-translation. Hilda Napier played the lead in *Iphigenia in Tauris* in the translation later introduced to the London stage by Lillah

McCarthy. The most distinguished actress the OHS produced before
Maggie Smith was Margaret Rawlings, who arrived from Japan in 1920
and was accepted 'because of worthy and scholarly letters' written
by her clergyman father. Rawlings was an exemplary product of the
school who, before gaining a reputation as an outstanding classical
tragedienne, graduated from Lady Margaret Hall in the University.
Her best friend was one Leonora Corbett who also became an actress
and played Elvira, the ghost-wife, throughout the New York run of
Noël Coward's *Blithe Spirit*. Leonora, recalled Margaret Rawlings, used
to arrive late each term and regularly confessed to her house mistress
that she was plagued by 'carnal thoughts'. She was invariably consoled
with cocoa and bourbon biscuits.

Another OHS actress of a more local provenance, and just a few
years ahead of Maggie, was Judith Stott, whose family had a grocer's
shop in Walton Street. She remembered Maggie tap-dancing at a bus
stop in Headington. Judith Stott's example must have been a spur
to Maggie's ambition. After training, she became a prominent West
End juvenile, playing the young girl in *The Chalk Garden* opposite
Edith Evans in 1956. Judith Stott appeared in countless plays wearing
Clark's sandals and white ankle-socks. She crisscrossed with Maggie
for many years subsequently, appearing with her (and Dame Edith) in
a television version of *Hay Fever*; succeeding her in the Peter Shaffer
double bill of 1962; and remaining friends throughout two decades,
during which period she was married to the Irish comedian, Dave
Allen: 'To me, she's just my Margaret. She's laughter and tears, and
part of my life for so many years.'

Margaret Smith does not loom large in the school history and
magazines. She played tennis once for her house, West Club. She
earned 'special congratulation' as Puck in the lovers' quarrel scene
from *A Midsummer Night's Dream*, which her house performed in the
Shakespeare Competition (East Club, with 'the pick of the acting', took
the palm). And a contributor to Violet Stack's 1963 school history, a
senior girl of the day, wrote in half-apologetic retrospection: 'Could
one have attempted to keep in order the naughty little red-headed
fourth former, even as far as we tried, if one had known that Maggie
Smith would today be playing to packed houses in the West End?'
Miss Stack, who had previously taught at Holloway prison, had been

headmistress since 1937. She replaced Miss Gale, who was struck by lightning on holiday; the school magazine reported that 'although this terrible accident was fortunately neither fatal nor completely incapacitating, it made a return to work impossible'.

The school's reputation for drama had dipped a little during the war, but that was put to rights by the advent of Dorothy Bartholomew. Miss Bartholomew arrived at the OHS in 1948 and stayed for five years and one term. She was later headmistress of Norwich High School for twenty-two years and retired to a quaint little house in the cathedral close: 'Margaret was in the Upper Fourth when I arrived and they were very lively, both lots. I thought they were going to be my undoing. I remember her as a very private person. She was certainly naughty, but it was an attractive naughtiness, in a way. I think, looking back now, she already saw where she hoped to go, and maybe we missed out.'

Margaret felt she missed out badly by not being cast as Viola, a fact she would sometimes bitterly refer to in later life. But although Miss Bartholomew saw the Viola Margaret eventually played with the Oxford University Dramatic Society in 1952, and admired it, she still harboured reservations:

> I think she had more the seed of a Beatrice than a Viola. She was very good at the pert parts; she's not really, or wasn't then, my idea of a Viola. When I joined Letty Stack, we hadn't done a Shakespeare for about seven years. The old building was the last word in girls' schools when it was built, and it was still the last word. We had this one hall which had double-glazing – of necessity as the London lorries thundered past – and this is where we did the plays. Letty was keen we should do *Twelfth Night*. Margaret did, I am sure, understudy Tessa Collins as Feste, but Tessa was so healthy she was never likely to miss the performance. I think, in the end, Margaret could not sing very well, either.

Miss Bartholomew was quite right. Although adept at 'putting across' a revue number, Maggie was never really happy with music on stage and was only too keen to escape from revue the moment she had made her mark in it. Classroom contemporaries Margaret Bonfiglioli (née Slater) and Bridget Davidson (née Senior), who were later respectively head girl and deputy head girl, confirmed that Margaret did rehearse as Feste, and was funny, though she was more renowned as a general wag and everyday comedienne than as a conscientious performer. They deny that Miss Bartholomew had a down on Margaret, even though she was obviously a cantankerous handful in the classroom. But there remains a puzzle as to why she was not cast in the main school production when, according to Margaret Bonfiglioli, 'her real acting talent had become evident in her inspired and inspiring playing as the Porter in *Macbeth* in the Shakespeare Competition'.

Margaret's nickname was 'Woozler'. Everyone, says Bridget Davidson, called her that, but nobody, least of all Maggie herself, recalls why. Perhaps it was a result of some rustic mimicry, a precise evocation of the Banbury or Bidford inflections which the mature Maggie would later evoke so thoroughly as Margery Pinchwife in *The Country Wife*. Of the two lots of the Upper Third in 1947, Margaret, testifies another contemporary, Ruth Clarke (née Ayers), was in 'the other form'; those girls were inferior except when it came to the Shakespeare Competition, whose trophy, the Power Shield, was named in honour of the Power sisters. In this one aspect of competitive school life, says Ruth Clarke, the 'other form' was formidable opposition indeed:

> Jean Wagstaff, who everyone knew wanted to be an actress, played the straight lead . . . If there was a comic part, it would be played by Margaret Smith. She made us laugh, but we never saw her having a possible future on the professional stage. It was a great surprise to us when she left school 'early' to go to the Oxford Playhouse School with Jean Wagstaff. We received the coded message that Margaret was a 'failure'. Everybody was a failure if they didn't go to university. I was a failure because I went to London University, not to Oxbridge.

Miriam Margolyes, who was at the school from 1945 to 1959, from the infants through to the sixth form, and who would appear with Maggie in the Harry Potter series and in *Ladies in Lavender*, felt uncomfortable at the school, even though she was 'a responsible form leader' and left with an Exhibition to Cambridge, where she emerged as a comedienne of a thousand voices. Her family was Jewish, her father a doctor, and definitely not part of the University milieu.

It might be an absurd over-sensitivity, but I also felt a tinge of anti-Semitism. Like Margaret, I was a bit of a clown. But I'm sure the school confirmed an air of snootiness that made her feel that she had to emerge in her own right, that she couldn't be part of this world and that she had to forge her own steel out of another factory.

That factory would be the Oxford Playhouse. Another school friend, Verena Johnston (née Hunt), who, like Ruth Clarke, lived in Cowley, went to the Smith home 'on at least two Saturday mornings' to play Monopoly with Margaret and her brothers. Her father, Tommy Hunt, was a theatre fanatic who collected playbills and programmes all his life, and used to take Verena and Margaret to both the New Theatre and the Playhouse. Verena Johnston does not recall Margaret 'shining' at school, nor being aware of any class difference between herself and the other girls. But Margaret, she says, was adamant by the age of fifteen or sixteen that the stage was 'the only thing' for her. Tommy Hunt advised her of the many pitfalls. She should only go ahead, he said, if it was the only thing in the world she wanted to do. It was.

3

Clown of Town and Gown

Margaret had decided she wanted to go to drama school in London. She had set her heart on RADA, the Royal Academy of Dramatic Art, but her parents said she could not leave home in Oxford. Meg wanted her to go to secretarial college and unhelpfully suggested that she could not hope to be an actress 'with a face like that'. Nat was torn between obeying his wife and pleasing his daughter.

Oxford High School had only fanned the flames of an ambition that was engendered outside. Margaret Smith was, and Maggie Smith is, a voracious reader. During her years at the High School, she devoured a popular fictional series by Pamela Brown, who wrote a children's novel about the theatre, *The Swish of the Curtain*, in 1941. The book was written because its author, a fourteen-year-old wartime evacuee to Wales, wanted to sustain her playtime theatrical fantasies with her best friend in London. By an extraordinary coincidence, the lodgings which Ian and Alistair had taken in Peel Street, Kensington, were in the house owned by this same Pamela Brown and her husband Donald Masters, a repertory actor. Margaret had read all of Pamela Brown's 'Blue Door' series, and she talked about them with the author when she visited her brothers. Pamela Brown had trained as an actress at RADA and had adopted the stage name of 'Mela Brown' in order not to be confused with the famous actress of the same name. She had then become a producer of plays for children on BBC television.

The books exactly reflected Margaret's developing situation. In *The Swish of the Curtain*, a group of enthusiastic junior amateurs, the Blue Door Company, who have created their own theatre and presented a series of Shakespearean and vaudeville concerts, all progress from Fenchester (a country town of historic interest modelled on Colchester in Essex) to drama school in London; all, that is, except for young Maddy, the cheeky girl who becomes the heroine of the series. In *Maddy Alone* (1945), Maddy's career takes off in spite of not going to London when she becomes embroiled in professional show business on her doorstep: a film is made for which there is a part for a local twelve-year-old. Later books, *Blue Door Venture* and *Maddy Again*, recount, respectively, the founding of a professional theatre company in Fenchester and the launching of Maddy's career in television. This last book appeared by popular request in 1956, just as Margaret Smith became Maggie and leapt from miscellaneous work in theatre and television to Broadway.

Pamela Brown died in 1989, shortly after several of her books had been reissued for a new young readership. If Margaret was ever stage-struck it was when she read Pamela Brown. In later life, she often quoted with approval the other Pamela Brown, the actress who, like her namesake, trained at RADA and who played Ophelia to Robert Helpmann's Hamlet and Millamant to John Gielgud's Mirabell. This Pamela Brown said, 'It's the audience that's stage-struck, not me.'

In 1951, Margaret was unhappy at school and unhappy at not going to RADA. This tense situation was resolved by Nat going to see Isabel van Beers, a drama teacher who had a travelling brief among the Oxfordshire schools with a regular port of call at the High School. Margaret had responded to her, and Mrs van Beers had been a good deal more encouraging than Miss Bartholomew. Nat had heard she was starting a drama school based at the Playhouse in Beaumont Street. Mrs van Beers, who had spotted Margaret's 'built-in timing', accepted her immediately as one of the first intake of the Oxford Playhouse School of Theatre. Thus she embarked on a two-year course which was to pitch her into the ferment of both the hard professional theatre and the softer, more glamorous whirlpool of University productions. Oxford made her. Over the next four years, she broke many hearts, played countless leads, became a fixture in University revues, a personality in her adopted city and a toast of the Edinburgh Festival.

The Playhouse School was her passport and Mrs van Beers her Svengali. Originally trained in ballet, the formidable and vastly experienced teacher had been sent to study acting in Oxford at the end of the 1920s. Like Margaret twenty years later, the budding actress had plenty of opportunity to rub shoulders with the best. In 1932 and

1933, Isabel van Beers appeared, in a minor capacity, in two of the most renowned of all OUDS productions: John Gielgud's version of *Romeo and Juliet*, and Max Reinhardt's outdoor *A Midsummer Night's Dream*. She had married Stanley van Beers, a stage manager with Lilian Baylis at the Old Vic, and before the war worked in repertory in Leeds, Bradford and Coventry. The couple were later divorced, and Isabel took to teaching, basing herself in 28 Wellington Square, just off Beaumont Street and a stone's throw from the Playhouse.

The idea for the school at the Playhouse was hatched with Nevill Coghill, the Fellow of Exeter College who was at the heart of Oxford theatre for more than thirty years. Morning classes were held in a little church in St Cross, and the Playhouse stage was made available, five afternoons a week, from 2.30 to 5. Most importantly, the school had an arrangement with Equity, the actors' union, to provide students for twelve small parts a year within the professional company. Students were also encouraged, if invited, to take part in University and college productions. Thus the students could 'learn to handle their audiences' by listening to them, flushing them out and adjusting to their funny ways and habits. This was the most important skill, in Isabel van Beers's book, and one for which Maggie Smith would become renowned. The fees were twenty guineas a term. The reward was a certificate in acting from the Guildhall School of Music and Drama in London, of which Mrs van Beers was an honorary member.

Margaret had made a great impression on Mrs van Beers on one of her visits to the High School. The tutor gave her a speech of Helena's in *A Midsummer Night's Dream*. 'She sent it up! A child of fourteen. And I thought, oh my word, this is interesting. She had, even then, marvellous comedy timing, and she never made a mistake. By the time she came to the school it was obvious she was going to be something. She was on one track and her sights were at the top.'

Thus, in October 1951, Margaret Smith made her first appearance on the Playhouse stage as Jean in *The Pick-Up Girl* by Elsa Shelley. A photograph shows her leaning over a banister in a silk shirt, mouth half-open, looking sultry. And in June 1952, as she completed her two-year course, she at last played Viola, in the OUDS *Twelfth Night*. The President of the OUDS, John Wood, renowned later as a leading Royal Shakespeare Company actor, played Malvolio ('Looking as lean, lanky and statuesque as Don Quixote,' said the *Oxford Mail*), the future television executive Patrick Dromgoole was Sir Toby ('A dapper little man . . . [not the usual] gross-bellied understudy of Falstaff') and the founding director of the Royal Exchange Theatre in Manchester, Michael Elliott, who would one day direct Maggie as Miss Julie, was Antonio.

Margaret Smith – the unfamiliar name fooled the OUDS historian, Humphrey Carpenter, who made nothing of it in his celebratory book – shivered in the gardens of Mansfield College every night, praying for rain. As Viola/Cesario she wore black tights, a white full-sleeved blouse and a sword, and she promptly collected her first rave review. The *Oxford Mail* was more than complimentary: 'Margaret Smith, whose loveliness has a boyish quality about it, made Olivia's infatuation for her seem quite natural . . . I was much struck by the simple sincerity of her acting. She approximates very nearly to the Viola of our dreams.' In the summer vacation, the production toured to Clermont-Ferrand in France, and the Hebbel Theatre in Berlin as part of the Berliner Festwochen.

Margaret was now fully immersed in the life of the University theatre, and its centre was the Playhouse, where the director of productions was Frank Shelley. She threw herself energetically into productions of both town and gown at a time when the Playhouse was a staging post for the leaders of tomorrow's theatre, and the OUDS full of ambitious undergraduates and future stage and television luminaries.

One such Oxford idol was Ned Sherrin, whose participation in the University revues was a crucial formative influence on Maggie: 'I think as she became older she became a little more extravagant, but I remember her as a quiet little thing, rather like one of Trollope's little brown girls. She obviously had tremendous talent, but she was not flamboyant.' She did not, for Sherrin and his contemporaries, have the glamorous, remote mystique of Zuleika Dobson in Max Beerbohm's Oxford love story: 'Our own Zuleika was a girl called Jennifer Weston who married a property tycoon, and of course Antonia Pakenham [later Lady Antonia Fraser] was up at the same time, floating around town on her bicycle. Margaret was simply considered to be one of the very best actresses.' But she did make some impression on Oxford fashion. Patrick Dromgoole says that in 1952 she was the first person he knew who bought a pair of jeans and sat in the bath water while wearing them, 'allowing them to dry to shape around her figure'.

Home was still 55 Church Hill Road, and Meg would dispatch Nat to walk halfway into town if they thought Margaret was being detained at rehearsals beyond a proper hour. They were grudgingly reconciled to Margaret's ambition and may have been comforted by a perceptive progress report which Frank Shelley sent to Nat in January 1953: 'As raw material for the stage she is second to none in the school. But ... I suspect that her very quickness and impatience to improve herself may at times get in her way, and make her her own "worst enemy". She must find patience towards her less gifted fellow pupils, and also towards the tutors at the school ... Margaret has the essential stuff in her. It takes too long to try and define it; but some of us can recognise it.'

The *Oxford Mail* certainly had. Two months before Frank Shelley wrote his report, he had directed Margaret and Ronald Barker as two naughty children in *The Housemaster* by Ian Hay. The public-school farce also had Francis Matthews in the cast, but the *Mail* was more taken by the OUDS Viola transformed into 'Button' Farringdon: 'How John Betjeman would have approved of Margaret Smith, all legs and too brief "briefies", in which she hoarded hot sticky chocolate, destined in no time at all to become that great mountainous sports girl, Joan Hunter Dunn. She came as near to being a Great Dane puppy as any mortal, unhelped by Barrie, dare hope. I adored her.' But not everyone saw her potential. Ronald Barker, destined to become one of Britain's most popular television comedy actors, was a member of the Oxford Playhouse Company throughout Margaret's apprenticeship. Years later, at the height of his fame, Barker told a correspondent, B. A. Young, that all he remembered of young Margaret Smith was that he advised her to give up the profession 'as I didn't think she had the qualities or the talent necessary! How wrong I was.'

It is worth noting at this early stage that Margaret was as much in demand for serious drama as she was for revue. Either side of her final year at the Playhouse school, she appeared in T. S. Eliot's *Murder in the Cathedral* with the University Poetry Society (the poet Adrian Mitchell was the First Priest) in St Peter-in-the-East Church; with the University Players in Andreyev's *He Who Gets Slapped* (as Consuela, the doomed love object and bareback rider, to whom, said Frank Dibb in the *Oxford Times*, she brought 'both vernal freshness and a never self-conscious humour'); and with the OUDS again in February 1954 as Gertrud in Michael Meyer's first play, *The Ortolan*. Meyer, the Ibsen biographer and translator, was then a tyro novelist and playwright, and his symbolic drama about a young poetess, the protégée of an older woman who cannot have children and seeks fulfilment in the girl's success, was favourably reviewed by four undergraduates nursing bright futures: Sherrin, Michael Elliott, Peter France, the television presenter, and Monty Haltrecht, the novelist.

Patrick Dromgoole, who appeared in the play and shared Oxford digs with Haltrecht, remembered his friend's description of Margaret in a minor role: 'frail as an opalescent moth'. She was, said Dromgoole, 'the perfect illusion, terribly beautiful, her colour fairly startling, and she was impossibly young, or seemed so, and a bit distant in the sense that no one ever felt very near her'. Harold Hobson, the critic of the *Sunday Times*, found his way to Marston Hall to see *The Ortolan* and was similarly struck: '. . . at one point, when she speaks of a working girl's dreary chances of a cheap pick-up at Saturday night dances, Miss Smith makes a brief foray out of the play's general atmosphere of intellectual efficiency into the realm of theatrical emotion'. This first notice in the national press was not only typical of Hobson's acumen and ability to spot new talent; it isolates for the first time the Maggie Smith way with unsentimental expressions of sadness. The loneliness of her childhood found an outlet on the stage, and it remained characteristic of her first maturity that her flights into Restoration comedy, as well as her swoops into simple revue material, were invariably shot through with a stinging and truthful pathos.

She signed her first professional contract with the Oxford Repertory Players at the Playhouse on 12 June 1954, as an assistant stage manager at a salary of four pounds and ten shillings a week. Her professional commitments, apart from making the tea, included walk-on roles in a series of productions in 1954 and 1955 by Peter Hall and Peter Wood, both of whom were to become distinguished directors. Shortly after Frank Shelley had written Margaret's progress report, the Playhouse was taken over by Thane Parker, chairman of the London Mask Theatre, a company responsible for the Westminster Theatre and

J. B. Priestley's productions. Parker also administered a little touring outfit called the Elizabethan Theatre Company, which had been formed by a group of Cambridge graduates including Peter Hall and Peter Wood. Parker appointed Hall to the artistic directorship of the Playhouse, where he stayed for nine or ten months before accepting a more promising post at the Arts in London. Peter Wood succeeded him.

In Peter Hall's version of Gogol's *The Government Inspector*, Margaret played the wife of the schools' superintendent in a company which included Billie Whitelaw, Derek Francis, Tony Church, Peter Jeffrey, Frank Windsor, Michael Bates, Toby Robertson, Ronald Barker and Clifford Rose. Philip French, the film critic who was then an undergraduate, vividly remembers her singing 'The Boy I Love is Up in the Gallery' in a music-hall compilation supervised from the piano by Peter Hall in a moustache. 'She was absolutely wonderful,' says Hall. 'She sang that song with such wit and pathos, it was simply spectacular. The ironic side to her means she can be pathetic without ever being self-indulgent. I didn't think she would develop the range that she subsequently has, but I did think she had star quality.' Hall also directed her as the West Wind 'in a lot of green make-up' in the 1954 Christmas musical by Vivian Ellis, *Listen to the Wind*. By 1955, Hall had taken over the Arts and hit the West End with *Summertime*, Ugo Betti's play starring Dirk Bogarde, at the Apollo. Peter Wood took over in Oxford, and Margaret appeared in his productions of Pinero's *The Magistrate* and Sheridan's *The School for Scandal*.

She therefore brushed with the past and the future of the British theatre. Maggie Smith became a star in her own right, but she was also one of the last generation of beneficiaries of the regional repertory system. Peter Hall would go on from Oxford to produce the key new modernists, Samuel Beckett and Harold Pinter, in London, and to found the Royal Shakespeare Company in 1960. Peter Wood, who later followed Peter Hall to the Arts, directed Pinter's first play, *The Birthday Party*, in 1958. Wood's busy parallel career in television embraced Maggie Smith in her first major small-screen role, also in 1958, and he would work with her many times in the West End, in Los Angeles, on Broadway and at the new National Theatre, of which she was a founder member in 1963.

Even more immediately important than her Playhouse connections was Margaret's involvement in student revues. These were bright days for the University theatre, which had been galvanised in the postwar years by the activities of Kenneth Tynan, John Schlesinger, Sandy Wilson, Tony Richardson, William Gaskill and Lindsay Anderson. The early professional success of such people prompted a rush of energetic talent towards the stage and the rapidly expanding new world of television. The Oxford Theatre Group was formed in 1953 to take plays and a revue to the fringe of the Edinburgh Festival. It hired professional directors, Casper Wrede and Frank Dunlop, to direct Strindberg's *Miss Julie* and Molière's *Tricks of Scapin*. In the revue, *Cakes and Ale*, Margaret Smith performed three solo items: a song about a cinema usherette, 'Première', for which lyrics had been written by Ned Sherrin and music by Andrew Johnston ('It's my première tonight, and I'm scared as scared can be . . .'); a marionette musical number by Johnston, 'Invisible Strings', which became her party turn; and a sketch about bedtime drinks by Leonard Webb called 'Somnos' (Webb as a fireman fell asleep on the job while his wife, Maggie, is incinerated at home: 'It's getting very close, this fire unkind; the margarine is basting my behind').

The professional highlight of the 1953 Edinburgh Festival was the Old Vic production of *Hamlet* starring Richard Burton and Claire Bloom. The actor playing Bernardo ('Who's there?') was Jeremy Geidt, and his visit to the damp attic in Riddle's Court off the Lawnmarket, where the OTG performed, was particularly significant. His brother-in-law, Peter Dunlop, was to become Margaret's long-term agent and confidant as a direct result of this encounter. Geidt, who later worked in Boston as a senior actor with Robert Brustein's American Repertory Theatre, recalled that the audience at *Cakes and Ale* was pretty sparse. But he was totally smitten by 'this Titian-haired beauty, sitting on a stool in a haze of cigarette smoke'. With a mutual friend, Margaret later visited Geidt in his dressing room at the Assembly Hall and said, 'I hear you think I'm good; what do I do now?' Geidt said he would arrange an introduction to Peter Dunlop of Fraser and Dunlop in London. And he did.

At some point over the next year, Margaret visited Peter Dunlop's office, situated at the wrong end of Wardour Street over a tailor's shop. On his desk, Dunlop kept a heavy Venetian glass stone. In the course of the interview, Margaret fiddled with it, picking it up and putting it down. Dunlop eventually said, 'Oh, for heaven's sake, leave that alone,' and you can imagine now the electrified reaction of hurt dignity that was flashed by the girl across the desk, the pained, piercing look of 'Well, if that's how you feel about it . . .' Despite this incident, the agent and the actress took to each other immediately. Dunlop, who had acted through Charterhouse and Cambridge and on the London stage, was not remotely theatrical. He much preferred country life and spending time with his family circle. He was Margaret's type of agent and they remained together for nearly thirty years, although she never signed a contract. 'She couldn't be bothered,' says Dunlop with a chuckle.

She went back to Oxford and waited for something to turn up. Even without professional work, she was in demand. According to Ned Sherrin, if you wanted success with a University show, you tried to get Margaret Smith in the cast. And, on a personal level, there were countless admirers of this waif-like, clownish chanteuse whose timing and stillness on a stage marked her out from the crowd.

One of the most fervent was John Beary, a young actor four years her senior who was smitten during a six-month attachment to the Playhouse as an assistant stage manager and bit player: 'We were both innocent, and both romantics. We walked into the night along the Oxford rivers, and cuddled in punts moored under bridges.' Beary, who became a writer and director in America, remained devoted, though he did concede that he lost her when she was 'taken up' by the undergraduates. One such was Michael Murray, in later life a professional actor, who became Margaret's favoured 'boyfriend' after Beary, and another keen admirer was Andrew Johnston, who wrote much of the University revue material and, on graduating, pursued a notable career in advertising. Both, along with the rest, were kept at arm's length. Margaret was a properly brought-up young girl and was in no great hurry to yield her mysteries. She soon learned to protect herself from regular exclamations of sexual adoration. The physical side of life was fairly unimportant to her, and her upbringing certainly pre-empted any idea of dalliance, let alone promiscuity.

In December 1953, yet another undergraduate was entranced by the vivacious redhead, and his long-term campaign was ultimately to prove successful. Beverley Cross came up to the University, to read history at Balliol College, in the Michaelmas term of 1952. He therefore missed Margaret's Viola, but he was aware of her reputation when he met her for the first time during rehearsals for a charity gala organised by Ned Sherrin in aid of the Greek earthquake victims. Margaret did several of her increasingly renowned sketches, including her Joan Greenwood impersonation (as Gwendolen in the just-released Anthony Asquith film of *The Importance of Being Earnest*), and Beverley played his guitar. Beverley joined the queue of unappeased Oxford suitors, tucked in just behind Michael Murray and Andrew Johnston. The friendship simmered on the back burner for a few years before it became serious at the end of the decade.

Margaret was far more interested in reading than she was in canoodling. Having grown out of the runaway adventures of the Blue Door Company, she came across a more acidic, more sophisticated and deeply sympathetic literary rebel: Holden Caulfield in J. D. Salinger's *The Catcher in the Rye*. If there is one literary example for Maggie's acute allergy to phoniness, it is Salinger's young hero, the world-weary urban cousin to Mark Twain's Huckleberry Finn. She was deeply impressed by Salinger's book about a boy who ran away from school and had harsh words for everyone, including Laurence Olivier and the Lunts.

She had been given some Salinger stories to read by John Beary, who had laid his hands on copies of the *New Yorker*, where they were published, through the Ford Foundation. The whole Playhouse company was badgered into reading Salinger by his new champions, Beary and Margaret Smith. Beary then wrote to Salinger, telling him about Maggie, his 'comrade-in-arms', and asking for his advice. Salinger replied to them both, telling Maggie that she had better get a move on and marry this boy who doted on her. Beary, who formally proposed marriage to Margaret in 1953, says that Salinger told him to make up his mind one way or the other. The correspondence must have been one of the very few Salinger entered into in Britain, apart from that with his publishers, before becoming almost entirely reclusive in 1965, 'the Greta Garbo of American letters'. As the poet Ian Hamilton recounts in his *In Search of J. D. Salinger*, the author gave his last interview to a couple of American schoolgirls in 1953, at just about the same time as John Beary was writing to him. *The Catcher in the Rye* was not yet the cult manual of adolescent outsiderism it became in the 1960s, and was not all that widely read. The paperback only became available in 1956. Although it prefigured the 'youth quake' whose icons were James Dean and Elvis Presley, the appeal to Margaret, and to the teenage Hamilton in Darlington, County Durham, lay in its gloriously impatient tone of voice and in Holden's coruscating contempt for cant, pretension and phoniness.

Maggie was affected not only by *The Catcher in the Rye*, but also by the short story 'For Esmé – with Love and Squalor', whose war-damaged American hero is offered succour by a precocious young girl he meets while stationed in Britain towards the end of the Second World War. It is unfortunate that Meg, incensed by her daughter's literary adventurism and certain that such carryings-on would lead to immoral contamination of some kind, destroyed the letter Maggie received from the American author. This bitter experience probably put Margaret off letter-writing for good (she is a lax correspondent to this day, and no great emailer, either) and did nothing to improve her relationship with her mother. It must have steeled her, too, in her determination finally to escape the asphyxiating intimacy of the semi-detached house in Cowley.

Material from the 1953 Edinburgh revue, and the gala, was incorporated in a BBC television programme, *Oxford Accents*, transmitted on 26 February 1954 as part of a series on Oxford. The linking commentary was delivered by Brian Johnston, the cricket correspondent, and the event marked the television débuts of both Maggie Smith and Ned Sherrin, who was given a 'producer' credit. In the summer term, Margaret was photographed in the press with the twenty-one-year-old President of the Oxford Union and future Cabinet Minister, Michael Heseltine. They were discussing details of a cabaret for the presidential ball. In later life, Maggie Smith and Michael Heseltine, nicknamed 'Tarzan' or 'Goldilocks' on account of his flowing mane of blond hair, would share the same hairdresser, Patricia Millbourn.

The OTG's revue for Edinburgh in September 1954 was *On the Mile*, presented in the late-night spot in Riddle's Court after a production of *The Dog Beneath the Skin* by W. H. Auden and Christopher Isherwood. Philip Purser of the *Daily Mail* confessed that he fell 'swiftly, completely in love' with the 'infinitely talented' young actress and invited her to accompany him to see Ruth Gordon in *The Matchmaker*, the international Festival's main attraction. Years later, Maggie would remind Purser that he had started her off: 'That's when I realised you can be a comic and yet be an actress. If she [Ruth Gordon] can do it, I thought, so can I.' An amalgam of the best recent Oxford revue material, with Margaret Smith in the cast, was presented in London in October 1954 at the New Watergate Theatre Club in Buckingham Street, off the Strand.

Ian and Alistair began to appreciate the company of their sister, whose visits to London were increasingly frequent. The boys were working as dogsbody assistants in an architectural firm and decided that they would separate to acquire experience and later form a joint practice (they never did). In 1951, Alistair had worked with a company designing the gardens in Battersea Park for the Festival of Britain before starting his two years of National Service with the Royal Engineers (Ian was rejected on health grounds). The brothers had moved from Peel Street to another flat in Kensington, and by 1954 had moved again into a large top-floor flat in Belsize Park, Hampstead, with two other professional colleagues. The friends soon disappeared and the apartment began filling up with Margaret and other aspiring young actresses. Ian remembers this as a 'very jokey' establishment: 'And also very proper, I might say. Margaret had really blossomed, but the Swinging Sixties weren't remotely in sight. Margaret was buzzing around, almost waiting for something to happen.'

Peter Dunlop found her little bits of television work. She was a hostess on ITV's quiz game *Double Your Money*, which required her to look decorative and to introduce the show's star, Hughie Green, thus: 'We'd like you to meet the man with the biggest head in television, the man with the greenest hue . . . Hughie Green!' With Jeremy Geidt, she 'walked on' in the first BBC television version of John Galsworthy's *The Forsyte Saga*. Geidt recalls that he and Margaret, playing a young couple at a party, asked the director, Tony Richardson, if they should chatter only when the microphone boom materialised above them. Richardson launched into a long Stanislavskyan lecture on how really good actors never stop acting. When the scene restarted, Smith and Geidt danced meaningfully around the studio and, oblivious to the action on the set, carried on acting, and dancing, down the stairs, out of the building and into the car park, while Richardson was reduced to a state of white-knuckled fury on the balcony. As he recounts the incident, Geidt has a memory flash of bright eyes, smiles, irreverence and high spirits: 'Magical moments, like a diamond shining, giggles while strap-hanging on the underground.' But, he added, this same Margaret Smith was 'incredibly self-anchored; she had what the Georgians called "bottom". She knew who she was, and she had this absolutely fearless quality.' The wide world beckoned.

Equity, the actors' union, had informed her that there was already a Margaret Smith on their books and would she mind changing her name. In September 1955, the programme for her second New Watergate revue, *Oxford Eight*, reveals that she was now Maggie Smith. Peter Dunlop's partner, Jimmy Fraser, who handled the film side of the business, went along one evening with Leonard Sillman, the New York producer, who was planning a Broadway presentation of *New Faces*. Maggie's reviews were good: she was described as 'a rich comic talent' and 'a comedienne of some versatility'. Sillman was impressed and invited her to meet him in his hotel suite. Her initial reaction was sceptical. She had no intention of falling for that old trick, the one where a slick American producer with a suite at the Savoy fancies a girl in the revue and asks her over to challenge her defences. She stood him up. The next day a colleague told her she was mad, did she not realise that this man presented new talent on Broadway? She agreed, reluctantly, to go and see him. She had very nearly blown her big chance. Leonard Sillman assembled his cast for *New Faces 1956* with an opening date of 14 June at the Ethel Barrymore on Broadway, and one of the unknowns he engaged was Maggie Smith.

4

New Revue and Old Vic

Maggie Smith, the new comedienne of Broadway, was twenty-one years old, five feet and five inches tall, with blue eyes, red hair and a bright, occasional smile. She lived in Greenwich Village and she was paid $350 a week by Leonard Sillman, of which 10 per cent went to her agent, Milton Goldman, who acted in New York for Fraser and Dunlop. She was not happy. She sent Meg a magazine cutting in which she was photographed wearing a silk evening gown and a forlorn expression. Across the bottom she wrote: 'I look very sad! Mummy, I'm not as sad as I look.' Working for Leonard Sillman, a pushy hoofer from Detroit who had once employed Tyrone Power as his chauffeur, was not a barrel of laughs. Maggie was required to play several old ladies when *New Faces 1956* opened in Boston, but she put her foot down and had them deleted before New York. Sillman was a devious and unpleasant character by all accounts, but he did have a nose for talent. Typically, he thought great acting was to do with being stingy. There is, however, something in his theory of the hoarding of gifts, holding back, teasing an audience. 'The young English actress, Maggie Smith, who appeared in the last *New Faces*, has it,' he observed in his 1959 autobiography, 'and it will make her a star.'

The title 'New Faces' had been suggested to Sillman by the financier Otto Kahn, as a contrast to Ziegfeld's expensive *Follies*. The first show was in 1934. Henry Fonda sang, and Imogene Coca did a striptease. Tallulah Bankhead, according to Sillman, smoked like a furnace throughout the opening night's performance. In 1936, Gypsy Rose Lee nearly appeared alongside Van Johnson but withdrew at the last minute. Sonny Tufts was in the 1938 version, but 1943 was a non-vintage year. Sillman's reputation took a dive. After the war, Maxwell House Coffee (with whom, ironically, Maggie was to make her only television advertisement, during the run of *Lettice and Lovage*) sponsored *New Faces* on the radio, and CBS TV gave their new revue show not to Sillman but to Ed Sullivan.

But in 1952 Sillman had bounced back with his fourth *New Faces* in which a comic actress called Alice Ghostley was an overnight sensation and young Eartha Kitt stopped the show with 'Monotonous'. It ran for a year, and then went on tour. In 1956 Sillman was ready to fire once again with a new assemblage of hopefuls. They came from all over: India, Sweden, the Virgin Islands, Italy, France and Puerto Rico. The star, however, proved to be T. C. Jones (long since forgotten and dead), a drag artist from San Francisco who opened the show as the husky Tallulah with a throaty, mannish laugh and a series of insults aimed at the serious theatre of Stanislavsky and Elia Kazan. The critics were sold on T. C. Jones. Walter Winchell devoted a column to him. In their reviews, neither Brooks Atkinson in the *New York Times* nor Walter Kerr (later an admiring fan) in the *Herald Tribune* mentioned Maggie Smith, though the cast album and production photographs suggest there was something worth noting. A cod Ziegfeld tribute to the all-American girl closed the first half. Following 'Miss Jungle Madness' and 'Miss Fisherman's Tail', Maggie jerkily descended the staircase as 'Miss Bowls of Sunshine', covered in dozens of oranges, and sang, to a slow foxtrot rhythm, in a voice of adenoidal, strangulated lack of conviction: 'I'm a vision of beauty, and the beauty part, is the beautiful feeling, I feel in my heart.'

Maggie's Englishness was also exploited. In one sporting sketch where cricket was derided, she responded, aghast, 'Anybody who'd say that would strike the Queen!' Although the Broadway list of that season included such archetypal American hits as Paul Muni in *Inherit the Wind*, Sammy Davis Jr in *Mr Wonderful*, and *The Pajama Game*, New York was in the grip of one of its periodic bouts of showbiz Anglophilia. Rex Harrison and Julie Andrews, who had opened in March in *My Fair Lady*, were the toasts of the town, and Maggie was soon taken up. She became good friends with Julie Andrews and her husband, the designer Tony Walton, and through them met the agent Lou Wilson, who rescued her from the shark-like attentions of Milton Goldman. Alice Ghostley, too, became a lifelong friend and would collect Maggie's first Oscar for her in 1970. She joined in the celebrations for Eliza Doolittle's twenty-first birthday (Julie Andrews was twenty-two, the same age as Maggie) at the 21 Club on 1 October. In November, the artist Feliks Topolski invited her to a party with Rex Harrison, Harrison's lover Kay Kendall (he was still married to Lilli Palmer, but later married Kendall, who died of leukaemia in 1959), and the distinguished Scottish-born actress Eileen Herlie. Lou Wilson took her on a trip to Puerto Rico. Maggie liked New York, up to a point. But the showbiz social whirligig was never her scene and she was relieved when *New Faces* closed after a seven-month run. She returned to England, and the boys' Belsize Park apartment, to capitalise on her Broadway status.

The obvious next step was to establish her revue credentials on British soil, and Maggie was signed up by the ambitious and stylish young impresario Michael Codron for the London première of *Share My Lettuce*, 'a diversion with music' by Bamber Gascoigne, which featured an offbeat, quirky score by Keith Statham and Patrick Gowers, and one lyric by Michael Frayn. More importantly, Codron teamed Maggie Smith with Kenneth Williams, another rising star who had made his name as the Dauphin in a 1954 revival of Shaw's *Saint Joan* and in Sandy Wilson's exuberant musical *The Buccaneer*. Gascoigne had launched *Share My Lettuce* at Cambridge University, where he was an undergraduate. It caught something of a new surrealism in revue pioneered by the choreographer John Cranko's *Cranks*. It was bright and bubbly, slightly bizarre, with no hint of the 'satire boom' inaugurated by *Beyond the Fringe* three years later. Gascoigne says he 'sat and stared in fascinated amazement at all that went on' and recalls the wonderfully snide verbal wit of Williams in rehearsal and the fun and vitality of Maggie Smith. He thinks she was a little plumper round the shoulders in those days.

After a couple of flops, Codron needed a hit. *Share My Lettuce* proved a lifeline leading to innovative West End presentations of Harold Pinter, John Mortimer, Sandy Wilson, more revue, and something like solvency in the mid-1960s with Terence Frisby's *There's a Girl in My Soup*.

Kenneth Williams shared his lettuce with a white rabbit which he kept in a box. There were eight colour-coded performers – Williams was 'lettuce green', Maggie 'orange' – who were heralded by a bebopish overture in the early style of Leonard Bernstein. The sketches included a Pinteresquely menacing encounter in a railway compartment and an almost mathematically precise party scene in an army mess where all the officers were called Michael and all their girlfriends Susan. In 'Party Games', Maggie played the rapidly articulating hostess: 'Here's a pencil and pad and you won't find it bad these are games that we all of us know; pass 'em on as you write 'em and ad infinitum it's just party games that make a good party go.' Kenneth Williams said that Maggie sang this number while fiddling with a rope of beads, twirling them round her neck and then, amazingly, around her waist. 'Just as they seemed to be heading for her ankles, she deftly altered their course and the beads ended up round her neck again. She finished the song looking as immaculate as when she started.'

The show opened on 21 August at the old Lyric in Hammersmith. Williams, said Milton Shulman in the *Evening Standard*, 'capers across the stage like a tipsy pixie getting sloshed on champagne bubbles', while Richard Findlater in the *Observer* lauded this 'elegant, faintly macabre, and immensely funny' new talent. Williams had been around a little while. Nearly nine years older than Maggie, he came from an ordinary London Cockney background (his father was a gentlemen's hairdresser in King's Cross) and had found his show business feet towards the end of the war, and just after it, entertaining the troops while based in Singapore. On being demobbed, Williams worked around the country in repertory theatres and made his first real impression in *Hancock's Half Hour*, a BBC radio series starring the melancholy Tony Hancock, in which his fruitily intoned camp persona, unprecedented in public broadcasting, delighted the listening multitude. Williams was outrageous, but brilliantly fast and funny. His acting had a brutal, Japanese style to it, and his mask-like pixie face was likened by Kenneth Tynan to that of Jean-Louis Barrault in a farce. He had first seen Maggie in that Oxford revue at the New Watergate. He told Tynan that he had gone along with John Schlesinger and had been immediately struck by her magnetic quality:

She was like an extraordinary cat, and indeed her eye make-up was positively feline. When we worked together, the way she invented that business with the rope of pearls was definitely a result of her

thing about Bea Lillie. I loved her urchin quality, too. She's physically adroit and can fold her arms in such a way that they disappear.
The other quality in her work is a sort of basic American feel that
must have come from *New Faces*.

It is the lot of all gifted performers to be 'discovered' in their
early years with the regularity of a cuckoo emerging from its clock.
But Maggie's comic personality, the essence that was to make her a
star, was already apparent. Codron knew she was special: 'She was
always extraordinary, even at the very beginning. She came down to
Hammersmith and took one look at a set that was on the stage for
another show and said, "I didn't know they still designed sets like
that!" I was flabbergasted. But her assurance had nothing to do with
pomposity or silliness; she was completely herself, and very funny.'

Share My Lettuce transferred to the Comedy Theatre in the West End
in September and moved on to the Garrick in the New Year. Maggie
groaned, 'This must be the longest tour in town.' More substantial
television work began to be offered. The first major role Maggie played
on British television was that of Susie, a dumb blonde waitress, in *Boy
Meets Girl*, a Hollywood comedy by Bella and Sam Spewack which
Independent Television broadcast in its 'Play of the Week' slot in June
1957.

One consequence of West End exposure was being spotted for the
movies. Dennis van Thal, Michael Balcon's chief talent scout at Associated British Studios, Elstree, signed her on a seven-year contract at the
same time as Shirley Anne Field and Ann Firbank; they joined a stable
which included Richard Todd, Sylvia Syms and Janette Scott. Very
little was subsequently found for Maggie to do. She always rejoiced
in the first monthly fan-mail report she received. It consisted of one
word: 'Nil.' However, during the run of *Share My Lettuce*, she did make
her first feature film, *Nowhere to Go*, written by Seth Holt (who also
directed) and Kenneth Tynan. She had only crossed Tynan's path once
before. As an Oxford schoolgirl, she claims to have knocked him over
with her hockey stick in the High while jumping off a speeding bus.
She had no idea who he was, but told her brothers that she had felled a
man in a purple suit. They knew that only one man wore a purple suit

in postwar Oxford: the already famous undergraduate Tynan, whose middle name was not Peacock for nothing.

Tynan was now working as both a drama critic on the *Observer* and a script editor at Ealing Studios. Maggie was cast as Bridget Howard, a rich, lonely, slightly snooty but inquisitive girl who has run away from five schools and who now befriends an unsuitable confidence trickster, played by the well-built Canadian actor George Nader. One of only two black-and-white movies she made (the other was *The Pumpkin Eater*), *Nowhere to Go* was Seth Holt's first film in a career which, unlike Maggie's, never fulfilled its promise.

The opening prison break-out in *Nowhere to Go* is a rightly renowned sequence of great excitement, and a fine cast includes the silent-screen star Bessie Love as a wealthy widow, Bernard Lee as a dangerously smiling 'Mr Big', Harry H. Corbett as an obstreperous crook and Andrée Melly as an Irish night-club girl. It is a flinty, technically assured film, full of shadows and twists, with a good jazz soundtrack by Dizzy Reece. Bridget stays loyal to conman 'Greg' (Nader), takes him home for Christmas in the family cottage in Brecon and ends up being arrested herself. Under that cover, Greg tries to steal a getaway bike, is surprised by a farmer and fatally wounded. As he lies dying in the road, Bridget returns from the police station to find his last message – 'Tell your friends to look somewhere else' – and walks away over the fields into the middle distance, sad and alone once more, a prisoner of her own background and the British class system. Maggie was a different kind of young film heroine, edgy, sensitive and intelligent. One popular newspaper declared that she made 'bosomy blondes old-fashioned', while the more sedate C. A. Lejeune in the *Observer* looked forward to seeing her again: 'She looks as crisp as a celery stick and speaks like a girl who has a good mind of her own,' she wrote.

Since working with her at the Oxford Playhouse, Peter Wood had developed a parallel career in television. The West End producing company, H. M. Tennent, run by Hugh 'Binkie' Beaumont, had an arrangement with ITV to present new work, and one of Wood's 1958 projects – the year in which he also directed Pinter's *The Birthday Party* – was *Sunday out of Season*, 'a gentle, sensible little play', according to one critic, by a West Country potter called Peter Draper. For 'Binkie-vision', as the set-up was known, Wood wanted to cast the girl he remembered from Oxford as a defensive student from London University who goes to a small Welsh seaside resort to recover from an unhappy love affair. She embarks on a tentative new friendship with a local boy whose father is suffering from silicosis and who is also in flight from emotional turmoil. This role was taken by Alec McCowen, who had worked with Wood at the Arts and who had already made a West End reputation in several plays, including that same production of *The Matchmaker* (opposite Ruth Gordon) Maggie had seen in Edinburgh.

McCowen was enormously taken with her: 'I remember thinking, when is she going to do something? I looked at her face and nothing seemed to be happening. But when I looked on the monitor, I realised everything was happening. Her acting was all in her head and very underplayed. It was a tender little play and she gave a very sensitive performance.' Peter Wood says that he had to hold the viewfinder up to his eyes so that the actors could not see him snivelling: 'The periphery of the emotional situation was very precise; they acted beautifully, in concentric rings. Alec's role was tenth cousin to Jimmy Porter [in *Look Back In Anger*], only Welsh, and Maggie had come to commune with herself.'

It was because of *Sunday out of Season* that both McCowen and Maggie were invited by Michael Benthall to join the Old Vic in 1959. One detail of this transaction still rankles with McCowen. During early rehearsals for that first season, the actors were marking out the moves when Benthall shouted at Maggie and McCowen from the back of the stalls: 'You'll have to speak up, we can't have any of this television acting here.' This insult to two of our most conspicuously audible actors was doubly hurtful because they were only 'blocking': 'But he was a strange man, Michael Benthall,' says McCowen, 'who used to give with one hand and take away with the other. He didn't much like people liking him, I don't think.'

Maggie completed a hectic television schedule which included Christopher Fry's *A Phoenix Too Frequent* and Somerset Maugham's *For Services Rendered*. Most of Maggie's early work on television has been lost or wiped. The cavalier attitude of its own custodians towards the nation's small-screen culture, in the age before video recordings, let alone DVDs, is a scandal of the postwar era; in Maggie's case, the loss is particularly regrettable if one judges it by the quality of her performance in the Maugham, which has luckily been preserved. She plays Lois, the youngest of three daughters in a country household torn apart in the dreary aftermath of the First World War. Maugham's bitter 1932 play was confirmed as a Chekhovian classic by this production, and its urgency and pathos are well served by the immediacy of a 'live performance' on television. The male casualties of war sit on the sofa, though Maggie as Lois is threatened less by bombs than by bombazine. She wants out, action, the bright lights, something to look forward to. She paints a serious, thoughtful portrait of a girl waking up to her own ability to exert power over men. She exudes confidence and poise, and does not use her 'revue' intonations, but the clear, cool voice of the real actress. It is a lovely performance, truthful and sharp, in a very good company.

At the end of 1958, Maggie appeared briefly in the only out-and-out West End flop of her career, *The Stepmother* by Warren Chetham-Strode. The débâcle was most keenly felt by Kate Reid, the distinguished Canadian actress who was making her London début. She played the new wife of a man haunted by the memory of his crippled first wife, and Maggie flitted on as a variety agent's secretary called Vere Dane, stealing the notices in a scene where she instructs an office boy in the art of coping with a would-be trainer of performing elephants. On tour, Maggie's humour and pathos were noted in the *Yorkshire Post*. Desmond Pratt said that her brash Cockney forthrightness was mixed with 'a deep sympathetic understanding of the secretly forlorn'. *The Times* approved 'a delightfully wristy performance'. Kate Reid recalled that Maggie's hair was dyed 'very, very blonde, almost pink' and that she cried a lot in rehearsals.

Maggie took this role partly on the rebound from a strange rebuff by Charles Laughton, in which her old Oxford admirer, John Beary, also played a part. Beary had been working in Ireland, but was now employed as an assistant to Laughton, who was appearing in, and directing, *The Party* by Jane Arden. Laughton went to see Maggie in *Share My Lettuce* at Beary's suggestion, invited her to audition for the role of his daughter and subsequently to dinner. Beary saw the whole affair as his great chance of reclaiming Maggie. Laughton said that she 'showed some signs of genius' and reminded him of Laurette Taylor.

But the next morning, the final girl came in to audition. It was Ann Lynn, and she was cast on the spot.

Beary says that Maggie was so shocked by this apparent rejection that she decided at that moment to do no more revues and to enter the lists as a serious actress. She became a contender. And Beary was romantically thwarted for the second time. In June 1959, the *Sunday Times* identified a representative cross-section of the British cultural élite, and the film critic Dilys Powell nominated in their number Maggie, whom J. W. Lambert apostrophised as 'a popper-in of great talent'. In August, Maggie returned to Edinburgh with the Old Vic company as Lady Plyant in Michael Benthall's production of Congreve's *The Double Dealer*.

Benthall had run the Old Vic since 1953, and Maggie was one of several newcomers who bridged the gap between these last days of the old rep and the incoming era of subsidised theatre. In 1963, Laurence Olivier would take over the Old Vic as the first artistic director of Britain's new National Theatre, and Maggie would be one of his twelve contracted actors, most of them unknown or recruited from the Royal Court. At the end of the 1950s, she represented the transitional phase, as well as that future in embryo, along with Judi Dench, Barbara Jefford, Alec McCowen, Stephen Moore and John Woodvine. John Moffatt recalls that she fitted into a very happy company which is 'unfairly despised' because of what happened afterwards. The leading actors were Fay Compton, Joss Ackland, Walter Hudd, Robert Harris, John Justin and Donald Houston. In 1960, Judi Dench and John Stride would make their names in Franco Zeffirelli's production of *Romeo and Juliet*. Michael Elliott ran the final Old Vic season after Benthall left in 1962, and then everything changed.

Judi Dench, Moyra Fraser, Maggie, John Moffatt, Alec McCowen and Joss Ackland became a particularly close group of friends within the company. They had Sunday lunches in each other's houses and suppers after the show. For McCowen, it was 'by far the happiest company I have ever worked in. That company symbolises for me the theatre and my time in it. Some of the productions were terrible, but not all. The happiest show I did there was *The Merry Wives of Windsor*, which was appalling, but a riot to be in. It was always very hard to get up the stairs in the interval because Moyra Fraser and Maggie had invariably collapsed with laughter and were rolling around hugging each other in these huge skirts.' Although Maggie was ever a worrier and self-doubter, McCowen says she 'was not so much a moaner in those Old Vic days'. He noticed the difference, the more downbeat approach, years later when they filmed *Travels with My Aunt* with George Cukor. 'Every morning on *Travels*, the greeting would be "Don't feel like it today" or some such phrase; but then this spirit for comedy bubbles out in a totally mysterious way.'

Judi Dench shared a dressing room with those very merry wives. 'Maggie always had the most beautiful clothes. She taught me always to buy not one pair of shoes but two or three identical pairs of what suited you. I had never met anyone like that before, and I've always done this ever since. She came to see me at the Vic the year after she left and she was wearing the most beautiful white coat. I jumped on her back and she spilt a glass of tomato juice all down the front. But I don't think she had two of those! To me, she's always been immensely funny, and always so chic with that wonderful, shiny hair.'

Judi and Maggie got to know each other in Edinburgh because Miles Malleson, a senior character actor who was as renowned for his bottom-pinching exploits as he was for his halitosis, was pursuing both of them. Judi Dench says, 'We were rather frightened of him, but I expect he only wanted to take us out to tea.'

The Double Dealer had not been produced since 1916, and Alan Pryce-Jones in the *Observer*, lauding Congreve as 'a supreme poet of the corrupt ephemeral', declared, presciently, that such a rare approach to playwriting needed a National Theatre to do it justice: 'Since the contemporary theatre has no experience of Restoration comedy, the company must be congratulated on doing as well as they do. They must not, however, sneeze when they take snuff.' The London reviews were generous, but it was Bernard Levin in the *Daily Express* who really threw his hat in the air, and not for the last time:

> ... shining over all there is the captivating, brilliant, champagne-bubble performance of Miss Maggie Smith as Lady Plyant. Miss Smith is a walking, talking flame. She has a squeal of pretended virtue with undertones so lascivious that it turns my bones to water. And I swear she never puts foot to ground throughout, but floats a yard above the stage.

Lady Plyant is a tyrant at home, a coquette abroad. Maggie, consigning her elderly husband to a permanent state of subjection and sexual starvation, must have driven poor old Miles Malleson as potty on stage as she did off. The spirit of independence in marriage and the enunciation of wittily brutal conditions laid down within and without the married state are hallmarks of the comic heroines who became Maggie's speciality: Rosalind, Beatrice, Silvia, Mrs Sullen, Margery Pinchwife, Maggie Wylie and Amanda Prynne. From Shakespeare to Restoration comedy, J. M. Barrie to Noël Coward, Maggie knew instinctively how to make herself stylishly available on her own terms. Levin declared that *As You Like It*, in which Maggie played Celia to Barbara Jefford's Rosalind and Alec McCowen's Touchstone, marked the end of a seven-year lean spell at the Vic, and that the theatre was now 'a place to visit for pleasure rather than duty'.

But new notes of critical dissension heralded a debate over mannerism which was to loom large across the years in any discussion of Maggie's acting. In the *Sunday Times*, J. W. Lambert entered the first caveat: 'Maggie Smith mangles her phrases [as Celia] with a quite striking absence of ear'; and Edward Goring in the *Daily Mail*, noting that previous queens in *Richard II* at the Old Vic included Peggy Ashcroft, Margaret Leighton, Renée Asherson and Claire Bloom, stated that Miss Smith 'is more suited to comedy . . . The flat, tremulous voice manages a tear-choking note but carries stronger echoes of Maggie, almost of our Eth of *The Glums*. Regal robes and one of those medieval gilt hairnet affairs sit uneasily on the dizzy bombshell of *Share My Lettuce*.'

Her extraordinary inflections have always been part of her repertoire. Alec McCowen can still hear today the sonic imprint Maggie left on Celia in phrases such as 'lame me with reasons' ('lame' given syllabic extension and a mocking, viperish tincture); 'like a dropped acorn', said of Orlando found lolling under a tree; 'I like this place and willingly could waste my time in it' on arrival in Arden; and 'Alas, poor shepherd', a poignantly heartfelt ejaculation. McCowen, no technical slouch himself, says that this colouring of the words, the unexpected highlighting of phrases that normally pass unnoticed, put her, for him, in the same class as Edith Evans. 'We knew she was a very special actress, even in that company; we were all pretty good.

But to do this with Celia! Barbara Jefford was a bloody good Rosalind, but she must have been quite surprised.'

Maggie was disappointed not to be playing Rosalind herself. She was also passed over for Gwendolen in *The Importance of Being Earnest* (again, Barbara Jefford, still young but vastly more experienced, got the role). Michael Benthall made amends by giving her the leading role in J. M. Barrie's *What Every Woman Knows* and thus set the seal on her stardom. The opening night was 12 April 1960. The *Daily Sketch* reported twelve curtain calls under the heading of 'Maggie – a Star at 24'. The *Daily Mail* review was headlined 'Maggie's night at the Old Vic', and the critic reported 'very loud cheers' and 'the arrival of Maggie Smith as a fully-fledged comedienne'.

Barrie's play, dating from 1908, when it was seen as a loose retelling of the early career of the Labour Prime Minister, Ramsay MacDonald, had not been seen in London since 1943. For the first time, Maggie was able to conjure the Celtic side of her background in the character of Maggie Wylie, an allegedly spinsterish ugly duckling whose father and brothers marry her off to a working-class upstart who has breached the family home in order to steal knowledge from their library. The 'wee wifey' becomes the inspirational support for the Scottish autodidact's political success, but she is taken advantage of, and proceeds to redefine her position by renegotiating it with evidence of marital infidelity. Some critics, including Alan Pryce-Jones, thought Maggie was too straightforwardly entrancing: 'Far from being unmarriageable, she would have had all Kirriemuir at her feet at a turn of the wrist.'

The production was given for only twenty-five performances, but the acclaim was tumultuous. John Moffatt, playing a diplomat, remembers that, on the first night, he came on 'and she had her back to me; it was the first time I had met her in the play and she was bent over a desk. She turned, and it was one of those extraordinary moments when I didn't see Maggie Smith there. I saw this other Maggie, Maggie Wylie, and it quite startled me. I hadn't seen this in rehearsals. I suddenly thought: this is a great actress.' The impact of Maggie's Maggie Wylie was considerable. The West End, and in particular the all-powerful Binkie Beaumont, sniffed out a new star. John Moffatt, looking back, is adamant about her right to supremacy.

Maggie always behaved instinctively like a great star. There was never any question of dirty words or taking her clothes off. This was, and is, inconceivable to her because of an idea of what the public will accept. And it was nothing to do with being 'grand' or 'theatrical'. With Maggie, the work always came first. When I was a young man, there were many great untouchable stars in the West End: Cicely Courtneidge, Marie Tempest, Noël Coward, John Gielgud and Beatrice Lillie. Maggie is the last one of that breed. And her privacy, her dislike of giving interviews and appearing on television chat shows, is all part of that. She respects the public too much to disappoint them with bad manners or odd behaviour.

The London publisher Hamish Hamilton wrote to Maggie on the very next morning: 'Your performance is enchanting, and I wish Barrie could have seen you. I'm sure he would have agreed that you are every bit as good as Hilda Trevelyan [the original Maggie Wylie], and much better than anyone else since. I haven't enjoyed an evening in the theatre so much for ages. My congratulations and thanks.'

One month after *What Every Woman Knows* opened, 'Binkie-vision' presented the première on ITV of Noël Coward's *Hay Fever*. Although Maggie's loyal champion Philip Purser thought that the 1925 comedy was 'rather a fraud' and that the production, directed by Casper Wrede (who had directed Maggie in *The Ortolan* at Oxford), suffered from its curiously haphazard camera work, the event was important in many respects, not least the distinction of its cast list. Maggie played the bashful, giggling flapper, Jackie Coryton, alongside Edith Evans as Judith Bliss, George Devine as David Bliss, Paul Eddington as Sandy Tyrell and Pamela Brown (the actress, not the author) as Myra Arundel. This latter role Maggie was to make her own ('This haddock is disgusting') in the famous National Theatre revival four years later, when Edith Evans would repeat her somewhat over-age version of Judith.

Coward had been off the agenda for a few years and had suffered setbacks in the theatre. *The Times* wondered at Edith Evans never having played Judith before and surely anticipated 'Dad's revival' (as Coward himself called it), which began with a 1963 production of *Private Lives* at the Hampstead Theatre Club, in declaring *Hay Fever* to be Coward's best play 'and one of the most perfectly engineered comedies of the century'.

The Bliss family entertain four guests for the weekend and subject them to mild humiliation and eccentric diversion between Friday evening and Sunday morning. Jackie is an effectively dumb role which Lynn Redgrave later occupied with considerable flair at the National. Maggie had her eye on Myra (*The Stage* complimented Pamela Brown on her 'darkly etched vampire') and, in the long term, Judith, the devastatingly hare-brained and incorrigibly vain actress who is teetering on the brink of middle-aged retirement. Meanwhile, *The Times* found this version 'a delicately timed, stunningly stylish production', and noted Maggie Smith's 'beautiful study of flaxen inanity'.

Maggie appeared 'by permission of Associated British Picture Corporation Ltd, and the Old Vic'. She was now definitely in demand. Michael Codron wanted her to appear in another revue with Kenneth Williams, but she was determined to continue her education as an actress. While Maggie made waves at the Old Vic, Codron presented two more shows with Williams, *Pieces of Eight* (1959) and *One Over the Eight* (1961). The Williams/Smith partnership was not over, though. They remained in touch and would team up again before long in the West End.

Maggie was flat-sharing with a girlfriend, Juliet Duncombe, in Eldon Road, Knightsbridge, and spending a lot of time with Ian Bannen, a Scottish actor six years her senior who had been in the Stratford-upon-Avon company with Beverley Cross and who, in 1958, had scored two great personal successes in the plays of Eugene O'Neill, *The Iceman Cometh* and *Long Day's Journey Into Night*. Bannen was a soft-spoken, introspective character whose melancholic disposition was ideally suited to the dark complexities of O'Neill. And, like the loyally besotted John Beary, he was a Catholic. Maggie was very taken with him, and also with a close friend of Bannen's, a stage-struck cleric called Adrian Arrowsmith, who began giving Maggie instruction in the Catholic faith. There was even talk at one stage of a great wedding in Westminster Cathedral. Nat and Meg must have been horrified at the thought of their daughter converting from their Presbyterian and Anglican persuasions. In the event, the friendship with Bannen petered out and Maggie never became a Catholic, although it was a close-run thing. Bannen was married only much later in life, after a turbulent career in movies and television.

Beverley Cross reappeared on the horizon. His first play, *One More River*, had opened successfully at the Liverpool Playhouse with a young actor called Michael Caine in the cast, and it was scheduled for an October 1959 presentation by Laurence Olivier's production company at the Duke of York's in London. He knew very well that this might bring him closer to Maggie once more, and although he was married to another Oxford contemporary, Elizabeth Clunies-Ross, he declared himself 'absent without leave', and reported devotedly to the stage door of the Old Vic in order to renew his lifetime's mission of courtship.

5

West End Calling, Screen Testing

The reappearance of Beverley Cross was to have a decisive effect on Maggie's career. His rock-like imperturbability complemented her anxiety and defensiveness. Until his death in 1998, as Maggie made her way through the early and middle ages of her fame and career, Beverley's companionship was the essential safety net for the high-wire tension of her performing style.

Beverley's mother, Eileen Dale, was a dancer and actress who claimed to have been pestered at the stage door of the Hippodrome by a 'frightfully dull' man called Evelyn Waugh (their brief correspondence is lost). She also appeared in the London premières of *Our Town* and *A Streetcar Named Desire* (she played Eileen Hubbel in Laurence Olivier's 1949 production headed by Vivien Leigh, Renée Asherson and Bonar Colleano). In 1936, when Beverley was five, Eileen married George Cross, a theatrical manager of such stars as Godfrey Tearle and Jack Buchanan, and later a long-serving house manager of the Ambassadors Theatre.

Beverley attended the naval college at Pangbourne during the war, joined the army and then postponed his arrival in Oxford by taking a berth in the Norwegian merchant navy. After Oxford, he joined the Shakespeare Memorial Theatre Company at Stratford-upon-Avon, but was discouraged from developing his acting career by a remark of John Gielgud, in whose production of *Much Ado About Nothing* he played Balthazar: 'You'll never make an actor; you wear your doublet and hose like a blazer and flannels.' He stopped acting almost immediately and wrote two novels, some television plays and *One More River*. His varied writing credits include two Tommy Steele musicals, two Richard Rodney Bennett operas and the new version of *The Scarlet Pimpernel* for Donald Sinden, directed by Nicholas Hytner at Chichester and Her Majesty's in 1985. In the late 1950s, he was one of the first recipients of the new Arts Council playwriting awards, for each of his first two plays, *One More River* at Liverpool and *Strip the Willow* at the Nottingham Playhouse. But the fashion in new playwriting was moving away from Beverley's style of work towards the rougher, working-class prescriptions for British society delivered by John Osborne, Arnold Wesker and the angry brigade at the Royal Court.

The link between the old West End order to which Beverley aspired and the new Court generation was Laurence Olivier. While his presentation of Beverley's *One More River* enjoyed a modest run at the Duke of York's and then the Westminster, Olivier himself was starring in Ionesco's *Rhinoceros* at the Royal Court, where he had scored one of the greatest successes of his career as Archie Rice in John Osborne's *The Entertainer*. Olivier, still married to Vivien Leigh, was appearing opposite Joan Plowright, with whom he was in love. When *Rhinoceros*, directed by Orson Welles, transferred to the Strand Theatre, Olivier's affair was reported in the newspapers and Plowright was compelled to leave the production because of the uproar – and, it was alleged, gastroenteritis. Plowright stayed on at the Court and made the biggest splash of her career as Beatie Bryant in Arnold Wesker's *Roots*. Guess who stepped into the Ionesco?

Maggie Smith took over as Daisy to Olivier's Berenger on 8 June 1960 for a six-week run. The show was the hottest ticket in town; it was said to be harder to get into than *My Fair Lady*. Other London hits of the moment included Donald Pleasence in Harold Pinter's *The Caretaker* at the Duchess, Paul Scofield in Robert Bolt's *A Man for All Seasons* (as it happens, the first play I saw on the London stage) at the Globe, Alec Guinness in Terence Rattigan's *Ross* at the Haymarket and the Lunts in Peter Brook's production of Dürrenmatt's *The Visit* at the Royalty. Maggie had instantly signed up to the élite. The *News Chronicle* described her as 'cool, crisp and wonderfully matter-of-fact as Daisy, the last woman in the world to join the rhinoceros ranks'. Maggie had little rehearsal time with Welles, but remembers being fascinated by the size of his feet. Olivier was suffering from gout at the time and Maggie set the pattern for their warily competitive relationship by sitting on the gouty leg during rehearsal.

Levin in the *Express* admired the way Maggie tamed her 'natural razor-sharpness . . . into the simple, consoling girl she should be' and

The Stage averred that she was 'gradually developing into an actress of distinction'. But *The Times* thought that she failed in the final long duet with Berenger: 'Her coming to look after him in a world beset by rhinoceroses is all too casually presented to us as a matter of comparative unimportance, so that her eventual desertion does not shock us as it should. Miss Smith's charm and lightness are not quite all that are needed here.' This idea that Maggie might be out of her depth in serious stage drama was one she never completely shook off, though there is ample evidence from Maggie Wylie onwards – through Desdemona and Hedda Gabler to her blistering performances in Edward Albee in the 1990s – to contradict it.

The force of her comic and indeed sexual presence certainly impressed Olga Franklin in the *Daily Mail*, who reviewed a television adaptation of Somerset Maugham's three-act comedy *Penelope*. Maggie played a doctor's wife who wins back an errant spouse by affecting indifference. Franklin said that the production's one weakness was that 'the beautiful Maggie, dressed to the nines with more sex appeal in her little finger than Monroe and Bardot in the nude, made it seem hopelessly unconvincing that her doctor husband should prefer another woman'.

The ripening of Maggie coincided with her appearance in Beverley's crucial second play. After the première of *Strip the Willow* in Nottingham, a new pre-London tour was presented in Cambridge, Newcastle and Brighton in September. Maggie was cast as Kathy Dawson, a politician's mistress sheltering from an imminent nuclear attack in a decaying West Country folly, along with an archaeologist (played by Barrie Ingham) and a private detective (Michael Bates, who had also been in *Rhinoceros*). Beverley had inverted the Judgement of Paris myth by requiring Kathy to choose the man with whom she would begin procreation after the bombs had fallen in the first interval. For one reason or another, Maggie spent much of the play wearing very few clothes.

Maggie's decorative qualities were politely referred to on the road, but *The Times*, venturing forth to the Hippodrome at Golders Green, last stop before the West End, ran a review under the unpromising headline 'Britain Wiped Out in Comedy's First Act', while the *Daily Telegraph* killed kindly, but killed nonetheless, with 'Horror Comedy a

Bit Flat'. Beverley wrote his personal tribute to Maggie in the form of a stage direction at Kathy's entrance: 'She is about twenty-five and very beautiful. As elegant and sophisticated as a top international model. A great sense of fun. A marvellous girl.' Binkie Beaumont of H. M. Tennent, who had gone to Golders Green at Beverley's invitation, told him that the West End did not like ironic comedy but that 'the girl is very, very good'. So good, in fact, that he started planning her West End career while putting a stop, for the moment, to Beverley's: *Strip the Willow* never made it onto Shaftesbury Avenue.

Also in the cast was a young Australian actor, Michael Blakemore, who, thirty years later, would direct Maggie in *Lettice and Lovage*. He played an American soldier on security patrol after the fall-out.

It was an odd play, derived from drawing-room comedy and Peter Ustinov's *The Love of Four Colonels*. But I had this long and very delicious scene with Maggie, which she played in a bathing suit. We tended to giggle a lot, but playing with her was thrilling, because of her sense of stage reality. Like all remarkable actors, she can live in the moment. She organises a part so that every single moment is accounted for, but she still has the flexibility within that framework to do something marginally different each night. She is also incredibly generous. The prerequisite of the very best acting is the ability to listen; and there's no actor I know who's a better listener than Maggie. She was on her way to becoming a star in those days, but she wasn't there yet. She was just an extremely brilliant actress that everyone had their eye on and had great hopes for.

Maggie and Beverley were now living together in the Eldon Road flat in South Kensington. Beverley was otherwise based at the White House at Beaumont in Hertfordshire, which he shared with his chow dog, Tuffet. His first marriage had broken down irretrievably, but there was a delay in arranging the divorce. Most friends of Maggie and Beverley regarded them as unofficially engaged. Beverley went off to location in Jordan to do some second-unit script editing on the David Lean film of *Lawrence of Arabia* ('action stuff with camels'), while Maggie squeezed in another television role before joining a production of Jean Anouilh's *The Rehearsal*, which Binkie Beaumont was supporting at the Bristol Old Vic and bringing into the Globe. The television play, only the second that survives on tape from her early career, was *The Savages* by Peter Draper, the author of *Sunday out of Season*. This was another 'Binkie-vision' project in which Maggie plays Rose, a Cockney prostitute who steals the heart of a young boy starved of affection at home. It is a sentimental and naïve piece, but not without its moments. The best scene is that between Maggie and the boy, who tells her that she is the most beautiful person he has ever seen. Maggie has a tumbled, fresh-faced look about her and the sympathetic listening she lavishes on the boy makes a nice change from all the 'entertaining' she has to provide at other times.

Maggie was a more respectable child-minder in *The Rehearsal*. She played the young girl employed to care for the orphans in the west wing of a château where a party, rehearsing the performance of a Marivaux play, unconsciously echoes its own romantic intrigues. The girl, Lucile, is heartlessly seduced by the debauched hero, called Hero, played by Alan Badel. The assistant director was a young working-class son of a Home Counties gardener. He was called Robin Phillips and Maggie later spent a crucial working period of her life with him in Canada, where he was director of the Stratford Festival Theatre in Ontario. But in 1961 he was a nobody. And a dogsbody.

The director, John Hale, left him to run through a rehearsal of the seduction scene, which was not going well, on what happened to be Phillips's nineteenth birthday: 'Badel was very much the star, sitting centre stage, and Maggie was hugging the walls.' When they cried out for help, he tentatively suggested that the scene might be more effective if Maggie sat centre stage and Badel encircled her. 'I don't think it was a particularly clever suggestion, but they tried it, and of course the scene immediately worked. It was quite nice. I could see Maggie's eyes twinkling at the suggestion. She didn't say anything... but they whisked me off for a birthday drink because they were so pleased.' Phillips was to become one of Maggie's favourite and most influential directors, but not for another fourteen years.

After the first night at the Globe on 6 April 1961, Robert Muller in the *Daily Mail* declared the scene to be 'one of the most affecting things to be seen in London at the moment'. Levin in the *Express* commended Maggie's 'pretty dash and honesty'; Hobson in the *Sunday Times* found her 'touching, sincere and sometimes devastating.' Tynan in the *Observer* applauded everything about the play and production except her contribution: '[She] never quite captures the luminous gravity that Anouilh demands; instead of silver she gives us tin,' hinting at Portia's casket scene in *The Merchant of Venice* which Maggie played on television ten years later. *The Rehearsal* moved next door to the Queen's Theatre in May but Maggie was back at the Globe, and reunited with Kenneth Williams and the director Peter Wood, one year later in Peter Shaffer's double bill *The Private Ear* and *The Public Eye*. Her success here ensured that she was discovered yet again. Binkie Beaumont was clasping her to his scheming and all-powerful bosom, and literati even more distinguished than the critics were sitting up.

Evelyn Waugh visited the Globe with Lady Diana Cooper and wrote to Ann Fleming on 2 July 1962:

We (Diana and I) went to the theatre and saw a brilliant (to me) actress named Maggie Smith. We couldn't get seats and then said 'How about a box?' 'Oh yes, of course there's always a box. Do you really want one?' So we sat cheek by jowl with Maggie Smith and admired her feverishly . . . Miss Smith is a fair treat and the two little plays she is in give her a chance to show it. She will become famous. Perhaps she is already and it is like me saying, keep an eye on a clever young American called T. S. Eliot.

In the first 'little play', *The Private Ear*, Maggie was Doreen, an office typist on a first date with a nervous music-lover in his Belsize Park flat; in the second, *The Public Eye*, she was Belinda, the young wife of a jealous accountant who sets an eccentric private detective, Julian Christoferou, on her trail. Julian munches macaroons in a mackintosh and becomes the surrogate lover who never existed to start with. The role was taken by Kenneth Williams, but Beaumont considered him too outré for the sensitive musical wooer, and that part was played by a prominent juvenile of the day, Terry Scully, who gave up acting shortly afterwards. According to Peter Wood, the double bill's director, it had initially been offered to Michael Caine, though Caine himself has no memory of this. A trailblazing young romantic actor who did not sound like a RADA-trained minor public schoolboy, Caine was on the brink of a movie career which would eventually pair him with Maggie in *California Suite*.

Shaffer, of course, wrote the two triangular pieces with a view to the same three actors appearing in each. Instead, Williams made a mark as the strange detective and Maggie increased her reputation for versatility. Many critics expressed disappointment in the quality of the plays, but Shaffer only offered them as *jeux d'esprit*. Both Shaffer and Wood took every opportunity to observe the extraordinary rapport between the two young stars. Shaffer remembers a Sunday lunch at the Bear Inn, Woodstock, en route to the pre-West End touring date in Oxford. He asked Maggie if she liked salmon and she replied that she did if it was good; if it wasn't, it tasted like old blankets. The phrase lodged. The small restaurant was full of sober, respectable families. The situation acted as a spur, says Shaffer, to Williams, 'who invented an invisible man standing at the table exposing himself, with Kenny in that very loud fruity voice protesting "I've had just about enough of this, I'm not interested in your dick, do you understand that?" and so on. Maggie was in part delighted, but really rather disapproving. She hardly ever performs like that in private, let alone in public.'

As for their work together, Wood says it was simply dazzling. 'They were like greyhounds, the speed at which they could bat and ball it.' Wood dismisses as 'facile rubbish' the common accusation that Maggie picked up her exaggerated campy nasal twanging from Williams:

> She has an idiosyncratic inflection process that is all her own. Kenneth, too, had this way of splitting the inflection, the 'ee-aw' thing which is immensely valuable and which Katharine Hepburn and Jean Arthur also had. This skill allows you to lift the end of a line so that it is properly heard and available for another actor to respond to. It's quite a rare gift nowadays. Maggie and Kenneth adored each other primarily because of their common speed and brilliance: it was like Boris Becker and John McEnroe meeting each other on the tennis court having never played anyone else as good as themselves.

Maggie's great moment in *The Private Ear* arrived when the hapless would-be seducer fed his behemoth of a sound system the love duet from *Madame Butterfly*. Wood devised a six-minute mime, each move of which was timed 'not to the bar, but to the note' and, at the point of seductive would-be resolution, Maggie slapped Scully's face. Shaffer recalls Maggie not doing a sketch, but suggesting a woman in a terrible situation in a fake ocelot coat, entangling herself in that coat, taking a cigarette, burning the coat out of nervousness. His climactic stage direction in the published text describes exactly what she did: 'Doreen slaps the boy's face – then, horrified, takes it between her hands, trying to recall the blow.'

These were happy days, symbolised by the fact that Beverley, Maggie and Beverley's stepfather, George Cross, were working in adjacent theatres on Shaftesbury Avenue: the Apollo, the Globe and the Queen's. Beverley had a great commercial success with his English adaptation of the French farce *Boeing-Boeing*, starring David Tomlinson; Maggie was working with the actor she liked above all others, Kenneth Williams, while Richard Pearson, who played the jealous accountant, became a good friend to both; and George Cross was managing the Queen's and playing host to Anthony Newley's hit musical *Stop the World – I Want to Get Off*. Williams said in his autobiography that the warm summer 'seemed never ending' and he would spend weekends blackberrying in the Hertfordshire fields and chasing the dog around the gardens at Beaumont and nearby Broxbourne with Maggie and Beverley. One blazing Sunday morning, Maggie drove Williams to Beckenham in Kent for a day with Richard Pearson and his family. She wore a pink dress with a matching hatband round a straw boater: 'It was an open car and, at every traffic light, motorists and lorry drivers looked twice at this elegant lady motorist. I felt very proud sitting beside her.'

Feature articles about Maggie began to appear more regularly, and she covered her embarrassment with giggles. She told the *Daily Express* that she had no idea where she was going: 'I just drift into things and I've been lucky. I live for today. I'm restless. I put off everything,' adding with a nice touch of mysteriousness, 'I'm always living behind myself.' Evasive tactics were momentarily dropped when she told *Woman's Own* magazine that she would not return to revue: 'To go back to anything is bad. In revue you have to make your impact in three minutes flat. It's agony...' Nor was she brimming with fashion tips for the readers: 'I can't wear any kind of jewellery, and hats look ghastly on me.'

Her performance in the Shaffer plays secured her the first of her many major awards: best actress in the *Evening Standard* drama awards for 1962. Maggie had beaten off challenges from Brenda Bruce, Geraldine McEwan, Dorothy Tutin, Siobhán McKenna and Sheila Hancock. That year's best actor was Paul Scofield in Peter Brook's great production of *King Lear*. Maggie accepted the prize on 28 January 1963 with the words, 'I did seem to get through at O-Level. I do promise you I'll try very hard next term.' She was escorted to the dinner at the Savoy by Beverley, and wore a long black skirt and a bronze-coloured top which, said the *Express*, reflected 'the deep glow of her lovely auburn hair'.

She had left the Shaffer plays and taken a three-week holiday with Beverley in the winter sun on Tobago. 'Next term' would bring a fateful invitation to join the National Theatre. But she was concentrating for the moment on her third big West End role for Binkie and H. M. Tennent, Mary McKellaway, in Jean Kerr's *Mary, Mary*, which opened at the Queen's at the end of February (*Stop the World* had completed a run of just over a year). Jean Kerr was the wife of the prominent American drama critic Walter Kerr. She never saw Maggie in her play because she refused to board an aeroplane. The Canadian actor Don Harron was the trusted repository of her views on how the play should be produced. Mary in the play is a journalist, precariously married to the publisher Bob McKellaway (Harron). Within a fortnight of their divorce, a question of income tax reunites them. A flirtation with a film star enlivens Mary and rekindles her marriage. The rows were redolent of Coward's *Private Lives*. But Mary's barrage of wisecracks – 'By the time she is thirty, a starlet has been carefully taught to smile like a dead halibut'; 'This man writes like a sick elf' – was insufficient to save a piece most critics deemed second-rate. Levin, who had moved to the *Daily Mail*, said it was constructed on 'the washing-line principle', with funny lines hung out to dry between the posts holding up the plot. But the comments on Maggie's performance were uniformly complimentary.

The most interesting and sustained appreciation came from Bamber Gascoigne, who had recovered from the agreeable shock of seeing Maggie in his own revue and taken up a column in the *Spectator*.

Miss Smith's performance is extraordinarily mannered – but then this is largely its strength, since the mannerisms are so completely and unmistakably her own. Most great comediennes have this quality of unique oddity; anyone else borrowing their gestures or tricks would look plain ridiculous, but in them, the effect is superb. If Beatrice Lillie is suavely mad, and Joyce Grenfell is gawky, the word for Maggie Smith is probably akimbo. When motionless she looks as trim as a kitten, but the slightest shock – a seductive innuendo from a dark, handsome film star, or the blast of light when the curtains are drawn in the morning – is likely to send her billowing across the stage, her legs and arms flapping about in a welter of confusion like a puppet whose puppeteer is about to sneeze.

The breakthrough was now fully accomplished. She was working with the élite, and the future élite, of her profession, but I was surprised to learn that she was also, in these first couple of years of the 1960s, participating in some informal workshops with the directors Lindsay Anderson and Anthony Page (years later she would work with Page on three of her finest mature stage performances in plays by the American playwright Edward Albee). Page, after graduating from Oxford, where he had seen Maggie in the student revues, had studied at the Neighbourhood Playhouse School of the Theatre in New York, an offshoot of the Stanislavsky-influenced Group Theatre of the 1930s and the Actors Studio founded in 1947 by Elia Kazan and Robert Lewis. It was a form of Method acting that, in the system developed by the director Sanford Meisner, replaced the Stanislavskyan use of affective memory with an emphasis on 'the reality of doing'; in other words, it was a performing technique devised to find a new, or fresher, way of an actor speaking the truth. Anderson and Page ran these sessions of improvisatory scenes in different locations around town – Ronnie Scott's jazz club in Soho, various houses in Chelsea – and invited actors to do exercises, and improvise scenes, outside of the performances they were already giving in London theatres.

Maggie went along several times, in company with such budding young actors of the day as Albert Finney, Daniel Massey, Georgia Brown (who had scored a hit singing 'As Long as He Needs Me' in Lionel Bart's *Oliver!*), Donal Donnelly and Alfred Lynch. Page recalls:

I don't know if anyone learned anything, but it was great fun and very amusing. You don't think of Maggie, then or now, as a workshop sort of actress, but she seemed to enjoy it. I was absolutely possessed by this Meisner system at the time, almost like a born-again. She had then, as she always had, a great curiosity and appetite for her work, and she is of course incredibly intelligent, with very strong instincts, and fantastic powers of concentration. She doesn't really like being told if she's done something well because she's very aware that if it all comes back at her, she perhaps can't hit it in the same way, so everything has to stay provisional, incomplete; and that's at the root of her having a very instinctive way of acting.

In movies, too, Maggie was on the brink of stardom. Her seven-year film contract suddenly yielded a sprightly role in an eminently watchable crime comedy, *Go to Blazes*, for which the Irish wit and raconteur Patrick Campbell co-wrote the screenplay. Maggie played Chantal, a French shop girl in a Berkeley Square fashion house run by a queenly couturier majestically played by Coral Browne. They become involved in the escapades of three amiable crooks – Daniel Massey, Norman Rossington and Dave King – a pyromaniac 'Mr Big' played by Robert Morley, and a struck-off fire chief, played by Dennis Price, who educates the gang in fast getaway techniques by appropriating an old fire engine and securing immunity against red lights, traffic police and other civil obstructions. The film suffers an almost fatal attack of lethargy during an overextended farcical interlude with Derek Nimmo as a domestic flood victim but the rest is bright and charming, with lovely vignettes from dear old Miles Malleson as an excitable antique fire-engine curator and the legendary Wilfrid Lawson as a junk-yard manager.

Maggie appears at her most lushly glamorous in this film and she knocks Daniel Massey for six at their first encounter. Her figure is sensuously outlined in a stylish olive-green dress when Massey, on the run, backs into a roomful of models and disrupts a fashion show. He passes himself off as an aristocrat from the Foreign Office. Their romance founders when their cover is blown. For not only is the Massey character a fraud, so is Chantal: when Coral Browne tells Maggie the firm is going bust, her French accent evaporates in a Cockney howl of 'Blimey, can't we 'ave a lovely little bonfire, and collect?' Coral Browne's shop eventually goes up in flames as Massey and Co. raid the next-door bank. But the getaway is interrupted by a real forest fire and, in their efforts to act responsibly for once, the crooks forfeit their booty. Sackfuls of banknotes are blown into the sky. Prison looms once again.

Nowhere to Go had been made in a spirit of antagonism towards the Ealing comedies but, in the positive destination of *Blazes*, Maggie relished just as readily the genuine, slightly quaint and old-fashioned article. The contrast is a clear demonstration that she would never distinguish conclusively between the serious and the trivial in her work; she respected both and was unhampered by too many artistic pretensions. She knew as clearly as anyone, and better than most, the difference, say, between Congreve and Peter Shaffer. But both could supply appropriate raw material for the exercise of her artistry.

Finally, it was in *The VIPs* that Maggie created an international stir. MGM's two-hour blockbuster, scripted by Terence Rattigan and directed by Anthony Asquith, was in part devised as the second film after *Cleopatra* to enhance the romantic fairy-tale legend of Elizabeth Taylor and Richard Burton, the biggest gift to showbiz gossip writers since the heyday of Douglas Fairbanks and Mary Pickford. A sort of *Grand Hotel* of the airport lounge, the film crams an array of star actors – among them Orson Welles and Margaret Rutherford – into a fog-bound Heathrow, where they await a delayed flight to Miami. Elizabeth Taylor is on the point of leaving her shipping-millionaire husband (Burton) for a fling with Louis Jourdan. Maggie appears as Miss Mead, a loyally inventive and romantically disposed secretary to a brash Australian tycoon played by Rod Taylor (the same sort of relationship was repeated opposite Rex Harrison in *The Honeypot*). She fidgets effectively in a sensible coat and beret while Rod Taylor receives bad news; he has one last chance to beat off a corporate challenge in America, but no cash. Meanwhile, Burton goes grovelling to

Elizabeth Taylor with apologies and new intentions, but an almighty row ensues.

At this point, Maggie has her big scene, requesting help for her boss from the wealthy Burton. She plays it on the edge of tears, while Burton, boiling inside with his own frustrated devotion, recognises her advocacy as an expression of unrequited love for Rod Taylor and signs a blank cheque. It is a beautiful encounter, expertly and tenderly played on both sides. Burton certainly recognised Maggie's quality. He later said that she didn't just steal the scene; she committed 'grand larceny'. He never worked with her again.

She had kissed the Canadian George Nader in *Nowhere to Go*. Her second screen kiss with a hunky colonial leading man (Rod Taylor was Australian) was gratifyingly received and she delicately touched her lips with the tips of her long fingers. Off screen, Rod Taylor had fallen very heavily for Maggie and was even said by Robert Stephens to have proposed marriage to her in the first week of shooting. She did not entirely reject his advances, although he was a married man, and the romance blossomed in their second film together, *Young Cassidy*.

While Maggie continued to draw the town in *Mary, Mary*, Kenneth Williams came out of the Shaffer plays and persuaded Beverley to accompany him on a holiday cruise to the Greek Islands. Williams was quite happy sipping his eau de vie on deck, but Beverley ploughed ashore to visit the hallowed sites on Delos, Lemnos and Skiathos, though he did manage to drag Williams up to the Parthenon when they dropped anchor at Athens. As these two stalwarts of the commercial theatre were trudging through the ruins, Laurence Olivier was gathering around him a hand-picked caucus of personnel for the new National Theatre he had launched at Chichester in 1962. As fellow directors, he enlisted William Gaskill and John Dexter, both from the Royal Court, where he knew, through Joan Plowright and from first-hand experience, that the most exciting new theatrical energy was being unleashed by George Devine.

Each director had a say in the recruitment of actors. Dexter and Gaskill insisted on three Royal Court actors, in addition to Plowright: Robert Stephens, Colin Blakely and Frank Finlay. In carving up the repertoire, Gaskill agreed to do a Restoration comedy, Farquhar's *The Recruiting Officer*. He told Olivier that the only actress he knew who could play Silvia was Maggie Smith, whom he rated 'the new Edith Evans', though he later qualified that to say she didn't really resemble her at all (there was nothing of the clown in Evans, he said): but he had seen her as Lady Plyant in *The Double Dealer* at the Old Vic and said that 'she spoke the brilliant, difficult text as if it were the most natural expression of the character'. Joan Plowright, now married to Olivier, obviously had his ear on account of its proximity to hers on the pillow. She had also been aware of Maggie for some time. She remembers rehearsing *The Entertainer* and reading Jean Rhys and, not surprisingly, feeling a bit low. Two friends took her to see *Share My Lettuce* and she thought Maggie was 'divine': 'Way before the National Theatre started, Larry was drawing up a list of people to be considered, and I persuaded him to go to see Maggie in *The Double Dealer*. Larry came back and said that an actress who can play comedy as well as that can also play tragedy, if she really wants to.'

As a result, Olivier, who of course now knew Maggie at first hand from *Rhinoceros*, invited her to lunch at the Ivy, the theatrical restaurant opposite the Ambassadors Theatre. She was a percentage star in the West End, earning 7.5 per cent of the gross box-office take, with a more than promising film career taking shape. The offer had to be good. Olivier was unable to put a great salary on the table, but in addition to Silvia, he unexpectedly threw in Hilde Wangel in Ibsen's *The Master Builder*, and Desdemona in *Othello*. Maggie was so surprised she nearly choked on her food. Binkie Beaumont, she knew, had more plans for her. And, in spite of the Old Vic season, she felt she was inexperienced in the highbrow classical repertory. She gave Olivier a definite 'No' and rushed home in a blind panic to Eldon Road. Beverley was horrified at her decision. He talked her down, and round. First thing next morning, Maggie sent Olivier a telegram reversing her decision and accepting his invitation to join the National Theatre.

She was one of twelve actors placed on a three-year contract. Robert Stephens was another and, as Beverley jovially admitted in later life, in persuading her to join the National at the Old Vic, he pushed her into the whirlwind of a relationship with Stephens, followed by marriage and two children with him. For a time in the 1960s, it seemed as though the English-speaking theatre had found, in Maggie Smith and Robert Stephens, its new ideal star couple, fit successors to the Lunts and the Oliviers.

In November 1963, *Time* magazine picked out Maggie Smith and summarised her career as she prepared to test her mettle with Olivier. Earlier in the year she had given a rare and most revealing interview to Nancy Banks-Smith in the *Observer*. Nothing she has said since summarised so well the life she had found as an actress in flight from both the pressures of the real world and the deficiencies, as she saw them, in her own personality:

I'm never shy on the stage. Always shy off it. You see, the theatre is a different world. A much better world. It's the real world that's the illusion. It's a world whose timetable is more precise than anything else on earth. Outside, trains can run late. But trains in the theatre are always on time ... It's strict. It's secure. The theatre is full of people looking for prefabricated security. They find it there. Nowhere else. Outside, marriages crash ... life goes wrong ... the thermometer freezes. Inside, the walls are padded against the world.

6

Surprises with Olivier at the National

Maggie has always had a habit of stepping from one job to another with scarcely a break and often a too busy period of overlap. She joined Olivier's National as a West End star, and extended her night shift on Shaftesbury Avenue in *Mary, Mary* during the opening rehearsal period. She left *Mary, Mary* on the last night of November 1963 and ten days later opened as Silvia in *The Recruiting Officer* at the Old Vic. The curtain had gone up on the new National on 22 October with a fair-to-middling production of *Hamlet* guest-starring Peter O'Toole. *Saint Joan* and *Uncle Vanya*, both great successes, joined the repertoire from the Chichester Festival Theatre, where Olivier had been preparing and half-launching the operation for two summers.

The Recruiting Officer had not been seen in London since 1943 and it was the first real test of how the mixture devised by Olivier and his subalterns would work. Olivier himself appeared as Captain Brazen, alongside Max Adrian as Justice Balance, ex-Royal Courtiers Stephens and Blakely as Captain Plume and Sergeant Kite, with new names Derek Jacobi and Lynn Redgrave in support. An unknown Michael Gambon played a tiny role. William Gaskill, who had been flatteringly wooed away from the Royal Court by Olivier, recalls the flurry of excitement which attended these early days:

I don't remember Maggie coming in like a visiting star, not for a moment. I did a lot of improvisations, so everyone was in the same boat. The starting-up of the company was exhilarating and that generated a kind of equality, with of course Larry having the status that he always had. Everyone was in a sense less experienced and less important than he was.

The production is renowned in retrospect as signalling the restoration of Restoration comedy. It was light and clear, with a beautiful outdoor Shrewsbury townscape based by the designer René Allio on the redbrick Queen Anne buildings of the main street in Amersham. It had architectural airiness without pastel-coloured cuteness. Bamber Gascoigne, who had succeeded Kenneth Tynan on the *Observer*, said that 'every scene on this stage acquired an air of sharpened reality, like life on a winter's day with frost and sun'. The old 'gadzooks' fan-flapping Restoration frills and frippery were out. The playing was tough, quick, ebullient, and Felix Barker in the *Evening News* confidently proclaimed that 'a new tradition was born in the English theatre . . . [with] no straining after effects, no twiddly bits' in Gaskill's quietly orchestrated production. Olivier's entrance, after a big build-up in the early scenes, was at first subliminal, as he flashed hilariously across the back of the stage without a word. Maggie spent most of the evening in travesty, with a cork-black moustache and knee-high black boots which, as B. A. Young said in *Punch*, gave her 'a curious gait with a suggestion of the goose-step about it; just to see her walk across the stage is a comic treat in itself'. Gaskill thought she was not immediately happy in the role, but improved as the production matured in the repertory. Her amorous pursuit of Captain Plume resulted in a fraternal clinch with Robert Stephens, who exclaimed, oddly bemused, 'S'death! There's something in this fellow that charms me!'

There was indeed. He and Maggie embarked on a clandestine affair in early 1964 that was initially an inevitable consequence of working proximity. In March, at Lynn Redgrave's twenty-first birthday party, only two people – Lynn and her father's dresser, Christopher Downes, who became a close friend (and dresser) to both Maggie and Robert – knew of the liaison. Robert was married, for the second time, to the actress Tarn Bassett. They had a daughter, Lucy, born in 1963, who became an international lawyer. Robert had met Maggie at a party several years earlier and considered her 'a rather sad-looking creature'. During rehearsals of the Farquhar she made him laugh a lot: 'She was very raunchy. She didn't drink like a fish, but she swore like a trooper. I thought it was just going to be one of those theatrical romances which can happen, but she was much more serious about it than I was.' Robert was three years older than Maggie. The son of a West Country master builder, he left home in Bristol to train in Bradford with Esmé Church and arrived in London via a stint with the Caryl Jenner touring company and repertory in Morecambe. Tony Richardson, George Devine's assistant at the Royal Court, brought him down to join the English Stage Company as a founder member in 1956. It was there, in 1958, that he played the title role of *Epitaph for George Dillon* by John Osborne and Anthony Creighton. The production transferred to Broadway.

The future looked good. And so, for a considerable time, and mostly with Maggie Smith, it was. But Robert, who died in 1995, was a complex, troubled character whose immensely likeable volatility became too much part of his stage persona. William Gaskill, who had also been introduced to the Court by his fellow Yorkshireman Tony Richardson, was the director of *George Dillon*. He once pinpointed Robert's special quality as an actor: the ability to understand the nature of failure. In the last act of *George Dillon*, after the hero has enjoyed some success as a hack writer, he is given a present by his family. Gaskill recalls that, as he unwrapped it to discover a typewriter, Robert registered layers of reaction that convinced you this man would never write anything worthwhile in his life. There was a similar moment of volcanic poignancy at the end of *The Recruiting Officer*, when Plume renounces his job: '...the recruiting trade with all its train of lasting plague, fatigue and endless pain, I gladly quit...' Stephens invested the lines with what Gaskill calls 'a shadow quality', bringing to the conclusion something over and above what the play actually says.

Robert had returned to the Court after New York and joined Olivier's new venture at Chichester in 1963. He had already played the Dauphin in *Saint Joan* and Horatio in the O'Toole *Hamlet* before Maggie came spinning into his life as Silvia. The relationship, artistic and personal, gathered speed throughout 1964, with Maggie playing Desdemona and Hilde Wangel opposite first Michael Redgrave and then Olivier, and Robert scoring his greatest National Theatre triumph as Atahuallpa, the Peruvian sun god in Peter Shaffer's historical epic *The Royal Hunt of the Sun*. Within the same twelve months, Maggie's second major film, *The Pumpkin Eater*, was released, and she answered a call from Rod Taylor to play opposite him in the Dublin shooting of a film about the early life of Sean O'Casey, *Young Cassidy*. This hectic year ended with the all-star National production of Noël Coward's *Hay Fever* and preparations for Franco Zeffirelli's riotously Italianate *Much Ado About Nothing*, in which Maggie and Robert sealed their pact with the public as Beatrice and Benedick.

The cast of *Othello* assembled to read the play on 3 February 1964. As recounted in a famous rehearsal log book kept by Kenneth Tynan, Olivier, who had been talked reluctantly by his dramaturg into playing the last great tragic role available to him, 'delivered the works – a fantastic full-volume display that scorched one's ears, serving final notice on everyone present that the hero, storm-centre and focal point of the tragedy was the man named in the title. Seated, bespectacled and lounge-suited, he fell on the text like a tiger.' Olivier had enrolled at a gymnasium and worked hard at unravelling a new baritonal lower octave to mix in with his steel and whiplash tenor. His make-up was incredibly elaborate. He aimed at a blue-black Nubian colour and, at every single performance, covered himself from top to toe in three layers, allowing each one to dry. This process took three hours. His dresser then polished him with a piece of chiffon until he shone. His hair was cut short so that his wig could be glued to the back of his neck, deleting the possibility of a recalcitrant hedge effect when his neck muscles bulged. Finally, he was sprayed in a very fine mineral oil. He was literally, and metaphorically, untouchable. Maggie felt that in the scene when she welcomed him back from Cyprus, there should be physical contact. Olivier refused, and she exclaimed in one rehearsal, 'I've come all the way from Venice to see you, you've won the war, I'm pleased to see you, what do you want me to do, back away in fuckin' 'orror?' Olivier took Robert, who was not in the production, to one side and said, 'Please tell her to stay away from me on the stage. I don't mind if she looks like a cunt, but I'm buggered if I'm going to look like one.'

The production opened on Shakespeare's birthday, 23 April. There was a brittle wariness and rivalry between Olivier and Maggie. She was possibly the only member of the company of whom he was secretly afraid, simply because he knew how good she was. She could give as good as he gave, and was probably twice as fast. One night Olivier took her to task for the diphthongs she would form on her vowel sounds. As the daughter of an important senator, he felt she would speak impeccably and not sound quite so common. She took the point and poked her head round his dressing room as he sat there in all his black and naked glory: 'How Now Brown Cow!' she mockingly and immaculately intoned. Olivier either didn't get the joke or refused to be riled: 'That's much better, Maggie darling,' he said. Christopher Downes remembers, too, that Maggie sent the boss a postcard of Cassius Clay, then at the height of his boxing fame, on which his boastful tag-line – 'I'm the greatest, I'm the greatest' – was prominently displayed: 'He didn't get it at all. He had very little sense of humour about himself.'

John Dexter was the director of *Othello*, and he encouraged Maggie to be stronger, stiller and more serene than are most Desdemonas. According to Riggs O'Hara, the American actor who lived and worked with Dexter for thirty years, the director saw the steel and iron in Maggie and disliked the more girlish, vulnerable side of her acting. In his diary notes, Dexter wrote after the early casting sessions: 'Nobody wants her [Maggie]. I do. A strong-willed mature woman who's been around and knows what she wants. She wants that big black man. Isn't everyone tired of pretty blonde ingenue Desdemonas?'

Maggie surprised everyone in the role. As O'Hara says, 'She sailed down from the back of the stage through that copper arch in a blue paisley dress with that wonderful brown chiffon over-sash Jocelyn Herbert had designed for her, the air billowing out under it; it was quite spectacular. I'd never seen her be that magisterial.' John Gielgud thought she was 'extraordinary casting' but that she pulled it off splendidly. Tynan thought that she revealed something new – 'an ability to play serious characters whose approach to sex was affirmative and aimed at total erotic fulfilment'.

In spite of Olivier's 'hands-off' instruction, the couple kissed when Othello arrived in Cyprus, with a hint of dreamy sexuality on both sides. In pleading for Cassio, Maggie played sweetly but strongly right down the middle of the argument. And when Othello struck her round the face with the proclamation he had received from Lodovico her reaction was not, as Tynan noted, the usual collapse into sobs, but 'one of deep shame and embarrassment, for Othello's sake as well as her own. She is outraged, but tries out of loyalty not to show it. After the blow, she holds herself rigidly upright and expressionless, fighting back tears. "I have not deserved this" is not an appeal for sympathy, but a protest quietly and firmly lodged by an extremely spunky girl.'

This scene spawned another anecdote often recounted by Maggie, corroborated by Robert and by Derek Jacobi, who played Cassio. Some months into the run, Olivier was trying to persuade Maggie that she should appear in Thornton Wilder's *The Skin of Our Teeth*, but Maggie was resisting the idea, and one or two other suggestions. Olivier was so incensed that he slapped her with particular force across the face with his hand rather than with the proclamation. She was knocked cold and Edward Petherbridge, playing an attendant supernumerary at the start of his distinguished National career, emitted an audible gasp of 'Oh, Mags!' Frank Finlay had to improvise a new piece of business for Iago: carrying an unconscious Desdemona from the Senate House. And when she came round in the wings, she woozily exclaimed: 'Well, that's the first time I've ever seen any fucking stars at the National!' Diana Boddington, Olivier's loyal and devoted stage manager, disputed this story. She said it was Orson Welles who nearly killed his Desdemona, Gudrun Ure, and she stage-managed that production, too. According to Boddington:

> My only problem with Larry's Othello was the long dress Maggie wore. Larry played in bare feet and as Maggie came on upstage she at first used to bring on with her all the cigarette ends that she'd gathered in her progress along the corridor from the dressing room. Larry used to go berserk. The only solution, finally, was to ban smoking in the corridors on *Othello* days.

Most of the reviewers moved into sonorous top gear to try and do justice to Olivier's performance. The production itself was competent enough, but Frank Finlay's Iago was clinically devious and efficient rather than crawling with theatrical malice. Olivier had no intention of being upstaged by his lieutenant. But some dissenters, notably Alan Brien and Jonathan Miller, took exception to Olivier's adoption of what they described as 'nigger minstrel' characteristics. The languorous, rolling gait, the swaying from the hips, the full-throated imprecations and the open-palmed, eye-rolling, tongue-lolling insouciance all conjured a white man's vision of an exotic, alien paramour, very probably with enormous sexual apparatus, who had transgressed the decorum of polite society. Which is exactly Shakespeare's point about Othello. It was Olivier's unapologetic sensuality which raised hackles. Looking back, the performance was poised at the very last moment at which the liberal theatre-going audience would accept the impersonation of a demonic black character by a white actor. Subsequent made-up Othellos have dodged the problem by playing martial dignitaries (Brewster Mason and Donald Sinden) or Moorish outcasts (Paul Scofield and Ben Kingsley). And when Michael Gambon hinted that he might approximate to Olivier's tidal waves in an intimate and heavily cut Scarborough revival directed by Alan Ayckbourn, the show never saw the light in London. Today, the role is the preserve of black actors only.

Olivier's daring interpretation, certainly unrivalled by any white or black actor since, was probably the last great romantic tragic performance of our theatre. The epileptic fit was amazing, terrifying, and the final deathbed aria over Desdemona's corpse – 'Wash me in steep down gulfs of liquid fire', arms supplicating with the elements – before slashing his throat with the concealed stiletto, one of the most animal feats of acting I have seen. Zeffirelli told Tynan: 'It's an anthology of everything that has been discovered about acting in the last three centuries. It's grand and majestic, but it's also modern and realistic. I would call it a lesson for us all.' Maggie herself was quietly touching, though *The Times* felt she was on distant terms with the part: 'Obviously a mettlesome girl who would not for an instance have endured domestic tyranny, she introduces facetious modern inflections (for instance her giggling reference to "these men" in the bedchamber scene) which clash destructively with the character.'

In July, the production moved down to Chichester for just sixteen highly applauded performances. Robert Stephens was already embarked on *The Royal Hunt of the Sun* on the open festival stage. John Dexter, directing, had been attracted to the play by the challenge of a single stage direction: 'They cross the Andes.' Robert's primitive icon was in part homage to Olivier's Othello, but mostly an extraordinarily vivid and powerful performance in its own right. No one knew what an Inca god might have sounded like, so Robert created an entirely new world of vocal sound based on bird cries, throat clickings and glottal stops. He also became a burnished figure of sensual athleticism. Shaffer recalls Maggie sitting in on rehearsal and giving them both a lift back to the house in Bosham which Maggie shared for the season with Derek Jacobi and Edward Hardwicke. She was flitting around between London and Dublin (where she was filming *Young Cassidy*) and Jacobi recalls how, at one point, she returned from Dublin and announced she was going to bed for two days. On the third day, he took a cup of tea upstairs and opened the door to find Robert there, too.

The Master Builder, directed by Peter Wood, had opened at the Old Vic in June, and was promptly hailed by Bernard Levin as the National's 'first catastrophe'. Michael Redgrave as Solness appeared not to know his words, and people in the theatre, as well as in the audience, assumed he was drunk. In fact, he was suffering from the onset of Parkinson's disease and would switch alarmingly from one scene to the middle of another in the next act. As Hilde, the reviving demon from the architect's past, Maggie was in the firing line, desperately trying to keep the show on the road. Olivier was furious with Redgrave and made that fury quite clear. After the first-night performance on 9 June, he burst into Redgrave's dressing room, dragging Peter Wood after him, and delivered an almost incoherent tirade, telling Redgrave in no uncertain terms that there was nothing wrong with 'this boy's' (Wood's) production and that he would play Solness himself. He did so, on tour in Oxford in November, prior to returning to London and dividing his Solness between two Hildes: Maggie and Joan Plowright.

When the press was invited to see Olivier's Solness, one reviewer was bold enough to say that Maggie acted Olivier off the stage. On the second night, Robert was sitting in her dressing room when Olivier called by and said, en passant, 'Oh, by the way, I understand that one of the critics says that you almost act me off the stage. If I may say so, darling angel, heart of my life, in the second act you almost bored me off the stage, you were so slow.' Slowness was about the last accusation you could ever level at Maggie. Robert watched the performance that night and witnessed her rip through the play like a jet-propelled aeroplane.

She picked up her cues so quickly, you couldn't slip a razor blade between the lines. Larry fluffed and dried all over the shop. He paid for his mistake by being made to look like a complete monkey. It was after that experience that he said to me in the street he would never act with her again. Nor did he. They were both brilliant, but in completely different styles. He worked inwards to a role from the outside; she works always on her breath-taking comic instinct, about which she can tell you absolutely nothing.

Even at loggerheads, Maggie and Olivier struck great sparks off each other. Peter Wood says that one morning of rehearsal for *The Master Builder*, the scene of their first encounter, was 'the greatest moment in the theatre I have ever known'. Gaskill saw one performance 'at which they were electric. I shall never forget it; it was as good as anything I've ever seen, a kind of excitement had taken over.' Irving Wardle summarised the transformation:

This Solness is a thirsting vulgarian who has hoisted himself to middle-class status, but whose manners still compare coarsely with those of the doctor and his bloodlessly genteel wife. His fear of heights, later to take on a cloudy significance, is thus firmly rooted in the fear of losing his precarious foothold in society . . . Maggie Smith's Hilde has developed almost beyond recognition . . . her scenes with Solness now carry an erotic charge which visibly augments the characters and forms a natural bridge to the mighty symbolic outbursts of the last act.

Internal relations were not made any easier by the fact that Joan Plowright scored less of a success in the role of Hilde than did Maggie. She had also been ill, suffering a miscarriage which prevented her from opening opposite Olivier as planned. But when she did face the critics, Clive Barnes in the *Daily Express* said that the play sagged with Plowright and that Olivier could not strike the sparks that flared up with Maggie's Hilde, a creature of 'fire and ice'. Maggie herself was too busy to take much notice of Olivier's anguish. She probably enjoyed the fact that he needed her lustre in the company but resented its shine. Younger company members appreciated her industry and example. Lynn Redgrave found both her and Robert endlessly helpful and encouraging. 'I loved watching Maggie, and learned an awful lot. It must have been hell for her rehearsing at first with my father, but she was extraordinarily sympathetic to him. He, I know, thought she was brilliant.'

Her stock continued to rise in the film world. It is an odd coincidence that just as the erotic fulfilment Tynan noted in Desdemona and Hilde must have been fuelled by the affair with Robert, so she played crucially catalytic girlfriends in her next two movies at a time when three men – Beverley, Robert and Rod Taylor – were competing for her decisive favours. In Jack Clayton's exceptionally frank *The Pumpkin Eater*, with a screenplay by Harold Pinter adapted from Penelope Mortimer's novel, Maggie plays the relatively small role of Philpot, a children's nanny in the household of Peter Finch and Anne Bancroft. The latter is excessively philoprogenitive, that is to say, cannot contemplate sex without parturition. She has eight children by three marriages. Maggie is a fecklessly destructive foil to Bancroft's invincibly productive wife and she is easy pickings for Peter Finch, though the affair is cloaked in secrecy and never explicit. We first see Maggie in the kitchen, sitting skittishly on the sink with legs and arms akimbo, informing Bancroft that she (Philpot) is frigid. Finch is a scriptwriter; Maggie, lolling mischievously in her bedroom, opines to Bancroft that 'it must be wonderful to have a man working in the house'. An indelible comic mark is made on a deeply depressing, sometimes slow, but fascinating black-and-white film, with Bancroft sinking further into decline and despair, breaking down in Harrods and failing to rescue the marriage after visits to an abortionist, a doctor, a psychoanalyst and even her first husband (played by Richard Johnson). Dilys Powell in the *Sunday Times*, detecting the influence of Antonioni, applauded a 'beautifully devised' film which, for once, looked with women instead of at them. Years later, Clayton pulled off a similar feat with Maggie in the central role of another piece about tragic disintegration, *The Lonely Passion of Judith Hearne*.

Maggie's Dublin sojourn yielded a piece of work which would provide good material for a specialist film buff's interrogation on television's *Mastermind*. Which film did John Ford abandon after shooting just twenty minutes? In which film does Rod Taylor, as an

Above left Margaret, aged three, on the front gate at 68 Northwood Gardens, Ilford

Above right Day trip to Sandringham, September 1938, with her mother and brothers Ian (left) and Alistair

Above left Aged ten, parading her membership of the Vera Legge School of Dancing in the back garden at 55 Church Hill Road, Oxford

Above right Meg and Nat in Washington, DC, for Ian's first wedding, 1965

Above In *Twelfth Night* for the OUDS, 1952:
'The Viola of our dreams,' said the *Oxford Mail*

Left Oxford High School for Girls, 1951

Maggie as Orange with Kenneth Williams as Lettuce Green (centre) in Bamber
Gascoigne's revue *Share My Lettuce* at the Comedy Theatre, 1957

Maggie as Bridget with conman George Nader in her first feature film,
Nowhere to Go (1958), co-written by Kenneth Tynan for Ealing Studios

Above Preparing in her dressing room as
Mary McKellaway in Jean Kerr's *Mary, Mary*
at the Queen's Theatre in 1963. It was her
third, big West End role for all-powerful
producer Binkie Beaumont

Left In Beverley Cross's second play, *Strip the
Willow* (1960), Maggie played a girl described
by the author as 'very beautiful, elegant,
sophisticated . . . with a great sense of fun'

With Laurence Olivier in the film version of *Othello* (1965): Maggie's Desdemona surprised critics and the public alike when John Dexter's production opened at Chichester and the Old Vic in the early days of the new National Theatre. With an 'untouchable' Olivier, said Tynan, she proved she could play characters 'whose approach to sex was affirmative and aimed at total erotic fulfilment'

As Beatrice and Benedick in Franco Zeffirelli's exuberant Sicilian production of *Much Ado About Nothing* at the Old Vic in 1965, Maggie and Robert Stephens forged a relationship with the public that established them as favourites for several years

Maggie plays the flute to a suitably unimpressed Peter Ustinov in a comedy of conmen, *Hot Millions* (1968): 'A woman's place is in the 'ome, innit, making money!'

The Prime of Miss Jean Brodie (1969), set in Edinburgh in the 1930s, proved a career game-changer for Maggie at home and in Hollywood. A glacial but glamorous admirer of Mussolini and General Franco, Miss Brodie believed her pupils were the crème de la crème: 'Give me a girl at an impressionable age, and she is mine for life.'

Above Tigbourne Court, the Edwin Lutyens house near Guildford that Maggie and Robert bought and shared with her brother and sister-in-law in 1968. The house was sold in 1981

Right Proud mum with second son Toby, two weeks old in May 1969

Below Maggie celebrates her Oscar victory on the night of the Hollywood ceremony in the stalls bar of the Old Vic, after the first performance of *The Beaux' Stratagem*, with Robert and (to his left) their friend and dresser Christopher Downes

As Hedda Gabler, a performance of neurotic intensity
at the National, and Maggie's favourite production,
directed by Ingmar Bergman in 1970

Irish playwright built like an Irish navvy, say 'All the world's a stage, Mick, but some of us are desperately under-rehearsed'? And in which film does Michael Redgrave as W. B. Yeats walk on a stage and shout at a rioting audience, 'You have disgraced yourselves again'? The answer to all three questions is *Young Cassidy*, which must be classified as compellingly bad. It tells the story of playwright Sean O'Casey, 'John Cassidy', his life and his loves, and his association with the Irish Citizens Army and the Abbey Theatre during and after the Easter Rising. It ends with him boarding a ship for England. Tynan, who was writing film reviews in the *Observer* while working at the National, sneered, 'This is O'Casey spruced up for export and audience identification.'

The project was beset with bad luck. Sean O'Casey, who vetted the use made of his volumes of autobiography, died during the shooting. John Whiting, who had been commissioned to write the screenplay, died a few months before shooting started. And John Ford, whose career was winding down, took to his bed with illness after getting only a few reels of film in the can. Lindsay Anderson had first been approached, and had thought of Richard Harris as the roistering O'Casey the producers had in mind. But, by the time Ford became involved, the MGM executives forced him to have Rod Taylor. Ford supervised a few scenes between Taylor and Julie Christie, who played the first of Cassidy's three girlfriends (the others were Pauline Delaney and Maggie), and also the funeral of Cassidy's mother. Although *Young Cassidy* is still labelled 'a John Ford film', the bulk of the work was taken over by Jack Cardiff.

The movie opens with a slightly work-soiled but mostly glistening Rod Taylor digging in a sewer. At home, Flora Robson makes stew and Jack McGowran dresses up as Richard III. The tram strike looms, Rod writes a pamphlet. Suntanned, fleshy, square-jawed and large, Rod declares that 'there is too much in this country going to waste' and starts filching books from a bookshop where Maggie Smith slaps his wrists and charges him sixpence. Maggie's character, Nora Creena, appears, respectfully portrayed, in one of O'Casey's plays, *Red Roses for Me*, and also in one short chapter of his autobiography. She was far too religious for O'Casey to bear and he wrote, 'Free thought to her would be but blasphemy and ruin eternal.' Instead, Maggie plays a sturdy slip of a girl, her long ginger hair tied in a black bow at the back, in whose eyes O'Casey sought 'a soft, shy shelter', as a sensible, sensuous support system to his ambition. Their courtship is the central theme of the film, pushing aside all other political and cultural developments. On a spree in the countryside, Rod pulls Maggie down on top of him and the camera cuts to a bubbling, picturesque river. There follows a sweet and sickly sequence of post-coital languor, with a certain amount of kissing, cuddling and singing. Maggie, it must be said, looks positively radiant and old hot Rod pretty pleased with himself.

When Cassidy and Nora visit Lady Gregory at Coole Park, we are treated to the sight of an imperious Edith Evans waited on by a skivvy played by O'Casey's real-life daughter, the actress and director Shivaun O'Casey. Rod carves his initials on the tree alongside those of Yeats, Shaw and Augustus John, and is told by Michael Redgrave's monocled poet that he, John Cassidy, is the Irish Dostoevsky and that he must be prepared to be inspired by the Arctic waste, not the warmth of his girl's body. The uproar at the first night of *The Plough and the Stars* is summarised by the brother who accuses Cassidy of showing his countrymen to be knaves and fools, and of 'putting our room on the stage and me in it'. Redgrave's Yeats, however, tells Cassidy that the world and its playhouses belong to him. Encouraged, Rod asks Maggie to marry him in the dark of an empty Abbey auditorium. 'No, Johnny,' she says, abandoning him to the world; she needs a simple life, not his terrible dreams and anger, and she backs away up the aisle and out of the theatre. Rod boards a ship and the credits roll.

In her personal life, Maggie made a similar decision. The hurly-burly of life with a Hollywood star was not something she ever seriously contemplated. Beverley's quiet loyalty was taken for granted, but he was beginning to lose touch. His first wife was still being difficult about a divorce and while Maggie had become embroiled at the National, he had spent time in Australia directing the première there of *Boeing-Boeing*. Maggie, thanks to Beverley's encouragement, had discovered a new life at the Old Vic, and her creative partnership with Olivier and, especially, Robert Stephens, held promise of unlimited excitement and glory. Most importantly, the work was challenging and adventurous, though the inscrutable, demanding William Gaskill thought that the bloom had already gone off the National's ensemble pretensions: 'In the second season at the Vic we had Noël Coward trying to get Dame Edith to remember her lines in *Hay Fever*, Franco Zeffirelli camping it up in *Much Ado* and a set for *The Crucible* that looked like a gnome's tea-party. I could see the socialist ensemble was not going to happen.'

Another way of looking at it was that the National Theatre was entering a richly popular phase and that the ideals of a committed company formed along the lines of the Berliner Ensemble were an impracticable option, anyway. They probably always were with Olivier at the helm and the flamboyant, eclectic Tynan, the archetypal champagne socialist, at his side. The actors themselves knew they were part of something exciting, whatever its intellectual pedigree, and they worked harder than ever. At the centre of the company, Maggie and Robert became box-office magic, attractions second only to Olivier himself, and a couple living out their supposedly private bliss in the glare of public adulation.

7

Romance with the New Lunts

Having made her mark at the National in two demanding tragic roles, Desdemona and Hilde Wangel, which altered the public's perception of her, Maggie renewed her comedy career with especial relish. In the middle years of the 1960s she and Robert enjoyed the razzmatazz of being 'the new Lunts'. They were married in 1967, shortly after the birth of their first son, moved house, acquired a country property, had another son, and were cast in leading roles in major films: Maggie as Miss Jean Brodie, Robert as Billy Wilder's Sherlock Holmes. Maggie's film would make her an international star. Robert's failed to do the same for him and married life became much trickier. The time arrived when they could no longer share equal billing. These tensions were disguised for some years within the apparent democracy of a theatre company.

Maggie and Robert were cast in *Hay Fever*, which, in spite of the problems with Edith Evans as Judith Bliss, became one of the National's greatest hits. On the first day of rehearsals, Noël Coward addressed the cast: 'I'm thrilled and flattered and frankly a little flabbergasted that the National Theatre should have had the curious perceptiveness to choose a very early play of mine, and to give it a cast that could play the Albanian telephone directory.' Although about ten years too young for the part, Maggie always saw herself as Judith Bliss, and her sights on it must have been sharpened now. She 'covered' the role and very nearly took it over. As things turned out, she made a fantastic comic creation of the vamp Myra Arundel, and will forever be associated with the show-stopping delivery in Act Three of the previously unremarked line 'This haddock is disgusting.' (The haddock was not really that bad; stage management provided mashed bananas.)

Derek Jacobi, who played Judith's son Simon Bliss, recalls how battle lines were drawn between Dame Edith and Maggie at the first dress parade:

Maggie came on in this ravishing black cocktail number for Act Two which had an eye-catching long fish-tail fan at the back. The Dame put her elbow on the sofa where Maggie had to sit, and as Maggie got up, there was this great tearing sound and the fan came off. 'Oh, that looks so much better, Maggie,' said the Dame. At the next rehearsal, Maggie returned not only with the fish-tail back on, but also with an immensely long cigarette holder around which, before she sat down on the sofa, she twirled the fish-tail. She then sat down, unpeeled the holder from the fan and put it in her mouth. Of course this remained in the show and more or less stopped it every night.

Dame Edith was far too old for Judith, but Coward, who directed, was monumentally patient, a fact enshrined in Tynan's account of one of the Master's most renowned mots. Dame Edith insisted on saying in rehearsal, apropos of the weekend cottage's Thames-side situation in Cookham, 'On a very clear day you can see Marlow.' Finally Coward could stand it no longer and yelled from the back of the stalls, 'Edith, the line is "On a clear day you can see Marlow." On a *very* clear day you can see Marlowe and Beaumont and Fletcher.' The actress herself became suddenly aware of her predicament as she travelled up to Manchester for the out-of-town opening with her friend, Gwen Ffrangcon-Davies. She was going through her lines and came to the scene where she is defending her flirtatiousness to her own children: 'Anyone would think I was eighty the way you go on.' She stopped, stared at Ffrangcon-Davies and said, 'But I *am* nearly eighty. I'm seventy-six. I can't play this part.' In Manchester, Dame Edith took to her hotel bedroom and refused to emerge until earnest representations had been made by Coward, Olivier and John Dexter. She told Coward, who found her moaning on her bed, that she had 'a dry mouth and a dropped stomach'. She agreed finally to play the dress rehearsal, to which an audience had been invited, only after Coward had decided 'to give the Dame hell' and had berated her for being a disgrace to herself, the theatre and Christian Science. The audience was sent home.

When the play was run for a second time, the Dame was allowed back to the hotel, and Maggie stood in as Judith. Diana Boddington was stage-managing and remembers a riot: 'Well, Maggie just sent up Edith's performance something rotten. The mimicry was unbelievably funny. We were all – Noël, Larry, everyone – laughing so much we were lying around on the floor.' No doubt hearing that Maggie, or 'the little Smith girl' as she called her, was more than capable of stealing her thunder as Judith, Dame Edith agreed to play the week in Manchester on the odd condition that Gwen Ffrangcon-Davies was allowed to sit in her dressing room, presumably as a last line of defence against any dreaded Maggie intrusions. But Maggie never allowed respect to swamp her adversarial instincts. She knew, and loved, the Dame's reported comment on *Share My Lettuce*: 'It is unprofessional, and cissy.' Lynn Redgrave recalled that, later in the run, Dame Edith imperiously accosted Maggie backstage: 'I understand that you are covering the role of Judith Bliss. I should like to tell you here and now that I shall not be off.' Maggie, quick as a flash, replied, 'Well, I sincerely hope not, because the costumes won't fit.'

'The Dame, God rest her soul,' says Jacobi, 'was not the most generous of actresses. She was certainly hideous to us youngsters, giving us notes and summonses and tellings-off and I think to a certain extent Maggie was standing up to her for everyone else in the cast.' Nothing, not even these peccadillos, could tarnish Dame Edith's reputation or the profound respect in which she was held. But by this time in her career she was a sad and loveless old lady, and her example in private life was probably something Maggie was afraid of. One way of ensuring against complete emotional isolation would be to have children. Dame Edith had a few loyal friends, but no family; and not much peace at the Old Vic this time round. Jacobi remembers that Maggie and the Dame occupied adjoining dressing rooms and, between shows on matinée days, Maggie would play a favourite record, 'Baby Love' by the Supremes, at full blast 'so that the Dame could not sleep and would be too tired to cause trouble in the evening performance'.

On the first night, 29 October 1964, Coward sat in the stalls next to Judy Garland, just behind Lena Horne and quite near Rudolf Nureyev.

It was that sort of evening. In a programme note, Tynan reminded a generation for whom Pinter was the new master of elliptical style that 'Coward took the fat off English comic dialogue; he was the Turkish bath in which it slimmed.' Style apart, Herbert Kretzmer declared in the *Express* that *Hay Fever* was 'one of the few plays I have seen that is about nothing at all'. Each member of the Bliss family invites a guest for the weekend. Charades are played after dinner. The guests leave in the morning before breakfast. A generally observed point was that the guests now seemed more eccentric than the hosts, whereas the reverse was true when Marie Tempest led the 1925 première. Certainly none was more eccentric than Maggie's Myra Arundel in green cloche hat and matching shoes, looking, said Felix Barker in the *Evening News*, 'like an Anita Loos heroine drawn by Aubrey Hammond'. Myra is described in the play as a girl who goes about using sex as a sort of shrimping-net. With her fluttering eyelashes and anaconda smile, Maggie was a picture of enamelled, nauseated horror as she stroked Derek Jacobi's hair and found her fingers covered in grease, or scooped her train into position with the cigarette holder and faced yet another doomed assault upon her lethal defences.

If *Hay Fever* unleashed a comic genie from the National's bottle, the Zeffirelli production of *Much Ado About Nothing*, so despised by Gaskill and some of the more high-minded critics, let slip the dogs of merry war. The costumes were coloured and padded out to resemble Sicilian confectionery dolls. Maggie looked at her most edibly beguiling in a red dress and blonde wig. Robert was a swarthy swaggerer with heavily pomaded hair and massive dark glasses. The contest between Beatrice and Benedick was that of two razor-sharp habitual antagonists who were in love with each other to start with. It opened on 16 February 1965 and stayed in the repertoire for several years. The audience loved it. Philip Hope-Wallace in the *Guardian* gave the most vivid overall picture of its free-wheeling opera buffa provenance:

> The lancers in Messina? But that is nothing. Some of the girls have strayed out of Goya or Fuseli, the lordlings are from Visconti's *The Leopard*, Dogberry leads them in a chorus of *La traviata*, Leonato has escaped from *Don Pasquale* and later turns up (in mock mourning for his daughter) got up like Papa Ibsen. There is a

town band; a female bicycle; umbrellas; human statuary; bowler
hats and a measure of mugging and gesticulating which make
the films of Gloria Swanson or the farces of Labiche look like
tableaux vivants of unwinking decorum.

Against this, the killjoys, led by Bernard Levin (who reported 'one
of the more excruciatingly tedious evenings at present obtainable
this side of Hell'), booed from the cheaper seats as well as from the
review pages. But however reprehensibly glib was Zeffirelli's irreverent
approach to the comedy, we can see it now as the first of a whole
string of major Shakespearean knees-ups in the latter half of the century. Within two decades, the RSC would present other comedies by
swimming pools, on motorbikes and as thinly disguised sub-Broadway
musicals. One serious point at issue had been Tynan's recruitment of
the poet Robert Graves to 'clarify' some of the more recherché jokes
and references. Over three hundred minor alterations were proposed
and many adopted. But Maggie refused point blank to accept any
alteration on 'I had rather lie in the woollen', and proceeded to show
Tynan and Graves how to convey the meaning and gain the laugh.
One key to Maggie's greatness in Shakespeare is her genius for unlock-
ing abstruse meanings with unerring perception and comic timing.

Albert Finney made his NT début as Don Pedro and played him,
said Levin, 'as though he had a red-hot poker stuck in his trousers,
staggering about backwards and talking like an itinerant ice-cream
pedlar with a cleft palate'. Another NT débutant was Ian McKellen,
whom Maggie herself had recommended as Claudio on the basis of his
touching performance in James Saunders's *A Scent of Flowers*. Finney
subsequently blossomed in *Miss Julie* and *Black Comedy*, both with
Maggie, while McKellen did not find a congenial casting groove and
postponed his passage to the top flight for a few years, building his
reputation elsewhere.

Maggie was unhappy before the opening. She told Christopher
Downes that she was going to put on a wig and dark glasses and go
to the Isle of Man. But anyone who saw this deliciously irrespon-
sible and joyous production has memories of two particular Maggie
moments. When Don Pedro concluded that, out of question, she was
born in a merry hour, Maggie stopped the scene for just one half-line

of piercing pathos with 'No, sure, my lord, my mother cried...' and immediately revived the antic mood on 'But there was a star danced, and under that was I born.' The pain of childbirth was the price of her jocund animation, and Maggie turned the scene right round on the proverbial sixpence. Later, in the church, she is asked by Benedick what he might do to soften Hero's agony at her supposed betrayal. Zeffirelli had wanted her to play for another big laugh. Instead, she yelled 'Kill Claudio' with unexpected savagery. This outburst of towering, disinterested rage stunned the audience to silence and so petrified the scene that you felt the entire production might have to be abandoned, like an unruly football match suddenly blanketed in freezing fog. Robert held a very long pause and whispered, almost under his breath, 'Not for the world.'

Two weeks after the opening of *Much Ado*, Maggie took part in a Sunday night Bach–Handel concert at the Royal Festival Hall to raise money for the Save the Children Fund. She admitted to Sydney Edwards in the *Evening Standard* that she could play Bach's easy pieces for the piano, but confined herself to the recitation of a script based on a play by Colly Cibber and a contemporary account of a temperamental clash between two of Handel's sopranos. She was asked about her NT touring schedule: 'I'm going on tour – to Glasgow, Nottingham and Manchester. It always happens to me. I make a film and get sent to Cricklewood and everybody else goes to Tahiti.' In addition to gadding around the industrial north, the National maintained its connection with Chichester on the softer South Downs, where they presented a fourth summer season in 1965. Maggie opened in July in a double bill of Strindberg's *Miss Julie* and a new farce by Peter Shaffer, *Black Comedy*.

Miss Julie was cast first and Tynan approached Shaffer with a commission to write something to go with it. Shaffer revealed that, ever since he had seen the Peking Opera, he had wanted to write a farce involving the 'black theatre' of one of their most famous sketches, where battle is joined on a fully lit stage by combatants plunged into total darkness. Although late with a film script, Shaffer was told to get on with it by Olivier who, Shaffer recalls, as a result of Tynan's enthusiasm, simply looked straight through him and said, 'It's all going to be thrilling.' Shaffer immediately developed a writer's block because he'd agreed to do it before working out a plot. Olivier's only suggestion was that Maggie's part shouldn't be too long as she was working very hard and seemed to be frail.

The plays went into rehearsal in Chichester and although the Strindberg, translated by Michael Meyer and directed by Michael Elliott, was relatively straightforward, John Dexter was directing the Shaffer from a script that seemed to change every day. Maggie's role as Clea, the jilted mistress, was an unresolved hotchpotch. One day, according to Riggs O'Hara, she stood up and said she had the perfect answer: 'As I slit my wrists in the first play, why don't I cut my throat in the second?'

Both productions were seen to better advantage, however, when they arrived at the Old Vic in the following March. You could sense more of Miss Julie's gathering horror and there was clearer delineation of both her social superiority and her sexual desire. Ronald Bryden in the *New Statesman* took a well-timed and perceptive long view of Maggie's career. Over her performance as Miss Julie, he said, hung the burning question of whether she could go on to become the National's tragedienne: whether she might some day tackle Hedda, Phèdre and Cleopatra, or continue on her present course towards Rosalind, Millamant and Wilde's Gwendolen. As it turned out she would have to go to Canada to play Cleopatra, Millamant and Rosalind. Hedda was a few years off. Phèdre beckoned but never materialised, and Gwendolen was submerged in Lady Bracknell. In 1965, the issue of her tragic aspirations remained, for Bryden, in the balance. She was much less a seductress, he felt, than a hypnotised victim, although she managed a momentary comeback in the second half with her long history of a twisted upbringing. Although one or two critics acclaimed this Miss Julie as a great performance, Bryden was nearer the mark in alleging that the bloodthirsty diatribe against men, as well as the desperate lesbian appeal to Christine, was beyond her range. It was a pointer to what she might achieve, rather than a fully accomplished tragic portrayal. The play's impact was softened, muted.

Although some critics were mean and sniffy about *Black Comedy*, the piece was a riotously funny addition to the repertoire and one of the most expertly played farces London had ever seen. *Black Comedy* opens, in complete darkness, with an effete sculptor, Brindsley Miller

(Derek Jacobi), showing his debby, squeaky-voiced fiancée, Carol (Louise Purnell), into a flat he has furnished with antiques 'borrowed' from a neighbour, Harold Gorringe, in order to impress her father, who is about to arrive. A motley crew of unwanted visitors included Maggie as the irate ex-mistress queering Brindsley's romantic pitch. So this, she haughtily declared, was what he meant by a blind date. Shaffer arranged a delayed entrance for Maggie in order to allow her to wind down from Miss Julie, and she came on and topped everyone with a classic display of mischievous outrage culminating in her impersonation of Brindsley's ancient Cockney cleaning woman, Mrs Punnet. Maggie spilt the beans from a great height dressed only in a borrowed pyjama top: 'Water? Good 'eavens, I must have upset something. It's as black as Newgate's knocker up 'ere. Are you playing one of your saucy games, Mr Miller?' The point about the performance, though, apart from its surface brilliance, was the element of desperation in Clea's attempt to hang on to Brindsley. She had walked out on him after four years and had thought of nothing else for six weeks. Her affection was riddled with guilt, and her revenge tempered with pathos and the threat of loneliness.

It would be crass to suggest that Maggie's coruscating Clea fed off the confusion in her personal life, but by the time Robert and Maggie were back in London in 1966, Beverley was rumly contemplating the four or five years he had spent as Maggie's unofficial fiancé. He had divorced his first wife and left his two daughters to be with her, and now Robert was about to be divorced by Tarn Bassett. Things were coming to a head.

The National visited Oxford in April with the double bill and also Pinero's affecting backstage comedy *Trelawny of the Wells*, in which Maggie had taken over as Avonia Bunn, a part which, like Clea, allowed her to parade a splendid pair of legs. John Higgins told *Financial Times* readers that she played Avonia as 'a fourth-rate trouper with a heart as high as the Post Office Tower and a turmoil of emotions that run from jubilation to despair in a matter of seconds'. Robert Stephens gave a marvellous, heart-rending performance as the budding new playwright of the future, Tom Wrench, a companion portrait to his George Dillon and a roseate premonition of Chekhov's cynical poet Trigorin, one of Robert's outstanding performances ten years later.

By June, Robert had taken over from Finney as Harold Gorringe in *Black Comedy*, and the farce was paired with a new John Osborne script, *A Bond Honoured*, directed by Dexter, in which Maggie and Robert played an incestuous sister and brother. The text was derived from Lope de Vega's *La Fianza Satisfecha*. It was a strict and very classical, rather Oriental, production. Maggie wore a not very becoming black wig and black contact lenses, and when she died, she made a turn and pulled red ribbons out of her belt to indicate the blood. She was again disciplined by Dexter to control her natural gestural brio. Dexter was renowned for the abrasiveness of his tongue and the total demands he made on actors. A side effect of his obsessive style was that he could be deeply unpleasant to them. Maggie never worked with Dexter again. Riggs O'Hara recalls meeting Maggie years later at one of Olivier's Christmas parties. She was moaning about some director or other. He asked her why, in that case, did she never ask for John? 'And she said she could no longer stand being shouted at.' O'Hara coldly enquired whether she wanted a director, or a friend.

The friendship with Robert was overpowering her loyalty to Beverley. For a time, the domestic equilibrium was maintained. In June 1965, with Maggie tied up at the National, Beverley and Kenneth Williams departed on another holiday together. This time it was a month-long jaunt to Crete and Turkey, and Beverley worked out the itinerary: London to Athens, boat to Istanbul, then Heraklion, then boat to Naples, and home. Once again Beverley went off in search of the sites of classical legend, including the palace of Agamemnon, Knossos, Phaestos and Sitea. At home, the crunch finally came in the summer of 1966, when Maggie disappeared to Rome for a few weeks to make a film with Rex Harrison called *The Honeypot*, an amazingly cumbersome rewrite by Frederick Knott and the director Joe Mankiewicz of Ben Jonson's *Volpone*. Robert followed her there, and Maggie finally wrote to Beverley with the bad news. He had been aware of the developing romance with Robert since his return from Australia, where he had spent three months directing *Boeing-Boeing*. 'I was more than hurt, I was murderous. So in order not to murder anyone, I got married again quickly and went to Greece and France to keep out of their way.' His second wife was Gayden Collins, a model, and Beverley kept travelling, and working on his screenplays and libretti, for the next six or seven years. He had waited for Maggie before and he would wait for her again.

By the end of the year, with Beverley gone, Robert had moved into Eldon Road. Maggie continued playing Myra Arundel, Beatrice, Desdemona and the double bill in the Old Vic repertoire. She started to do less when she realised that, at the age of thirty-two, she was pregnant. Joan Plowright took over, not all that happily, in *Much Ado*, which Robert redirected on behalf of Zeffirelli (Robert was shortly afterwards appointed an associate director of the NT), and Desdemona was passed to Billie Whitelaw. Maggie was named in Robert's divorce from Tarn Bassett and the baby arrived in the Middlesex Hospital on 19 June 1967. *The Honeypot* had overshot its schedule by many weeks, and Maggie had not seen a gynaecologist in Italy. The baby was upside down and had to be delivered by caesarean operation. Maggie said later that this made her feel as though she had just popped out to Harrods for it. The boy was named Christopher, after his godfather Christopher Downes. Everyone had expected a girl, including Zeffirelli, who had pre-christened the baby 'Daisy'. Maggie received a telegram from Zeffirelli in Italy which read: 'Congratulations on Christopher. I shall spend all my life trying to turn him into Daisy.'

Ten days later, Maggie and Robert were married in Greenwich registry office. This was arranged by the National's press officer, Virginia Fairweather, who wanted to keep the wedding private and well clear of the inevitable media glare at Caxton Hall. Fairweather explained to the Greenwich officials that Maggie's brother, Alistair, lived in nearby Blackheath (true) and that Maggie had been staying there for several weeks (less true). Virginia and Christopher Downes were the witnesses, and the quartet was in and out of the Greenwich back door and sipping celebratory champagne in Eldon Road by midday. The sipping stopped while Robert went off to perform a *Royal Hunt* matinée. In the evening, the party decamped to a favourite Italian restaurant in Beauchamp Place known privately as the 'Trattoria Hysteria', and a few other friends arrived. Albert Finney's nativity present was the recently released Beatles' *Sergeant Pepper* album. The first the public knew of all this – indeed, the first official announcement of any sort on the subject – was an article written by Barry Norman, then showbiz correspondent of the *Daily Mail*, on 20 August 1967. The ginger baby was two months old, and Robert said that his arrival had slowed Maggie down: 'She isn't so frantic to be working.'

The whole business had confused Maggie's parents, though of course they took delight in their new grandson. On the day of the wedding, 55 Church Hill Road was besieged by reporters, who parked out in the public house across the road. Nat was convinced that Maggie only married Robert because she was pregnant by him. Nat retired in the same year and offered his life's work of jottings, pamphlets, papers and sundry little publications to the Bodleian Library. He was so upset when they rejected his offer outright that he took all the papers down to the bottom of the garden and burned them. He resolved on the spot to renounce his medical and scientific interests and to devote the rest of his life not only to keeping the archive of his daughter's career, but also to catching up with her world of literature and the theatre. He went down to Blackwell's bookshop in Broad Street and stocked up on Penguin classics and Elizabethan poetry.

Maggie's maternal purdah didn't last long. Almost immediately, she and Robert made television versions of two cut-glass old English comedies: Somerset Maugham's *Home and Beauty* and Frederick Lonsdale's *On Approval*. The latter also starred Judi Dench, who remembers that they all 'corpsed' terribly and were threatened with the sack. Dench then came down the stairs wearing a tartan cloche hat, which was 'too much' for the fourth member of the cast, Moray Watson, who promptly 'collapsed all over again'.

By the end of the year, Maggie was back on a film set, starring opposite yet another distinguished old bear of English comedy, only slightly less grizzled than Rex Harrison, Peter Ustinov. Ironically, Maggie was offered the part of Patty Terwilliger in *Hot Millions* because the shooting had been delayed and Lynn Redgrave, the original casting, had become too heavily pregnant to continue. On the parturition front, Maggie came full circle by introducing Christopher, aged eight months, to show business in this film.

Christopher's screen début comes in the scene where the apparently incompetent Maggie has taken a job as a bus conductress. She helps a mother and child off the bus and lingers on the pavement to admire the swaddled infant. The bus moves off and Maggie turns in panic to chase it down the street.

Maggie starts the film as a failed traffic warden who has a room in the same lodging house as Ustinov, alias Marcus Pendleton, a.k.a. Caesar Smith, an embezzler turned criminal computer programmer. Overstressing her character's inclinations towards flirtatious scattiness, Maggie inveigles herself into Ustinov's firm as his new secretary. She is brittle, funny and defensive, somewhat frozen, with long false eyelashes which reinforce a strange resemblance to the puppet Lady Penelope in *Thunderbirds*. But she melts in the touching scene where she and Ustinov eat an improvised sausage supper and discover a shared love of music. They are, of course, a pair of lonely misfits. Ustinov's cosy, reassuring manner elicits a sudden, moving declaration: 'I'm so lonely I could scream it from the roof-tops.'

In their next scene together, Maggie proposes marriage. Soon, she is sitting at home, pregnant, while Ustinov disappears, mysteriously, to one of his various European 'offices'. Through the London contact of a deliciously nasty and lubricious executive played by Bob Newhart (' 'Ere, what we doing in the park?' asks a mini-skirted Maggie when Newhart offers her a lift home), she ingeniously uncovers the criminal operation. She then quietly outmanoeuvres them all. She has been embezzling funds from Ustinov – whose businessman alter ego, Caesar Smith, is really Robert Morley – and reinvesting them with spectacular financial results. She is offered a place on the board, but declines it with the imperishable line, 'A woman's place is in the 'ome, innit, making money!' The film ends with Maggie playing the flute in a Haydn concerto conducted by Ustinov in a sequence recorded in Watford Town Hall. *Hot Millions*, scripted by Ustinov and Ira Wallach, and directed by the Canadian Eric Till, is in some ways a feminist comedy. It is not a great film, but it is entertaining and it did give Maggie plenty of scope to combine comedy with pathos. There is also an implied paradigm of her own career at this stage in its assertion that you can both have a successful home life and shoot to the top of the professional tree.

Maggie must have taken some assurance from this, though she soon found out how difficult it was to balance the private life with the public demands of her talent. For her, the career always came first, not out of cunning or strategic necessity, but out of her incurably obsessive drive to be working. And she had a sure instinct about what work to do.

To start with, she and Robert were equal married partners. The liberating physical relationship with Robert and the birth of the first of her two sons had enriched Maggie's womanhood, with incalculable benefits to her acting. But neither she nor Robert yet knew how very difficult it would be to sustain such an exhilarating partnership.

—8—

The Prime of Miss Maggie Smith

The Prime of Miss Jean Brodie, released in 1969, eight years after the publication of Muriel Spark's novel, remains the film most readily associated with Maggie Smith. It certainly symbolises the period of her working life in which she first achieved her greatest fame. It is a good film, not a brilliant one, and Maggie becomes camp although, as Peter Hall says, Maggie only really resides on the cusp of camp. She does not go the whole hog; there's too much going on inside. But Maggie had certainly commanded a camp following in *Share My Lettuce* and *Mary, Mary*. As Jean Brodie, the Edinburgh schoolmistress of the 1930s whose pupils were the 'crème de la crème', she had a much wider audience and a proportionately larger camp following. For the first time, her stardom was totally secure. She had, as Peter Wood describes it, 'a telepathic ray' with an audience in the theatre; on screen, the same thing happened. Maggie won her first Oscar and entered the international arena on her own terms. As Cecil Wilson said in the *Daily Mail*, 'After repeatedly stealing other people's pictures, she now becomes a star in her own right.' And *Jean Brodie* was the first X-rated movie to be chosen for the annual Royal Film Performance.

Robert was also in *Jean Brodie*, and indeed gave a fine performance as Teddy Lloyd, the raffish art master who paints a nubile schoolgirl (Pamela Franklin) in the nude, has an affair with her, yet desires the spinsterish Miss Brodie all along. The director was Ronald Neame; his grandson, Gareth Neame, who would grow up to be the executive director of *Downton Abbey*, features here, too, as a little boy painted on his potty in one of the art works strewn about Teddy's studio scene of seduction. But from the moment we see Maggie stiffly cycling through Edinburgh in her sensible coat and hat, signalling a right turn into the Marcia Blaine School for Girls with the grim determination of a comically blinkered road menace, the movie belongs to one person. Muriel Spark's novel had been adapted for the London stage in 1966 by Jay Presson Allen, and the title role taken by Vanessa Redgrave, succeeded by Anna Massey. Presson Allen did the screenplay for the producer Robert Fryer, who was adamant that Maggie should play the role. Executives at Twentieth Century Fox were much keener on the idea of Deborah Kerr.

It is tempting to see Maggie's creation as a subtle revenge on her Scottish puritanical mother and indeed on the Oxford High School, which had, as Maggie admitted in an interview, more than a touch of Marcia Blaine. In her gingery blonde, glistening Marcel-waved wig and no-nonsense, shoulder-shuffling walk, Maggie was a comic totem of unbending rectitude. Her dictatorial aphorisms in the classroom – 'Prop up your books in case of intruders,' 'Give me a girl at an impressionable age, and she is mine for life' – were cloaking something more sinister, a seditious intent to inculcate enthusiasm among her charges for the men she most admired, Mussolini and General Franco. This darker side of Jean Brodie's fanaticism escapes Maggie. You do not really feel that the performance acknowledges the mixture of bland academic exhortation and dangerous brainwashing in Spark's heroine. (Her declared motto of 'Lift, enliven, stimulate!' was reworked for Lettice Douffet by Peter Shaffer as 'Enlarge, enliven, enlighten!') Her 'gels' must be prepared, she says, 'to serve, suffer and sacrifice'. And she precipitates the death of one of them (played by a young Jane Carr), who rushes off to Spain and inadvertently joins the Fascists while her brother is fighting for the Republicans. Maggie plays a Brodie who lives immune to the world and even her own beliefs. But she also presents a chilling portrait of bottled-up sexuality and dazzling irony. Walk with your head up, she instructs the gels, 'like Sybil Thorndike, a woman of notable mien'. The joke here, of course, and one of which Brodie is unaware, is that Sybil Thorndike was also a woman of notable left-wing spirit. Maggie's laugh is gained on the glacial camp delivery of the line, without a trace of sarcasm. Miss Brodie is betrayed finally by the girl who is her sexual substitute in the life of Robert's infatuated married art master. Maggie's anguished cry of 'Assassin!' is not as blood-curdling as it might be. The nastiness of her character has been swamped in the enamelled perfection of her comedy performance.

The film opened almost simultaneously in New York, where the critical response was tumultuous. In the *New York Times*, Vincent Canby said there had not been such a display of controlled, funny, elegant theatricality since Laurence Olivier soft-shoed his way through *The Entertainer* nine years previously, and was one of many to comment on Maggie's complicated and judiciously executed array of counterpointed moods, switches in voice levels and obliquely stated emotions. The cultish impact, and this is the first evidence of an intensely camp admiration that has attached to Maggie ever since, was registered by the influential columnist Rex Reed, who said that Maggie had made the profoundest effect on him of any actress since Kim Stanley in *The Goddess* in 1957. He drooled on prophetically in *Holiday* magazine about 'one of the most magnificent screen performances in the history of the medium by Maggie Smith who takes the film into the realms of immortality. Words could never do justice to her work, to the skill and wit and sureness. If critics could give Oscars, she would already have one from me.' Whatever the quibbles, Maggie's Miss Brodie, far more severely and accurately Scottish than Vanessa Redgrave's admirable stage performance, would enter a pantheon of flawed, inflamed schoolteachers on celluloid: Robert Donat in *Goodbye Mr Chips*, Bette Davis in *The Corn is Green*, Michael Redgrave in *The Browning Version*, Sidney Poitier in *To Sir, With Love*, Sandy Dennis in *Up the Down Staircase*, and Robin Williams in *Dead Poets Society*.

While filming continued on Jean Brodie, the ever-solicitous Christopher Downes was helping Maggie and Robert to house-hunt. Maggie's agent Peter Dunlop also gave advice and extended his range of interests in Maggie's life from contracts and tax demands to domestic requirements, especially nannies. Something larger than Eldon Road was now needed, and a 1902 villa on four floors near the Fulham Road seemed just the job. It remains in Maggie's possession to this day. While the move was in hand, Maggie, Robert and baby Christopher stayed in Penelope Gilliatt's house in Chelsea. Gilliatt's marriage to John Osborne had just broken up, and their daughter, Nolan, was brought back to England by the nanny, Christine Miller, to visit her father. 'Big Chris', as she was affectionately known by the boys when older, immediately hit it off with Maggie and helped out with the baby because Christopher's own nanny had suddenly left. She stayed with Penelope Gilliatt and Nolan for over ten years and later worked for Maggie and Beverley in Canada.

It began to make economic sense to think of a second home, a place in the country, and Maggie turned to her architect brothers for advice. Or rather, she turned to one of them. Ian had gone to America in 1959 and stayed there, building up a successful practice in civic architecture and specialising in big stores and university developments. Ian married in 1965, was divorced four years later, and remarried, acquiring a stepdaughter in the process. Alistair had married in 1963 and settled with Shân and their son, Angus, in Blackheath, where they became friends and neighbours of the actress Margaret Tyzack and her husband, years before the two Maggies won their Tonys in *Lettice and Lovage*. Prior to that, they had lived round the corner from Eldon Road. Shân had done a lot of Beverley's typing for him. Alistair's firm, Norman and Dawbarn, which specialised in designing hospitals and aerodromes overseas, was based in Guildford, Surrey. In 1968 he and Shân decided to move nearer the office. The plan was to find a big house suitable for dividing in half and sharing with Maggie and Robert. Guildford was only about thirty miles from London and easily reached at weekends. The first place Alistair saw was Tigbourne Court, an 1899 house designed by Edwin Lutyens, probably the most gifted and influential of British architects since Sir John Vanbrugh and Nicholas Hawksmoor. Lutyens was active in this part of Surrey at the turn of the century, and Tigbourne Court at Witley, one and a half miles from Chiddingfold and a few more from Guildford, was one of his most original and unusual inventions.

The main gate loomed suddenly on a busy road: a symmetrical entrance screen disguised an unusually asymmetrical house. The loggia of the main entrance had a three-gabled wall above, and each of the other entrances an independent forecourt formed by the shape of the building and the use of different paving. The walls were made of Bargate stone, drilled with lead, and there were red bricks in the chimney stacks and window surrounds. A pergola led to a garden of four acres, landscaped by Gertrude Jekyll, and a well. This was a very far cry from the cramped living conditions of Maggie's childhood.

But there was no intention of turning the address into a fashionable weekend bolthole for favoured showbiz chums as, for instance, Olivier and Vivien Leigh had done with Notley Abbey. Maggie has never been a great party-goer, let alone anything at all of a party-thrower. At first, the two families occupied one half of the house while the other half was redecorated, and then Maggie and Robert moved into the main suite of rooms. Alistair and Shân stayed in the servants' quarters, which nonetheless had six bedrooms. Shân supervised the gardening and developed all the local contacts needed to run such an establishment. When Maggie and Robert appeared at weekends, usually late on Saturday nights, the two families could be as intimate or as separate as they wished. The arrangement worked very well.

Maggie fitted in a quick guest appearance in Richard Attenborough's posh, gargantuan but irresistible film-directing début, a version of Joan Littlewood's *Oh, What A Lovely War!* She appeared, in Judith Crist's phrase, 'raucous and insidious as a Lilith of the music hall', a bespangled coquette singing the recruiting song 'I'll Make a Man of Any One of You'. In a way, she expressed the soul of the film, which is about enlistment through seduction, and death as a payment for experience. The sudden close-up on the grotesquely made-up Maggie at the end of her song is one of the movie's most indelibly vulgarian images.

With transatlantic stardom and two new homes came another major award and a second dose of maternity. In March 1969 Maggie received the Variety Club award for film actress of the year in *Hot Millions* (other recipients included Jill Bennett and John Gielgud for stage performances in plays by John Osborne and Alan Bennett, and a twenty-eight-year-old Tom Jones as show-business personality of the year). One month later, on 21 April, Toby was born. Like Christopher, he was delivered by caesarean in the Middlesex Hospital. He had been expected two days later, but Maggie was impatient to get it over with and remembers more or less pushing Tommy Steele's wife out of a hospital bed so that she could jump into it. Within six weeks, Maggie was rehearsing for a Chichester Festival Theatre revival of Wycherley's *The Country Wife*.

She had been stung into action by a major rebuff at the National Theatre, where Olivier had asked her to choose between Viola in

Twelfth Night and Rosalind in *As You Like It*. When Maggie sought to take the matter further, Olivier, who was increasingly jealous of Maggie's and Robert's appeal to the public, tartly informed her that he was going to produce an all-male version of *As You Like It* (he did, with Ronald Pickup as Rosalind) and a revival of *The Way of the World* with Geraldine McEwan in the 'Maggie role' of Millamant. This news was hurtfully imparted by letter after a particularly convivial weekend Maggie and Robert had spent with the Oliviers in Brighton. The hurt was not lessened by the fact that Olivier had posted the letter before his guests arrived.

Meanwhile, Maggie told Catherine Stott in the *Guardian* that she found babies fascinating once 'they stop being the wobbly turnips they are for so long . . . One has lived selfishly for so long that it is suddenly rather an appalling thought that you really need to think about so many people, small people who really need to be thought about.' Robert needed to be 'thought about' too, perhaps. During the Chichester period he collapsed for the first time with one of his subsequently regular bouts of acute depression aggravated by heavy drinking and overwork.

Margery Pinchwife was Maggie's first new stage role for three years. The Chichester season was no longer an extension of the National. John Clements had succeeded Olivier as artistic director, and his *Country Wife* production team reflected his sober West End pedigree: it was directed and designed by two 'old school' veterans of the Binkie Beaumont era on Shaftesbury Avenue, Robert Chetwyn and Hutchinson Scott. The plot revolves around the untrue declaration of an incorrigible rake, Horner, that he is impotent and therefore to be trusted with other men's wives. Margery, like Lady Plyant in *The Double Dealer*, is married to a jealous old fool, and in her major scene she writes a letter of rebuttal to Horner, dictated by Pinchwife, through which she refracts her own lascivious invitations.

Maggie risked the bucolic accent of the country cousin but made it a specifically consistent one. In a prim cap and low-cut dress, sensuously wielding the fateful quill pen, she emanated a twinkling air of wistful sexuality. Ronald Bryden observed how, in trailing a nasal, farmyard drawl about the stage, she made Margery's stifled talent for living seem like some monstrous escaping vegetable, burying the rest of the play knee-deep in eager, luxuriant greenery. She put the seal on her performance, as any great Margery must, in the letter scene where, panting and hanging her tongue almost to her chin, she climbed half onto the writing-table with anxiety, and caught the quill successively in her hair, her eye and her inkwell. Christopher Downes likened Maggie in this scene to Ethel Merman doing a big Cole Porter number. Its effect on the audience was galvanic. The night Downes went, the inkwell fell off the table and Maggie caught it just before it hit the floor. He thought this one of the most incredible pieces of 'business' he had ever seen, but Maggie assured him afterwards that it had never happened before. At the end of the scene, 'poor old Gordon Gostelow' as Pinchwife came on with the line, 'What have you done?' and of course, says Downes, 'got a huge laugh; he was ever so pleased with himself'.

Although Maggie has made several recordings of Shakespeare, and there is both a record and a film of the NT *Othello*, *The Country Wife* is the only play she has ever recorded in an original production for BBC Radio. She did so in 1985, with Jonathan Pryce as a darkly lubricious Horner (Keith Baxter was silkier but less dangerous at Chichester), Barbara Jefford as the fulsomely insatiable Lady Fidget and John Moffatt as the surely definitive Sparkish. Maggie's radio performance, though slightly riper, is very much a recreation of the Chichester version: as crisp and rosy as a fresh young apple, with a precise Oxfordshire accent and a musicality unsullied with mannerism. When you hear Maggie, spuriously concerned about her husband, her 'dear Bud', ask, 'Why dost thou look so fropish? Who has nangered thee?', savouring those two unexpected syllables of 'frop' and 'nang', you cannot imagine anyone else ever sounding so charmingly mock-innocent or so deliciously flavoursome. These months mark the high point of Maggie's stage career in Britain. The fact that Robert played Archer and Tesman to her Mrs Sullen and Hedda, two of her greatest stage performances, indicated that, although the marriage still prospered, Robert's visible, public role in it was becoming more of a supporting one. And by winning an Oscar, Maggie changed her footing within the profession and upped her market value way beyond Robert's.

The Beaux' Stratagem opened in Los Angeles, where the NT was on tour, in January 1970. Billy Wilder took Jack Benny to the first night.

According to Christopher Downes, the great comedian recognised the gift for which he himself was renowned above all other entertainers. 'Gee, what about that girl's timing!' he said of Maggie to Wilder. The three-week season in the huge and intimidating Ahmanson Theatre was the first of several appearances Maggie and Robert made there over the next few years. She had a ready-made Hollywood following, on account of the success of *Jean Brodie*. And in the New Year's Honours list back home, she had been appointed Commander of the British Empire, CBE, along with Joan Plowright and Kenneth More. The Los Angeles season also featured Olivier's production of Chekhov's *Three Sisters*, in which Robert played the louche battery commander Vershinin and Maggie played Masha, the middle sister whose dull marriage to a schoolmaster is briefly, and tragically, enlivened by her infatuation with the visiting army officer. Masha was really Plowright's role, but she had been unable to make the trip. The Ahmanson was picketed during the opening night intermission by student radicals accusing the National Theatre of being 'an airless mausoleum'. The reviewers thought otherwise. Maggie's reception was ecstatic. The Los Angeles drama critics gave her their best actress award. Olivier never allowed Maggie to share Masha in London with Plowright. He could not afford another blow to his wife's pride comparable to those she had already suffered over Hilde Wangel and Beatrice. In any case, Plowright was an exceptionally fine Masha. The production was recorded, like the *Othello*, on film.

Christopher and Toby were left at home with their grandparents while Maggie and Robert took a house in Malibu for the duration and soaked up the adulation. In the *New York Times* of 22 February 1970, under the headline 'The New Young Lunts?', Walter Kerr (husband of the author of *Mary, Mary*) applauded two performers who subtly signalled that they were fighting hard for an eternal promise that was probably going to turn out to be false. When they were at last torn apart, Kerr noted Maggie's discovery of sounds below the level of speech that would interest, and perhaps surprise, Jerzy Grotowski. This reference to the fashionable Polish avant-garde guru hinted at something disturbing and elemental in the performance, and the significance of acting with her volatile and seductive husband added another layer to the mixture. Robert's flirtatiousness was almost his professional trademark. On being chided by Olivier for this, he retorted, 'But I learned how to do it all from you!'

Maggie told the author and critic Ronald Hayman, 'I think of Robert as an actor when we're working, and not as my husband. But I can see that it's easier for an audience to watch two people who are married playing two characters who are married. It's all done for you.' For his part, Robert told Hayman that their work on stage was never staled by custom or familiarity: 'I'm always constantly surprised by Margaret. There are certain actors and actresses with whom you can never vary anything... But I wouldn't say that I knew beforehand the way in which Margaret was going to speak some line. I'm constantly dazzled by a different reading or a different approach to a line.'

If they were the new Lunts, there seemed little chance of a repeat of the famous occasion when Alfred Lunt and his wife Lynn Fontanne 'dried' on stage together. The deathly silence was broken by the audible delivery of the next line by a prompter. Still neither actor spoke, and the prompt came again. Silence. Another prompt. Alfred turned crossly to the stage-management corner and hissed, 'We know what the line is, but which one of us says it?' Maggie also relished the story about Lunt's failure to get an easy laugh on a line in which he requested a cup of tea. After weeks of puzzling over this, Fontanne finally asked her husband why he didn't simply ask her for a cup of tea instead of asking the audience for the laugh. The Lunts, like Robert and Maggie, had made their own way as actors before appearing together for the first time in the 1924 production of Molnár's *The Guardsman*, source of both the above anecdotes. The difference was that they were married while working separately for a long time prior to that historic success. Marriage for Robert and Maggie was inextricably linked to their work together, specifically at the National. Maggie eventually performed Molnár's comedy not with Robert, but with Brian Bedford in Canada. There were, however, many plans to exploit the marriage on stage and screen, most of them emanating from Robert. It is ironic that this should have been so at the very time when Maggie, in Farquhar and Ibsen, portrayed the richly comic and profoundly tragic consequences of a wretched marriage.

She and director Gaskill picked up exactly where they had left off in *The Recruiting Officer*, and by the time *The Beaux' Stratagem* returned

from Los Angeles and opened at the Old Vic on 8 April, Maggie's Mrs
Sullen was a full-blown masterpiece of comic acting. At six o'clock
that morning, Maggie heard that she had won the best actress Oscar
in Hollywood. Her friend from the *New Faces* days, Alice Ghostley,
collected the award on her behalf in the Music Center adjacent to the
Ahmanson. She had unexpectedly beaten off challenges from Jean
Simmons in *The Happy Ending*, Liza Minnelli in *The Sterile Cuckoo* and
Jane Fonda in *They Shoot Horses, Don't They?* Her triumph was shared,
at a distance, with John Wayne, who belatedly won his first Oscar for
True Grit, and John Schlesinger, who was declared best director for
Midnight Cowboy, which was also voted best picture. This was second
time lucky for Maggie: she had been nominated in the supporting
actress category for *Othello*. Gaskill recalls thinking how oddly low-
key, and typically English, was that first-night reception at the Vic for
someone who had just won an Oscar.

Farquhar's last play is about divorce, with many references to the
poet John Milton's tracts on the subject. Two buccaneering gallants,
Archer and Aimwell, arrive in the sleepy town of Lichfield and upset
various apple carts. Archer homes in on Mrs Sullen, a London beauty
driven frantic by boredom and shrewish by a sodden, elderly husband.
Gaskill cleared the stage, and his designer partner on *The Recruiting
Officer*, René Allio, delicately, but not preciously, conjured an English
cathedral city in russet canvases and Queen Anne interiors, with an
ochreously shaded High Street and a glimpse of the church beyond.
The atmosphere was light and vaporous, conducive to the tasteful
expression of high spirits. Benedict Nightingale in the *New Statesman*
noted Maggie's artful aggression and its effect on Robert:

> A purr becomes a quiet growl becomes an ecstatic snap of the jaws:
> the cat turns chameleon turns crocodile, and it's scarcely surprising
> that Stephens responds as he does. Who ever saw such biological
> bravura in a woman? Swagger and sally as he may, a kind of artless,
> rather awkward wonder never quite deserts him: he seems a man
> transfixed.

Of all Maggie's stage performances, it is Mrs Sullen that inspired
the most impressively evocative writing from the critics, just as Edith

Evans had started critical adjectives dancing in 1927 when she scored the biggest success of her career thus far in the same role. Maggie's tilted nose and chin conveyed a heavenly contempt for men that was irresistible; her surreptitious smile betrayed a willingness to forgive a lesser species; and her swooping descent from decorum to appetite was epitomised at the moment when Robert's Archer refused her money with a bow and she stood, purse held in her still-outstretched hand, while her eyes ran like zip fasteners up and down his extended leg.

She was a tight-laced beanpole, graceful, swaying and tender, who thawed among her own languid phrases and angular gestures. Her playing drew from Ronald Bryden a splendidly phrased comparison with some exquisite Douanier Rousseau giraffe, peering nervously down her nose with huge, liquid eyes at the smaller creatures around, nibbling off her lines fastidiously in a surprisingly tiny nasal drawl. The overall and overwhelming beauty of Maggie's Mrs Sullen derived from the fact that her humorous façade masked the imminent possibility of tragedy and despair. And it proved, perhaps more so than any other of Maggie's London performances, that the best of comedy always fends off disaster and that whereas farcical comedy ends in laughter, the true spirit of emotional comedy could just as easily end in tears. Gaskill thought she had matured immeasurably as an actress since they had worked on *The Recruiting Officer*, and remembers most the way she handled the speech which closed the first half. Gaskill adored Farquhar, but knew this poetic passage was feeble. He wanted to cut part of it, but Maggie asked for it back and, he says, 'shaped it wonderfully. She played it in a pure classical style, quite breath-takingly':

> Wedlock we own ordain'd by Heaven's decree,
> But such as Heaven ordain'd it first to be;
> Concurring tempers in the man and wife
> As mutual helps to draw the load of life.
>
>   ·   ·   ·   ·   ·   ·
>
> Must Man, the chiefest work of art divine,
> Be doomed in endless discord to repine?
> No, we should injure Heaven by that surmise;
> Omnipotence is just, were Man but wise.

Maggie and Robert themselves were getting along quite well, but they were certainly not of 'concurring tempers'. In late June they opened at the Cambridge Theatre in *Hedda Gabler*, and John Moffatt, who was playing Judge Brack, overheard many big rows through the dressing-room walls. Robert would occasionally forget to waken Maggie at the appointed time as she slept between matinée and evening performances, and she would fly into a rage. The National had extended its activity into the Cambridge, and the Ibsen was joined in repertoire there by *The Beaux' Stratagem* in August. Ingmar Bergman's celebrated Stockholm production of *Hedda Gabler* had visited the Aldwych Theatre as part of the World Theatre Season of 1968. Bergman had never directed a play outside Sweden, but was coerced into doing so in London by Olivier, to whom he habitually referred, with heavy sarcasm, as 'the Lord'. Michael Meyer, whose translation was used, has recounted the dim view Bergman took of the play and expressed his own view that the production was a very striking evening, but only for someone who neither knew nor liked Ibsen.

The text was heavily cut. Great liberties were taken, some of them repeated in later productions, most notably the collaboration between the director Deborah Warner and the Irish actress Fiona Shaw at the Abbey in Dublin in 1991. There was no portrait of General Gabler and there were no vine leaves in Loevborg's hair. Instead of the controlled revelation of Hedda's pregnancy, Maggie appeared in a wordless prologue, pushing frantically at an unwanted bulge in her stomach, apparently on the point of vomiting. But there was some-thing electrifying about this production, and certainly about Maggie's performance. Robert Stephens says, quite unequivocally, that it is the best production of anything he has ever been in. John Moffatt says that, years later, he talked about it with Maggie and they agreed they had not encountered an experience like it since, nor a director: 'What that man could do in a few seconds, the way he could transform a performance with one little remark. I could go on all day about it.'

Bergman was going to set up the recreation of his Stockholm version for about ten days and leave London to fulfil other commit-ments while Olivier took over. The billing would read something like 'Ingmar Bergman's production supervised by Laurence Olivier'. But he suddenly found he could rejig his plans and return for a week or so before the opening. He repeated an experiment he had tried, with success, before. He left the actors with masses of notes, asked Olivier to relinquish his 'assistant director' role (Olivier was only too happy to oblige) and instructed them to rehearse for a maximum of four hours a day, on their own. No one was to disturb their work. In his auto-biography, Bergman says that the only reason he did *Hedda* in the first place was that the brilliant actress Gertrud Fridh had no leading part that autumn. He set about his task with some reluctance, but found that 'the face of its weary supreme architect was unmasked' and that 'Ibsen lived desperately entangled in his furnishings, his explanations, his artistic but pedantically constructed scenes, his curtain lines, his arias and duets. All this bulky external lumber hid an obsession for self-exposure far more profound than Strindberg's.'

Michael Meyer, on the other hand, rated *Hedda Gabler* one of the most economically written of all great plays, which Bergman cut as though it were a film. Much of the humour, said the increasingly humourless Meyer, went out of the window. So, for that matter, did the windows. The stage was a red vault with a screen down the middle. On one side, the text was enacted while, on the other, the actors, primarily Hedda, explored unspoken emotions. Bryden assumed that this interpretation was based on the Freudian case history of Emilie Bardach, the elegant, repressed Viennese woman Ibsen had met and flirted with on a Tyrolean holiday in 1899. And he thought that this admittedly brilliant but non-naturalistic treatment deprived the play of its mystery and Maggie of the opportunity to exploit her gift for lacing her games in polite society with scornful artificiality. Irving Wardle, too, considered the device distracting, though Maggie Smith's reactions, he said, like those of Gertrud Fridh, were 'powerful and stylistically beautiful'.

For others, myself included, the performance, given without an interval, was revelatory, a long rehearsal for the suicide Hedda executed in full view of both herself and the audience (the actress usually leaves the stage). When the producer Michael Codron went to see it, a woman seated behind him turned to her companion as Maggie picked up the gun and whispered, 'Now does she do it, or does she chicken out?' The issue was in the balance while Maggie's Hedda turned again and again to the mirror, vainly seeking to unlock the puzzle of her existence by contemplating her troublesome physical reality. Finally she peered accusingly into the glass for the last time and continued peering as she pulled the trigger. Bergman's opinion of Hedda was that she was a creature of complete vanity. He told Robert of a lady critic in Stockholm who was madly in love with a theatre director and who, when the director ran off with another woman, was found lying in bed having cut her throat, with an open razor in one hand and a mirror in the other.

The first night was distinguished by the presence of Tennessee Williams sitting in a box, pretty far gone, laughing loudly at all the wrong moments. He alone seemed oblivious to the fact that the play, as *Time* magazine put it, had been removed from the sitting room into the psyche. It was clear that Judge Brack's fondness for the back entrance in Tesman's house was an unconscious reference to sodomy. The emasculation of Loevborg was underlined in the account of the bullet lodging in his pelvic region. Olivier's original casting idea was for Robert to play Tesman, and Jeremy Brett Loevborg. But Robert persuaded him to reverse the roles. Instead of a beautiful Byronic wreck, Robert's Loevborg was a convincingly passionate creation, a memorable addition to the Stephens gallery of plausibly flawed writers. As Anthony Curtis noted in the *Financial Times*, he was not the usual weak intellectual, 'but a man of coarse and brutal strength and strong sexuality, out of D. H. Lawrence rather than Gissing. One really does believe that he might have a great prophetic book in him.'

There was a deliberate contrast between the predominant public image of Hedda and her pre-play manifestation in a white shift, shoulders bared, smoking a cigarette and shuddering with disgust, her thin, blanched face subject to spasms of tearing torture. With her severe centre parting, high forehead, tapering fingers and heavily corseted costume, Maggie's stark physical appearance was a puritanical complement to her Jean Brodie disguise. She was so highly charged and pent-up, you felt she might explode if touched, and only the slightest facial movement betrayed the intensity of Hedda's welling emotion. Harold Hobson concluded that Hedda had been profitably deprived of sympathy and that her performance was so generally terrifying that, when she nearly ripped out Mrs Elvsted's hair, he jumped out of his seat. Considering that Hobson was severely crippled and had to be hoisted between chromium-plated wheelchair and plush velvet fauteuils for most of his working life, the accolade was great indeed. We must assume that Maggie's Hedda, as far as he was concerned, was truly miraculous.

The *Evening Standard* drama panel agreed: on 25 January 1971, Maggie received the best actress award for the second time. It was handed over by Bergman, but not Ingmar – Ingrid. John Gielgud and Ralph Richardson were jointly voted best actor for their performances in David Storey's *Home*. Whenever leading actors of the day were discussed, Maggie and Robert, but especially Maggie, were now mentioned. The great director Tyrone Guthrie, in a book on acting published at this time, said, 'I certainly do not expect to coach or teach actors to play their parts. It would obviously be wild if I were to give lessons to Maggie Smith on how to make a line sound witty, or to suggest inflections to Sir John Gielgud.' The film mogul Daryl F. Zanuck, thinking of teaming Maggie with George C. Scott, termed them 'the greatest living actress and actor in the world'.

A week after Alice Ghostley had collected the *Jean Brodie* Oscar on her behalf, Maggie had a couple of days free to attend the Tony Awards ceremony in New York. She and Robert flew the Atlantic and presented a special award to Alfred Lunt and Lynn Fontanne. A direct succession was implied. But the next few years saw the alliance crumble and Maggie's career take a few wrong turnings. She was moving past Jean Brodie's prime, and well into her own as Mrs Sullen and Hedda Gabler.

9

Prickly Pain in Private Lives

'I think very few people are completely normal really, deep down in their private lives. It all depends on a combination of circumstances. If all the various cosmic thingummys fuse at the same moment, and the right spark is struck, there's no knowing what one mightn't do. That was the trouble with Elyot and me, we were like two violent acids bubbling about in a nasty little matrimonial bottle.'

Thus Amanda sums up the situation in Noël Coward's *Private Lives*, the last play in which Maggie and Robert appeared as a partnership. The tragic dilemma of two people who love each other too much to be able to live together was horribly appropriate. In real life, the simulacrum of their on-stage liaison, Maggie and Robert just ran out of steam. But 'deep down' there was always a scar left by the sparks of the fusion. After *Jean Brodie*, Robert was keen to press home the advantages of working with the film's producer, Robert Fryer, who was in charge of the Ahmanson Theatre in Los Angeles and host to the National on their successful visit with *Three Sisters* and *The Beaux' Stratagem*. A producing company was formed of Bobby, Maggie and Bobby – BMB – but the only fruit was a production in Los Angeles of Coward's *Design for Living*, in which the Lunts and Noël Coward had originally made up what the play's standard prig calls 'a disgusting three-sided erotic hotch-potch'. The idea had been hatched during *Hedda Gabler* at the Cambridge, where it had been decided that John Moffatt, who was Judge Brack, would play Leo to Maggie's Gilda and Robert's Otto. American Equity kicked up a fuss and, in spite of receiving a three-page cable from Coward himself on the matter, denied Moffatt permission. Denholm Elliott, who already had a green card, played Leo instead. Also in the cast, as the prig, Ernest, was Roderick Cook, who had known Maggie since Oxford revue days and appeared with her and Kenneth Williams in *Share My Lettuce*. The director was the ever-faithful Peter Wood, whom Robert usually translated as 'Pierre Bois'.

Once again Maggie and Robert rented a house on the beach front at Malibu, a forty-five-minute drive from the Ahmanson. Wood stayed out there after dinner one night and travelled into rehearsal with them the following morning in the Rolls which Fryer sent each day to collect them. It was driven by Fryer's assistant, an orphan from Bristol, whom the director, himself a West Countryman, knew very well. Wood sat up front making animated conversation. Suddenly, in a voice Wood had never heard before, Maggie said, 'Would you mind not talking.' The process of concentration had already begun. Wood cites this not as an instance of grandeur or pretension, but of a perfectly simple, professional request. Silence was mandatory.

The production broke all box-office records during its seven-week run, and Maggie's 'ankle work' was widely approved: she wore an ivory-white satin sheath, cut on the cross, and sat on an enormous sofa, facing the front, sending semaphore signals with one leg dangled over the other. Robert made an impressive second-act entrance in a white camel-hair coat. But the reports were mixed on the impact made by the central trio, 'the three amoral, glib and over-articulate creatures, who cannot help themselves', as Coward called them. The unease in the off-stage marriage was unwittingly touched on by a Californian admirer, Mrs Jeannette Warnken, who wrote a letter which Maggie found hilarious and had posted on the noticeboard of the Ahmanson:

Your performance... is exuberant, delightful, flawless and frightening... I am concerned about your health. Anyone with a keen eye and sincere interest worries that YOU WILL NOT MAKE IT THROUGH THE RUN (Damn this typewriter, those capitals were unintentional). How exasperating it must be for you to be working with your charming chubby cherub of a husband who seems to rollick through his part without the slightest bit of tension. You are an enchanting and capable pair, but please do not attempt to keep up with him physically. Do take a REST after this run and have your face done... You are the greatest actress of our time. Please take care of yourself. We of the great mass audience depend upon you for our dreams.

The two Bobbies wanted to take *Design for Living* to Broadway, but Maggie insisted on coming to London and playing in repertory with another production, to be directed by Zeffirelli. The proposed play was Goldoni's *The Housekeeper* and the producer was going to be Eddie Kulukundis, the vast and genial scion of a Greek shipping family whose enthusiasm for theatre was never quite matched by his artistic acumen. Zeffirelli planned to infest the stage with crowds of villagers and donkey-drawn carts. The air would be heavy with cod Venetian accents, garlic and horse manure. Not surprisingly, Robert went slightly off his rocker at this stage, and the entire BMB project was abandoned. Binkie Beaumont was miffed that Robert and Maggie had gone to Kulukundis and not to him. His career as top dog on the Avenue had been in serious decline since the middle 1960s. The new boys there, notably Peter Bridge and Michael Codron, had taken over.

By the end of 1973, both Binkie Beaumont and Noël Coward would be dead. So the plan to revive *Private Lives*, directed by John Gielgud, starring Maggie and Robert, would be seen in retrospect as Binkie's last West End throw. It opened at the Queen's on 21 September 1972, and, according to close friends, was part of a desperate final attempt by Maggie to keep her marriage, and Robert himself, on the rails. Ten years later, John Gielgud wrote to B. A. Young confessing that he had heard rumours that Maggie was 'difficult', but that he found the experience a pleasure. She was, he said, 'a dream girl to rehearse. I never thought Robert at all rightly cast, and their marriage was running down in a big way, though neither of them showed when they were working that they were in the middle of emotional problems. She is a fanatic about rehearsals, always so full of new touches of invention that I found it difficult to decide which were the best to keep in.'

Gielgud's misgivings over Robert as Elyot were largely dispelled in a performance which dug deeper into the part than anyone thought possible. The overall effect was that he seemed not to be playing against Coward, but mining the text for even more intimations of mortality than are already there. A blasted intruder in the salon, rather like his Loevborg, Robert's Elyot caught both the savage hedonism of the character's proposals, and also the last-gasp quality of his life with Maggie: 'Let's blow trumpets and squeakers, and enjoy the party as much as we can, like very small, quite idiotic schoolchildren.

Let's savour the delight of the moment. Come and kiss me, darling, before your body rots, and worms pop in and out of your eye sockets.' Confronted with the bullish, unpredictable quality of this performance, it was little wonder that Maggie's Amanda stiffened into a frantic bundle of signals. The wide divergence of reaction – among audiences as well as critics – demonstrated the thinness of the line to be trod between style and caricature. Nonetheless, she looked stunning as an auburn-wigged, Marcel-waved Amanda, dressed first in flared pencil skirt and later in floral red pyjamas. The clothes were designed by another Shaftesbury Avenue legend, Beatrice Dawson, and the elegant curvilinear setting was the work of Anthony Powell, a quondam protégé of Gielgud who became one of Maggie's closest allies in this awkward period of her life.

Elyot is defined in the play as Amanda's first real love, a man who drinks and knocks her about and to whom only the worst part of her is attracted. Rarely can the pain of a disintegrating relationship have found such a poignant and direct artistic expression. 'Snap, snap, snap, like a little adder,' jeers Elyot; 'Adders don't snap; they sting,' scoffs Amanda. Robert snapped and Maggie stung. The strain of the private life finally took its toll on *Private Lives*, and the reviews, though for the most part highly favourable (the idea that the whole shebang was a critical disaster is entirely mythical), contained two attacks, by Jack Tinker, who had recently joined the *Daily Mail*, and Harold Hobson, of such concentrated vitriol that they were later said to account for Maggie's subsequent departure to Canada. There is only a partial element of truth in this. Tinker accused Gielgud of allowing Maggie her head, or worse, her hands. She had, he averred, hands of sand which got into everything. Hobson was even more destructive, suggesting that the youthful promise he had spotted in Michael Meyer's *The Ortolan* eighteen years earlier had been entirely traduced by experience: 'There was once a time, at the Old Hall in Marston, near Oxford, when Margaret Smith could make the heart stop for a moment with a forlorn word, a crushed gesture. In *Private Lives* she is merely a compendium of grimaces, an anthology of little squeaks, a catalogue of double-takes.'

The problem with Maggie had come to a head: you either found her weaponry of gestures and reactions wildly funny, a comprehensive guide to the nervous system which fuelled them, or you did not. And you did not even have to be for or against. You could be for one day, against the next, as critics whimsically proved down the years. The general rule, though, is that the mechanics of Maggie's acting, which are spontaneous and unrivalled, work best when she is relaxed and connecting fully with her emotional interior. This was certainly not the case in *Private Lives*, though the production as a whole had the considerable merit of confounding cosy Cowardian expectations and Gielgud's gentlemanly attempts to impose order. It was a bit of a riot, and swung around enormously during the run. After the first night, Coward went backstage and wagged his finger at Maggie, telling her off for overdoing it: 'You've got very common indeed. You're almost as common as Gertie.' Maggie told Alan Bennett that to be compared with Gertrude Lawrence, if only for overdoing it, seemed such a compliment that she instantly mended her ways.

Maggie was mightily relieved when, at the end of the year, Kenneth Williams moved into the Globe next door, in *My Fat Friend*, a comedy written for him by Charles Laurence. In spite of a difficult rehearsal period, the play had gone well and Maggie, who read other people's reviews even if she never read her own, left a note at the stage door: 'I've never seen such a wonderful crop of good notices. You may have been away from the theatre for a long time but you've certainly come back with a bang!' They had supper together again just before Christmas and harked back to their occupation of these same theatres ten years previously, when Williams was still in the Shaffer double bill and Maggie was in *Mary, Mary*. Williams said that God intended such things. It was 'the divine nature of special affections'. This unusually sombre conversation continued with Maggie declaring: 'It was all so carefree then, wasn't it? But the awful thing about success is that it gets harder every time, not easier. When we were young, arrogance blinded us to the pitfalls.'

Because of Williams, Maggie agreed to make her one and only appearance to date on a mainstream British television chat show, hosted by Michael Parkinson on BBC TV on 17 February 1973. The other guests were the footballer George Best, the poet John Betjeman and Kenneth Williams. Maggie appears in elegant black from top to toe, looking drawn and nervous to start with but loosening up as the interview proceeds. She quotes Pamela Brown's remark about the audience being stage-struck and how things get 'more and more difficult' the longer you go on. A couple of laboured clips from *Travels with My Aunt* do little to lighten the atmosphere. She answers the 'who influenced you?' question with Ingmar Bergman and William Gaskill, which completely silences the studio audience.

Maggie had done little television work altogether since the early days of her career: just two 'Plays of the Month' for the BBC which she recorded before *Private Lives* opened: *The Merchant of Venice* and Shaw's *The Millionairess*. Portia was clearly not her role and Maggie found no way round the triumphal priggishness of the *Merchant* court scenes. She later told Alan Bennett that, at the time, Robert was having an affair with the make-up girl on *The Merchant*, so, as far as she was concerned, the quality of mercy was pretty strained. Her Portia submitted rather sulkily to her father's conditions of marriage, mocked the suitors inordinately and was implacably cruel in driving home the letter of the law. You sense, though, that Maggie did not love Portia enough to play her very well.

She was far more temperamentally suited to Shaw's Epifania Fitzfassenden who, like Portia, is bound by a parental rule: any suitor for this woman worth £30 million must succeed in converting £150 into £50,000 within six months. The comedy eventually leads her to an Egyptian doctor (played by Tom Baker in dark pancake and a red fez) who has kept a clinic for penniless Mohammedan refugees. Under the rush and silliness of this technically engrossing performance, Maggie shot a bolt of profound loneliness. The final effect is one of helter-skelter skittishness subdued in scenes of limpid radiance. Cedric Messina assembled a fine array of supporting talent: Peter Barkworth as the solicitor Sagamore, James Villiers as Epifania's first husband (Villiers added distinction to the boring Victor in *Private Lives*) and Charles Gray as a barking city slicker.

Nancy Banks-Smith was seduced in the *Guardian*: 'From the hurly-burly of Epifania's entry, lashing her silver foxes like a tail, to the peace of the last scene when her doctor listened entranced to the slow sledgehammer of her pulse, it was mainly Maggie Smith singing Shaw. And that's well worth an hour and a half of anybody's life.'

'Can one live with a volcano, an avalanche . . . a millionairess?' cried Barkworth's Sagamore. Maggie saves her climactic transfiguration to the final great speeches, and the one about marriage and a thousand little infidelities – 'a wife is all women to one man . . . his comfort, his helper, at best his greatest treasure, at worst his troublesome but beloved child' – was as great, in her performance, as the best of Congreve and Farquhar. You realise, watching this again many years later, that such theatrically inflamed and stylish acting and writing on television are almost entirely a thing of the past.

An attempt to repeat the success of *Jean Brodie* in George Cukor's film of *Travels with My Aunt*, though not without its admirers, was a considerable failure, and further evidence that Maggie's career had peaked and not yet found a new direction. Robert Fryer had set it up with Maggie and the *Brodie* screenwriter Jay Presson Allen (with contributions from Hugh Wheeler) two years previously, but Maggie had rejected the idea. The property then went the way of Cukor and Katharine Hepburn, and Alec McCowen was hired to play Henry Pulling. McCowen had done a read-through thinking he was being auditioned, and at the end of it, Hepburn turned to him and said, 'How was I?' He was at first expected to address his Aunt Augusta as 'Mumsy', Hollywood's notion of how English boys spoke to their mothers. Hepburn was never happy with the script and started re-writing it herself. She was eventually fired by MGM for insisting on a longer schedule than the allotted fourteen weeks.

Robert Fryer persuaded Maggie, against her will, to take over, and Robert was cast as Visconti, the only man who ever really cared for Aunt Augusta and the first and only love of her life. The film took as long to shoot as Hepburn had forecast, chiefly because of Maggie's laborious make-up each day. Alec McCowen recognised that she was not in the best of spirits, because of the problems with Robert: 'She was only eating one meal a week, and that was a little smoked salmon or consommé or something. She fainted on the set one day, and yet this extraordinary energy came out. Cukor should have been a little more controlled, but he simply fell in love with her. Every time she did something, he loved it.' McCowen has no idea where Maggie's performance came from in these conditions. It was George Cukor's forty-ninth film. Aged seventy-two, he instantly admitted Maggie to his private pantheon of great stars he had directed – Garbo in *Camille*, Audrey Hepburn in *My Fair Lady*, Judy Garland in *A Star Is Born* and

Katharine Hepburn passim: 'She is resourceful, inventive, and she has mystery and power. Mystery in a woman is terribly important,' he told David Lewin in the *Daily Mail*.

One mystery was how Maggie, her face lined for the role like an old map of the Indies, managed to evoke comparisons with a Modigliani drawing, La Goulue in Toulouse-Lautrec's poster, and, as George Melly said in the *Observer*, 'a Beardsley lady or one of those wicked old trouts in the novels of Ronald Firbank'. Like some bizarre preparation for the other Aunt Augusta, Wilde's Lady Bracknell, Maggie sweeps through a survey of her own colourful past, dragging her impressionable 'nephew' in tow and reliving her affair with Visconti in some glutinous flashback scenes (in which Maggie, her flowing ginger hair restored, eyes sparkling, manages to resemble an attractive pubescent schoolgirl). Graham Greene's storyline, to say nothing of his superb comic dialogue, is entirely traduced and de-energised, and the unresolved ending, in which a future way of life is to be decided on the slow-motion toss of a coin which freezes in the last frame, is both idiotic and insensitive. The script, it now turns out, was mostly what Katharine Hepburn had written while holding everybody up. Jay Presson Allen told Cukor's biographer that only one big speech was hers, and that there was nothing of Hugh Wheeler's: 'It was Kate's script.' There are handsome location shots, especially in Paris in the George V Hotel and the buffet of the Gare de Lyon. And McCowen as Henry is superb, crusty and dry as an old biscuit. But, as George Melly said, the central quality of Greene's heroine, her irresistible charm, is missing. Maggie manages a few shafts of sudden emotion, but this is very much a performance most memorable for its make-up. And even that has the occasional, unfortunate effect of making Maggie resemble a male drag artist.

Much better, but less widely recognised, is her performance in the film she made just before *Travels*, Alan J. Pakula's *Love and Pain and the Whole Damn Thing*. This curious project, scripted by Alvin Sargent, was one of many follow-ups to the 1970 weepie *Love Story*, which portrayed romance vitiated by the fatal cancer of Ali MacGraw. In *Love and Pain*, Maggie plays Lila Fisher, a lonely spinster from Bournemouth who is dying of an unspecified incurable disease and who discovers passion on a Spanish holiday with the much younger Timothy Bottoms.

Bottoms, following up a notable début in Peter Bogdanovich's *The Last Picture Show*, was also 'crippled' in his role – by parental expectations, asthma and his own innate sensitivity. And Pakula was hot stuff after providing quirkily enjoyable vehicles for Liza Minnelli in *The Sterile Cuckoo* and Jane Fonda in *Klute*. The result was not a smash, nothing like, but here at least are the first outlines of Maggie's mature studies in emotional disintegration of the 1980s. One scene in particular prefigures *The Lonely Passion of Judith Hearne* in its glum, suicidal alone-in-a-hotel-bedroom despair. Maggie has collapsed again with her mystery illness, scrawled 'Adios' on the mirror and finished off the brandy, no doubt with a whispered toast of 'Bottoms up'. Earlier, Maggie has managed to shake off a few inhibitions at a flamenco club. Bottoms misreads the signals and jumps on her lustily when they return to the hotel. Rejected, he goes next door and tearfully smashes his fist through the partition. Maggie goes into his room, cleans up his hand and starts thawing out a little herself. However unlikely this situation seems at first, the playing of it is beautiful, funny and tender. When she gets out of bed, Maggie executes what the *New Yorker* described as the first sexual pratfall by a girl in a movie. She trips over her own panties. Vincent Canby of the *New York Times*, who had disliked her intensely in *Travels*, thought she was 'magnificently funny', while Dilys Powell in the *Sunday Times* said Maggie presented 'passion, shame, hysteria and a momentary disintegration which are the more telling for being muted, almost miniature'.

With her marriage under threat, there suddenly seemed a danger that aimlessness would overtake her career. She unexpectedly agreed to play Peter Pan at the Coliseum for the 1973 Christmas season. Captain Hook was not played by Robert – who would have been ideal – but by the Irish TV comedian Dave Allen, whose vocal projection over the orchestra pit left something to be desired. Allen was an old friend of both Robert and Maggie, and was at that time still married to the actress Judith Stott, Maggie's example at the Oxford High School.

Accounts of Robert Helpmann's production vary a great deal, but Christopher Downes, who was dressing Maggie, recalls one matinée she played barefoot, with a dreadful hangover, and the special silence she won with her query to the audience on the subject of their faith in fairies. Lauren Bacall was in the stalls with her child, and so was

Peter Eyre, the actor. Of that one performance, Eyre said to Downes, 'I think this is not the performance of the year, but the performance of the decade.' Michael Billington was impressed by Maggie's Peter:

> Like Dorothy Tutin before her, she rescues the role from thigh-slapping archness and presents us with a complex manic-depressive trying to ward off internal demons by surrounding herself with young people. Desperation is never far away as she talks of the barred maternal window or asks us if we do really believe in fairies; and, alone in the House of Trees at the end, her Peter becomes a potentially tragic Tennessee Williams hero living off memories and music in a warm climate.

The weather had changed. Peter Hall had taken over from Olivier at the National Theatre, and the Old Vic company had been altered and overhauled in the new master's likeness in preparation for the move to the South Bank in the mid-1970s. Binkie Beaumont and Noël Coward had died. But Maggie herself was no back number. In a *Times* survey of the 'top of the pops' people of 1973, the British high-profile élite of sixty men and sixty women included, on the distaff side, Edith Evans at number fourteen and Maggie 'when playing the Master' at number thirty-one. Vanessa Redgrave just scraped in at number fifty-seven.

Maggie needed a new West End break. A play was commissioned from Charles Laurence, whose play for Kenneth Williams had been a big hit. The result was *Snap* (originally 'Clap', the slang word for gonorrhoea), a loose reworking of Schnitzler's *La Ronde* in which everyone received sexual infection thanks to Maggie's character, Connie Hudson. It was awful. Peter Dunlop was informed by his wife that he was so drunk on the first night that he was incapable of speaking to anyone. Clever ploy. Christopher Downes maintains that audiences howled with laughter during the previews, but the critics descended like a ton of bricks and killed off all expectations. The producer, Michael White, is reputed to have asked Maggie whom she would like as a director, to which she languidly replied, 'I dunno, Ingmar Bergman or Bill Gaskill.' Gaskill she got, and he always maintained that *Snap* was the one piece of work in his long career of which he was thoroughly ashamed. It opened at the Vaudeville in

March 1974. In the programme biography, Maggie listed her favourite role as Mrs Sullen, her favourite food as oysters, her favourite music as applause and Bach, her favourite sport as watching Wimbledon and her ambition 'to dance and sing and keep on working'. General critical uproar ensued over cheap tricks, mannerisms, prostitution of her high-class skills and an alleged inability to distinguish between rubbish and true comedy. Maggie gave it the works, jumbling her knees and elbows, falling over her own ankles as readily, said Alan Brien in *Plays and Players*, as she collided with her own syntax. But the effort was unworthy of the play, which sank like a stone the more frenetically Maggie tried to administer the kiss of life.

This débâcle coincided exactly with the final, inevitable break-up with Robert. What had gone wrong between them? Their relationship, forged in the white heat of the National Theatre's inception, had been sustained by physical attraction and common purpose at work. Maggie had gone to the National as a West End star, Robert as a leading representative of the new intellectual theatre. Maggie took artistic respectability from her association with Robert; he assumed that her stardom and glamour would rub off on him. This happened for a while, but the mistake Robert made was to assume that Hollywood stardom would automatically follow. Admittedly he was unlucky. But he never attained the eminence on screen of his wife, nor did he win an Oscar, and William Gaskill bluntly declares that, when the balance sheet is totted up, Maggie is the greater and more resilient performer.

Robert's understandable inability to accept this was a major factor in driving the couple apart. Temperamentally, too, they were a mismatch. Maggie's idea of fun is to shut the door against the world, immerse herself in a couple of good books, a hot bath and the bedroom comforts of an early night. Robert liked noise, people, flowing cups and piled-high plates, and as much social brouhaha as could be mustered.

In early 1969, Robert had been signed up by Billy Wilder to make *The Private Life of Sherlock Holmes*, a film that was going to do for Robert's international career what *Jean Brodie* had done for Maggie's. He was convinced that it was going to be his 'great statement', like Peter O'Toole's in *Lawrence of Arabia* or Albert Finney's in *Tom Jones*. Wilder assured him that the film would make him a star.

He was upset that, on the occasion of his 'one big chance', Maggie promptly moved down to Tigbourne Court for five months, with children and two nannies, leaving him to rattle around and fend for himself in the Fulham house during the six-month filming. He asked her to read the script, which Wilder had written with his regular and distinguished collaborator, I. A. L. Diamond. Robert complained that she couldn't care less about it. To be fair to Maggie, she had plenty on her own plate at this time, organising her work on *The Country Wife* at Chichester, coping with the disappointment of Olivier's rebuff and caring for the baby. And Tigbourne was only half an hour's drive from Chichester. She and Robert were committed to return to the National for Gaskill's production of *The Beaux' Stratagem*, and Maggie regarded the Chichester jaunt as a means of limbering up.

Robert's view of this period was understandably tarnished by the fact that *The Private Life of Sherlock Holmes* was a disaster; ironically, today it is something of a cult favourite, one of those films that gradually draw their audiences into the game of it. Still, the feeling at the time was that the script fell below expectations, the acting misfired and Wilder's direction, for once, was wayward and cumbersome. Seeds of resentment were sown which yielded poisonous fruit. Robert took the failure of this film very badly and his behaviour became increasingly erratic. He was also prone to fits of violence. But only furniture was at risk with Robert around, never life or limb.

Design for Living in Los Angeles was an attempt to sustain the great success Maggie and Robert enjoyed in *The Beaux' Stratagem* and *Hedda Gabler* in 1970, but the writing was already on the wall. During this period, Peter Wood, who was directing them, reckons that Robert's various little compensatory infidelities and peccadillos were becoming intolerable to Maggie. But his behaviour was not all that unreasonable given the pain of so many dreams evaporating. Robert always flirted and dallied, sometimes drank too much and was generally at his best, his most attractive and also his most dangerous, when he was having a good time. He was, in every way, as Wood says, 'an adorable rogue'. The relationship became a trial of strength, and Maggie was never unduly bothered, at least on the surface, about showing how strong she could be. She felt deeply that marriage was for life, for children and for loyalty between the protagonists, however much the career took over. And so did her parents. Meg and Nat got wind of trouble brewing and began to suspect that their worst misgivings about Robert were likely to be fulfilled, especially when he exacerbated the situation beyond redemption by conducting his affairs with Antonia Fraser and Vanessa Redgrave in the full public glare of the gossip columns.

Maggie's husband in *Snap* was played by Barrie Ingham, who had appeared with her in Beverley's *Strip the Willow*. It was hardly surprising, therefore, that Beverley should re-enter Maggie's life at this point. He had tracked Maggie from a distance and had often spoken to her parents in Oxford. Nat was always convinced that Maggie would one day end up married to Beverley. Beverley had also kept in touch through the proxy of Kenneth Williams. He certainly knew that the marriage was in trouble. Early in 1972 he had rented a converted farmhouse at Seillans in the Var, in the South of France, and Williams had travelled across to stay in a nearby *pension* for a few days, to talk over old times and have dinner in St Tropez.

Beverley returned to London in 1973 to work on the Tommy Steele musical, *Hans Andersen*. He sensed that now was the time Maggie needed him most of all. He called backstage at the Vaudeville, ostensibly to greet Ingham, but really to catch up with Maggie. Over a period of several days, Maggie told him the whole saga of her marriage to Robert, the children and how her silently enraged parents were sitting at home in Oxford muttering 'I told you so' to each other, and to her. With the failure of *Snap*, there was renewed talk of taking *Private Lives* to Los Angeles, Toronto and New York, though not with Robert. Audiences would have to make do with just one of the 'New Lunts'; John Standing, who had taken over from Robert at the Queen's (playing opposite Jill Bennett, who had replaced Maggie), would be hired to play Elyot. Beverley convinced Maggie that this was the right thing to do, just as he had persuaded her in 1963 to accept Olivier's invitation to join the National.

Maggie, much to John Gielgud's amazement, insisted on three weeks' re-rehearsal before going to America, and the company moved into the vast expanse of Drury Lane, rattling out Coward's brittle prose in the incongruous shadow of the set for the Billy Liar musical, *Billy*, in which Michael Crawford was enjoying a huge success. Gielgud, an inveterate film-goer, had of course been to see *Travels with*

My Aunt since he had last crossed swords with Maggie at the Queen's. One day in rehearsal he dropped one of his celebrated bricks when he interrupted a scene to give an impulsive note: 'Oh, don't do it like that, Maggie, don't screw your face up. You look like that terrible old woman you played in that dreadful film . . . Oh no, I didn't mean *Travels with My Aunt*.' Gielgud remembers her working furiously even after he had left Drury Lane at about tea-time to prepare for his own nightly stage performance as Shakespeare in Edward Bond's *Bingo* at the Royal Court. It was odd that, once again, Maggie should be playing a comedy about returning to a first love.

Beverley was far from boring, but he had more of Victor's solidity than of Elyot's raffishness, though he certainly shared Elyot's enthusiasm for travel. *Private Lives*, a crucially symbolic play in Maggie's life and career, was now an almost inverted paradigm of her situation. She had lived through the rough and tumble of life with Elyot (Robert Stephens), but was returning to the calm and safety of her sensible Victor character (Beverley Cross).

Maggie set off on her American tour with her sons. Christopher was now seven, Toby five. Divorce papers were issued between Maggie and Robert, and between Beverley and his second wife, Gayden Collins. The minute she arrived at the Ahmanson Theatre in Los Angeles, where *Private Lives* played from the second week of October 1974, Maggie started experimenting with Coward and Amanda Prynne. Shutting out the pain of the break-up went hand in hand with stripping down the engine of her comedy technique. She admitted privately that the harsher critics had been right about her performance in London. She had settled into automatic and then shot into overdrive when seduced by the audience. That was always the most dangerous seduction. John Gielgud had written to B. A. Young, in comparing her with Gertrude Lawrence, whom he had seen in the original production, that 'her main trouble lies in her inexhaustible vitality and invention (much like Miss Lawrence) and a good (or bad) audience is inclined to go to her head'. The only real corruption Maggie has ever suffered is that meted out by an enthusiastic crowd in the stalls.

The Victor and Sibyl in London, James Villiers and Polly Adams, were replaced by the Americans Remak Ramsay and Niki Flacks. The

set designer Anthony Powell travelled to Los Angeles where, at one of
the previews, Powell says, the play suddenly leapt to life:

> She threw away everything she had done in the past and played it as
> though it were Ibsen or Strindberg, pushing everything as far as she
> could. She tested it for all that poignancy of two people who cannot
> either live with, or without, each other, and it was unbelievable. I'd
> never seen anything like it in my life. The audience was spellbound.

At the same time, according to Powell, she refined some of the London
performance and knitted the two versions together. But on the first
night in the Ahmanson she chickened out and reverted to the old
trickery, settling for the easy laughs. 'I went round in the interval and
she just burst into tears and said, "Don't say a word. This is one of the
most horrible moments of my life; I know what I should be doing and
I can't do it." But within a week or so she was back on track, working
at the role as she had been before.'

Dan Sullivan of the *Los Angeles Times* had given the first-night
performance a polite, respectable review, but heard from a friend of
the subsequent transformation. He returned to the Ahmanson in the
last week of the run and delivered an unequivocal rave, saying that
Maggie's Amanda was now more human, more genuinely mixed up
and not at all the study in external flamboyance he had first seen.
The production moved on to Chicago, Boston and Denver, and then
visited the huge Royal Alexandra Theatre in Toronto just prior to the
five-week engagement in New York. Gielgud was at last free to see what
she was up to. He arrived from London for a matinée in Toronto and
thought her acting was 'absolutely perfect'. The critic of the *Toronto
Star*, Urjo Kareda, who had seen the performance in London, said
that Maggie had now found something else, a new, faintly perceptible
murmur of apprehension.

Maggie returned to New York for the first time since *New Faces*
and was applauded as a more than worthy Broadway successor to
the Amandas of Gertrude Lawrence, Tallulah Bankhead and Tammy
Grimes. Clive Barnes in the *New York Times* declared that either
the London reviews had been libellous or Maggie had transformed
herself. The outrageous triple take she executed on seeing Elyot

unexpectedly materialise on the balcony had been retained, followed by the hilarious crumbling spin across the stage. But, as Jack Kroll said in *Newsweek*, you also got a sense of heartbreak in this first act for which the four-square reliability of Victor was real compensation. In Coward's play, Amanda and Elyot have been married for three years and divorced for five. Maggie and Robert had been married for the same total of eight years, with an almost identical period of separation within the marriage. Their divorce went through in April 1975, just after Maggie returned from New York. And on 23 June she and Beverley were at last married in Guildford registry office. The guests were Alistair and Shân, their son Angus, and Christopher and Toby. Maggie wore a beige trouser-suit.

Important plans for a new life had been laid one fateful day in Toronto when Robin Phillips, newly appointed as artistic director of the Stratford Festival in Ontario, sent Maggie a telegram which read simply, 'If you want to escape for a weekend I'll come and collect you.' Beverley had flown out to Chicago to join Maggie and the boys after the opening of *Hans Andersen* in London. They said they would love a weekend away from the touring grind, so Phillips asked one of his board members at Stratford if they could borrow her holiday cabin on Lake Huron for the weekend. Joe Mandel, Phillips's friend and partner, collected Maggie and Beverley in Toronto and drove to Stratford to collect Phillips. The party drove on for another hour to the cabin. Robin Phillips recalls that Maggie was wrapped in mink, delighted to be free and 'absolutely hysterical'. After a good night's sleep, they all went for a long walk. It was an exceptionally cold winter. Only when the ice melted in the following spring did Phillips realise that Maggie had in fact been walking on the lake. Over the weekend, Phillips drove Maggie and Beverley back into Stratford and showed them over the theatre and around the town. They looked in on a rehearsal. At some point on the second or third day, Beverley said to Phillips, 'You know, I think if you asked Maggie, she would be quite interested in coming here to do something.' The conversation turned to Cleopatra and Millamant. And the next stage in Maggie's professional life was agreed on the spot. She would return to Canada in a year's time and join Robin Phillips in his second season at Stratford. By then she would be married to Beverley and she could start over, with a clean sheet.

Robert's divorce from Maggie was much more of a defeat for him than it was for her. He had envisaged a royal progress through the National, the West End, Broadway and Hollywood. He wanted to be a star very much more than she did, and she was one anyway. He was merely a very fine actor, one of the finest. After the London run of *Private Lives*, it was his turn to retreat to Tigbourne, which he now said he always hated, and to play a season at Chichester as Trigorin in *The Seagull*, directed by Jonathan Miller. The production was revived in 1974 in an interrelated Freudian season at Greenwich, the Chekhov presented alongside Ibsen's *Ghosts* (Robert as Pastor Manders) and *Hamlet* (Robert as Claudius). It was excellent work, but it was not the Big Time. All hopes were now pinned on a 1975 Anthony Shaffer commercial thriller, *Murderer*. Unhappily, this proved to be yet another disaster and not, as intended, the new *Sleuth*. This, after the failure of *Sherlock Holmes*, was a second body blow of ferocious impact. Robert was sent reeling around the ring, having lost his wife, his foothold at the National, his chance of film stardom and now his promise of a compensatory financial windfall in the West End theatre.

He reacted with a terrible wildness and for a short time became socially impossible and virtually unemployable. Luckily, during *Murderer*, Robert had fallen in love with the talented actress Patricia Quinn (best known for her appearance in the stage and film versions of *The Rocky Horror Show*). They forged a relatively secure domestic relationship which lasted right through to Robert's death and proved his partial salvation. In the post-Maggie years, Robert had his professional ups and downs, with some good seasons at the National Theatre under Peter Hall and several notable television and film appearances. But his unrivalled gift for projecting a sense of tragic waste would never encompass the greatest heights of Macbeth or Antony. However, in 1991, just turned sixty, he made a remarkable return to the top Shakespearean flight at Stratford-upon-Avon as both Falstaff and Julius Caesar. He had been invited to join the RSC by that company's new artistic director, Adrian Noble, who, as a schoolboy in Chichester, had undergone a Pauline conversion to the idea of a career in the theatre thanks to Robert's performance in *The Royal Hunt of the Sun*. And then, in 1993, he scored an ultimate triumph as an immensely moving King Lear, again directed by Noble, at Stratford-upon-Avon.

Lovable, unpredictable, noisy and in many ways reprehensible, Robert remained a true vagabond of the British stage to the end, but one whose real glory was in a distant Camelot, first at the early Royal Court and later at the Olivier National, in harness with the woman he could neither live with for ever nor quite stop loving. He was out of the hunt, but he would always be Elyot Chase:

You're looking very lovely, you know, in this damned moonlight. Your skin is clear and cool, and your eyes are shining, and you're growing lovelier and lovelier every second as I look at you. You don't hold any mystery for me, darling, do you mind? There isn't a particle of you that I don't know, remember and want.

10

Canada Home and Dry

That weekend discussion at Lake Huron with Robin Phillips did indeed prove the basis of Maggie's first season at the Stratford Festival, Ontario. She signed up to play Millamant and Cleopatra, and she added her second look at Masha in *Three Sisters* and a vignette as Mistress Overdone, the noisy bawd in *Measure for Measure*.

She arrived to join rehearsals in the trim, quiet and prosperous festival town on 1 March 1976 in the middle of a violent storm. She would return for three more seasons, avoiding the worst winter weather by making films in Hollywood, to complete what many colleagues and critics would hail as her regeneration. A qualifying opinion often expressed of this supposed exile was that nobody saw her work there except a few London critics and a lot of lucky Canadians. But London is often less of a theatrical world centre than its practitioners and critics allow. The greatest summer theatre festival in North America is not just a magnet for visitors from all over Canada. It attracts, at its best, keen attention in New York and sends reverberations right through the continent. This was certainly the case in the Phillips years of 1975 to 1980. Maggie was Queen Guinevere in her second Camelot, a golden era indeed comparable in some ways to the Olivier years at the Old Vic, though without the acting in depth or the intellectual spine provided by Tynan. In Brian Bedford, the company's outstanding actor, Maggie linked up with one of her most trusted leading men, her Lancelot. And in Robin Phillips, King Arthur, she had found one of her most crucially influential and sympathetic directors.

Maggie was at last married to the man she began to say she should have married in the first place: 'My Bev. Nice, my Bev, isn't he?' The house in Fulham was kept on but rented out, and would remain so until 1986 when the boys were old enough, and only too eager, to colonise it. For now, Christopher and Toby, aged nine and seven, were enrolled in a Stratford school. The traumatic accumulation of Maggie's unhappy London experiences – marital collapse, rejection by the National, strain and controversy in *Private Lives*, critical disaster in *Snap* – would be cleansed by the concentrated process of work in a permanent ensemble on challenging roles no one had offered her at home. In Canada, Phillips says, Maggie felt relieved of 'the demons and pressures that haunt and taunt'.

Bedford, a perceptive Yorkshireman of working-class background who had made his career mostly on the other side of the Atlantic since going to New York in John Gielgud's production of Peter Shaffer's *Five Finger Exercise* in 1959, offers one of the most striking diagnoses of the 'Maggie' condition. He says that, for her, just the journey from breakfast-time to lights out each day is very difficult and fraught with problems: 'She's not at all affected, you know. I often think that her blood is of a different temperature to the rest of us. And that must be the Scottish side. I've always suspected that the chilliness, the rather bleak "Highlands of Scotland" element in Maggie comes from her mother.'

Maggie's parents were relieved that she was reunited with Beverley. They understood him in a way they did not understand Robert. Beverley had a bona fide association with the University and often mulled over the old days in Balliol with Nat, much to the old man's delight. Nat liked nothing more than to relish his association with the medical and academic life of the city, and Beverley knew how to show a lively interest. Throughout what became known as the period of separation from Maggie, Beverley had kept in touch with her parents. Robert was not someone to whom they felt they could safely entrust their daughter. He didn't fuss and guard her in the way they knew Beverley had, would and wanted to. From the moment Beverley achieved his life's aim of marrying Maggie, he exchanged his former domestic life completely for hers. For Nat, especially, Beverley was another son. Beverley returned the compliment: he saw much less of his own two daughters and committed himself wholeheartedly, and without a moment's hesitation, to becoming 'Dad' for Christopher and Toby.

Maggie asked Christine Miller, who had left Penelope Gilliatt's employ in 1975 and had been working in New York, to join them as child-minder, shopping companion, cook and general helpmate. She got on well with Beverley. She stayed for two and a half years and laughed a great deal for most of them. And she adored the boys: 'Toby was a bit more what I'd call ballsy; he was wonderful when he was little, a real boy, very naughty. He got stuck in there straight away, went fishing with his mates and did all the "boy things". Chris was a little more ethereal, more reflective, more stay-at-home.' When Maggie went on tour with *Private Lives*, the boys had been sent to a school in Los Angeles where most of the children were 'kids of posh lawyers'. They hated it. The fresh air, lack of pressure and informality of Stratford were as welcome to them as was the whole change of pace and climate to their mother.

The new family was billeted in a rambling 1894 three-storey house on Cambria Street. Built in red brick and Queen Anne style, with an odd little decorative black spire, the house was the work of Thomas Trow, a well-known local architect whose granddaughter, Eva McCutcheon, rented it out to the festival. Maggie and Beverley liked the house – it had a very large kitchen and dining area and a beautiful sitting room – but it was slightly too big for their purposes. In subsequent seasons they rented a more compact and practicable white clapboard house on Norman Street, previously occupied by Jessica Tandy and Hume Cronyn.

Mrs McCutcheon kept one cupboard in the attic of 220 Cambria Street locked, saying it contained precious mementos for her grandchildren. This attic was a large room, ideal for the boys to romp and run around in with their friends. Late one night, after a certain amount of running and romping had been perpetrated, Maggie and Christine returned from the theatre to find the lights on and the forbidden cupboard half-open on its chain. Curious to see what treasures the cupboard contained, Maggie got down on her knees and rummaged around with her long spindly arms. She brought out first a tiny toy house covered in pebbles, looked at Christine and said, 'Ooo-er,' then produced a set of tiny gardening tools, a little window box and a mangled shoe. The accidental discovery of these worthless signs of dwarfish domesticity – not at all the silverware or jewellery they expected to find – caused the two women to collapse in gales of uncontrollable laughter. They were only subdued by an angry, Malvolio-like intervention by Beverley in his dressing gown.

In Stratford, such an event counts as a dramatic highlight. Compared to Stratford, Ontario, sleepy old Stratford-upon-Avon is a seething metropolitan centre. Both Stratfords are dedicated in the summer months, and increasingly the early winter ones, to a festival of drama based on the works of Shakespeare. In the middle of the prosperous south-western Ontario farmlands, in a town most renowned for being a glorified railway junction, this is more unexpected, obviously, than in the town of Shakespeare's birth. The idea of following the English example, but using that example to forge a national classical theatre of Canada, was hatched by a remarkably imaginative and persistent Stratford-born journalist called Tom Patterson.

The quiet, determined, bespectacled and altogether unlikely man who inspired Canada's most prestigious cultural institution was, according to the Canadian critic and Stratford historian Martin Knelman, 'less interested in the aesthetics of Elizabethan theatre than in finding economic salvation for a town that was losing its chief industry – a repair centre for railway steam engines'. Patterson's 'impossible dream' was launched in the spring of 1952, when he wrote to the Irish director Tyrone Guthrie, who had worked for the Canadian Broadcasting Company in his youth, inviting him to supervise a festival in 1953. The standing joke was that Patterson, who had only seen one play in his entire life, knew he wanted Guthrie but did not really know who he was until he looked him up in the local library's *Who's Who*. He was instantly less of a joke when he caught his big fish and pulled the entire financial and political community of Stratford behind him. On 13 July 1953, the venture took off, locally and internationally, with Alec Guinness and Irene Worth leading the new festival company in *Richard III*.

They performed in a large canvas tent on the riverside site where the theatre, designed at Guthrie's insistence on a thrust-stage principle by Tanya Moiseiwitsch, would open four years later. All the money was raised on subscription, appeal and donation. The Festival Theatre combined the thrust stage with a wrap-around auditorium similar to that of a Greek amphitheatre, with seating for 1,800 people. A second festival venue was acquired and refurbished during the 1960s: the downtown Avon Theatre, an imposing vaudeville house seating 1,100 people. A third, smaller arena was added in 1971.

By the time the actors occupied the pillared and porticoed thrust stage in 1957, Guthrie had moved on and the artistic directorship was in the hands of the British director Michael Langham, who consolidated the festival's reputation and nurtured many important native careers. He was succeeded in 1968 by the more controversial, and less successful, Jean Gascon, a French Canadian who started his regime in harness with a Canadian administrator, William Wylie, who died, and a fellow Canadian director, John Hirsch, with whom he rapidly fell out. The general impression was that the exciting, heady days of the festival's birth had been lost in a routine and slightly predictable repertory, and that Gascon's stilted efforts at more adventurous productions inevitably proved disastrous.

When Robin Phillips arrived in 1975, a new impetus was sought and soon found. The 1953 festival was a six-week season of forty-two performances playing to 68,000 people and grossing $206,000 Canadian at the box office. In Phillips's first season in 1975, a twenty-one-week season of 362 performances played to 437,000 people and took $2.6 million. Maggie's impact in 1976 was immediate: in a twenty-two-week season of 338 performances, the overall attendance jumped to 518,000 and the box office gross to $3.7 million. In 1975, the government grants amounted to about 20 per cent of the total income of $3.7 million Canadian. Five years later, when Phillips left an operation which had more than doubled its income to $8.3 million, those government grants, an almost standstill figure, constituted just 10 per cent.

The nearest equivalent in Britain to the Stratford Festival Theatre is the Chichester Festival Theatre, which was conceived partly in response to Tom Patterson's adventure, with a similar mobilisation of private money and local involvement at business and management levels. Chichester's theatre, which opened in 1962, and where Maggie had worked in Olivier's National company, also has a thrust stage but one that is not nearly as effectively designed. The Stratford stage is surprisingly small and seems at first limited in its potential. In fact, its simplicity allows for endless variations in the actor's relationship with the audience, which is clustered around the acting area – no spectator is more than sixty-five feet from the stage – in a much more intimate and successful way than at Chichester, even after the £22 million makeover finished in 2014.

The main attraction to the Stratford visitor at festival time is the predominant air of holiday high spirits emanating from the river and the theatre. There are delightful walks through the woods and along the bankside, and the richness and variety of the domestic architecture – streets of sturdy brick houses and clapboard villas set among perfectly manicured lawns – are considerable compensation for the somewhat deadening respectability and almost shocking cleanliness of the town. The Festival Theatre is just a few minutes' walk from the centre, surrounded by greenery and adjacent to a public baseball pitch where theatre patrons can prepare for fictional heroic encounters by witnessing a few minutes of the real thing: a schoolboy match is in progress on most summer evenings. Flags are flown and a brass anthem played by musicians before each performance. There are crowded bars, hot-dog and sandwich counters, a bustling bookshop and a pleasant air of delight at the fact that anything cultural is happening at all in so seductively bland and untroubled a setting.

Phillips was surprised to find that Maggie was more 'ready for escape' than he had thought, and detected a determination to rethink not only her art, but also her life: 'I don't actually believe that England has ever seen that Maggie, the one we had for six years. She found new muscles and toughness. Her voice became an incredible cello, no longer a violin.' At the same time, Phillips came under continual attack from the nationalist faction who resented the import of British stars, and indeed his own presence as a British director entrusted with the future of the Canadian classical theatre. The private salvation of Maggie's acting career was bound up in a wider maelstrom of the debate about the festival's identity. These tensions had been endemic to the enterprise from the very beginning. But Phillips was a charismatic personality who unwittingly fanned the flames of the dispute to a new level of intensity. There were orchestrated campaigns against him in the press, and private hate mail, too.

In London, Phillips had most recently presented a striking selection of productions at the Greenwich Theatre, with glossy, eye-catching designs by Daphne Dare (who came with him to Canada) and notable performances by a string of outstanding actresses: Elisabeth Bergner,

Joan Plowright, Penelope Keith, Mia Farrow, Geraldine McEwan and Lynn Redgrave. He seized the biggest opportunity of his career so far with both hands, and his invitation to Maggie was a masterstroke. As a result of her coming to Stratford, Brian Bedford agreed to join the company for three years from 1977. Phillips's work-rate was phenomenal, and his ability to generate extremes of loyalty and exasperation among colleagues and journalists almost unrivalled. In general, and on balance, he created a perfervid atmosphere of expectation and excitement.

In the mid-1960s, there were just two regional theatres apart from the Stratford Festival and the nearby Shaw Festival at Niagara-on-the-Lake (the latter was launched in 1962). In Toronto, outside of the main houses, there was no fringe or supplementary theatre venue at all; today, there are over fifty small theatres. As the critic Martin Knelman wrote, Canadian actors become stars by not staying in Canada, and he cited the careers of Donald Sutherland, Genevieve Bujold, Christopher Plummer and John Colicos. To them you could add Hume Cronyn (who, with his London-born wife Jessica Tandy, was a frequent festival star), Kate Reid and Colleen Dewhurst. In a rapidly changing theatrical environment, fraught as much with burgeoning patriotic pride as with its attendant parochial cringe, the commitment of the Stratford Festival to the idea of a classical company was important, and absolute.

In Guthrie's first company, Douglas Campbell was generally recognised as the leading native member. But nationalist malcontents could sourly note the fact that, in Maggie's first season, her two leading men were both British: Jeremy Brett was Mirabell and Keith Baxter, Antony (although the latter was, admittedly, a last-minute replacement for John Colicos). The paying customers, of course, did not worry too much about these niceties. And Maggie herself was both immune to the wrangling, almost impervious to it, and wildly popular within the acting company. As far as they were concerned, she brought them full houses to play to; she was demonstrably a great performer; and she worked as hard as, and probably harder than, anyone else. Richard Monette, a native Canadian actor who had lately returned from working abroad (he was in the London production of *Oh! Calcutta!*), says that this combination of box-office success, magic and technical discipline was 'very important in sustaining a classical company for that long'. Monette, who later returned as a director and then artistic director of the theatre, voiced the general consensus of opinion about that 'golden era': 'Everybody adored Robin and Maggie. Maggie paid the ticket for all the young Canadian actors, and everyone got a piece of the pie.'

Another key witness to this period was Ronald Bryden, who, after serving his stint on the *Observer,* had joined the RSC as a play adviser to Trevor Nunn. Bryden had been educated in Toronto (before going on to Cambridge University) and had returned in the mid-1970s, after his RSC attachment, as head of the Graduate Centre for the Study of Drama in the University. He says that while it is obviously not true that Robin 'turned Maggie into a great actress by bullying her out of her mannerisms', he certainly removed what Phillips himself calls 'that nasal thing' from her voice and all superfluous flutterings from her wrists. Bryden had been instrumental in Phillips's appointment. 'We think of those years as a Camelot. Nothing as good, certainly, has happened there since.' Even so, Bryden sounds a convincing note of dispassionate objectivity when he looks back and tries to sum up Robin Phillips's work:

> I think it was brilliant, some of the finest theatre I saw in my life. But there was always a kind of sleight of hand involved in it, because of the nature of the casts he was working with. After Maggie, Brian Bedford and Canada's one great home-grown actress, Martha Henry [who was born in America], he was working with a middle level of character stalwarts who would have seemed slightly over-parted in the Old Vic of the 1950s, and below them a ruck of young Canadians of uneven natural talent and almost uniformly inadequate training. With enormously careful casting and direction, he could assemble these disparate materials into gorgeous arrangements, but you were always aware that his bouquets were artfully surrounding orchids with wild flowers.

London critics were flown over by the Canadian authorities to report back on the new regime and their encomiums would have looked slightly more suspect, perhaps, had they not chimed with what most of the Canadian and New York critics thought as well. There was a concerted campaign to restore Maggie to her pinnacle. Also, as Bryden shrewdly remarks, the London critics had become more accustomed in the mid-1970s to the prevalent austerity of most British classical productions, certainly at the RSC. The Stratford lushness came as a surprise, and possibly a relief.

The Way of the World and *Antony and Cleopatra* opened within two days of each other at the start of June. The hidden eddies of insecurity in the Congreve comedy were spotted by Walter Kerr, whose account in the *New York Times* suggested that Millamant's prattling was a defensive measure and that she was the most vulnerable character on the stage. The tone of her proviso in the marriage-contract scene with Mirabell was altered utterly, said Kerr, with not a flick of her heavy-lidded eyes and an insistence on 'one small, ordinary, unmistakably human need: the barest minimum of privacy'. She brought the scene to a heart-stopping standstill, says Phillips, just as she would once again in the Chichester revival directed by William Gaskill in 1984. Maggie's Cleopatra was one of her more unexpected performances, though Bryden reckoned that Phillips was wrong to batten onto a suggestion of Keith Baxter that the two protagonists, rather like Elizabeth Taylor and Richard Burton, were no longer in love with each other but keen to sustain their public image. There was no direct physical comparison with Taylor: Maggie wore a long red wig and a succession of simple kaftans. B. A. Young reported in the *Financial Times* that she was 'not visually voluptuous, but wiry and active' and that there was not an inflexion or gesture that was not fresh and personal. Caryl Brahms opined in the *Guardian* that Maggie's Cleopatra was placed at that stage 'where incandescence flowers into a steadier flame' and that she was particularly touching when, reconciled with the stricken warrior, she 'like some compassionate dragonfly, drooped her azure wings to cradle her dying mate'.

Many of the Stratford productions were preserved on video for archival purposes. These records of actual performances, shot in black and white on a still camera at the back of the auditorium, are by no means fully reliable guides to the shows themselves, least of all to the detailed physical and facial work of the actors. However, in studying them, one can breathe the atmosphere of a production and, especially, sample its vocal qualities. The *Antony* video, one of the earliest in the archive, is a bit of a blizzard to inspect. But you do hear the general unaffected purity of Maggie's delivery and, having learned of the demise of Antony's paragon of a wife, the wonderful laugh she wins on 'Can Fulvia die?' There is sob-bolstered anguish on 'Oh, withered is the garland of the war.' In calling for her crown and owning up to those immortal longings, Maggie, now 'fire and air', picks up the slack and consigns her other elements to baser life. Her embrace of death is lightly, almost ecstatically, phrased and is the more moving for being so.

Richard Monette, playing Lucio in *Measure for Measure*, used to walk off the stage as she went on as Mistress Overdone.

> She used to say, 'How's the house, Richard?' and I would say, 'Dreadful, I didn't hear a titter.' All she then did was cross from stage right to stage left. She managed to get an entrance round, three of the hugest laughs I've ever heard and an exit round. And as she passed me, she'd say, 'I don't think they're so bad, Richard.' She could see where the audience was and simply conjure their reaction. Every time. This alchemy is hard-gained through experience and technique. And of course, with her, there is the recognition factor. But it is also evidence of inbred comic genius.

And in *Three Sisters*, directed by John Hirsch, Maggie recycled her beloved Masha in a company at least the equal of the National's: Martha Henry was Olga and Marti Maraden, Irina, with Keith Baxter as Vershinin. Nicholas Pennell, an English actor who had made his name in the definitive BBC television version of *The Forsyte Saga* alongside Eric Porter, Kenneth More and Nyree Dawn Porter, had been a Stratford Festival regular since 1972. He rated this *Three Sisters* the best he had ever seen, and Maggie herself wanted to know where John Hirsch had been all her life.

So greatly did Maggie enjoy this Stratford season that some observers sensed that she might emigrate to Canada entirely. She turned down a West End opportunity to star in Neil Simon's *Plaza Suite* (she made the film, titled *California Suite*, two years later) because of the commitment she had already made to a second Stratford season, where Phillips had promised her Rosalind and Judith Bliss in *Hay Fever*. She had already become a founding member of Canadian Actors' Equity, which had declared its independence from the American organisation. She watched some of the archival videos of Brian Bedford's work in the 1975 season, when he had played Angelo in *Measure for Measure* and Malvolio. Bedford was returning to Stratford to play Richard III, Jaques in *As You Like It* and, Maggie willing, her opposite number in Molnár's *The Guardsman*, which was scheduled for a December opening at the Ahmanson in Los Angeles before joining the Stratford season in the Avon Theatre at the beginning of June. Maggie was willing. Little Toby asked her what was she going to play in *The Guardsman*. She said, 'The Actress,' to which he replied, 'But I thought you were one of those already.'

Trying to arrive at the heart of what Maggie achieved in Stratford, Phillips states categorically that she has two talents, as a clown and as an actress in both comedy and tragedy. 'The first talent is beyond imagining in its skill and technique; I don't know about it, but I can watch and admire it. The other persona, the actress, is the one I've always worked with.' Phillips had seen the clown element starting to play in the Toronto *Private Lives* and did not like the crossover of the two talents. Personal taste comes into all this. Gielgud felt the Toronto performance to be almost perfect. And it would be impossible to pretend that Maggie's work in Canada was instantly, or ever totally, purified of those inflexional idiosyncrasies and gestural extravagances that are part of her registered weaponry and comic personality. But the tendency was for Maggie to work through her technique to the outer limit of her potential, and not be satisfied with what came easiest to her, the automatic vaudeville of the clown side of her talent. In the high-style, high-tension comedies of Molnár and Coward (*Hay Fever* in 1977, *Private Lives* for the last time, with feeling, in 1978), Maggie put her new resolutions to their severest test.

Maggie and Brian Bedford assumed the Lunt roles in *The Guardsman*, a basically silly play in which the Actor, cognisant of the Actress's energetic cultivation of lovers before their wedding, investigates his new wife's fidelity after six months of marriage by disguising himself as the supposed man of her dreams, a romantically impetuous Russian officer in full military regalia. The ruse is finally exposed, but not before the audience has to decide at what point the Actress, like Falstaff in the Gadshill escapade, recognises her sparring partner and justifies her protest that she knew it was him all along. By all accounts, the comedy rattled rather noisily around the Ahmanson. Phillips was not impressed. Peter Wood, who watched from the stalls, was horrified to find that Maggie and Bedford were flashing their considerable techniques at the audience like knives. On her fifth outing to the Ahmanson, Maggie still found the big theatre hard work.

Maggie's Judith Bliss finally emerged from its impatient chrysalis in September. She entered through the French windows and went straight behind a sofa, where she stood like a restless heron, arranging some flowers and putting them on a piano. When she finally moved round in front of the sofa, the audience noticed for the first time that she was wearing her garden wellies. This speed and constant element of physical surprise galvanised the production. At the first hint of her husband's philandering, she seems to swoop down the staircase in a single motion. And, on the video, something very peculiar but extraordinary is going on in the tea scene. Maggie is downstage in her floppy hat, checking through the contents of every single sandwich on the silver stand. The audience is convulsed with laughter for minutes on end. Where Edith Evans was dotty and vague, Maggie was distracted, yes, but acid and sharp. She was a portrait not of woolly vagueness but of rampant vanity, and also a credible object of young Sandy's sexual desire, however casual. There's a way in which she delivers the line 'I've been pruning the calceolarias' that is almost the final explanation for everything. Myra Arundel raises hardly a titter on 'This haddock is disgusting.' The central, manipulative consciousness of the comedy is indisputably Maggie's Judith, with her menacing control of the charades and her string of bitchy prophecies thinly disguised as helpful advice ('Men don't grow old like women, as you'll find out to your cost in a year or two, Myra').

The following summer, Maggie was ready for her third and final assault on Amanda Prynne, having fine-tuned her working relationship and personal friendship with Bedford. 'By the time we got there, we really did love and hate each other, which was just right,' her partner confessed. Bedford had played Elyot as a RADA student directed by his contemporary Albert Finney, and again on Broadway opposite Tammy Grimes in 1969. This time, Bedford says, 'we did it very seriously, less of a comedy of manners and more like Chekhov. It seemed very real to us.'

> SIBYL (*rushing after him*): Elyot, where are you going?
> ELYOT: Canada.

The tart exchange implying a random and inappropriate choice of escape route was extremely funny, especially in self-conscious Canada. Maggie told the *Toronto Sunday Sun* that there would be no more triple takes, as there had been when she played it with Robert Stephens:

> Seriously, now, if that really happened, if someone you had loved walked in unexpectedly, you wouldn't do a triple take, would you? . . . Mind you, if my first husband walked in right now, I'd feel very, very odd. But it doesn't require a triple take, does it . . . I mean, he might get one. I mean, he would certainly get one if he walked in right now. But it's not quite the answer, is it? If you know what I mean.

Instead of bounding across the stage like a headless chicken when Elyot appeared on the adjacent balcony, Maggie merely executed a svelte double take and leaned back on her chair. Her gestures, as Bryden had noted in *The Guardsman*, had acquired the refinement and perfect elegance of a Japanese print. One hand is forever fluttering to her forehead or the nape of her neck. The effect is beautiful and not irritating. When she tells Victor that 'Men are transparent, like glass', her right arm shoots straight up in the air, slightly crooked, and shoots straight down again, as if rapidly closing a blind. The gesture punctuates the line itself and conveys, in the quickest of flashes, an extraordinary complexity of descriptive thought: contempt, spelling out the obvious for a backward listener (Victor), the sheet of glass, a literally penetrating observation, a joke, an assertion of superiority.

At the same time, Nicholas Pennell, who played Victor, felt that Maggie allowed for enough resonance in their relationship to suggest there might have been something in it in the first place. And the second-act quarrel is preceded by the hilarious sequence of Maggie trying to get comfortable on the sofa, adjusting her limbs, jostling, lying down and moving agitatedly about for a full two minutes. 'To use a Maggie phrase,' says Bedford, 'there is nothing to discuss about those arms. There is nothing like them and I don't think there ever has been.'

Bedford's Elyot was hailed by Jay Carr in the *Detroit News* as a brilliant black diamond of a performance, generous and solidly motivated. The emotional undertow was not as pronounced as it was with Robert Stephens, but the style combined truth with polish. Maggie was good for Bedford because of the demands she made on him: 'In *Private Lives*, I always used to go into her dressing room during the half and she was usually very low. One day she was sitting with the mascara brush just gazing into the mirror. "How are you, darling?" I said. "Oh, darling," she replied, "one is nothing, off!" And of course the phrase has entered our repertoire.' Along with 'ghastly', 'richocheting around', and 'deranged'.

Back in Oxford, just as *The Guardsman* was about to open in Los Angeles, Meg suffered a cerebral haemorrhage in the front room of 55 Church Hill Road: she had always enjoyed good health, apart from the recurrent minor affliction of sinusitis. Nat had gone upstairs to write a letter and she called him down to the front sitting room, said she was tired, put her arms around his neck and collapsed. She lay for seven weeks in a coma in the Radcliffe Infirmary before passing on, in a freezing cold January, at the age of eighty. Nat was grateful that Meg never recovered from the stroke. She would have been a helpless invalid, a vegetable. But he was devastated. A month before he died himself, fifteen years later, he tearfully pointed out that nothing much had changed in the house since that day: 'I've kept up the repairs. But the furnishings and the photographs of Margaret, all of that, has never been changed. And I never will. If I changed that, I'm going to change the vision that's been built up over the years. It would have been lovely for Meg to know that Margaret had become a Dame.'

Maggie was by no means indifferent to her mother's collapse, but having been assured by Nat that there was nothing to be done while she was in the coma, and that obviously she could not communicate with anyone, she felt obliged to continue in *The Guardsman* at the

Ahmanson. During this period, she had taken serious stock of her own health and had been to a Chinese hypnotist in Stratford in order to give up smoking between the first two Stratford seasons. In California, where she was filming, she visited a psychic nutritionist whom Bedford had recommended to her. She spent a lot of time 'shrinking into elevators' to avoid guests who mistook her for Vanessa Redgrave. She also spent more time not explaining herself than was her wont. She told Gina Mallett, the sharp critic on the *Toronto Star*, who monitored the Phillips regime as carefully as anyone, that she only felt real on stage: 'I don't like myself very much. I'd much rather be someone else.'

When Meg had eventually died, Maggie had been unable to return to England for the funeral, unwilling to break her overriding commitment to the public and the management at the Ahmanson. *The Way of the World* from the 1975 season had initially been booked to cover her release, but the expense of such a large-cast show was prohibitive. Phillips, Maggie and Brian Bedford had agreed to fill the schedule with the Molnár. 'What could I do?' exclaimed Maggie to Gina Mallett. 'One can't just chuck a show.' Even as a girl, Maggie had never been close to her mother. In adult life, she remained even more distant. And no one – Robert, the boys, Beverley, her parents, dead or alive – took precedence over her professional duties, as she saw them. This was never a matter of choice or decision as far as she was concerned, but of simple fact. She did feel the loss endured by Nat but she did not return to Oxford for a good few years.

After two years in Los Angeles and two years in Canada, Chris and Toby now returned to Surrey and Tigbourne Court, where Alistair and Shân Smith took charge. They were enrolled at a local prep school and spent most of their time at home in their aunt and uncle's side of the house. Years later, Christopher said that, while he enjoyed 'the brilliant gardens' of Tigbourne, he was 'freaked out' by spending most of his time living in one half of the 'Gothic pile' and looking through the windows into his own house. Toby, too, found this 'quite unpleasant'. The prep school had an 'incredibly religious headmaster', and the boys found themselves seriously behind the rest of the school because they had not learned any Latin or French in Canada. Christine Miller had outlived her usefulness, though not her capacity for friendship. Beverley had more time to deal with the domestic arrangements as well as his own writing and paperwork, and the boys had gone. Maggie was in the middle of some of the most taxing roles of her career. Christine slipped away to work as a secretary and house-minder for members of the *Monty Python* team.

Christine always felt that Maggie was much closer to Nat than to Meg: 'Meg wasn't a very soft person and she had some strange, old-fashioned ideas about discipline. I once took the boys to Oxford and left them there for a few days. She seemed to me just like a very stern, staid old lady.' Toby remembers Granny Meg as 'always knitting. She terrified the life out of Nat, who liked his drop of whisky at night. He'd creep around the house avoiding her like the plague and pouring out his toddy.' The boys thought of her as 'quite warm, really'.

She had not seemed warm to Maggie, but at least she could no longer advise her daughter to complete a secretarial course as a safeguard against the possibility of failure in show business. But Maggie's career had baffled Meg. She took little pride in it and probably never understood what she had done to deserve such a peculiar and unconventionally successful little girl.

11

Salvation in Stratford, Stoppard and Virginia Woolf

With the boys tucked up safely in Surrey and Nat pottering around happily in Oxford, Maggie settled in at Stratford feeling reasonably content, or as near to that condition as she would ever be. Beverley told Gina Mallett that the only serious worry in life was luggage, and Maggie, flitting between England, Hollywood and Stratford added, 'I don't honestly know where home is. We're nomadic. It is odd, but it doesn't worry me very much. I guess I'll go where the work is. It's a marvellous new kind of life.'

Britain was denied not only some of her greatest performances, but also some of the best Shakespearean productions of the decade. Few critics had seen the equal, for instance, of Robin Phillips's production of *Richard III* with Bedford as Crookback and Maggie as Queen Elizabeth. Ronald Bryden said that, on that evidence, Phillips was fit to join the inner ring of great directors – Peter Brook, Peter Hall, Ingmar Bergman, Roger Planchon and Jerzy Grotowski – capable of orchestrating a disparate group of actors into an entity. Margaret Tyzack had also joined the company, replacing Kate Reid, who was ill, to play the Countess in *All's Well That Ends Well*, Queen Margaret in *Richard III*, and Mrs Alving in Ibsen's *Ghosts* (in which she scored an unequivocal triumph).

Maggie's high, light comedy was rightly seen within the proscenium Avon Theatre, but all the major Shakespearean work was on the Festival thrust stage. Phillips had concocted an imaginative and intuitive response to Maggie's personality. He knew that Cleopatra was the first of the Ptolemies to bother to speak a variety of languages, as did Elizabeth I. He felt that, in Maggie, there was an extraordinary link with past times:

During a totally lively, modern conversation, you can see right through her skin to almost every period back through time. Her skin is very thin, translucent, and you become aware of those strange medieval eyes, eyes of the palest blue, watery, liquid, limpid. Her skeleton actually represents English history. I do think of everything about those Elizabethan miniatures of Hilliard when I look at her.

The 1977 season – Robin's third, Maggie's second, and the twenty-fifth anniversary of the Stratford Festival – coincided with the Silver Jubilee of Queen Elizabeth II. Phillips revived his 1976 *A Midsummer Night's Dream* with Maggie succeeding Jessica Tandy as both Hippolyta and Titania. She was, in fact, those characters as dreamed by Elizabeth I, and the production opened with Bottom's Dream sung on tape by Hippolyta attired as Gloriana herself, in gold and black with a wig of startling crimson ringlets. Not so much Bottom's Dream as Gloriana's trip, mused Michael Billington: the queen saw herself not only as Titania and Hippolyta, but also as Helena, as played by Martha Henry. Maggie's articulation of Titania's 'These are the forgeries of jealousy' speech, delivered standing stock still, her arms extended, was reckoned magical by all; its devastating simplicity and masterful phrasing and control are apparent on the video. Referring to the Indian boy, the bone of contention between Titania and Oberon, she reveals that his mother, 'being mortal', of that boy did die. It is a moment lit with sudden pathos, similar to the moment in *Much Ado About Nothing* where Maggie's Beatrice invoked the pain her mother endured in childbirth. Gloriana also commandeered the 'lunatic, the lover and the poet' speech of Theseus in Act Five as a sort of explanation of her intervention in such 'shaping fantasies'. Robin confesses he was unable to have Maggie on the stage as Elizabeth-cum-Hippolyta and not allow her mind to encompass that speech: 'She is in tune with Shakespeare, as she is with both sexes. Which is why I think of her as a creature. There are things which she hasn't learned, but which she simply *knows*. She knows about the Elizabethans, and she knows how to speak Congreve, and lots of other things that you can't possibly know from having gone to Cambridge,' a sly dig at the Oxbridge directors who dominated the British subsidised theatre after Olivier, and certainly at the National; Peter Hall, Trevor Nunn, Richard Eyre and Nicholas Hytner were all Cambridge graduates.

She knew, too, how to stand still and not move her hands. For all its imperfections, the video of *Macbeth* shows Maggie in her long black wig and floor-length black dress standing centre stage, pencil-thin and sleek, hands by her sides, calling on spirits to unsex her here and take her milk for gall. As Bryden says, she, not Macbeth, was 'the great imaginer' in this production – 'I feel the future in the instant' – rhapsodically ahead of the game and in for a penny, in for a pound. She moves her right hand to her left breast on 'I have given suck and know how tender 'tis to love the babe that milks me.' (Maggie always considered it cruelly ironic that she, who has splendid breasts, had experienced difficulty producing milk for her own sons.) The hand scythes down again on 'dash'd the brains out'.

Maggie had arrived late from Hollywood for rehearsals (*California Suite* was overrunning), so her Macbeth, Douglas Rain, had rehearsed for several weeks, and worked out his own performance, with a stand-in. The result was unevenness and uncertainty all round, but Maggie made sure she took care of herself. She had asked Coral Browne for advice. 'It's a fucker, darling,' Miss Browne had soothingly replied, 'and all I can say is keep your eyes open in the sleepwalking scene. For some reason, it rivets the fuckers.' Thus reassured, Maggie did precisely that, gliding hauntingly through the scene in a long white nightgown, reaching out for only the second time in her performance (the first is on 'Full of scorpions is your mind') on her quadruple 'Come' when she hears the echo of the knocking at the gate.

Richard Eder of the *New York Times* thought that this final wandering speech, 'rubbing her hands, recalling her action in a broken voice and reaching for the husband who has moved into a separate nightmare', was 'pure grief'. But the production divided critics and audiences alike. Ronald Bryden was more enthusiastic than most: 'It is hard and dark as onyx, austerely unfamiliar, jumping over time and expectation like a bad dream. But few Macbeths can have looked deeper into Shakespeare's inferno.' After the dead-of-night murder of Banquo and the escape of Fleance, there was delivered one of Phillips's most spectacular coups, Bernard Levin recalls, as the lights came up almost immediately on the banquet – 'tables, glasses, everything. They must have done it in fifteen seconds and there was no noise at all. It was astounding, and a complete gasp went up from the audience.' Maggie told Levin later that she knew nothing of how it was done, was totally in the dark and had to be led to her place for the scene.

No such guesswork attended her Rosalind, one of the roles about which Maggie had rightly felt proprietorial for many years. It seemed absurd that she should have had to wait until the age of forty-three to play it, older even than was Edith Evans, the other most famous 'over-age' Rosalind (Dame Edith played the part aged thirty-eight, and then again aged forty-nine). Phillips set the comedy in the late eighteenth century, the period of George III, and Robin Fraser Paye's design was of a single large gnarled oak tree on a grassy knoll, the actors dressed in big hats, flowered skirts, bustles and riding breeches. The stage shimmered like a watercolour painting by Thomas Rowlandson.

As You Like It opened in August 1977, but most of the critical approval was clustered around the revival in June 1978. Watching the video, you can hear the audience falling in love with Rosalind, just as she had fallen in love with a younger man. As with her Millamant, the performance is perfectly balanced on that razor's edge between tears and laughter, with the underlying urgency of a woman energetically seizing her last chance for love. And of course the speed and wittiness of Rosalind's interventions in the forest were exactly matched by Maggie's qualities as an actress, and her physical beauty was compounded by a strange, ethereal sadness.

Orlando was played by a blond, fresh-faced and well-built Canadian actor called Jack Wetherall. Brian Bedford chipped in with a darkly confidential Jaques, punctuating his 'Seven Ages of Man' speech with some wonderful pauses. The rest of the performances look, frankly, a bit dodgy, but the balancing and pacing obviously carried the night and day. Levin was convinced that Maggie's Rosalind was one of the definitive performances of his lifetime. He detected the fuller music of her marvellous voice and approvingly observed that, although she had rid herself of the old vocal mannerisms, she could still go knock-kneed at the slightest provocation. Levin was never outdone on the effect of Rosalind's adieu: 'She spoke the epilogue like a chime of golden bells. But what she looked like as she did so I cannot tell you; for I saw it through eyes curtained with tears of joy.'

Robin Phillips felt that the clown tendency in Maggie's Rosalind
had been exorcised in a particular morning of rehearsal when they
were considering the Rosalind/Ganymede protestation of how tur-
bulently she would be in love: 'more jealous of thee than a Barbary
cock-pigeon over his hen, more clamorous than a parrot against
rain, more new-fangled than an ape, more giddy in my desires than
a monkey'. Encouraging Maggie to be serious, Robin suggested that
she should first of all make it as funny as possible. She improvised an
entire menagerie and monkey-house, squawking and swinging around
the tree that was the single feature of the set. The entire company was
laid out on the floor with laughter and Robin recalled how remarkable
had been the evocation of the tree where no tree stood:

> Everybody stopped and looked at an empty rehearsal room with a
> blank wall. They stared at a space where she had just been halfway
> up a tree and swinging in its branches. To this day, I cannot tell
> you how she did it, how she swung from those branches without
> leaving the ground. I don't understand it, but she did it. We all
> saw her in the tree. I called a coffee break and people dispersed in
> stunned silence.

On resuming rehearsal, Phillips took the scene in the other direction,
towards the pain of the disguise and protection, and, because of what
had gone before, 'Maggie was able to do that in a remarkable and very
moving way. And of course that was finally in the production.'

Maggie's idea of social life was, and is, extremely limited, so she did
not feel particularly deprived in Stratford. If a performance had not
gone well, or even if it had, she would philosophically inform Brian
Bedford that there was nothing for it but 'to get untimely ripped', and
quantities of champagne or white wine were duly consumed. Cold
meats and the occasional cooked goose were laid out for friends at
home after the shows. Nicholas Pennell recalls one lively evening
in the large kitchen in Cambria Street when Bernard Hopkins, an
extrovert member of the acting company, was calling everyone 'she',
and a conversation at one end of the table with Beverley was cut across
by Maggie savagely intervening from the other, 'Will you please not
call my husband Mavis.' The centre of social life was the Church

restaurant, which Robin's partner Joe Mandel had opened, retaining the spacious ecclesiastical open-plan interior, the Gothic windows and the stained glass, and painting the walls in a restful coffee colour. The food was excellent, the prices beyond the pay packets of the humbler company members. Maggie and Robin, Beverley and Joe would always sit at the first table on the left by the front door, and this area became known by other festival personnel as 'bomb alley'. The assumption was that it was wired for sound and microphoned to pick up any passing gossip or unofficial information.

Robin says that he never really socialised with Maggie at all. He had dinner at Cambria Street just once, during the first year. 'Our relationship through work is probably deeper and closer than any has ever been, but it is entirely work, work as we think of work, a very intimate relationship.' After their time in Stratford, Maggie visited Robin and Joe on the farm they had bought in Ontario. She and Robin were looking through the window at the lakes and fields, the chipmunks and the squirrels in the feeder. And the birds. Talk had turned to yellowhammers and speckled tits. Suddenly Maggie said, 'There's a yellow screwdriver.' Robin, an English country boy, knew rather less about Canadian bird varieties than about the robins and chaffinches in his native Haslemere, and had certainly never seen such a creature. He wanted to see it, looked hard, couldn't, and became furious. Finally, he saw what Maggie was agitatedly pointing out: a workman's tool for putting in screws, lying on the garden path. Phillips says that they could not speak for three hours afterwards and were so helpless with laughter that they had to go off on separate walks to relieve the agony. Soon afterwards, Robin came to England to direct a rock opera about Joan of Arc at the Birmingham Rep. He checked into his hotel room and went to the bathroom. On the towel rail, resting on the towel, was a tiny yellow screwdriver. It had somehow been pressed against the wall and had become stuck to the towel. At first, he believed Maggie had arranged for it to be left there. But she hadn't.

That whole story is a perfect example of our six years together. In many respects, life happens to Maggie. And I think that's to do with her being connected to all those periods, right back through the Victorians to the Elizabethans and the Ptolemies. I think she is a creature, an animal, in a sense. I don't mean she's not human. But she has senses that are more than human. In humour, certainly. She can respond to something that perhaps only squirrels would sense in the air. And I think that comedy, travelling around in the atmosphere, finds out her. Absolutely finds out her. I remember our time in Stratford in the way one remembers childhood summers. They were immensely hot and golden, those days, and the boys would get suntanned and Maggie would whizz home for dinner before coming back to the theatre.

During *As You Like It*, when she was off stage, Maggie used to walk through the park because Robin had suggested that it would be a good idea to remain in contact with the trees. People would sometimes stop and stare when they came across her in costume, apparently nowhere near the theatre. But she always was. And she walked, every Rosalind day, through the trees.

The Canadian adventure was to a large extent subsidised by three Hollywood movies Maggie made, none of them masterpieces, but all guaranteed to maintain her international profile and keep her in good screen company. As she restored herself as a stage actress, so she underpinned her screen status. Two of the three films involved Neil Simon, whose revue sketch Maggie had performed in *New Faces* at the start of her career. Two featured David Niven, who became a good friend of Maggie and Beverley, and one of them won Maggie her second Oscar.

The wackiest was *Murder by Death*, which was Neil Simon's first original script for the cinema (most of his screenplays are adapted from his own stage hits). The director, another débutant, was Robert Moore, responsible for Broadway's first commercial gay play, Mart Crowley's *The Boys in the Band*, and for Simon's musical (with a score by Burt Bacharach) *Promises, Promises*, itself adapted from an earlier movie, *The Apartment*. *Murder by Death* is a witty attempt at a parody of a murder mystery in which send-ups of fictional detectives, each with a motive, are summoned to 'a dinner and a murder' at a fog-bound manor in California. The host is Truman Capote, making his acting début as the sinister connoisseur, Lionel Twain, abetted by a deaf- and-dumb cook (Nancy Walker) and by a blind, inscrutable butler (Alec Guinness). The butler's name is Bensonmum, confusedly thought to be Benson by the ma'am who enquires after it. Guinness can then say that, no ma'am, the name is not Benson, ma'am, but Bensonmum, ma'am.

Peter Sellers as Sidney Wang is a glorious steal of Charlie Chan, and also Lionel's resentful stepson; the other detectives are near misses for Hercule Poirot, Miss Marple and Dashiell Hammett's Sam Spade. And David Niven and Maggie are Dick and Dora Charleston (as opposed to Nick and Nora Charles in Hammett's *The Thin Man*), heavily in debt to the old rogue. The delicious barminess of the script and the expertise of the acting from such a blissfully ideal group of performers never quite coagulate into screen magic. Maggie has her moments, as do they all, and she looks ravishing in a low-cut white dinner gown. She and Niven are billeted in Wang's wing of the manor and, darting an appalled look at the blind butler, Maggie half-mutters to Niven, 'Don't let him park the car, Dickie.'

Similarly, Capote, who propels himself around the dining room in a wheelchair and at one point whizzes rapidly backwards out of sight, prompts Maggie to comment, half-interestedly, 'I hope he knows how to stop that thing.' The dénouement hinges on the removal of a face-mask and a riddle of double identity, after the detectives, with the exception of Peter Sellers, appear to have been bumped off.

The 'real' Poirot appears in the pear-shape of Peter Ustinov in *Death on the Nile*, where Maggie picks up the thread not only with her old sparring partner in *Hot Millions*, but also with Niven, the costume designer Anthony Powell, who deservedly won an Oscar for his work on this film, and Jack Cardiff, whose superb cinematography is one of the best elements of John Guillermin's somewhat leisurely overall direction. The movie was a sequel to the hugely successful *Murder on the Orient Express*, in which Albert Finney had concocted his version of Poirot – strenuously bizarre, less urbane than Ustinov, at least as memorable – for Sidney Lumet. It had a screenplay by Anthony Shaffer, Peter's twin brother, author of *Sleuth* and the unhappy Robert Stephens vehicle, *Murderer*, with music by Fellini's regular composer, Nino ('The Glass Mountain') Rota; sumptuous Egyptian locations in the first half; lush on-board period interiors (the year was 1937) in the second; and a cast list including Mia Farrow, Angela Lansbury, Jane Birkin, Jon Finch as an incongruous Marxist in a beret, and a hopeful new heart-throb, soon to become a fixture in American television soaps, Simon MacCorkindale.

Whereas in Stratford, Ontario, Maggie was an inspirational cog in the wheel, here she was merely one of several extraordinary spokes. The film spooled round and she did her stuff. She played Miss Bowers, a severe travelling companion, masseuse and secretary to a rich widow, Mrs van Schuyler. This would not be all that significant had Mrs van Schuyler not been played by Bette Davis, enshrined in a series of exotic costumes and complicated headpieces like a glittering lizard encased in a mummy's tomb. Within the limitations of the film's dramatic potential, this double act, played almost as a shadow duel to the chummily conspiratorial 'old pals' act of Ustinov and Niven, looks like one of the great cinematic liaisons of the day. In their scenes together, you sit watching an old legend slugging it out with a new pretender. And one leaves the film rather regretting that we do not follow Maggie and Miss Davis on their next expedition to the Gobi desert; Maggie receives news of this plan with all the enthusiasm of someone being sentenced to death.

The story's murder victim is a grotesquely rich honeymoon girl, Linnet Ridgeway, played by the beautiful Lois Chiles, whose father ruined Miss Bowers's family on his ascent to the financial summit and thereby doomed Maggie to a life of grumbling servitude. Mrs van Schuyler's holiday on the Nile is rife with the possibility of fall-out. Davis slaps Maggie down with a warning to keep a civil tongue in her head or she'll be out of a job, to which Maggie scathingly replies: 'This town is filled with rich old widows willing to pay for a little grovelling and a body massage ... You go ahead and fire me!' By the time they clamber aboard the steamer in Alexandria, the double act is bristling with an air of uneasy truce. Maggie confides to the captain that 'the roasting afternoon sun will do wonders for those jaundiced jowls of hers', while Davis acidly apologises for Maggie 'accidentally' barging into Lois Chiles with the excuse that she once went fifteen rounds with Jack Dempsey. Shaffer's script glints and ripples along like this for well over two hours, but the second half of the film is fatally devoted to awkward flashbacks following up each possible enactment of the murder and an extended resolution, again using flashbacks, of what actually happened. Maggie and Bette Davis slip tantalisingly away, but not before Maggie makes the most of one heavily inflected hint at her spiritual condition. Consoling Mia Farrow after yet another surprise revelation, she conveys the whole history of her character by confessing that 'It's been my experience that men are least attracted to women who treat them well.'

This sexual defensiveness, compounded with a deep sense of injury, is a common trait in many of Maggie's performances. The prickliness, combined with vulnerability, is a distinctive element in a great many of her heroines, and is rather obviously exploited in *California Suite*, where Maggie plays the actress Diana Barrie, vaguely anticipating the receipt of an Oscar for her performance in a movie she thoroughly despises. That Maggie herself went on to win an Oscar, as best supporting actress, is an irony that was never lost on her. Nor, indeed, was it lost on her loyal father. Nat was reported in the *Oxford Mail* as saying that he was delighted, but surprised, as 'the film itself was somewhat bitty'.

As with the murder films, *California Suite* was constructed on the '*Grand Hotel* and fill the screen with stars' principle. Simon adapted his four short 1976 Broadway plays to show five couples simultaneously checking into the Beverly Hills Hotel for different reasons. Jane Fonda is a divorced career journalist locked in a child-custody battle with Alan Alda. Walter Matthau has arrived ahead of Elaine May for his nephew's barmitzvah and is assigned a prostitute as a gift for the night by his brother. Bill Cosby and Richard Pryor as a couple of accident-prone doctors are on vacation from Chicago with their wives (they crash the car en route to a Japanese restaurant). And Maggie is in town for the Oscars with her wayward bisexual husband, Michael Caine, who sells antiques and purchases young men.

Michael Caine, one year older than Maggie and busy in movies since 1956, remembers *California Suite* as 'a very enjoyable film'. But director Herbert Ross continually badgered Maggie for not, in his opinion, doing enough. 'I thought you were supposed to be funny,' he would yell at her, an approach which did not go down all that well, especially as Maggie was determined not to make a meal of a script heaving with quite enough coarseness already. 'As a result,' says Caine, 'she spent a lot of time on the set in floods of tears.'

Caine could have worked with Maggie on *The Private Ear* and *The Public Eye*, but he denies any knowledge of having been first-choice casting as the besotted music-lover in the first play. Their chemistry in *California Suite* is just right, in spite of the mawkish romanticism of a script which requires Maggie to pull her errant husband down on top of her in bed and, in what Kael describes as 'one of the most degrading of all scenes: a woman pleading with a man – who does not desire her – to make love to her', request servicing: 'Screw the Academy Awards, screw the Oscars, screw me, Sidney, please . . .' Caine wears his role of an automatic filling station with dignified levity. Maggie despises him because he has used her celebrity to mark his dance card. She finds him doing this at the end of the tawdry ceremony and, after an evening of ups and downs, crunchingly invites him to continue the motion.

Back at the hotel, Maggie cleans her teeth in the nude. As she slips on her nightgown, we catch a fleeting glimpse of her full left bosom in profile. 'Never again,' exclaims Walter Matthau after the prostitute passes out on him after consuming a bottle of tequila. You can imagine Maggie muttering the same phrase through clenched teeth along the corridor as Ross bullies her through the bedroom scene with Caine. The final straw for Diana Barrie is that the film with which she has failed to win an Oscar is being shown on the flight back to London after the junket. Caine says that Ray Stark, the film's producer, was so taken with the characters he and Maggie played that he promised to get Neil Simon to write a sequel for them alone. This never materialised, though the dream partnership was belatedly renewed twenty years later in Peter Yates's misfired *It All Came True*.

Caine and Maggie liked each other a lot. Both hail from the wrong side of the tracks, both have a devastating sense of humour and neither tolerates very much of the bullshitting hyperbole and self-importance that surround their industry. Caine, the ultimate screen professional, plays every scene knowing exactly where the director has placed his cameras. He was enthralled by Maggie's indifference to such technical niceties, noting how all her concentration was channelled into the details of the performance itself. The rest she left entirely in the lap of a director who, for some reason, had decided that the best way of handling her was to reduce her to tears. Caine jovially offered Maggie cold comfort: 'As long as they're on your back, that's all right because they're not on mine.' Caine had a good time. He said that acting with Maggie was like attending a one-woman masterclass on comic technique, adding that he would gladly enrol again – 'as long as they provide plenty of handkerchiefs'.

Pauline Kael said that Maggie performs in this movie like a professional who is used to doing the dramatist's job for him. Frank Rich, writing in *Time* magazine, thought that Maggie gave her best screen performance to date:

> Alternately buoyant and defeated, youthful and ageing, she transforms a potentially campy character into a woman of great complexity and beauty ... Caine sets off Smith's brittle wit with soothing tenderness. Together these actors prove that a marriage of convenience can be a dynamic emotional affair. They also demonstrate that Simon, when he puts his mind to it, can be a worthy American heir to Noël Coward.

The critical reception was generally more enthusiastic in America than in Britain. Maybe this was because Diana Barrie had triumphed in triviality, bitten the bullet and sold out to Yankee showbiz; she had spent eight years with the National and had finally been nominated for an Oscar because of her work on 'a nauseating little comedy'. America staked its final claim on British talent in the bestowal of its ultimate accolade. In *California Suite*, Maggie articulates the dilemma of the great actress in search of a proper reward in the face of personal disappointments. For all its faults, the film memorably recounts the price of that struggle in the partnership of arguably our greatest postwar British screen stars, Maggie Smith and Michael Caine.

When she was nominated for the Oscar as best supporting actress in *California Suite*, Maggie stayed in the Beverly Hills Hotel, where the film itself was set, with her friend and hairdresser Patricia Millbourn. In the film, the Jane Fonda character describes Hollywood as 'like Paradise with a lobotomy'. Diana Barrie (Maggie) doesn't understand why she's attending the Oscars ceremony: 'Glenda Jackson never comes, and she's nominated every goddamn year!' The spooky reality of her and Patricia's experience was echoed in its celluloid representation. On screen, Diana Barrie says, 'No woman can look good at five in the afternoon – except possibly Tatum O'Neal!' Maggie and Patricia did indeed have to be ready and all dressed up in the middle of the afternoon. And, as in the film, champagne and caviar had been sent up to the room. Or rather, round to their allotted cottage in the hotel grounds, well away from the central brouhaha. They stood under a lamp-post waiting for their lift; in the film, Maggie sweeps imperiously through the front entrance through a riot of fans and photographers ('Christ, the royal treatment!').

Patricia Millbourn recalls that Maggie had prepared nothing to say in the event of winning the Oscar and that, when she won, she duly said it: 'I didn't think I had a hope in hell.' She was only the third actress ever to win in both the best actress and the best supporting actress categories, following the fine examples of Ingrid Bergman and Helen Hayes.

California Suite is in part about not winning an Oscar, but the ceremony is not depicted. Instead, Maggie's actress acidly remarks on the general decline in the standard of face-lifts and hair-transplants, and the fact that a prize has duly gone to 'Miss Teeth and No Talent'. The words could have been taken out of her own mouth. After the real-life ceremony, a big, informal party was thrown as usual by the agent Swifty Lazar and theatre producer Irene Selznick, but Maggie found herself herded towards the official reception for the winners. She was terrified of not knowing anyone there, so she slipped away to find friends, including Patricia, at the alternative bash. 'I hope you don't mind me coming to this one instead,' she said to Miss Selznik. 'Oh no,' replied the hostess, 'it's perfectly all right, because you won!'

With Maggie seemingly lost to Robin Phillips in Stratford and the film moguls in Hollywood, offers of work in the London theatre had temporarily dried up. But when Tom Stoppard completed *Night and Day*, his 1978 West End comedy about freedom, journalism and politics, one of the first actresses considered for the role of Ruth Carson, bored wife of a mining engineer based in a fictitious African country, was Maggie Smith. It is something of a rough irony that Maggie's agent, Peter Dunlop, was not impressed with the play and returned it to Stoppard's agent without passing it on. Maggie certainly never read it until the opportunity arose to take the play to Broadway and she prepared for her third New York appearance on condition that she could perform the role in London first. This she did, in July 1979, taking over from Diana Rigg, who had scored a big personal success when the play opened in the previous November.

As things worked out, *Night and Day* only ran a couple of months in New York at the end of 1979, and Maggie was therefore free, having missed the 1979 festival, to return to Stratford for Robin Phillips's last season; from there she fortuitously made a resounding London come-back as Virginia Woolf in a tailor-made vehicle by Edna O'Brien. As usual in Maggie's career, everything fell into place without anything much having been planned. She was as strangely resigned as ever to her obsessional calling, her fate. Nothing much had changed in that respect, as she told the *New York Times* before opening on Broadway: 'Acting is what I do. One is nervous, every single time, to go on a stage at all. But it's the only way I've lived. I've never been in a position to question it. It is my work.'

The background to the action of *Night and Day* is a rebellion against a dictatorial president. The press corps covering the story includes the tough nut Dick Wagner, a boastful and competitive 'fireman' ('I go to fires. I don't file prose. I file facts'), and the idealistic young freelance Jacob Milne, who has scooped Wagner in his own paper and is threatening to scoop him again with a presidential interview. The journalists' rivalry extends also to Ruth, in whose house the action is set. She has had an affair with Wagner in London, but Milne now strikes her as metal more attractive. Ruth herself has rather languid views on the ethical debate on journalism in the play ('I'm with you on the free press. It's the newspapers I can't stand').

Peter Wood was once again her director, and he cites one day of rehearsal where Maggie gave her greatest performance. At the start of Act Two, Ruth comes from behind a tree after a rather strange, un-settling scene with the younger journalist. Ruth, naked (in the guise of her double), walks across the stage and into the house, and Maggie walks round the tree:

She had this ability to communicate that what we had just seen
was a fantasy, but that was way down her list of priorities. What
Maggie offered was a woman appalled by the force of her own sexual
fantasy, unsteadied by it, so that when she came round the tree,
she shook it away. Then she wondered if it had been real, and her
hand came up to her face, and slowly she began to take a humorous
attitude towards her own fantasising. This was simply the most dazzling display. She did it on that morning in rehearsal, then she lost
it, got it back, lost it again, and by the time we got to New York she
had laid her hands on it very precisely. It triggered an immensely
complex audience reaction: a rapt silence, followed by this magnetic
power, the slow realisation that they'd been hoodwinked by the
dramatist... It was miraculous how Maggie handled the house and
finally persuaded them into an extraordinary, rueful laughter.

That, says Wood categorically, and the scene she rehearsed with
Olivier in the first act of *The Master Builder*, were the two greatest
moments he has ever known in the theatre.

Maggie opened with Patrick Mower as Wagner and Edward de Souza
as her husband, at the Phoenix. She made much more of Ruth's inner
turmoil, in contrast to the devastatingly cool, self-possessed and glacial version of Diana Rigg. As Michael Billington noted, Maggie's Ruth
was a nervy, vulnerable expatriate sending out periodic cries for help
which were totally ignored. In this way Maggie got closer, one felt, to
the tension Stoppard sought between the character's pronouncements
and, a subtle distinction, her speaking thoughts. Stoppard had evened
up some of the arguments about the press and wrote in a topical gag
which referred to the protracted strike at Times Newspapers in the
struggle between the unions and the management leading up to the
installation of new technology and the reduction of manning levels
required by the new proprietor, Rupert Murdoch. Ruth was asked if
the papers were flown in and she replied, 'I don't think so; we're still
getting *The Times*.'

During this summer, Kenneth Tynan, despite suffering horribly
from emphysema, was beginning work on a *New Yorker* profile of
Maggie, although his friend and researcher, Ernie Eban, had been
trying to persuade him to turn his attention instead to Bob Dylan.

Tynan lunched Maggie twice in L'Étoile, his favourite London restaurant, during June. When he went along to see *Night and Day*, he scrawled on his programme a reference to Maggie's long upper lip and 'some of the finest fingers in the business', noting that she distinguished ('where Rigg didn't') between the private thoughts and normal dialogue of a play in which she entangled herself like a vine. Tynan's profile never progressed beyond a few dozen small pages of spidery jottings; he died aged fifty-three in July 1980 in hospital in Santa Monica.

When *Night and Day* opened at the Kennedy Center in Washington in October 1979, the response was enthusiastic and the play sold out for six weeks. Joseph Maher, who was playing Maggie's husband, Geoffrey Carson, was convinced that New York was going to be 'colossal'. Tom Stoppard was elated by the performance and gave Maggie an enamel 'head girl' badge. He felt as blessed in her performance as he had been in Diana Rigg's:

> When it comes to humour, comedy on any level, Maggie perhaps has no rival. She can get more out of a phrase, sometimes a single word, than any playwright has a right to expect. She manages to inhabit a character totally while simultaneously standing outside the characterisation and making her own ironic commentary. This is an 'impossible' trick, like being in two places at once.

Dick Wagner was played by a perfectly competent actor, Frank Converse, but by the time the show reached New York he had been replaced by Paul Hecht. Maggie refused to comment on whether she had had Converse fired; Converse sued for the rest of his salary on his run-of-the-play contract. The producer Michael Codron reported to Maggie's dressing room in Washington and she said, talking into the make-up mirror, 'I'll say this for you, Michael, you sure can pick 'em!' Codron believes that he has never recovered from the Converse affair as far as Maggie is concerned.

Maggie's name was above the title outside the ANTA, later renamed the Virginia, and since 2005 the August Wilson, on 52nd Street. (ANTA was an acronym for the American National Theatre Academy, original home of the Guild Theatre.) As Ted Kalem said in *Time* magazine, 'playing the ANTA stage is like pitching a tent in the Sahara.' Maggie did not like it, and she did not like her dressing room, either. She had it painted and recarpeted and continued moaning about it in an interview with Rex Reed in the *Daily News*. She complained that she had to wash her hair at home each day as the sink at the ANTA 'didn't work'. Reed recorded the exasperated reaction of the theatre owner:

> That woman has made so many impossible demands that she's becoming damned tiresome. Nothing seems to satisfy her. We re-carpeted, relighted, repainted, and re-shampooed the theatre and it's still not enough. She even wanted the aisles changed. Helen Hayes, Kate Hepburn, Raymond Massey, Julie Harris – all occupied that same dressing room and never complained. Alfred Lunt and Lynn Fontanne even occupied it together, at the same time. No complaints about the sink.

Edward Albee's *The Lady from Dubuque* had recently opened on Broadway, and the title amused Maggie. Each night, Joseph Maher was touched to find Maggie standing in the wings holding a jacket for his very quick change and ready to assist in a rapid adjustment of his cravat. The job should have been that of a very fat, camp dresser who was working on the show, and over dinner one night Maher commented on her unnecessary kindness. 'Well,' said Maggie airily, 'we couldn't have the lady from Dubuque doing it for you, could we?' Another well-travelled anecdote attaches to one of the monologues, when Maggie had to say quietly to her confused self, 'Run, run, you stupid bitch.' She inserted the slightest of pauses after the first 'run' and, at one matinée, a deaf lady near the front loudly enquired of her neighbour, 'What did she say?' Maggie quickly continued, a little more forcefully, 'Run, you stupid bitch,' which the deaf lady took in quite the wrong way.

Maggie and Beverley were borrowing Ruth Gordon and Garson Kanin's house in Turtle Bay and often supped after the show in Gallagher's Steak House opposite the ANTA, usually with Joseph Maher, who became a close friend. Like Alec McCowen, he had a good ear for the distinctive quirkiness of Maggie's laser-like observations. One of the producers of *Night and Day* was the bustling, businesslike

Nell Nugent, and Maher remembers Maggie whispering sotto voce as she heaved into view one night, 'Oh dear, here comes Nell Nugent, mean as paint.' That sink in the dressing room still rankled.

The reviewers complained of too much plot and not enough coherence. Much later, Maggie explained the play's New York failure to Jack Tinker in terms that make very good sense: 'They simply couldn't comprehend why a woman would go out and have an affair just because she hadn't sewn Cash's tapes in her son's clothes when he went back to school. It may be a very stupid reason to have an affair. But there isn't a woman in England who wouldn't understand.' Katharine Hepburn, when she visited backstage in her flat shoes and raincoat, told Maggie and Maher, 'The audience hates this play.' There was no way round it. One night, Maggie took her customary solo call in front of the cast, and two people stood up in the front stalls and offered a weak 'Bravo'. 'Oh dear,' Maggie muttered as she shuffled back into the line, 'deep sarcasm!'

Within a few months of opening in New York, *Night and Day* closed. Maggie had received an Edna O'Brien script about Virginia Woolf, a writer she much admired and one who preyed on her subconscious. She had once told an interviewer that she wished she had a strong, large face like Virginia Woolf's: 'Mine is very, very small. Too small.' The novelist had written the play, *Virginia*, with Eileen Atkins in mind, but Kenneth Tynan read it, suggested Maggie and made sure she received a copy of the script. Edna O'Brien did not know Maggie at this point, but she shared the same hairdresser, Patricia Millbourn, and the latter acted as another go-between. Robin Phillips liked the script and agreed that Maggie could do it at Stratford. It was to be a highlight of their last season together.

Things had gone slightly awry in Ontario. During rehearsals for *Private Lives*, Robin had been taken ill and Maggie was not planning to return for the 1979 season. In the event, he recovered, but this period was rife with speculation as to who would succeed him. Nonetheless, the 1980 season was a memorable last thrash. Maggie scored a sensational triumph as Virginia Woolf at the Avon, while she said farewell on the Festival stage with a second look at Beatrice in *Much Ado About Nothing*, perhaps her final exorcism of the partnership with Robert Stephens, and as Arkadina in Chekhov's *The Seagull*.

Her favourite sparring partner, Brian Bedford, was Trigorin; her golden
Orlando, Jack Wetherall, was Konstantin, and a trio of Stratford's own
biggest stars – William Hutt as Dorn, Roberta Maxwell as Nina and
Pat Galloway as Masha – added more lustre.

Maggie's Beatrice was a much more stately affair than the reading
à la Zeffirelli at the Old Vic. She still punctuated the laughter on the
line about her mother's cry of childbirth but, on the video recording,
'Kill Claudio' elicits a huge laugh, albeit one mixed with shock and
disbelief. Lavishly costumed by Robin Fraser Paye in the English Civil
War period, Maggie and Bedford struck a handsome cavalier partnership that is most notable, perhaps, for its air of civility and relaxation.
The edge and the bite have given way to an almost total luxuriance in
the security of a comic partnership. Michael Billington thought they
now sparked each other off like Spencer Tracy and Katharine Hepburn.
With Maggie's maturity came a richer, more gravelly voice and the
almost imperceptible shading of tears into laughter, of exquisite
pathos, that characterised all her work with Robin Phillips.

She was exactly the right age for Arkadina – forty-three, going
on thirty-two when her son's not around to contradict her – and
she played the comic-monster side of the character to the hilt. The
silliness and volatility of Arkadina are apparent, but above all the
impression you get is of an absolutely rampant stinginess. Just as she
used elements of her mother's Scottish Calvinism for Miss Brodie, one
senses Maggie harking back, in a subconscious way, to Meg's well-
intentioned but ferocious penny-pinching in Ilford and Oxford. Twice
she declares, very firmly, to Sorin and to Konstantin, that she has no
money. Finally, she's had enough and stuns the audience with one of
the loudest and angriest explosions of her career: 'I'm an actress, not a
banker!' This meanness underpins the mercurial vanity of all she says
and is marked savagely on her departure, when she sweeps away from
the servants with 'Here's a ruble; it's for the three of you to share.'
But she kills incisively, too, on the simplest of phrases which are just
slightly inflected to cause maximum damage. 'The garden reeks of
sulphur; is that intentional?' she teasingly remarks, thus scuppering
at a stroke her son's serious artistic aspirations and his faith in her
judgement. And when this Arkadina states that she'd rather be in a
melodrama than perform the gibberish her son writes, you feel the

full force of a blow delivered by an actress who really does identify with that remark and has always preferred to line up with the tried and tested as opposed to the difficult and risqué.

The backstage politicking was hotting up and the theatre went through a period of financial decline and artistic uncertainty until John Neville, another British director, steadied the ship in the late 1980s. In due course, Robin was appointed artistic director of the Chichester Festival Theatre but resigned almost immediately for reasons that have never been made clear. He spent five years (1990–95) as artistic director of the Citadel Theatre in Edmonton, Alberta, before resuming a freelance career. Undoubtedly, Robin must be credited with salvaging and relaunching Maggie's stage career. And although his plans to re-enter London in triumph, with a full season including Ustinov as King Lear, were in tatters, *Virginia* and Maggie's performance would come to the Haymarket at the start of 1981. This event, more than the takeover in *Night and Day*, marked Maggie's official return to London.

The first-night audience at the Haymarket on 29 January 1981, which included John Gielgud, Ingrid Bergman, Joan Plowright, John Osborne and Harold Pinter, reflected the heightened sense of anticipation. The play begins and ends with the words 'Something tremendous is about to happen', a description of the one experience, death, that Virginia told Vita Sackville-West she would never describe. This paragraph was delivered by Maggie in a voice of quiet apprehension. At the end, her voice soared, exultant and golden. In between, we had an expressionistic distillation of what Virginia Woolf herself called 'moments of being'.

Throughout the 1970s, subsequent to Quentin Bell's Virginia Woolf biography, hardly a Sunday had passed, it seemed, without the publication in one of the newspapers of yet more revelations and secondary material about Virginia and the Bloomsbury set. Maggie's performance achieved the extraordinary feat of entering a plea for privacy on the writer's behalf. Edna O'Brien's script did not refer to the everyday trials and tribulations of running the Hogarth Press, and contained not a whisper of the pamphleteering literary feminist. The social whirl of London and the Woolfs' country retreat at Rodmell were vague, unpopulated backgrounds against which Maggie registered disgusted shivers at all intrusions, a shuddering distaste for the physical life in general and for copulation in particular, and an impatient desire to be left alone. As Quentin Bell said of the novels, an audience actually heard Virginia Woolf thinking.

Virginia had received only seventeen performances in Stratford, but Michael Billington caught one of them and declared this the best role written for a woman since Miss Brodie was in her prime. In London it was apparent that a great tragi-comic actress was restored in full bloom, and Jack Tinker's comment that Maggie's Virginia contrived to look 'as though she was indeed born with one skin too few to survive in this world' was prophetic of one or two self-lacerating performances to come. In the *Evening Standard* report of how the judges decided on giving Maggie her third best actress prize, Bernard Levin said that her achievement in keeping him awake and interested in a play about Virginia Woolf, a writer he hated, was not to be underestimated.

The production was minimalist, with photographic images of the eerily haunting branches at Rodmell and the streets of London projected on to an arrangement of scrims. There were no properties, and just two chairs. The whole presentation seemed designed to show how Maggie had stripped down her engine and reassembled the parts after giving them a good clean. Nicholas Pennell was Leonard Woolf and Patricia Connolly Vita Sackville-West, the latter playing a fine scene culled from the book written in her honour, *Orlando*. O'Brien had distilled the entire play from the novels, the diaries and Quentin Bell's biography. She described the process of possession to Lucy Hughes-Hallett: 'The play came from inside me, but it is all Virginia. I worked like a sleepwalker, like a medium. It is a wedding for the two of us. For her, I hope, it is a resurrection.'

Pennell and Connolly had come to London from Canada with Maggie and Robin. One night, there were flashing lights before the curtain rose, traced to a lady in the front circle wearing a dress heavily adorned with sequins. When told about it, Maggie asked, 'Is she hanging from the dome and revolving slowly?' But the sequins were not, it transpired, the real cause of the trouble. A light in the fridge in the downstairs bar had short-circuited all the auditorium lighting. Nicholas Pennell remembers above all the relish with which Maggie acted:

She'd say, 'A rose is a rose is a rose ... is it?' and she'd swivel round to me with those large eyes. It was never a question of whether she was going to get a laugh. Sure she was. But she was about to have the most delicious meal with it. It is a sheer joy playing with her. It's how I imagine downhill skiing must be: you know you're not going to stop once you're on the skis, and there's a helter-skelter sense of recurrent switchback. It is truly exhilarating.

Jollity took a jolt halfway through the twelve-week run when Maggie's brother, Alistair, dropped dead of a heart attack one Sunday in Tigbourne Court. His demise, at the age of fifty-two, was totally unexpected. He had no record of ill health. Ian was the twin who had been rejected for National Service in 1951 on health grounds. Pennell called Maggie to sympathise, assuming that the Monday-night performance would be cancelled. But she was determined to go on, and said she wanted 'to get concentrated'. Pennell and Patricia Connolly joined her in the theatre at about three o'clock and went through some physical stretching exercises for a couple of hours in the front-of-house area. They returned to the dressing rooms through the darkened auditorium. Pennell recalls that, as they came up the stairs to the stage and went through the proscenium arch that divides reality from fiction,

> Maggie went, she absolutely went. Trish and I sat on the steps by the orchestra pit and held her while she had a big cry. Then she had a big laugh, and she'd always say afterwards, when we went up those stairs, 'That's where I had my Waterloo.'
>
> We then had to go out in the first act and I'm reading a letter, the first line of which is 'I am so sorry to hear about your brother's death,' and I didn't know what would happen. Those glacial blue eyes looked straight back at me as she gave the reply, 'We don't talk about that in our family.' It was a very weird moment. I think that, like most great artists, Maggie stores up all her experience and dredges through it later.

Ian Smith, the surviving twin, thinks that Maggie has difficulty in expressing emotion and may sometimes give the impression that she does not care very much. She did care very much about Alistair's death, but she never transmitted what she felt to the family. The matter was simply not to be discussed.

Tigbourne Court, which had been bought for £37,000, was sold for £185,000. Shân, Alistair's widow, decided that she would not move with Maggie and Beverley, but that she'd be better off on her own. She found a comfortable house in Milford, three or four miles from Tigbourne, with stables for her horse. Beverley found a well-concealed farmhouse in Sussex. It was more manageable than Tigbourne, on two floors and not too big. The original farmhouse dated from the late fifteenth century and a farmer had added some rather fine Georgian extensions in the early nineteenth century. The place had fallen into disrepair until it was acquired by a prominent QC from a dowager aunt and fitted out with proper plumbing and other amenities. Maggie and Beverley moved in during 1981, lived there happily until Beverley's death in 1998, and Maggie is there still. The boys were enrolled at Seaford College, a minor public school situated on the downs between Petworth and Chichester which neither of them much enjoyed, though both proudly claim to have passed more O-Levels than their mother. Maggie had insisted on them knuckling down to their work. Christopher persisted into the sixth form and successfully took A-Levels in English, history and politics. Toby was mightily relieved to be out of Tigbourne Court, liberated from its airiness and bigness, and its situation on an increasingly busy main road. 'Also, Surrey is such a boring county, with horrible places like Godalming. Sussex is really nice.'

In the 1980s, Maggie appeared in some very reputable films, but still the 'great film' eluded her. On the stage she brought only one of her Canadian performances to London – Millamant, in a new production by William Gaskill. The decade ended with the tumultuous commercial and critical success of her performance in *Lettice and Lovage*. She would always remain imperishably funny. But perhaps those heart-stopping moments of doubt, insecurity and anguish as Stoppard's Ruth Carson and as Edna O'Brien's Virginia Woolf were indicators of some extraordinary non-classical tragic work to come, on both large and small screen.

12

Best of British Pork and Palin

One of the distinctive features of Maggie's film career in the 1980s was that she appeared in movies that had more appeal for her than for the accountants in her agents' office. In her time at Fraser and Dunlop, Jimmy Fraser handled the film contracts and Peter Dunlop the theatre business. However, their influence on what she actually did was minimal. Dunlop retired in 1980, shortly after the mix-up over *Night and Day*. In July 1981 Maggie announced in *Variety* that her sole worldwide representation was now handled by James Sharkey at Fraser and Dunlop. Or rather, Sharkey made the announcement, which featured a photograph of Maggie in *The Guardsman* at her most impishly soignée: hair up, eyes soft and sparkling, full lower lip, a jewelled halter. Sharkey was at that time the most widely respected and brilliant of all actors' agents. But Maggie didn't take much notice of him, either. By 1984 she had joined Laurence 'Lol' Evans, chairman of International Creative Management and Olivier's general manager at the Old Vic in the 1940s. Evans was the doyen of the ten-per-centers. His all-star list included Olivier, Rex Harrison, John Mills, Albert Finney and Peter Hall. Maggie was even more of a mystery to Evans and, in the serene, secure twilight of his career, he happily went along with anything she wanted to do. By the end of 1991, Evans, too, had become a back number as he was eased into a consultative retirement and the younger, more dynamic Duncan Heath took charge of Maggie's affairs at ICM. She summed up by commenting, 'Nothing ever seemed quite right after Peter Dunlop.'

Maggie was increasingly attracted to smaller-budget, reputable ventures in preference to the international blockbuster projects that left her little chance to get her teeth into a good part. On both stage and screen she can be squeamish about bad language, and in this respect is unprepared to betray either the propriety of her lower-middle-class upbringing or the genuine instinct she has for not alienating a broad popular audience. Like all the great stars of old, she believes in exercising good taste wherever possible in matters of apparel, manners, public statements and morality. She can, of course, swear like a trooper when she's in the mood and behind closed doors. When William Gaskill sent her a copy of Howard Barker's rewrite of *Women Beware Women*, she was aghast at the barrage of filthy language and explicit sexual discussion, and turned him down flat. She had also turned down his invitation to appear as a cannibalistic Queen Victoria in Edward Bond's *Early Morning*. Similarly, when she was invited to impersonate Peggy Ramsay, the straight-talking agent of the dramatist Joe Orton in the film *Prick Up Your Ears*, her reaction to Alan Bennett's screenplay, which dealt in homosexual promiscuity and murder, was to retreat behind the excuse of not wanting to embarrass or upset her sons by appearing in such a film (the role was memorably taken by Vanessa Redgrave, though the agent's bird-like frailty and coruscating waspishness were much more Maggie's forte).

But it would be wrong to claim that she was completely unadventurous in her choices of material. After her final seven-month season in Stratford, Ontario, she had a week's holiday and then, typically, went straight to Paris with Beverley to join the Merchant Ivory shoot of Jean Rhys's first novel, *Quartet*. Jean Rhys, a favourite novelist, was, like Virginia Woolf, someone whose every written word she had long since devoured. Like her responses to most things, Maggie's response to literature is instinctive and intuitive. In drama, the challenge of Shakespeare and Congreve is inexhaustible because the writing demands the utmost technical concentration. It also offers the attractive challenge of playing women who assert their individuality in the face of social and marital constrictions. For similar reasons, Maggie has always found inspiration in the high stylists of the feminine consciousness: Woolf, Rhys, Jane Austen, Charlotte Brontë, E. F. Benson and many of the women writers published or reissued by the distinctive and aptly named Virago Press. There is a definite link in the 1980s between the spiritual nutrition Maggie found in her reading and the projects she undertook. The producer of *Quartet*, Ismail Merchant, the director James Ivory, and their regular screenwriter Ruth Prawer

Jhabvala, were embarked on a series of literary adaptations on low budgets that found large audiences attracted to their visions of faithful and respectable nostalgia. Ivory is not a galvanic or deeply imaginative sort of director, but he does deliver pretty packages. As Pauline Kael has said, 'he's essentially a director who assembles the actors, arranges the bric-à-brac and calls for the camera'.

The autobiographical heroine, a doomed Creole waif, played by the beautiful Isabelle Adjani, is corrupted by the married partnership of the writer Hugh Heidler and the painter Lois after her husband has been convicted of trafficking in stolen works of art. The Heidlers, played by Alan Bates and Maggie, had been modelled by Jean Rhys on her Parisian Svengali, Ford Madox Ford, and his wife Stella Bowen. The setting was mostly Montparnasse in 1927, and the full period flavour was dutifully milked. There were stunning scenes set in their proper locations of Le Boeuf sur le Toit, a steely art-deco restaurant, and the virtually unchanged ballroom of the Hôtel Pavillon Opéra, where Maggie glittered menacingly in a silver sheath dress, green eye make-up, and a silver skullcap. Maggie had never worked with Alan Bates before (they both appeared, later, in *Gosford Park*), but the pairing is a major factor in the film's attractive surface. There is something compulsively sinister in Bates's devious hedonism for which Maggie dutifully pimps, confiding to Adjani through clouds of cigarette smoke that her husband is not always 'nice' to her, and that she is accustomed to his extramarital adventures. Like all the Merchant Ivory adaptations, however, the movie fed off the original by softening the novel and failing to match its essence with a transforming artistic identity of its own. It is also fatally careless with the storyline, so that it is almost impossible to know exactly what happens at the end. There is no such confusion or ambiguity in Rhys's narrative.

The acting all round was very good, with some delightful vignettes from British actors Sheila Gish, Anthony Higgins and Bernice Stegers, but Maggie walked off with the best actress prize in the *Evening Standard* Film Awards in an exceptional year for British movies. Other winners were *The French Lieutenant's Woman* (best film), Bob Hoskins making his decisive breakthrough in *The Long Good Friday*, and Colin Welland's screenplay for *Chariots of Fire*.

After the bohemian quartet came a thoroughly mawkish ménage à trois (at one point the film's working title), *Better Late Than Never*, written and directed by Bryan Forbes and a strong contender for Maggie's worst film. The main point of interest is that it was also David Niven's last picture (he died in 1983), and the third he made with Maggie. Niven played Nick Cartland, a seedy nightclub singer, 'England's soufflé of song', who is summoned to Monte Carlo by a lawyer (Lionel Jeffries) to compete for the guardianship of a ten-year-old girl, Bridget, who might or might not be his granddaughter. Maggie is the stern child-minder, Anderson, 'not Mary Poppins', whom Nick and Bridget tease with such rollicking wheezes as blue soap, rubber eggs and whoopee cushions.

The mechanics of the comedy are pretty hopeless and an overall air of shoddiness is not dispelled by some attractive locations in the South of France nor by the Niven character's bottom-chasing antics on the beach. He picks up an over-made-up pneumatic good-time girl called Sable who turns out, most unfortunately, to be an apprentice embalmer. Mixed in with the awful soundtrack by Henry Mancini and a charmless child actor, the film leaves a sour taste in the mouth.

After this aberration, Maggie's only two 'international' blockbusters of the 1980s – the mythical epic *Clash of the Titans* and a second Agatha Christie luxury-cast mystery insouciantly unravelled by Peter Ustinov's tunbelly Poirot, *Evil Under the Sun* – come as a considerable relief. Both have their merits. The first was scripted by Beverley, who had not worked with or for Maggie since she appeared in *Strip the Willow* in 1960 (a projected Stratford collaboration on a Cross script about the Brontës, *Haworth*, had been scrapped at the time of Robin Phillips's first illness in 1978; the play was premiered, starring Polly James, at the Birmingham Rep in 1981). The second reunited Maggie with several of the *Death on the Nile* team: screenwriter Anthony Shaffer, Ustinov, Jane Birkin and her favourite costume designer, Anthony Powell.

In *Clash of the Titans* Maggie plays the goddess Thetis, antagonist of Perseus, and tetchy inamorata of Zeus. As the latter is played by Laurence Olivier, presiding over an idealised, antiseptic Olympus where the other white-gowned goddesses include Claire Bloom, Ursula Andress and Susan Fleetwood, the ancient Old Vic rivalry is lightly resumed. Olivier had resolved never to act on a stage with Maggie again after *The Master Builder*, and Maggie's Thetis, albeit only in a reported incident, once again 'bests' the old boy: she recounts with relish how Zeus once disguised himself as a cuttlefish in an attempt to seduce her, but that she beat him at his own game by turning herself into a shark. Beverley had taken spirited liberties with Greek mythology in racily retelling the Perseus legend. Perseus is obliged to return to Joppa and rescue Andromeda from a deformed suitor, Thetis's son Calibos; he must answer a riddle, capture and tame the last of the flying horses, Pegasus, and enter the temple of Medusa; there, after being attacked by snakes and a two-headed wolf, he cuts off Medusa's head and, with her eyes, petrifies the monster Kraken, whom Zeus has unchained from the ocean bed to ravish Andromeda and destroy Joppa. ('Great Zeus,' says Maggie, 'it is now the eve of the longest day'; 'Very well,' replies Olivier, 'release the Kraken!')

The last sequence owes something to the assault on Fay Wray and New York City by King Kong, and indeed this homage is intentionally perpetrated by the film's co-producer and special effects wizard, Ray Harryhausen, who was a protégé of King Kong's creator, Willis O'Brien. Harryhausen, in addition to creating the pterodactyl which carried off Raquel Welch in *One Million Years BC*, had provided the special effects for another Beverley Cross-scripted film, *Jason and the Argonauts*. The influence of *Star Wars* could be seen, too, in Harryhausen's golden owl, a speaking mechanical android whose appeal to audiences was similar to that of R2D2 in the 1977 George Lucas fantasy. But the film really belongs to the general tradition of Hollywood escapist adventures, and Beverley had cast his net wide. The hairy, sexually frustrated Calibos was obviously related to Shakespeare's Caliban, and the sea-monster Kraken had arrived from Norse mythology via Tennyson. There were also magical swords, enchanted shields, invisibility helmets, the belief in the overwhelming power of a kiss and even three blind witches, the grotesque Graeae, who share one single crystal eye; they were unrecognisably impersonated by Flora Robson, Freda Jackson and the Irish actress Anna Manahan.

Maggie comes a cropper when the marriage of Perseus and Andromeda is anointed by Siân Phillips (playing Andromeda's mother, Cassiopeia): her statue crashes hilariously to the ground and breaks up

while her gigantic face continues to mouth demands for the life of
the woman who spurned her son. At least Maggie could not complain
in this scene that her head was too small. The effects of the flying
horse, the speaking owl and the disintegrating Kraken are indeed
enjoyable – in a *Harry Potter*-ish sort of way – even if in long shot
the bestiary now resembles those plastic animals one used to find in
breakfast cereal packets.

Not much more of a performance was demanded of Maggie in *Evil
Under the Sun*, and, as a result, she resorts to a lot of wrist-flapping as
the cheerfully coarse-grained Daphne Castle, a royal ex-mistress and
hotel proprietor, who is in love with the murdered woman's husband
(Denis Quilley). Christie's 1941 novel had been moved by Shaffer back
to the 1930s – thus justifying lavish holiday costumes and the songs of
Cole Porter – and transported from Cornwall to a remote Tyrrhenian
island. The principal location setting was Majorca, with its travel-
brochure beaches, craggy cliffs, turquoise lagoons and subtropical
gardens. Quilley's doomed wife, the actress Arlena Marshall, played by
Diana Rigg, represents a rivalry with Daphne going back to their days
together as chorus girls: 'She could always throw her legs up in the air
higher than any of us – and wider!' The twosome momentarily bury
the hatchet in a squirm-inducing, badly sung rendition of Porter's
'You're the Top'.

As Diana Rigg's character has already refused to appear in a show
called 'It's Not Right and It's Not Fair' because, she says, it sounds like a
black man's left leg, she receives no less than her just deserts when she
is strangled on the beach. The incident is presaged by one scene *Variety*
thought worthy of Luis Buñuel: Maggie is shocked on a walk through
the lush landscape by the sight of a dead rabbit with worms crawling
through its innards. Maggie, understandably, is anxious to pin the
murder on anyone but herself, and her performance improves slightly
as she is quickened into anxiety by circumstances. But Diana Rigg is
not the only stiff on board. The cast includes cardboard cut-outs by
Sylvia Miles as an importunate producer (incongruously paired with
James Mason) and Roddy McDowall as a campy showbiz columnist
called Rex Brewster, reinforcing the idea that he is a dull facsimile
of the real thing, Rex Reed, with a succession of lame and spiteful
aphorisms. Ustinov cumbersomely unravels the mystery in a narrative

punctuated by flashbacks. The movie was deemed inoffensive enough to be chosen as the Royal Film for 1982, the third time Maggie had been implicated in that command event (her other 'royal' films to date were *Jean Brodie* and *California Suite*, both considerably superior and more 'adult').

In concentrating on a now highly paid film career in between the seasons at Stratford, Maggie had not had time to take up any offers on television. She had not made any television appearances in Britain since going to Canada, but she now returned to the medium with a performance in a William Trevor story, dramatised by Bob Larbey, that is a crucial statement of poignant, funny isolation on the journey from Virginia Woolf to the fraught heroines of Brian Moore and Alan Bennett in *The Loneliness of Judith Hearne* and *Bed Among the Lentils*. She began to specialise in ladies on the brink, alone in their rooms and on the verge of some cataclysmic, menopausal breakdown. Essential to this is the cast of the actress's mind, which had always suggested that relations with the opposite sex were seriously overrated. Funny ladies – Beatrice Lillie, Ruth Gordon, Carol Burnett, Lucille Ball, Lily Tomlin – were traditionally slightly beyond the pale, freakish, sexually intimidating, even neutral. Maggie, with blazing individuality, combined their cavalier raucousness and low view of masculine rapacity with an aching physical plausibility, an obvious capacity for being attractive.

This unique admixture of spiritual hauteur and physical need set off some fascinating alarm bells in the gallery of characters she now began to create. In William Trevor's *Mrs Silly*, directed by James Cellan Jones for Granada TV as part of an 'All for Love' series, Florence Barlow is a divorced vicar's wife whose son, Michael, is wrenched from her by the expectations of a snobbish preparatory school which she visits like some pathetic intruder, clumsily mistaking the headmaster's wife for the matron.

Maggie's remarkable performance both prefigures and complements the more widely acclaimed interpretation of Susan, the vicar's wife, in *Bed Among the Lentils*. The overpowering sense of social ostracism is in both cases compounded by one of resilience and dignity in defeat, though Bennett provides an additional strain of sarcastic commentary. The Trevor heroine is less complicated, but conceived on the tragic scale by dint of piercing observation and emotional truth. Physically, Maggie's Florence has the stark angularity of a Modigliani portrait and the chattering, incipiently out-of-control disposition of any inner-city bag-lady. The looming gulf between herself and her son is a dark pit into which she is starting to fall.

Another small-screen project, a co-production between the BBC and Hungarian television, was not nearly so memorable. *Lily in Love* was an unhappy rewrite by Frank Cucci of *The Guardsman*, directed by Károly Makk and starring Maggie and Christopher Plummer as the married protagonists. Plummer played an actor, Fitzroy Wynn, a Broadway has-been with unfulfilled ambitions to be a cinema heart-throb, while Maggie was Lily Wynn, an authoress whose next comedy screenplay, with a good-looking, sexy male leading role, was deemed unsuitable for her spouse. The Molnár conceit is reworked as a ruse by Fitz disguised not as a Russian guardsman, but as 'Roberto Terranova', an absurd blond Italian actor from Parma (a town famous for its hams) who seduces Lily on location in Budapest. It is quite a controlled and attractive performance by Maggie, and she looks beautiful and elegant. She seems, for purposes of minimal plausibility, to suggest that she knows Roberto is Fitz all along. But everything that is funny and ambiguous in the Molnár play is trampled in a crassly inappropriate script which sounds as though it is being made up on the spot. Maggie confessed to an interviewer that work on the set was complicated because she had trouble understanding what the director was saying. She referred to the film as 'the ghoulash' (and to her co-star as 'Christopher Bummer'): 'It was all slightly horrendous. You didn't know where you were half the time. Usually in the wrong place.'

The British film industry of the 1980s was relaunched on a wave of investment and optimism unprecedented since the 1950s. Like all such hallucinations, it proved as temporary as it was briefly dazzling. The rise and fall of Goldcrest, the emergence of David Puttnam as an independent producer of real flair and the increasing investment raised by co-production with television companies were all significant elements in the boom. When the tide receded on this era in British movie-making, Maggie was seen to have been involved in at least two films of especial interest. They were both produced by HandMade

Maggie keeps an eye on Robert drinking backstage at the Old Vic in 1971

The calm before the storm in a Malibu beach-front rental while performing Noël Coward's *Design for Living* at the Ahmanson

Marriage in transit at the airport with Christopher and Toby in 1972

Left On set with George Cukor, director of *Travels with My Aunt* (1972), who adored everything she did as Graham Greene's gorgon Aunt Augusta; he also adored Maggie herself

Below Two classic roles for BBC TV in 1972: a cruel and mocking Portia in *The Merchant of Venice* and an even wealthier heiress, Epifania Fitzfassenden, in Bernard Shaw's *The Millionairess*, a glorious display of high-style bravura and limpid radiance

Pain and passion in close-up relationships: Robert and Maggie as Elyot and Amanda in the quarrel scene of Coward's *Private Lives*, a watershed production directed by John Gielgud at the Queen's in 1972; and running free with Timothy Bottoms in *Love and Pain and the Whole Damn Thing* (1973), an unlikely movie romance vitiated by incurable disease

Right The idyllic setting of the
Stratford Festival Theatre, Ontario,
where Maggie revitalised her stage
career at the end of the 1970s in roles
denied her at the National: (*below*)
Millamant in Congreve's *The Way
of the World*, with Jeremy Brett as
Mirabell; (*opposite, above*) a flame-like
Cleopatra in kaftans and a red wig;
(*opposite, below*) and a shimmering
Rosalind in *As You Like It*.

Hollywood murder mysteries featuring all-star casts: (*above*) with David Niven in *Murder by Death* (1976), a spoof detective thriller written by Neil Simon; (*right*) as a severe travelling companion to a rich widow (played by Bette Davis) in *Death on the Nile* (1978), an Hercule Poirot mystery scripted by Anthony Shaffer; (*below*) and with Diana Rigg in *Evil Under the Sun* (1982), another Agatha Christie story relocated by Shaffer to the 1930s, with Cole Porter songs

Maggie won her second Oscar for playing an actress who fails to win one in *California Suite* (1978), written by Neil Simon and co-starring another British film legend from the wrong side of the tracks, Michael Caine

A farewell on Mount Olympus to Olivier as Zeus (centre) in *Clash of the Titans* (1981), scripted by Beverley Cross. Screen goddesses (left to right) are Maggie (as Thetis), Claire Bloom (Hera), Ursula Andress (Aphrodite) and Susan Fleetwood (Athena)

Above left Betty the pig avoids the attentions of Gilbert and Joyce Chilvers (Michael Palin and Maggie) in *A Private Function* (1984). It was Maggie's first collaboration with writer Alan Bennett

Above and left Country life down on the Sussex farmhouse: Beverley and Maggie walk the dog while Chris watches Toby vault the gate on a rare family photo-shoot in 1986; and relaxing on the sofa in the sitting room

Films, the company financed and run by ex-Beatle George Harrison and producer Denis O'Brien, which had been responsible for such exuberant British movies as the Pythons' mock-Biblical *Life of Brian*, Peter Nichols's *Privates on Parade* and Barrie Keeffe's *The Long Good Friday*.

The first, *The Missionary*, starring and written by Michael Palin, is not a total success, but is certainly, as David Robinson said in *The Times*, 'a superior comedy as British comedies go'; the second, *A Private Function*, also starring Michael Palin but written by Alan Bennett, is not only one of the funniest, and most nearly perfect, British films of the century, but also, as Philip French said in the *Observer*, 'as authentic a picture of the darker side of postwar Britain as our cinema has given us'. I would be tempted to submit *A Private Function* as the best movie Maggie has appeared in. It is entirely typical of her that she should have fallen in with two of our most irreverent and talented satirists, Palin and Bennett. Both are university wits, performers with no formal training or theatrical background, and influential humorists. Palin, in his Monty Python mode, sparring partner to John Cleese and Terry Gilliam, operates in the robustly surreal and funny-voice tradition of Lewis Carroll and *The Goon Show* of BBC Radio in the 1950s (which starred Spike Milligan, Harry Secombe and Peter Sellers); while Bennett, who made his name alongside Peter Cook, Jonathan Miller and Dudley Moore in the revue *Beyond the Fringe* in the early 1960s, had emerged as a substantial playwright, mixing the incisive Yorkshire wit of his social commentary with beautifully rhythmed verbal tapestries.

Neither had had any previous contact with Maggie. Richard Loncraine, the director of *The Missionary*, had asked Maggie to take part in a Gerald Durrell film which never got made, *My Family and Other Animals*, and she had expressed interest. He sent her a copy of Palin's script for *The Missionary* and the two of them, Loncraine and Palin, went along to meet her at the Berkeley Hotel. Palin remembers being apprehensive because, as he says, he was still 'overawed by great names, and certainly theatrical great names; most of our work in Monty Python had been fairly self-contained up to that point. And we played all the women, too.' It was the day after Maggie had received the *Evening Standard* award for *Virginia* and Palin says that while she was not exactly disparaging about this, she was palpably uninterested in such highly organised expressions of adulation. She had a vodka and tonic and a chat. Palin and Loncraine were prepared to change the script, allow her to make her own schedules, and come in as late as she liked in a white Rolls-Royce. They would have done anything to have her in the film. But Maggie, as usual, specified neither ifs nor buts. She simply said she would do it. Palin asked Michael Caine for some advice when acting with Maggie. Caine merely said, 'Watch her. She'll have that scene from under your feet.'

Maggie plays Lady Isabel Ames, the sexually frustrated wife of the richest man in England (a classically gruff and treasurable performance by Trevor Howard in one of his last films). She offers to finance an Edwardian home for prostitutes in the East End of London if the do-gooding cleric, played by Palin, will go to bed with her. When she visits the home and finds three of the fallen inmates romping lasciviously with the missionary, she withdraws her support and the girls are thrown out on the streets once more. The priest is engaged to a girl (played by Phoebe Nicholls) who is afflicted with a perverse passion for filing cabinets. A rather messy plot separates these two, consigns Maggie to a bizarre shooting accident on the Scottish moors and sends Palin back to the East End, where Maggie joins him after the house of correction is closed down in 1907.

It is a lively but unsatisfactory film, made for a mere £1.5 million, a curious mishmash of Shavian morality, merry facetiousness and class-conscious satire. It prompts loose comparison with the famous 1930s case of the Rector of Stiffkey, who disappeared each Monday morning from his Norfolk parish to consort with shop girls and prostitutes before returning in time for the following Sunday's services. Just as the Stiffkey padre would solemnly inform his young ladies that God had no objection to sins of the body, only sins of the soul, so Palin embarks on his bedtime salvation duties with many a quotation from Saint Paul. Maggie looks marvellous in silks, brocades and fine hats and her acting is so good it nearly blows a hole in the mixed-quality fabric of the film itself.

For all its imperfections, Maggie much enjoyed working with Palin on *The Missionary* and was happy to join him again on *A Private Function*. Palin had interceded on Alan Bennett's behalf and they all had as jolly a time as it is possible to have on a film with Maggie Smith. It was mostly shot in Ilkley, in West Yorkshire, under the first-time direction of Malcolm Mowbray, whom Maggie would refer to alternately as 'Our great leader' and 'Moaner Mowbray'.

The film has a period setting, on the eve of the 1947 royal wedding between Princess Elizabeth (who became Queen in 1952) and Prince Philip, later the Duke of Edinburgh. Bennett's Yorkshire community is a microcosm of postwar 'austerity' Britain rekindling the pecking order in social aspirations against a still restrictive background of food and petrol rationing and busy licensing authorities. Palin is Gilbert Chilvers, a call-out chiropodist who uncovers a conspiracy to rear an unlicensed pig and slaughter it illegally for a civic banquet in celebration of the royal wedding. Maggie is Joyce, his ambitious wife, a piano teacher and cinema organist who wants her future to live up to her past; her father had a chain of dry cleaners and the family 'regularly used to take wine with the meal'.

Bennett, the Oxford-educated son of a Leeds butcher, is almost the perfect writer for Maggie: stylish, discreet, with a double purchase, affectionate and wry, on the everyday speech of ordinary people. His idiomatic style is perfectly matched by Maggie's scathingly risible determination to move up the social ladder. Taking afternoon tea in the Grand Hotel is her rightful milieu: 'This is where I belong; put me in a long dress and surround me with sophisticated people, and I'd bloom.' Bennett stings and stabs, but in the gentlest possible way. Those 'sophisticated people' would be anything but. Litotes, the expression of an affirmative in which the negative is ironically implied, is a speciality of both this writer and this actress. And Maggie, as she showed in Stoppard's *Night and Day*, loves to perform, simultaneously and miraculously, both inside and outside a character, precisely on the line while reinforcing either its inherent contradiction or an objective critical slant.

This technique is sometimes mistaken for mere camp. Camp comes into it, certainly. But, like Lettice Douffet, we must remain enemies of 'the mere'. There is something essentially funny, as well as genuinely subversive, in Maggie's comic shrugs of rueful and analytical scorn. As Joyce, the Lady Macbeth of Ilkley, she wickedly encourages Palin's delightfully slow-witted Gilbert to steal and kill off the pig, thus thwarting the local bigwigs who have denied her husband a new clinic in the High Street parade of shops. She will deal with them from a position of supremacy: 'It's not just steak, Gilbert, it's status'; or, more to the point, 'It's not just pork, Gilbert, it's power!' The other characters are written and acted with a lip-smacking Gogolian relish: Bill Paterson's sweatily dedicated food inspector, John Normington's lily-livered solicitor, Tony Haygarth's cowering, blotchily complexioned farmer and Pete Postlethwaite's amorous butcher, who fondles the buttocks of his beloved 'war widow' with as much loving attention as he devotes to the porcine carcass on his professional slab. Best of all is Denholm Elliott's intemperate doctor who deplores the spectre of a socialist Britain where 'scum' rise to the top and where, on the National Health Service, 'anyone can come and knock on my door and demand treatment'. He gives this country 'five years'.

Bennett is an intelligent satirist and a serious historian; the lingua franca of showbiz doesn't come into it, except obliquely. The 'private function' is both the projected dinner party and a reference to the grim habits of the pig. The farmer has placed his illicit charge on a diet of shredded rats and garbage, thus causing severe incontinence and an unprecedented pungency of domestic aromas in Joyce's kitchen area. Joyce's mother (the beatifically lobotomised Liz Smith), who lives in the same house, thinks that the furtive smuggling of the pig is something to do with getting her into an old people's home. 'I won't show her it,' says Maggie, 'she's seventy-four and it's past her bedtime.' Once Joyce has fixed her deal with the top brass, she turns with equal matter-of-factness to her own private functions: 'Right, Gilbert, I think sexual intercourse is in order.'

Several pigs were used in the shoot, but the main bulk of bacon belonged to Betty, a cross-breed of the floppy-eared Large White family and the prick-eared, more alert Tamworth clan. The supplier was Intellectual Animals (UK), a company specialising in clever beasts for filmmakers. Maggie was so impressed by Betty's talent and sensitivity that she said she would always think twice in future before referring to any colleague as 'that pig of an actor'. The pig brought out the best in Maggie. One instance of quick improvisatory thinking is treasured by Palin:

As in all the pig scenes, we rehearsed without the animal, which was then brought in like a great operatic star, or Liz Taylor. There would usually be endless takes into which the pig would sort of be fitted. On this occasion, the pig, for some reason, unerringly did what was required first time. She lumbered straight round the room and stuck her head in the oven. Maggie was suddenly trapped and only had the option of backing out of camera shot. But she didn't. She put one hand on the oven, the other on the table and executed this wonderful two-footed leap right over the more than oven-ready pig. It's in character, it's in the film and it's a brilliant moment.

The pig is finally slaughtered while Maggie drowns out its squeals with her piano-playing and the pageantry of England is celebrated in a party in the sitting room. Maggie's Joyce, succulently overdressed in a blue suit, declares, in a line that mocks generations of suburban gentility: 'I'm going to throw caution to the winds and have a sweet sherry.' As the film fades on the post-prandial dance, a smooching Denholm Elliott places his hand on Maggie's bottom, her features pucker into an expression of distaste that just stops short of a reprimand and Palin salivates over another sweet little piggy.

Michael Palin remained in awe of his co-star: 'Terrifying is too strong a word. But she's formidable when crossed. There's an intensity of animosity sometimes, which comes out in her acting and which can be quite chilling. Maggie in a bad mood is clearly a few degrees worse than most people in a bad mood.' Palin and his wife, Helen, subsequently drove down to visit Maggie and Beverley in Sussex, taking a vase they had bought for her in the Japanese shop in Covent Garden: 'The vase had lots of flowers with it, and paper blooms. As I gave it to Maggie, I realised the paper blooms were in fact very small price tags and, as we talked, Maggie idly picked off the tags, one by one, without causing any embarrassment. I remember thinking that this was a great actor at work!'

Alan Bennett says that Maggie was in a consistently good temper throughout the filming of *A Private Function*.

I was there most of the time. I used to go and chat. I was what one of the actors, Jim Carter, called 'continuity giggles'. One of the things about Maggie is that she is more intelligent than most actresses, much quicker, and so she arrives at what she wants to do very quickly. She easily gets bored and one has to be careful of that. She can't resist a joke, but I don't think she's malevolent. I do find her frightening when I think of her career and the people she's worked with. The same is true of Judi Dench, but I'm not frightened of Judi Dench, simply because she wouldn't let you be. Maggie has a reserve which you never penetrate, really.

The critical reaction to *A Private Function* was ecstatic on both sides of the Atlantic, though Rex Reed commented on the 'kinky humour' and 'riotous bad taste' which rendered it virtually a 'foreign' film in America. Vincent Canby, however, considered it 'the most high-hearted, stylish English film comedy since the Boulting Brothers and the golden age of English comedy' and Maggie 'ferociously funny' as Lady Macbeth's 'dainty, lower-middle-class spin-off'. In the 1984 British Academy of Film and Television Awards (BAFTA), the film split the honours with David Puttnam's *The Killing Fields*, and Maggie was declared best actress, with the prizes in the supporting categories claimed by Denholm Elliott and Liz Smith.

A second film with Merchant Ivory, *A Room with a View*, enjoyed enormous popularity but had considerably fewer teeth than the Bennett movie. Maggie was cast as Charlotte Bartlett, 'a terrible pain in the neck' and yet another chaperone, this time in charge of a somewhat bland Helena Bonham-Carter as Lucy Honeychurch, E. M. Forster's impressionable virgin who goes to Florence, sees a murder and is sumptuously kissed in a Tuscan cornfield by George Emerson, played by Julian Sands. Both *The Missionary* and *A Private Function* had been relatively low-budget affairs, and so was *A Room with a View*, although, at £2.4 million, with an eight-week shoot and four weeks on location in Tuscany, it cost twice as much to make as *Quartet*. It was co-produced with Goldcrest and Channel Four. A salutary and revealing comparison is with David Lean's E. M. Forster film, *A Passage to India*, which cost £16 million.

A crack British cast included Maggie's old friend Judi Dench as Miss Lavish, the ubiquitous novelist; Daniel Day-Lewis as Lucy's diffident bookworm of a fiancé, Cecil Vyse; and Simon Callow as Mr Beebe, the rumbustious young vicar from Tunbridge Wells. Denholm Elliott chipped in with another craftily understated performance, as George's father, and summed up the appeal of the project with delightful insouciance: 'You may not earn much money, and the lunches aren't exactly the greatest, but it is Forster, it is Maggie Smith and Judi Dench, and it is Florence. It's good upmarket stuff which I like to be associated with ... usually, I play abortionists.'

Chronologically, the film picked up where *The Missionary* left off, in 1907. And the Edwardian distance was maintained by a series of irritating chapter headings, faithful to Forster, but suggesting a lack of ideas about filmic adaptation. Pauline Kael felt that Helena Bonham-Carter was recessive and unradiant, depriving the movie of a centrifugal force; she certainly does not convey with any urgency the dilemma of a young girl torn between expressing her emotions and stifling them. Yet, as Kael says, the actors around her create a whirring atmosphere, a comic hum that makes the film completely watchable. Maggie, whose spinsterish Charlotte 'sees sins against propriety every-where', visits the Honeychurches in deepest leafy Kent and does not have the correct change for the cab-driver. Lucy's young brother pays the driver, but Maggie, over-emphatically and in order not to seem as impoverished as she is, insists on 'a settling of accounts'. As Kael exclaims, 'it's like a Marx Brothers routine, with the glorious Smith fingers and wrists fumbling and flying in all directions'.

Maggie's line on the pathos of the character – 'In my small way I am a woman of the world' – is absolutely straight and uninflected. She goes for a walk through Florence with Judi Dench's novelist, the person to whom she finally betrays Lucy with a description of 'the kiss', several inches taller than her keen and precise friend, head jutting and corkscrewing around like that of a startled chicken. She makes the expression of the romantic secret an inevitable, gushing release for her own bottled-up feelings and unfulfilled sexuality. Every glance is informed with a signal of despair, an excuse, a cry for help, a diversionary remark.

Even off camera, Maggie could be just as alarming, and just as funny. Simon Callow had hardly met her before they worked on the film. Ismail Merchant renewed their acquaintance in the foyer of the Excelsior Hotel in Florence before shooting started and promptly departed to make arrangements for lunch. Callow recalls that there was an awkward pause before Maggie, looking distractedly into the middle distance, said, 'I hope he won't be long. Fabia Drake's been sitting outside in that car for an hour and if she sits there any longer, she's going to turn into a monument.' After Callow had, as he admits, gurgled fatuously at this remark, he became tongue-tied once again before making his biggest mistake of all – blurting out praise for her most recent performance. Maggie suddenly turned on a bowl of flowers which she said she found 'worrying' and walked off to see the venerable actress and save her from the accelerating process of monumentalisation.

Once again, Maggie picked up the BAFTA best actress award. Judi Dench was honoured in the supporting category and the film itself was named best film. *A Room with a View* made profits for its six major investors, but not enough to put a brake on the decline of Goldcrest, the once-shining hope of the 1980s film industry, which was now in almost terminal economic trouble. Maggie's reputation, like that of all the fine actors she worked with, survived intact. She had impercept-ibly adjusted to the new mixed-economy realities of film-making and was as much in demand as ever. These first few years of the 1980s were as busy as any in her career. For, as well as making eight or nine films in six years, she had been trying to find her way back on a London theatre scene very different from that which she had abandoned for Canada.

13

Millamant, Poliakoff and Poppy Cocteau

Settling into the Sussex farmhouse was a pleasurable chore for Maggie and Beverley after the upheavals of leaving Tigbourne Court and the nomadic existence spent shuttling between Stratford and Los Angeles. Maggie's sallies to the film studios were invariably conducted from home base, with the boys reassuringly nearby at Seaford College and Maggie's father within easy reach in Oxford. The most striking aspect of the new house was its uncluttered, tasteful cosiness, a place to sink into and to hibernate inside. Maggie's bedroom had an unobstructed view of the surrounding fields, which made a more than welcome change from the busy main road that rushed by the bedroom at Tigbourne. On the landing outside hung her treasured collection of Erté's original costume designs for the Lillian Gish silent movie version of *La Bohème* (Gish disliked them, so they were never used). In the main sitting room, books everywhere, was an almost complete collection of the distinctive Virago reprints of classic feminist novels, and the latest clutch of literary biographies in hardback. The trophies were strewn discreetly around, serving as decorative props, not displays.

The duck pond was converted into a small swimming pool, and there were three listed barns on the property's couple of acres, an ancient bake house, an orchard yielding apples, plums, pears, mulberries and walnuts, awash with daffodils in the spring, and a vineyard. Beverley's plans included converting the old bakery into a summer-house and acquiring a cider press to crush all the apples in the garden and save money at Christmas. His home-produced tipple, a brew he dubbed 'Old Methuselah', was a lethal mixture of mildewed garden berries, sugar and vodka, left to ferment for a couple of years.

This new home was a great comfort to Maggie at a time when it was not clear what direction her career would take. The National Theatre was no longer a close-knit caucus of actors and directors working briskly and intimately in ramshackle but friendly circumstances on one repertoire for the Old Vic stage, but a conglomerate of companies entombed in the concrete anonymity of the new building on the South Bank. She was confused. She felt she did not belong anywhere, and that no one wanted her at the RSC (where she had no association) or the National and, as she told Sheridan Morley, although she did not at this point see herself as 'Dame Maggie', bravely battling on into her eighties – which, ironically, is precisely what happened – she did need someone like Olivier or Robin Phillips to tell her what to do next. 'I come back to a theatre which seems to have changed in some odd way during the years I was in Canada. Nobody seems to be in charge; just a lot of little groups all carrying on as best they can.'

One such little group, United British Artists, had received Maggie's blessing at the end of 1982. The alliance, announced by the entertainments mogul Lord Grade, constituted a peculiar and finally ineffectual bid to imitate the old Hollywood United Artists, which set its agenda according to the whims of a few all-powerful stars. The British theatre at the start of the 1980s was not remotely receptive to an attempt to reproduce the 1919 adventure launched by Mary Pickford, Charlie Chaplin, Douglas Fairbanks and D. W. Griffith. The board included Maggie, Diana Rigg, Glenda Jackson, John Hurt, Albert Finney and Peter Wood, and decided on more or less nothing. The attempt at least had the value of acknowledging the situation: the two big national theatre companies had become impersonal monoliths; there was no natural home any more for the star leading actors of the day; a most enormous chasm had opened up – notwithstanding the works of Alan Ayckbourn – between the best contemporary playwrights and the most commercially viable actors; the spirit of adventure had been replaced by a struggle for survival; companies, except on the defiant fringe, were a thing of the past. In such an environment, a star like Maggie might look increasingly anomalous.

There was nothing for it but to test the water by taking a familiar plunge. The new house, like Tigbourne, was within easy striking distance of the Chichester Festival Theatre. Just as Maggie had sprung free from disappointment at the National by giving her Margery Pinchwife there in 1969, so she relaunched herself in a home-grown

British production of another Restoration classic, albeit one she had 'tried out' in Canada. She and William Gaskill took up where they had left off in 1974 (with *Snap*) in a sumptuous revival of *The Way of the World*. The whole family, in fact, tuned in to the Sussex playhouse. Chris had done well at Seaford, but his plans for going to university were scuppered by the attractions of a student assistant stage manager post he gained at Chichester in the early days when, before the Minerva was built, the theatre's supplementary venue was informally housed in a tent. Beverley's playwriting career was also revived at Chichester. In the mid-1980s he titivated the old Fred Terry vehicle *The Scarlet Pimpernel*, directed with spectacular success by Nicholas Hytner, with a cast led by Donald Sinden (the production later transferred to Her Majesty's in London). Less happily, he adapted Goldoni's *La Locandiera* as *Miranda*, a vehicle for Penelope Keith at her most overweening in a slightly misfired analogue of Mrs Thatcher's Britain. You never really knew what Beverley might produce next. Toby described him affectionately as 'an incredibly taciturn bugger', and Chris was always convinced that there were some pretty major surprises in store. There were potential diversions. Almost every year, Beverley received an invitation, addressed to 'Mrs Beverley Cross', to mount the podium at the annual 'Women of the Year' shindig at the Savoy Hotel.

One of Maggie's major consolations in this period was her geo-graphical and neighbourly closeness to Lord and Lady Olivier. 'Larry and Joan' had been living in nearby Steyning, as well as at Brighton, with their growing family since the middle 1960s. Maggie's rivalry with Joan Plowright and the edgy hostility with Sir Laurence were finally forgotten in these years of friendship and camaraderie. The truce was sealed by Plowright's appearance alongside Maggie in *The Way of the World*. The contrast in the type of acting each expertly delivered was summarised for William Gaskill in their backstage preparations: 'If you went past Joan's dressing room, you heard her going through every line, from beginning to end. And as you went past Maggie's, you heard that wonderful record of Nellie Wallace's laughing song, which she played to put her in the mood.' Maggie returned to one of her greatest roles, and one with which she had begun her Canadian sojourn, or exile, Millamant. And Joan Plowright played Lady Wishfort, 'that old peeled wall, that famous antidote to desire'.

The Way of the World opened at Chichester on 1 August 1984. Maggie's Millamant was a gloriously emaciated, darting figure, using her wit as a cover to insecurity. She had been admired in Night and Day and in Virginia, but she had not been seen in her full comic flow on the British stage for ten years. The critical reaction reflected the sense of a starved theatre-going public reconnecting with one of its favourite icons. Jack Tinker said she finally displaced Edith Evans in the role. He was beside himself and 'once more at her feet'. Less gymnastically, Nicholas de Jongh in the Guardian said her 'stupendous' performance would surely rank 'as one of the great high-comedy achievements of the past three decades', noting how she charted the independent girl's progress from languid disdain conveyed from a great height, nose tilted skyward, to reach in her wooing scene with Mirabell (Michael Jayston) a tantalising mixture of role-playing and real feeling. The production was London-bound (it opened at the Haymarket in November) and had been given the works by director Gaskill. The design was by two of his former Royal Court associates – sets of oaken doors and evocative emblems by Hayden Griffin, and beautiful costumes of silks and quilts patterned with stripes, butterflies and birds by Deirdre Clancy.

The kinship structure of a complex plot in which, as Anne Barton reminded us in a programme note, 'everybody is a half-brother, niece, mother, cousin or nephew of somebody else', was cleanly exposed around the simple motivating mainspring of the chase for Lady Wishfort's money. One also felt, among all the couplings and liaisons, that this was a play about three widows: Millamant, Lady Wishfort and Mrs Fainall. This latter role was powerfully played by Sheila Allen.

The casting throughout was formidable. Above all, Maggie embodied what Hazlitt called 'that peculiar flavour in the very words' of Congreve's comedy and, once again, she convinced us in the great proviso scene that she really did set important store by her dependence on solitude and morning thoughts. This jocund marriage of style and gravity typified the light and adult plangency of Gaskill's exemplary production. And Maggie's brilliant and capricious creation, with wit her quick and deadly weapon, made her immune to all invasions. No one in the British theatre – and there have been Millamants from Geraldine McEwan and Judi Dench – can rival her in this vein. She could flourish a remark to create havoc and then retreat quickly behind her fan, as Michael Billington said, like a soldier behind a redoubt. And the repulsion of the rustic Sir Wilfull with a cry of 'A walk?' was that of a woman dealing brusquely with an indecent proposal.

Seven years later, the *Sunday Telegraph* ran a series in which actors and other artists recalled 'A Night to Remember'. Susan Fleetwood, no mean actress herself and one who had played several 'Maggie' roles (Silvia, Rosalind, Beatrice, Arkadina), picked this Millamant as the most outstanding performance she had ever seen: 'I think Maggie Smith is an artist of the high wire; and to be that can cost a lot. She avoids the cosy, she takes the risk of being unsympathetic. And yet, even when she's spitting venom, one's heart is broken for her . . . When I see Maggie act, I always feel tremendously excited that I'm an actor too. She just makes me feel good about the job.'

John Moffatt rekindled the joy of working with Maggie: 'I'd go on with her for the first entrance in the park and sometimes she'd say, "Moffatty Woffatty, surprise me." She liked to keep it all as fresh and flexible as possible. So I would say, sotto voce, "There's an awful lot of midges in St James's Park today," and we'd play that scene slapping midges, a great twinkle going on between us. It was subtle and the audience would not really notice. But the scene would be enlivened by this, and her own performance freshened.' Moffatt also testifies that Maggie's Oxford enthusiasm for J. D. Salinger had not waned. If a matinée was looming for which neither of them felt at concert pitch, she would gee up Moffatt and her other colleagues by invoking the showbiz motto at the end of Salinger's *Franny and Zooey*, 'Let's do it for the Fat Lady.' The Fat Lady is in every audience, the one person out there who is really waiting for the performance as the highlight of her day and a balm to all woes. Maggie never cheats on a matinée; she always does it for the Fat Lady.

Having given Barker and Bond short shrift when approached about them by Gaskill, Maggie was always liable to feel with especial keenness the dearth of new West End plays for actresses of her age and calibre. But within a year, she was acting with John Moffatt once again, in *Interpreters*, a Cold War comedy designed as a vehicle for her and Edward Fox by Ronald Harwood, whose early experience as an actor in Donald Wolfit's company had led to his backstage hit, *The Dresser*. Slightly schematic and finally hollow, *Interpreters* nonetheless did have some texture within which Maggie could rehearse her special line in despair and vulnerability as Nadia Ogilvy-Smith, a spinsterish Russian language interpreter known as 'the old maid of Whitehall' who, on the eve of a summit conference between the political leaders of Russia and Great Britain, recalls an old affair in New York with her randy Russian opposite number, Viktor (Edward Fox). Moffatt umpired their tryst as a ramrod-backed Foreign Office official.

For these past ten years, Nadia has kept passion at bay, walled up in a Kensington flat with a ninety-three-year-old grandmother who once danced with the Ballets Russes and knew Tolstoy and Chekhov. When Viktor calls to collect a copy of *Heartbreak House*, Nadia mistakenly believes that his ardour indicates a long-term emotional commitment. The comic climax of their renewed encounter occurs at a diplomatic pow-wow where Maggie plays footsy under the table. She manipulates her emboldened leg into the lap of the Soviet president and watches, stunned and alarmed, as Edward Fox calmly gets up and crosses the room. A lesser actress would have milked this moment for coarse laughter. Maggie did indeed win her laugh, but she made of it something more truthful and complex by immediately immersing us in the pain of her embarrassment.

Moffatt reports that Maggie was not very happy with this production and that the direction of Peter Yates, better known for his work in the cinema (he directed Maggie and Michael Caine in *It All Came True* twelve years later), was virtually non-existent. Maggie also hated the set, which was of a predominantly bilious green colour, with a lurid green carpet to match. Invoking the name of one of the outstanding snooker champions of the day, she would complain to anyone within earshot, 'When I get out on that stage I feel like Hurricane Higgins.'

Just over a year later, Maggie was snared in another Anglo-based Eastern European scenario of misunderstanding and despair, *Coming in to Land* by Stephen Poliakoff at the National Theatre. This was Maggie's first (and last) role on the South Bank, the occasion of a long overdue reunion with Peter Hall as her director and, considered in retrospect, one of the last significant British plays to examine the false visions East and West entertained of each other before the extraordinary political upheavals at the end of the decade. Poliakoff, who in 1980 had written a wonderful television film along similar culture-clash lines, *Caught on a Train*, for Peggy Ashcroft, sent the play to the National as he had promised his next one to Peter Hall. He had thought of Maggie as Halina Rodziewizowna, an unmarried Polish design student who seeks asylum at British immigration, because of the impression she had made on him in *The Prime of Miss Jean Brodie*, especially in the scene where she pleads with the headmistress Celia Johnson 'and suddenly becomes terribly moving'. When Maggie read it, she accepted the role at once.

Ironically, in a play whose main confrontation is set in an immigration office in Croydon, a bleak and soulless *quartier* of South London, Maggie found herself particularly alienated in real life in the concrete labyrinth of the new National. Poliakoff, whose reputation as a dramatist is rooted in the poetry of urban desolation, retains a vivid image of Maggie inhabiting those bleak corridors like a lost soul unhappily dislocated from her natural West End ambience of plush and gilt. John Moffatt sent her a poem which she carried close to her heart as she wandered, perpetually lost, between her featureless box dressing room and the awkwardly wide proscenium of the Lyttelton auditorium: 'Fuck and bloody arsehole, shit bugger damn; I don't know where the fuck I am.' Poliakoff had always wanted his play to be staged in the smaller Cottesloe (now the Dorfman) Theatre, but knew it would be nonsense to have Maggie confined there with a limited audience. He wanted to kid the audience with a seeming boulevard structure and then lead them into 'something messier'. Because Maggie came from that boulevard background, she took the audience on exactly the journey Poliakoff prescribed:

Of all my plays, this was the one which has had the best audience reaction. And a lot of that was to do with the great performance of Maggie Smith. She is brilliant at accents, and captured to absolute perfection this thing of Poles who speak wonderful, slightly flowery English, in the tradition of Joseph Conrad, or a comparable Czech example like Tom Stoppard. She has a brilliant ear. And she has a ready-made public. She walks on the stage and can say anything, even if it's just 'Have a cup of tea', and people start laughing. This is not true, necessarily, of Judi Dench.

Maggie's first entrance was indeed remarkable. Her character had spent twenty-nine years looking after her father, a disgraced Polish politician, and learning English in preparation for her own life. She appeared in a doorway, weighed down with her belongings in two vast plastic bags, wearing oversize boots and juggling a cigarette. Michael Ratcliffe in the *Observer* likened this aggressive manifestation to that of Sybil Thorndike entering in a scuffle of cardigans and bumping into someone expendable in N. C. Hunter's *Waters of the Moon*. It was at once clear that Halina would not go away. She personified and combined, said Ratcliffe, laziness, sensuality, reticence and indestructibility.

There was dispute over the merit of Poliakoff's play: 'a piffling piece of over-produced flim-flam,' said Jack Tinker, possibly because of a battery of television screens designed to fill up the cavernous Lyttelton in the hi-fi emporium where Halina has gained illegal employment; a 'thin and disappointing piece,' said Ratcliffe; 'Maggie Smith could not be this good if Stephen Poliakoff had not given her the material to work on,' countered Billington. There was elegant, silky support from Andrew C. Wadsworth as an oil executive and from Anthony Andrews as a show business lawyer, both allies to her cause for patriation in England. But the major sparks were fired in a half-hour scene in the second act between Maggie and Tim Pigott-Smith as a ruthless immigration officer who turns the interrogation screws rather like Porfiry in Dostoevsky's *Crime and Punishment*. Cutting right down to the bone, Maggie, in eye-catching scarlet, tore into the scene with an animal ferocity she had not tapped in London since *Hedda Gabler*, crying to be allowed into the country with, as Billington said, 'the naked desperation of the potentially stateless'.

Between these two contemporary plays she fitted in an appearance at the Lyric, Hammersmith, as Jocasta in Jean Cocteau's high-camp 1934 version of the Oedipus story, *The Infernal Machine*. This was a good example of Maggie being talked into something about which she had nurtured no previous ambition whatsoever. The person responsible was Simon Callow, who was infatuated with the play and saw in Maggie the Jocasta of his dreams. The role, he felt, was one which could accommodate her full range, demanding a woman who appeared, by turns, skittish, amorous, haunted, tender, stark and suicidal. The tragedienne in Maggie appealed above all to Callow and had inspired him to become an actor in the first place.

Cocteau has fallen from fashion in the British theatre, if indeed he ever fell into it. The reviewers remained sceptical. Michael Billington branded the play 'poppy Cocteau' (not all that risible a tag as the playwright had conceived of the piece in a haze of opium) and John Peter in the *Sunday Times* thundered about bad art being gloriously sent up. But Callow was sincere in his admiration for the play, which covers Oedipus's return to his mother's womb as her lover, after he has killed his father. There is a famous scene with the talking Sphinx, and a long bedroom scene in which mother and son, magnetised by sexual attraction, are permanently on the verge of sleep. Cocteau, said Callow, set out 'to write the great nightmare of Western civilisation as a dream play', and by using a brilliantly evolved technique of repetitions, non-sequiturs, unmotivated impulses, quotations and slangy anachronisms, created 'a hypnotised world moving imperceptibly from dream to reality and back' in which the characters, all variants of boulevard archetypes, are caught up in the cogs of the infernal machine, the plot.

One of Callow's other heroes, the Irish actor Micheál MacLiammóir, had produced the play in Carl Wildman's translation at the Gate in Dublin in 1937. Callow, who was convinced that, in the face of AIDS, nuclear war and starvation, it was harder to dismiss Cocteau's vision of life as a trap devised by a remorseless divinity, provided his own script, even racier than Wildman's and fragrantly sensitive to the tension, flipness, misery, extravagance and ecstasy of the original. Callow had long wanted to do the play and he knew that Peter James, the director of the Lyric, Hammersmith, an avowed internationalist with a liking for mad projects, might be interested. He was.

Callow was building up his courage to approach Maggie when he was thrown together with her on the film of *A Room with a View*. He was certain that she found him too noisy, but his dread dissolved when they acted together: 'The contact, concentration and responsiveness were thrilling.' Still, he remained tongue-tied on the subject of Cocteau and started to entertain thoughts of Jeanne Moreau. A chance meeting with the French film star in Florence, on a rest day from shooting the Forster film, resulted in a series of telephone calls and messages which finally, however, led to a stalemate. During *Interpreters*, Callow resumed his hunt for Maggie and was rewarded with a positive response first time. Over supper, he outlined how he would conduct rehearsals. He asked was there any method she particularly disliked? 'Only stopping work at four and going off to the Garrick for drinkies.' Without quite getting down to brass tacks, Callow arranged another dinner date with Peter James joining them. James made an impassioned speech about the need to take on Cocteau as the major subsidised companies weren't interested, and the supplementary need to present him as well as possible with someone who would bring in the audience and do justice to the play. 'I need you, or someone like you,' said the intrepid James. Callow froze. 'Someone like me?' said Maggie. 'You,' said James. 'I know what you mean,' said Maggie. 'Well?' said James. 'Well?' said Maggie. 'Will you do it?' A pause. 'I can't see any reason why not.' 'But will you do it?' *'Pourquoi pas?'*

And that, recalls Callow, was it. People told him later that Maggie had said to them that she didn't know why she was doing the play, or she was only doing it to spite her agent, or because Edith Evans had never done it. But she had been taken by Callow's enthusiasm and had herself found something worthwhile and compelling in the drama. It was typical of her that she should disguise her commitment in a battery of airily bemused disavowals. Having initially tried, and failed, to interest Alec Guinness in the role of Tiresias, Callow had landed a fine alternative: the blind seer was to be played by Robert Eddison, one of the great verse speakers in the old style. Oedipus fell to the French film star Lambert Wilson.

The rehearsal period was troubled. Eddison simply did not get on with Maggie. Maggie was also highly critical of Bruno Santini's set, which the designer had covered in cellophane. Each time anyone went near the surface, it crackled and rustled. Maggie took one look and protested: 'I can't ... d'you ... I can't ... I can't ... it's like a thousand sweets being unwrapped all at the same time.' The cellophane went. Three previews were cancelled and, at the last dress rehearsal, when the dry-ice machine had turned the stage into a skating rink, Lambert Wilson fell into the orchestra pit. At the first preview, Maggie was faced with a total disaster but refused to succumb. According to Callow, she just set to and saved the show. And halfway through, she probably realised that the rescue operation was only half necessary. Then she went through what Callow took to be an habitual rigmarole of ringing up and apologising:

'She fears disaster every day. It's her natural reaction. It's as though she is spontaneously on acid. Which is what makes her acting so great. She will take a word and plumb its depth both comically and tragically until it begins to assume as lurid a life for you as it does for her.'

Jocasta was not popular in Thebes: 'My clothes madden them. My mascara maddens them. My joie de vivre maddens them.' Her attention is caught by a handsome young soldier who reminds her of her son. He would be about the same age, nineteen, now. 'Zizi,' Maggie cooed to Tiresias, 'just look at those muscles... feel those biceps, they're like steel.' Michael Ratcliffe described how this darkly murmuring witch then sank 'with an opiate lassitude and gloom on to the enormous pile of furs where she will unknowingly consummate marriage to her son'. In the last scene, Jocasta appeared in black, in a trough of misery. And then – Cocteau's masterstroke, says Callow – she returns as an apparition, dead, all in white, after she has hanged herself and Oedipus has stabbed out his eyes with his mother's brooch. Suffused with maternal spirit and radiance, her effect on an audience was invariably profound. Callow had begged her to remain as simple as possible, and she did remain as simple as possible. 'She was just astonishing.'

Number one son Chris had been working in the West End. After Chichester, he gained a job through the Fox family connection. Edward Fox and Maggie had been presented in *Interpreters* by Edward's younger brother, Robert Fox, whom Chris had met over dinner. Thus Chris came to be crewing on the Harwood play, humping costumes and assisting in the scene changes, where he 'walked on' in his mother's shadow as a Foreign Office security guard. Chris and Toby then worked together for a season in the tent at Chichester before Toby, who had long since decided to be an actor, enrolled at a minor drama school for about four months, then auditioned for the major ones. He was turned down because he was too young – he had left Seaford without taking his A-Levels – and spent another season crewing at Chichester before he was accepted at the London Academy of Music and Dramatic Art (LAMDA). Chris, meanwhile, moved on to Andrew Lloyd Webber's *The Phantom of the Opera* (which dropped anchor at Her Majesty's after *The Scarlet Pimpernel*), where he caught the chandelier every night before it hit the deck. There followed stints at the Redgrave Theatre at Farnham, where he gained his stage-manager's card, and the Mercury at Colchester, where he served as deputy stage manager.

Both boys had kept their father's surname, Stephens, but Chris had to trade it in, just as his mother had had to adopt 'Maggie' in 1956, because another 'Christopher Stephens' was registered with Equity. He tried registering under his maternal grandmother's names of Hutton and Little but they, too, were taken. Maggie said that, as he liked the poetry of Philip Larkin, why not use that name? So Chris Stephens became, and remains, Chris Larkin. He now decided, after all, that he wanted to train as an actor. Chris, cheerful and lanky, followed his younger brother Toby, confident and barrel-chested, into LAMDA. The boys used the Fulham house as their domestic base for the last few years of the 1980s and beyond.

Toby had first seen his mother on stage in *Peter Pan* and had wondered 'what the hell she was doing swinging around on a piano wire'. In Canada, Christopher Downes remembers sitting with Toby, his face alight, at the end of the last performance of *As You Like It* as Maggie, triumphant in the epilogue, took her curtain calls and was showered with bouquets of pink and yellow roses which matched the colours in her dress. Downes knew at this point – Toby was eight – that he wanted to share what his mother was lapping up. Toby recalls that when he confirmed that he intended to go on the stage, Maggie quizzed him on how many Shakespeare plays he knew, how many speeches by heart. She did on one occasion bawl him out for never going to see anything and not reading enough. It is the one serious row Toby has ever had with his mother. He started to do as she ordered. He learned that if he was to be even half as serious about his career as she was, he had to start watching and reading immediately.

At about this time, Robert, who was playing a bleary-eyed,

unforgettably bloated double of King Herod and Pontius Pilate in Bill Bryden's production of *The Mystery Plays* at the National Theatre, drifted back into his sons' lives. They had gone seven or eight years without seeing him and were now old enough to take responsibility themselves for keeping in touch. Both parents were now seen by them in a more appreciative context: neither came from a family with a history in the theatre, and both had to work very hard to achieve a professional status. As far as Maggie is concerned, Toby acknowledges that her moderately austere lower-middle-class background, so formative an influence on her career and personality, was denied him and Chris. Maggie is hard on other people because she is primarily hard on herself. The boys knew they had to learn to combat the relative ease with which they could face the world thanks to their mother's efforts.

Maggie was no more relaxed about her work than she had ever been, but her security at home and the friendship of her sons were cause for at least some satisfaction. Although she immediately regretted it, she allowed the American-based *People* magazine to take a look round the Sussex fastness and to encourage her to put her past into perspective: 'The tumultuous period of my life, so much of it is such a winter in my head . . . that's not me; it's Christopher Fry.' Toby told the magazine that he and Chris had enjoyed a remarkably smooth transition 'from one father to another', while Chris declared that Beverley was the glue that stuck the family together. Maggie concurred: 'Bev is a rock. He took on a lot: me and these two boys. I'm just remarkably fortunate that it did happen. When you meet again someone you should have married in the first place – it's like a script. The kind of luck that's too good to be true.'

14

A Toast to the Bard with Levin and Lettice

Stephen Poliakoff and Peter Hall entertained hopes of Maggie moving to the West End with *Coming in to Land*, but the Jack Clayton film of *The Lonely Passion of Judith Hearne* was in the offing and, more to the point, the long-promised script from Peter Shaffer, *Lettice and Lovage*, was almost a reality. In his preface to the published text, Shaffer put the unfashionable view that his purpose as a playwright was to serve the actor's art:

> Great actors are now a species infinitely more endangered than white rhinos and far more important to the health and happiness of the human race. I am referring to 'live' actors, of course – not their manufactured images on screens large and small. In our age where most performers have been reduced to forms of puppetry – neutered by naturalism, made into miniaturists by television, robbed of their voices by film dubbers and their right to structure roles by film editors – the authentic Great Actor has almost disappeared from the earth.

Shaffer counted Maggie 'indisputably' great and dedicated his new play to this Wonder of her Art, 'who incarnates comedy with love'. *Lettice and Lovage* was scheduled for an autumn 1987 opening in the West End.

The year started well, with Maggie winning the best supporting actress in the Golden Globe Awards for *A Room with A View*, followed by a nomination in the same category for the Oscars (she did not win). As well as the BAFTA award, she collected a Variety Club award as film actress of the year. Even more unexpected was a curious invitation she received that spring from Bernard Levin, who had given up theatre reviewing, but not his passion for Maggie Smith. He had been asked by his close friend Arianna Stassinopoulos Huffington, the Washington socialite, writer and controversial biographer of Picasso, to arrange a Shakespearean entertainment for the third annual Founders Day dinner at the Folger Shakespeare Library in Washington, DC. This was Mrs Huffington's first chairmanship of a major Washington event and she wanted it to be a success. The guest list of 170 people, each one paying a thousand dollars for the privilege of attending, included several Roosevelts, Judge Webster, head of the FBI, and many senators from Capitol Hill. A reception in the Great Hall of the library was to be followed by dinner in the Reading Room and whatever appropriate cabaret Levin and Arianna between them might be able to concoct.

Levin had recently published a book, *Enthusiasms*, where, in a chapter on Shakespeare, he had cobbled into one gigantic paragraph all the phrases, first coined in the Bard, which had since assumed the status of common parlance. His script was built around this passage and he sent it off to Maggie, who was intrigued. She agreed with Levin that Alec McCowen would make an ideal partner for such an occasion and all three of them had a splendid meal at Simply Nico. The actors signed up in exchange for a suite each at the Hay–Adams hotel and a first-class fare. On arrival in Washington, Levin promptly took his charges out for yet another sumptuous dinner and McCowen half-remembers returning to the Hay–Adams very much the worse for wear and quite unable to stand still for long enough to insert his key in his bedroom door. Maggie descended less squiffily from her floor and kindly inserted the key for him, turned down the bed, drew the curtains and put Mr McCowen safely to sleep within his luxurious sheets.

Levin's account of 'a stupendous triumph' at the Folger on 10 April 1987 is slightly challenged by McCowen's recollection of 'utter chaos' at the library when they turned up to rehearse, though it is conceivable that he might have been suffering from a hangover. Maggie and McCowen insisted on someone turning off the central heating and the air conditioning, which made noises similar to those of a lavatory flushing. Americans, McCowen reminded his colleagues, simply did not hear such noises. The actors wanted Levin to rehearse them, but he protested, with many a 'good grief' and 'for heaven's sake', that he was in no position whatsoever to embark on a career in theatre directing, least of all at this latish time of life, and certainly not, for starters, with the likes of Mr Alec McCowen and, 'by the mass', 'by all the stars in God's firmament', as well as 'by untold varieties of heck', the further likes of Miss Maggie Smith. So he told them just to get up there and do the blessed thing on their own, which is, after all, what directors usually say most of the time anyway (he added, for good measure).

In the afternoon before the event, Levin recalls, Maggie Smith lost her handbag. She could not move without this handbag, it had everything in it and so on and so forth, and a hunt was mounted throughout the hotel. The handbag was finally found under Miss Smith's bed. Then Miss Smith lost her spectacles. She was in no position to read the menu, let alone Bernard Levin's script, without these glasses, but she did have a prescription about her person. Probably in the handbag. Levin volunteered to dive into the Washington maelstrom and find an optician who, for a consideration, made up another pair of glasses on the spot. Before the dinner and the recital, the artists were bidden to an extremely smart cocktail party at Mrs Huffington's, McCowen in his dinner jacket, Maggie in what she said was her 'only black dress'. The ride in the limousine was through the rush hour. It took, says McCowen, an hour and a half to travel approximately two kilometres in order to attend a party where he and Maggie knew nobody at all. They stood on the terrace and Maggie looked down the lawn and said rather grumpily, 'Very small pool!' Ten minutes later they piled back into the limo to go to the Folger and Maggie said, 'Well, thank you Bernard, that was a lovely glass of water.'

The library, manned by liveried footmen and populated by Washington's finest, had been transformed into a Midsummer's Eve bower, awash with flowers, moss, ivy, models of little woodland animals, plants and jungle greenery. A large ficus tree sparkled with lights and streamers, and the whole place had been lit solely by candlelight. 'It was magic, absolute magic,' says Levin. 'What I shall never forget was that, as the catalogue unrolled, you could hear the audience stop breathing at this flood of phrases. Maggie and Alec were wonderful. And the cheering. Well, it was unbelievable.'

The actors were more tense. The dinner, according to McCowen, 'went on for hours and hours and of course we both had to have it. I was sitting next to a very obscure Roosevelt. Then there were speeches, then we were given a medal and then it was time for the recital. At which point, as we started, about twenty-eight of the more elderly diners took this as their cue to go to the loo. Anyway, we got through it, and Bernard was overjoyed and very sweet and I had some gin and tonic and Maggie had some champagne and then we both went back to the hotel and behaved disgracefully with room service. It was a very jolly time.'

At all stages of her career, Maggie has, for the most part, remained curiously invisible in public. She rarely appears in charity shows, seldom lends her name to committees or educational institutions, and you hardly ever see her on television, or hear her on radio, discussing some forthcoming performance or other. John Moffatt once confessed to her that he felt he had all the makings of a recluse. And she said, 'Oh, I am a recluse. I haven't got any friends.' Although she knows an awful lot of people, she consistently gave the impression during the 1980s, says Moffatt, that the only place she really wanted to be was at home with Beverley and the boys and the dog and the garden and the books.

It is as if she hides away, nursing her gift, and then bursts forth in a new role. She certainly did this as Lettice Douffet, imaginative guide to Fustian Hall and daughter of a theatrical mother who toured the Dordogne with an all-female company, cheerfully swinging her Falstaff padding over her shoulder to play Richard Crookback. Unusually, Shaffer wrote a whacking great role for a leading actress who had to do all the donkey work of laying down the expository information herself. Several critics felt that these early scenes could be trimmed with little loss to the play apart from Maggie's delightfully pitched variations on the same theme. But the whole point of Shaffer's play was to expose Maggie's artistry, not win points in a good dramaturgy contest. Lettice remains one of Maggie's greatest successes, a role in which she combined bravura comic eccentricity with clear, sustained indications of private grief. The external signs of her extraordinary behaviour as a tourist guide stemmed from an inner need to dramatise. 'Enlarge! Enliven! Enlighten!' is her battle-cry, as she elaborates dull fact with colourful fiction in the drab country house hallway. The play opens with four revue-style snippets of Lettice in action, delivering an increasingly embroidered account of a royal visit and a noble intervention 'on these very stairs' for the benefit of her group of tourists. That group is joined by an academic cynic. Bending her neck, like a disturbed but curious swan, Smith addresses him sideways: 'Excuse me, but there is a hostility in your voice which implies that what I am saying is an untruth . . . [A characteristic pause and a deadly, sympathy-gaining inflection as far as the tourist group is concerned, who want to believe the unlikely] . . . that it is lacking in veracity.' The last word is laid out like a decorated corpse. The second, more decisive intervention is made by Lotte Schoen, a brusque and severe representative of the personnel department in the Preservation (National) Trust, who casts severely incredulous aspersions on the historical information Lettice is feeding the tourists, especially that story of John Fustian leaping upstairs to stuff fried hedgehogs into Queen Elizabeth's mouth directly from his fingers.

After a killingly long pause, Lettice counters with 'I'm sorry – but I cannot myself get beyond your own behaviour.' This lights the blue touch-paper, and the audience ignites with a great, whooshing roar of laughter. They now know whose side they are on. Lettice is summoned to Miss Schoen's office in Westminster to discuss her dismissal on the grounds of unacceptable embroidery of the dull truth, the everyday, the 'mere' as pronounced by Smith in one of her most contemptuous inflections. She arrives in Westminster dressed in a black cloak and beret 'like some medieval abbot'. It transpires that her mother ran a Shakespearean touring company in France. The inherited histrionic talent of Lettice is cruelly suppressed by the loss of her job. The women subsequently meet in Lettice's basement flat in Earl's Court, where antagonism slowly thaws into friendship. Their relationship matures through Lettice's enthusiasm for historical charades, though this leads to an unfortunate accident on Mary Queen of Scots's execution block, and requires the third-act participation of a bemused lawyer called Mr Bardolph. Lettice is consoled throughout by the attentions of her cat, Felina, Queen of Sorrows.

Maggie exuded a sense of theatre in the role as an aspect of personality. Shaffer's play was a metaphor of fictional, improved historical fact, of theatre as a truth beyond documentation. Lettice's self-absorption became a source of magnificent self-defensiveness. In the second act, Lettice lost her left hand momentarily in a big floppy sleeve. Maggie shook her wrist inquisitively and stared at the absent manual append-age with an air of bafflement. A slight, ten-second piece of outrageous comic business was transformed into a wholly comprehensible and revelatory comment on the character's enraptured scattiness.

With a twinge of near-painful recognition, Lettice's defiance of the grey, the analytical, the sensible, corresponded for me with the actress's reluctance to be drawn into direct personal combat. Lettice starts with dismay whenever the telephone or the front doorbell rings. And when Mr Bardolph seeks information for the impending court case on what exactly took place prior to the accident on the scaffold, Lettice gives the tape-recorder the most terrible stare, arching backwards from the contraption and responding frostily and monosyllabically – 'Correct!' – to the early questions. Interviews are not Lettice's forte. At the end of the London version of *Lettice and Lovage*, Maggie as Lettice and Margaret Tyzack as the reconciled Miss Schoen, having toasted each other by quaffing a goblet of the Elizabethan home-brewed 'lovage', embark on a course of architectural terrorism. They have formed END, the Eyesore Negation Detachment (as opposed to CND, the Campaign for Nuclear Disarmament), and begin preparing, as the curtain falls, to blow up a select list of modern architectural monstrosities with a petard, a medieval explosive device. This conclusion, although it uncannily anticipated the conservationist, anti-modernist debate perpetrated in Britain by Prince Charles, was generally thought to be unlikely and unconvincing. Shaffer himself wanted to rewrite it, but the actors were reluctant to accept the changes.

It now transpires that they didn't believe in the ending themselves. But Margaret Tyzack says that they didn't mind the preposterousness 'because we were of the mind that we couldn't run a wool shop. The idea that anyone else could believe that we really could get anything together was, to us, astonishing.' Michael Blakemore, the director, says that Maggie tried to convince him and Shaffer that the rewrite was no good by rehearsing it badly for a couple of weeks but that 'when she did it, and started getting her laughs doing her magic on it, she got to enjoy it a lot'. The new last (strictly, penultimate) line in

New York, after the play had come full circle by Lettice describing her own place, was 'On behalf of Miss Schoen and myself – a brimming goodbye to you!' Shaffer says that Maggie worried and worried about this line not being quite right before inserting the more rhythmically satisfying extra phrase: 'On behalf of Miss Schoen and myself – and all true enemies of the mere – a brimming goodbye to you!'

Shaffer acknowledges that there is a school of playwriting which is anti-effective and says to hell with all that sort of thing: 'I do not subscribe to that school. I'm on Maggie's side. You have to honour the musical and the rhythmic side of things, and you have to honour your actress. She wanted to achieve that joyous envoi, to seal her bargain with the audience. I believe she gave one of the great performances of our day.'

Michael Ratcliffe, dismissing the piece as 'a fey heritage comedy', declared that the play's greatest mystery was the failure of Lettice and Lotte to end up in bed together. Margaret Tyzack says that lesbianism, even crypto-lesbianism, was never even discussed by anyone on the production. The idea would certainly never have crossed Maggie's mind. She was absolutely aghast when Ingmar Bergman had asked her, during rehearsals for *Hedda Gabler*, apropos of her interest in Mrs Elvsted's long hair, if she had ever experienced any physical sensations towards her own sex.

This was Shaffer's first out-and-out comedy since *Black Comedy* in 1964, in which Maggie had also scored a great personal triumph, but as part of a coherent National Theatre ensemble. Shaffer is a magpie writer. The genesis of Lettice Douffet owed something not only to Jean Brodie, but also to E. F. Benson's overbearing heroine, Lucia. The reviews were generally uneasy about the play and divided on Maggie's performance. Irving Wardle tipped his hat to 'an original and hilarious treatment of an important and theatrically neglected subject' but complained that the play kept coming to a stop for memory speeches and that the two characters were of decidedly unequal interest.

And the issue of mannerism was reintroduced with unwonted savagery by Martin Hoyle in the *Financial Times*. There were no two ways about it: Maggie got right up his nose. He bemoaned 'another revue turn' and, having dismissed her Lettice as 'gratingly superficial' and 'a grotesque comic caricature', added insult to injury by complimenting

Judi Dench and Peggy Ashcroft on their method of using their own personalities to illuminate character before settling on Alison Steadman as the ideal example of an actress who is unrecognisable from one part to the next. Even if this were true, which in Steadman's case it is not, the assertion that a performance in the theatre should be as unrelated as possible to the fixed personality of the actor is as tendentious as it is impracticable. But it is a common assertion, and one that has been entered as evidence against many great actors, even those who are palpably 'self-transformers', like Olivier. The charge that an actor is always 'the same' seems to me to be self-evidently crass. The sameness of the actor from role to role is the most obvious thing about him, even if he starts each time with the blank neutrality of Alec Guinness.

As Michael Blakemore says, the making of a remarkable actor depends on the extent to which he is an interesting person in the first place. 'And Maggie is a very sharp, very intelligent, witty lady.' Dull actors are the actors whom you never recognise from one part to another, mainly because you can never tell what they are really like. The additional trouble with Maggie, of course, is the armoury of her technique. The wrist-flapping and whirring of circles in the air were a part of the comic apparatus that had got her into trouble before. But, as Michael Ratcliffe pointed out, following hard on the heels of her 'marvellous performances in plays by Cocteau and Poliakoff . . . we now know she is acting like this because she wants to and not because she can no longer do anything else'.

Maggie certainly felt the play needed cranking up and worked very hard, every performance, to get it going. But the idea that her gestures and inflections were some random selection of uncontrolled whimsicalities was surely wide of the mark. The play needed her gestural aggrandisement, even if, as John Dexter felt, the opening scenes were feebly superfluous. There was more of a hectic flurry to Lettice Douffet than to Maggie's stiller comic creations for the simple reason that Lettice was habitually putting on an act to disguise the emptiness within. And she was a frustrated thespian. The irritation quotient stems from the frantic pace of the sculptural gesticulation, which in Maggie's case is executed with the style and precision of a speeded-up Kabuki onnagata. The character's nerves are always likely to get on ours. For this reason, Maggie can simply fail to strike on your box, but such is the fate of any performer. She struck on Frank Rich's all right. The *New York Times* critic saw the play in London and guaranteed its safe passage across the Atlantic, hailing 'the camp performance of our time . . . she seems to be Mr Shaffer's sexually ambiguous answer to Auntie Mame, or perhaps his sentimental gloss on the Madwoman of Chaillot.'

Bernard Levin wrote a long letter to Maggie after the opening and she told him later that she had cried. 'This was not affectation,' said Levin. 'I think this wonderful brittle façade she puts up is in fact a sort of protection against her doubts about her quality. She shouldn't have any doubts, but she clearly does have them, to my astonishment, to everyone's astonishment, and that's the softer side of her, the vulnerable side. She had cried because I had told her how very good she was. And I was very touched by that side of her.'

The performance became the talk of the town. Fellow professionals wrote fulsome letters, and John Gielgud, who opened next door at the Apollo in February 1988 in Hugh Whitemore's *The Best of Friends* – his last stage appearance – asked Maggie to dine with him one evening, if she was not too tired. He thanked her for some flowers she had sent him and, moved by the extraordinary reception he had received on his own first night, said that 'now we can rejoice in each other's overflow'.

But Maggie did not feel like doing very much in the way of rejoicing. She found the play as draining as anything she had ever done, and she was not well. The thyroid condition which was eventually diagnosed as Graves' disease caused her acute discomfort. And she had been working on two films, both about alcoholics, one for Jack Clayton and one for BBC television, which had been among the most emotionally exhausting of her career. They had not exactly driven her to drink, but they had certainly pushed her as far as she had ever gone in her screen performances.

15

Alone without God

For someone who came from a strict and religious background and who had seriously flirted with the idea of converting to Roman Catholicism, Maggie's twin portrayal of ladies disappointed in God, Alan Bennett's Susan in *Bed Among the Lentils* and Brian Moore's Judith Hearne, drew on some deep reserves of feeling and confessional anguish. In her stage and screen work of the 1980s she had demonstrated that the pathos endemic to her work as a comedienne could be redistributed as the chief aspect of her acting persona. The comedy and tears of her earliest revue sketches, tempered by her years in the classic repertoire, equipped her to play the modern tragedy of an ordinary woman as well as any other actress of her day. And she had no qualms about making her spinsters spinsterish or her married frumps frumpish.

Jack Clayton had wanted to make a film of Brian Moore's first novel, *The Lonely Passion of Judith Hearne*, for nearly twenty years. A Catholic himself, Clayton responded profoundly to the novel's portrait of a spinster in conflict with the sensuality of her own nature, the screen of social desperation drawn like a mask over the heroine's loneliness and secret drinking. He was not the first with aspirations of a dramatic transfer: in her classic review of Clayton's film, Pauline Kael revealed that José Quintero had once hoped to stage the story with Geraldine Page; that John Huston envisaged the screen role for Katharine Hepburn; and that other nearly-Judiths included Rachel Roberts and Deborah Kerr. Nobody had matched the rights and the financing until Clayton, backed by Denis O'Brien of HandMade Films, cast Maggie as the impoverished spinster in a skilful and sensible adaptation by Peter Nelson. Nelson's main innovation was to move the action from Belfast to Dublin, with the consequent loss of one layer of Judith's spiritual alienation in a primarily Protestant community. Like Joyce in Bennett's *A Private Function*, Judith is a part-time piano teacher with hopes of self-improvement. But there is no materialism or dynamism of any sort attached to these hopes. They are merely tickled into something resembling life by the appearance in Judith's boarding house of her landlady's brother, the widower James Madden, played by Bob Hoskins, who has returned to Ireland after thirty years in New York.

This deeply courageous film about escape, dependency and betrayal is possibly the best rebuttal of my own submission that Maggie has often been conservative in her choice of role. There is no hiding place in this portrayal, and no attempt at softening any blows. Maggie's acting is of a complexity and technical perfection unsurpassed by any other British performer of the past few decades: there is not one single hint of false sentiment, superfluous gesture, inappropriate nasal intonation, attenuated diphthongs, wrist acting, brittle evasion or any other of the objections sometimes raised against her. Another crucial quality, noted by Victoria Mather in the *Daily Telegraph*, is that although Judith Hearne is a withered, drab and nervous figure on the outside, Maggie invests her with 'an inward soul of bright innocence'.

Maggie inspects the characters assembled at the boarding-house breakfast table with more nervousness than when she beadily contemplated the refined guests in the Florentine *pensione* in *A Room with a View*. The landlady's son, wonderfully played by the big-bellied RSC actor Ian McNeice, is a loutish poet, claiming several more years of pampered lodging at home while he writes his 'masterpiece' and slopes off to debauch the maid every night. The agony of eye contact with Bob Hoskins as the returning prodigal gives way to the most tentative of dimpled smiles when they make a date to go to church together. Maggie has to nudge him awake during the sermon and mildly rebukes him for dressing like a comedian. He has noticed her rings and, taking them to be a sign of wealth, cruelly arouses Judith's affection while planning to exploit her as a sponsor for his hare-brained scheme of starting 'an American eating-place right in the centre of town'.

He invites her to a movie and a meal. The movie is *Samson and Delilah* starring Victor Mature, of which Groucho Marx said, 'No picture can hold my interest when the leading man's bust is bigger than the leading lady's.' Judith's world is circumscribed by others' expectations, notably those of the Church and of Wendy Hiller as a cantankerously pious aunt whom she was obliged to nurse after she suffered a stroke and who continues her mawkish tyranny over Judith from beyond the grave. Judith has a mobile shrine of her aunt's photograph and a picture of the Sacred Heart of Jesus. But the shrine is really a devotional triptych, completed by the secret bottle. When she learns that Hoskins's bumptious James Madden is a fraud with a record of failure and footling menial jobs, she literally shakes with tears, turns the Sacred Heart to the wall and sips at her whisky. The camera stays on her unadorned face of pain for what seems like the time it would take to say a rosary.

We cut to the physical sweatiness of Hoskins boarding the landlady's daughter ('just a little fun' is his prelude to a rape) and back again to Maggie clutching her bottle and gibbering a banal song: 'When you're smiling, when you're smiling, the whole world smiles with you.' In the privacy of her room, prayers are followed by alcoholic wipe-out and unconscious reverie on the floor. Judith begins her descent to the abyss by losing some of her teaching jobs and confessing more than she has dared before to a priest who absolves her, but declines to give her a penance. She embellishes and twists the story of how Madden has proposed to her, clutching a third glass of sherry in a family sitting room, moving just slightly into overdrive, eyes big and absolutely open to the lens and the inquisition of an unseen audience. With the last of her money, and a bottle in her handbag, she moves into the Shelbourne Hotel. She tells the priest: 'I can't believe any more. I'm all alone . . . I just don't believe God is there any more.' And in the most extraordinary scene of all she runs up the aisle of the church and shouts, 'I hate you' at the tabernacle, repository of the living body of Christ.

In a nursing home, surrounded by white linen and the white habits of Carmelite nuns, Maggie's Judith acquires the mad and powerful radiance of Lady Macbeth sleepwalking, or of Lucia di Lammermoor singing her mournful aria, or of Mary Tyrone riding high on her sweet powders in the last scene of *Long Day's Journey into Night*. (Too late now, but Maggie should have played this role with Robert Stephens as her husband and their two sons as their two sons.) Her hair is plaited on one side of her face, her two holy pictures to hand: 'They always make a new place home.' Madden, now employed as a van driver, returns to pay a visit. At last, he proposes marriage to Judith, adding the disastrous rider that she must have some money after all, as he found out that she had stayed in the Shelbourne. When Judith later leaves the home, she hands a crumpled piece of paper to the taxi driver on which is written Madden's address. The camera once again lingers, searching for clues, anxious to know if, at last, this is to be the really brand-new start she deserves. But Maggie's taut mask, frankly lined with a history of disappointment, is giving nothing away.

The film was made quickly, in seven weeks, and Maggie was in almost every shot. Jack Clayton recalls that her concentration was unbelievably intense. She stayed in a different hotel from everyone else in Dublin, not to be awkward, but to concentrate on the loneliness. There was, however, something temperamentally suited to Maggie about Judith's condition and she submerged herself in the role with relish. Clayton says she hardly took advantage of the dialect coach provided, but her accent is, as usual, spot on and faultlessly maintained. The same cannot quite be said for Bob Hoskins's blustery Madden; he tackles the role like a rampant rugby player, diving in energetically and not all that convincingly as an Irish American. But his charm and emotional sincerity come through and he much enjoyed working with Maggie for the first time: 'What surprised me is Maggie's so generous. You think a talent of that quality would swamp you a bit. She doesn't.' Hoskins was also convinced that she would win her third Oscar: 'I think [the performance] will put another fellow on Maggie's shelf.'

Although Maggie was honoured with best actress awards from BAFTA and the *Evening Standard*, the film was never considered at the Oscars and its distribution was scandalously limited. Why? The matter rankled with Jack Clayton and points up the dangers inherent in the monopoly system of screen ownership. *Judith Hearne* was premiered in New York in December 1987, but did not reach London until exactly one year later. It was held up by a dispute between HandMade and Cannon, the distributors, over debts on another film. The dispute meant that Cannon dropped the film and it therefore found only limited showing in three independent London houses.

And in America, a small company handling the distribution failed to provide copies of the film to the Academy membership voting for the Oscars and subsequently went into receivership. Maggie seemed not to be bothered. As usual, all her concern had been focused on the work itself. Clayton confirms that she is unaware of where the camera is, unlike some of the old Hollywood stars, like Joan Crawford, who knew where every lens and light was stationed, and that she therefore trusts the director to an unusual degree. She never looks at rushes and indeed rarely watches the finished film. She is reluctant to join the publicity circus, as reluctant as the most difficult of donkeys being led to market.

Clayton knew that Maggie's 'difficulty' was not an affectation. 'I've worked with a lot of actors who didn't like doing publicity, but they always did it when asked on behalf of the film. Maggie is the only one who won't. But it's not just that. I've never seen her at a party. I usually have drinks on my sets every Friday and I used to have to really persuade her to come. Once she was there, of course, she enjoyed herself as much as anyone.' Clayton admits that he admires her as much as any of the great actresses he directed: Simone Signoret in *Room at the Top*, Deborah Kerr in *The Innocents* or Anne Bancroft in *The Pumpkin Eater*.

> She's not impossible, she's an angel. She needs very little direction except reining her in sometimes. I just love her. She can be very tetchy in the morning and I do know that she ran the wardrobe ladies on *Judith Hearne* a pretty dance. She is pernickety. But she is always right in the demands she makes, which is the difference between Maggie and people who are just awkward for the sake of it. She is unbelievably professional, and unbelievably instinctive. She is top of my list.

Bed Among the Lentils is a close companion piece to *Judith Hearne*. So close, it nearly overlapped in the shooting. Maggie went straight from one to the other, losing a week's holiday in between because of a slight hold-up on Clayton's film. This meant that she had to learn the new script during the first week of rehearsals. 'She was pretty exhausted,' remembers Alan Bennett, the author and director, 'but that turned out to be no bad thing, really. I didn't have much to do. She did it the first time just as she did straight on the screen. I was bothered that she might slightly camp it up, but she didn't at all. She's got very good taste. There's a bit at the end where she lets her voice break when she's talking about the affair she's had, but she does it without any self-pity. It's just wonderful and I think she did that on the last day of rehearsal, and then she did it on the take, but she fluffed the final line so we had to do it again and I was frightened to tell her, really. But she did it again, and in the end we used the first take anyway and lived with the fluff because the first take was better.'

Maggie's solo was one of six monologues by Bennett, produced by Innes Lloyd, which went out under the generic title of *Talking Heads*. Bennett himself delivered one of them, as a mother-fixated adult bachelor. Other studies in loneliness, compromise and bafflement were entrusted to four superb actresses – Thora Hird, Julie Walters, Stephanie Cole and Patricia Routledge. Each character was poised between black-outs in a purgatorial state of reflective isolation. And the impulse behind each monologue was a desire to make some-thing of recent events, or at least to explain them to anyone who might listen. Bennett's style is too idiomatic, inflected and poetically entranced with the material detail of ordinary life to be totally bleak. But there was something Beckettian about these cries from the genteel suburban wilderness. Life had been tested, ever so quietly, and found to be wanting: Beckett with knitting, place-mats and doilies. In his introduction to the published texts, Bennett wrote: 'Though much of the church stuff in *Bed Among the Lentils* (including Mr Medlicott the verger) comes from my childhood, the disaffection of Susan, the vicar's wife, I can trace to opening a hymn book in the chapel of Giggleswick School and finding in tiny, timid letters on the fly leaf, "Get lost, Jesus." '

Maggie's Susan was suspended between seething resentment and a sort of bursting sexual anger. She glared and vibrated like a terribly cross stick insect. The first line said it all, but there was plenty more to follow: 'Geoffrey's bad enough, but I'm glad I wasn't married to Jesus.' With bold, descriptive strokes, and bolstered by Maggie's perfectly pitched, semi-sarcastic delivery, the sanctimonious life of a village parish and its boyishly good-looking, ambitious young vicar, Geoffrey, was painted by Bennett in the first few paragraphs. In this first of five pungent little ten-minute scenes, Maggie's hair is severe, her make-up non-existent, her head tilted slightly into the camera. She is as spare and scrubbed as her own kitchen table. She lets slip that she spends a lot at the off-licence. She is despondently out of kilter with the smug little world she describes and is animated by expatiating on its deadliness.

Next, we see her in the church, on the steps of a side-chapel, wearing a brown coat and polishing a candlestick. She is describing a lunch she and Geoffrey have given to the visiting bishop: 'Disaster strikes as I'm doling out the tinned peaches.' Escape from the suffocation of serving as a wifely appendage is afforded by the regular trip to a little Indian shop behind the infirmary in Leeds. The owner is called Mr Ramesh and he sells everything. In the third scene, Maggie is at first standing in the kitchen near the Aga and then sitting down and leaning on her elbow, to the left, on a towel rail. Slightly more akimbo, her comic pulse races as she lays into the kind of activity she herself should have pursued as a member of the Women's Institute. Jam-making. And flower-arranging. 'If you think squash is a competitive activity, try flower arrangement.' She anatomises the show of 'forest murmurs' arranged by Mrs Shrubsole on the altar and recounts how she proves its threat to human well-being by kneeling down and falling over, banging her head on the Communion rail. Later that night she drives into Leeds and Mr Ramesh shuts up shop and takes off his clothes.

It is in a state of reasonable intoxication, on an improvised bed among sacks of lentils, and largely thanks to twenty-six-year-old Mr Ramesh, who has wonderful legs and a child bride waiting for him in India, that Susan, on the second Sunday after Trinity, discovers 'what all the fuss is about'. By this fourth scene in the vestry, Geoffrey's loyal parishioners, 'the fan club', are on red alert: the Communion wine has all gone! Susan is now reduced to knocking back the Benylin and driving more regularly into Leeds for physical consolation with Mr Ramesh.

In the final tableau, Susan has signed up with Alcoholics Anonymous, starchily attired in a suit, blouse and respectable brooch. But 'Geoffrey's chum', the deity, can take credit for this, too. Susan and

her plight are brandished as further evidence of Geoffrey's case for
ecclesiastical advancement. From being a fly in the ointment, she has
graduated to being a feather in his cap. Mr Ramesh has gone home to
collect his child bride and is rumoured to be setting up a new shop
in Preston. Although Maggie's eyes are filled with tears, she has all
but frozen over with fierce anger and her imprisonment is complete.

It is this glacial surface, rippling with animosity, tension, pain
and frustration, that makes the acting so profound and moving in
both *Judith Hearne* and *Bed Among the Lentils*. To an extent, these are
self-immolating performances just held in control by sheer technique
and the sustained effort, over the whole arc of a role, to let us see
straight through to the soul of a benighted but resilient human being.
Maggie's full comic armoury serves this purpose, lending sharp edge
and clear, high definition to the tragic expression. The characters
are never indulged and the actress never wallows. There is nothing
random or vague about Judith's or Susan's state of mind. The process
Maggie describes is one of truthful, clinical disintegration and the
residual but wholly rational manner in which the human spirit rallies
to defy the rampant claims of the abyss.

These performances are majestic and beautiful because they celebrate human dignity in conditions of weakness and stress. Maggie
had her own share of weakness and stress. After playing at the Globe
in *Lettice and Lovage* for a year, she went on holiday with Beverley and
Joan Plowright before the planned opening in New York. At Albert
Finney's recommendation, they all went to the British Virgin Islands,
and the fateful accident occurred on 29 November 1988 when Joan
Plowright left early to return to the ailing Olivier in Brighton. Returning on a bicycle from making her farewells, Maggie rounded a bend,
came off the road and the bicycle, fell over a smallish escarpment and
landed on her shoulder in a prickly bush. She had splintered the top
of her shoulder, and the slow and painful recovery entailed physiotherapy, long daily swims at the Goodwood country club, exercises
and a good deal of patience. At the same time, her eyes were causing
serious problems – to deal with them, she underwent surgery and a
course of radiotherapy.

This period of adjustment was also marked by Olivier's final decline
and his death on 11 July 1989. Maggie emerged from her gruesome

regimen of recovery, and from deepest Sussex, to attend his memorial in Westminster Abbey on 20 October. Her eyes were concealed behind great sunglasses and she cut a figure of stylish anonymity in a black-and-white checked coat, a black skirt and a wide-brimmed black hat. She joined a select band of leading actors associated with Olivier's career who processed slowly up the central aisle carrying mementos and symbols on blue velvet cushions, depositing them on the main altar before resuming their places in the nave. Douglas Fairbanks carried Olivier's Order of Merit, followed by Michael Caine with an Oscar, Peter O'Toole with the *Hamlet* film script and Ian McKellen with Coriolanus's laurel wreath. Maggie walked slowly alongside Paul Scofield, he bearing a silver model of the new National Theatre and she a similar emblem representing the Chichester Festival Theatre; 'Not the first time she's carried Chichester on her own, dear,' Jack Tinker whispered in the nave. Dorothy Tutin bore the crown Olivier wore as King Lear on television, Derek Jacobi the one he had worn on stage as Richard III.

Frank Finlay brought up the rear with Edmund Kean's Richard III sword, a gift from John Gielgud to his old sparring partner which more vividly than anything else symbolised the direct succession from Shakespeare, through Garrick and Kean, to Sir Henry Irving and Lord Olivier. Albert Finney read from Ecclesiastes, John Mills from Corinthians, Peggy Ashcroft the last thirty lines of Milton's 'Lycidas' ('At last he rose, and twitched his mantle blue: / Tomorrow to fresh woods, and pastures new'). And Gielgud himself, looking frail after recent illness, shook his fist at death in John Donne's 'Holy Sonnet' and Hamlet's 'We defy augury' speech. Alec Guinness gave a twinkling, dispassionate address in which he described the threat of danger that clung to Olivier, both on stage and off: 'There were times when it was wise to be wary of him.'

Maggie was seated between her Sussex neighbour Scofield and her one-time film partner Michael Caine, who had gained the friendship and respect of Maggie on *California Suite* and of Olivier on the filming of Anthony Shaffer's *Sleuth*. She stood sadly among her peers and colleagues, joining in the singing of 'Jerusalem' at the end.

Maggie and Beverley attended the post-ceremonial thrash hosted by Joan Plowright in the upper foyers of the National Theatre. Many actors and backstage people have no recollection of seeing Maggie at this party. For while old acquaintance was renewed all around her, Maggie sat quietly in a corner talking to a very close and very ill friend of Peter Shaffer. The friend subsequently died, but Shaffer says that he will never forget the tenderness and sympathy Maggie evinced during this painful period of his life.

Maggie's own powers of recovery amazed her sons. Toby said that, when his mother went back to see her doctors after a few months of physiotherapy and swimming for two hours every day, 'Their teeth fell out. They couldn't believe it. Most younger people, if they have that injury, just learn to live with the fact that they can't move their shoulders any more. She can now move her shoulder around better than I can. And I've never fallen off my bike.'

She was determined to go to New York with *Lettice and Lovage*. Maggie could face a new start in better health as Dame Maggie Smith: she was secretly delighted, and relieved, to be remembered by the Prime Minister's office one year after Judi Dench had been similarly honoured. On 25 March 1990 she opened in New York at the Ethel Barrymore, the theatre she had first played in *New Faces* in 1956.

In New York, she took up residence in the Wyndham Hotel on the west side of 58th Street. *Lettice* reduced her to a state of terminal exhaustion and she did not stint on a single performance. The result was that the gradual process of recovery from her other misfortunes – which were further complicated by some root-canal problems with her teeth – was compounded by galloping fatigue. She became more reclusive than Garbo, supping bowls of soup in the hotel suite and only venturing out of town at weekends to visit Joe Mankiewicz and his wife, and occasionally Hume Cronyn and Jessica Tandy.

Frank Rich hailed 'a spellbinding actress' and drew a distinction between this theatre acting 'of a high and endangered order' and the same actress's 'tightly minimalised film work'. The Biograph Cinema in New York honoured Maggie with a festival of her films in April, and she and Margaret Tyzack triumphed at the Tonys on the first Sunday in June. Tyzack was certain that Maggie would win the best actress, but she herself was a surprise winner in the best supporting slot, and remembers verbatim the acceptance speech she made: 'Peter Shaffer's written a wonderful play and I wish I had his eloquence in order to thank him and our marvellous director, Michael Blakemore, our producers, and, above all, Dame Maggie, whose inspired idea it was that I should play this part. I thank them, I thank you, the Tony voters.' Maggie has not a clue as to what she said when she was announced. She had not been in the best of health. She stood up and bumped her leg against the chair, executing an extravagant, laugh-winning double take on the offending obstruction, just as she had when rushing into an Oxford classroom thirty-five years previously.

Two weeks later, on 18 June, Maggie attended another memorial service, this time for Rex Harrison, at New York's Church of the Transfiguration. The glittering congregation included Douglas Fairbanks, Claudette Colbert and Zoë Caldwell. Harrison had been one of the first big stars she had met on her first trip to New York in 1956, and, although she had only worked with him once, she belonged to the same aristocracy of talent. Maggie's address complemented those of Harrison's two sons and of Brendan Gill.

As one who had successfully battled against being pigeonholed, Maggie rightly lamented the fact that we never saw Harrison in Molière or Shakespeare, claiming, surely with justification, that 'he would have been wonderful as Tartuffe, Prospero or King Lear'. Unconsciously, she confirmed the kinship of temperament in those who specialise in the rare, demanding skills of light comedy: 'A man of charm, affection and wit ... but his charm was often not evident offstage [laughter was reported] ... He was not one to suffer fools gladly, whether it was his director or an overbearing leading lady ... [He] gave every line, every thought, every movement, a bit of magic.'

She was happy, too, to renew her friendship with Brian Bedford, who was also in town with his one-man show. Most of Maggie's friends, with the possible exception of Robin Phillips and Gaskill, are in some way frightened of her. Bedford feels 'the eagle eye' on him all the time. He first met her in the late 1950s at a London party and remembers her crouching in a corner talking about her prevailing virginity. He has since, she has told him, often featured in her anxiety dreams, 'sometimes wearing a dress while being terribly well organised and saying "Oh, I've got it all together!" I don't know what the hell it means, but I think it's an aspect of her professional insecurity, that she would think I was not only getting something right but also threatening her own position.'

After she agreed to go out to supper with him – 'it was like pulling teeth' – Bedford said he would pick her up after the performance. He arrived at her stage door and as Maggie came off to her usual tumultuous applause, she swished past him with 'Did you hear them ovating?' 'Yes,' replied Bedford. 'Did it drive you mad?' stabbed Maggie. They fell laughing into the dressing room, with a bottle of champagne and a table booked for 11 p.m. Maggie was ready to relax. More bottles were opened; the stage managers and the doorkeeper were brought in. Bedford recalls suddenly asking someone for the time. It was five to three in the morning: 'We staggered out, Maggie's car's been waiting, and we disappear into another haze of white wine. I woke up late next morning in need of fresh orange juice. I go to a little hole-in-the-wall place on 57th Street and by this time they are serving lunch and I have to sit at the counter. I'm vaguely aware that some woman next to me is ordering black bean soup. This woman grabs me, and it's Maggie.'

She does surprise her friends all the time, but never with any ploys that are calculated or self-conscious. She once met Bedford's brother and his wife in Stratford, Ontario. Bedford was astonished to learn, some months later, that she had unexpectedly followed up the idle exchange of telephone numbers by ringing his sister-in-law in Yorkshire and asking for her Yorkshire pudding recipe. Maggie has never been a great letter-writer. But she does write very occasionally to give her friends fleeting encouragement about herself. After her father died, she wrote to Bedford, who had settled into a new Stratford season in a stable domestic relationship: 'I am glad you are enjoying Stratford. You are quite right. If you are happy on the domestic front, as they say, it makes a huge difference. I was so happy when I was there and that was, now I think about it, the main reason. It was terrific having Bev and the boys with me . . . Pissing down as usual in England. It's so cold even the sheep look wrecked.'

She had started her eventful imbroglio with *Lettice and Lovage* just three weeks after finishing work on *Judith Hearne* and *Bed Among the Lentils*. Both roles had left her feeling raw, she told an interviewer in the *Los Angeles Times*. 'I'd got so absorbed, and it doesn't go away from you.' She took a long time to get the rawness out of her system, and the feeling was one she said she had never known before. She was ready for anything. She told another interviewer: 'I wouldn't want to retire. I am sure there is something to do, even if it be a wardrobe mistress . . . I take things day by day. You can't plan. You hope.'

— 16 —

Tales of Ageing, Innocence
and Experience

A slightly alarming development in Maggie's career was the extent
to which she played old ladies before her time. In the end, of course,
this accidental tactic paid off handsomely and you could never be
quite sure if she'd caught up with herself or not. All the same, she
stuck out against old ladies right at the start, when Leonard Sillman
was unwise enough to foist some doddery dowagers on her during the
pre-Broadway try-out of *New Faces*. But after the blazing directness of
her tragic performances in *The Lonely Passion of Judith Hearne* and *Bed
Among the Lentils*, Maggie aged prematurely as the ninety-two-year-old
Wendy Darling in Steven Spielberg's Hollywood blockbuster *Hook* and
as the seventy-three-year-old but well-tended housekeeper Mrs Mabel
Pettigrew in the BBC television adaptation of Muriel Spark's *Memento
Mori*. By the time she played Lady Bracknell in *The Importance of Being
Earnest* at the Aldwych Theatre in 1993, she seemed, if anything, too
young for the part.

Hook is the ultimate Spielberg film in that it combined, at the time,
the director's twin obsessions: the glorification of childhood innocence in middle-class Middle America and an application of those
homey backyard values to the world of wistful adventure; *E.T.* meets
Indiana Jones. Glutinous and often torridly spectacular, the Spielberg
films nonetheless amounted to a significant strand in American
popular culture at a time when environmental pollution, urban
violence and poverty, and the general moral degradation of political
and public life, demanded some sort of compensating reply from art
and literature. The collapse of family life was especially exploited by
Spielberg. The tragedy of adulthood, as Spielberg was not the first to
observe, is the sacrifice we make of our childishness. In *Hook*, Maggie,

in the relatively peripheral role of Wendy, her large beseeching eyes daubed on her crinkled face like liquid pools of memory, lays down a single rule in her London house: 'No growing up.'

Peter Pan has forgotten his childhood and, in the shape of the impish Robin Williams as Peter Banning, has matured into a forty-year-old New York mergers and acquisitions lawyer, with a wife, two children, and a cellular phone. The family comes to London – by Pan Am, of course – Williams wrestling with his fear of flying, to see Wendy after a ten-year gap. Peter has married her granddaughter in a desire for parenthood. But he takes calls during his daughter's school play (a pleasingly gauche performance of *Peter Pan*) and misses his son's key baseball game (he sends along an office colleague with a video camera). The film opens directly into this contemporary scenario, with no credits and no fanfare. The sense of 'other-worldliness', the familiar Spielberg element of the light on the other side of the window, has an obvious significance in this case. Maggie provides the first shiver when she appears at the top of the stairs, rather like Judith Anderson as Mrs Danvers in *Rebecca*, as Peter and his family arrive: transfigured in the half-light, dignified by age and a walking stick, she intones 'Hello, boy' with the sinister implication of one claiming rights of possession.

When Peter tells her of his busy commercial life in New York, the sadness in Maggie's eyes is briefly enlivened with a twinkling regret: 'So, you've become a pirate.' The tension gathers at a grand dinner in aid of the Great Ormond Street Hospital (the beneficiary of J. M. Barrie's *Peter Pan* royalties) at which Wendy is honoured for her lifetime's work of rehabilitating orphans. One such was Peter, who makes the keynote, moving speech. This tribute is similar to that afforded Coral Browne as the very old Alice Liddell in Gavin Lambert's *Alice in Wonderland* postscript, *Dreamchild*. Wendy has no chance to reply before the fictional underworld rises frighteningly to reassert its claims on reality. As the ranks of fellow orphans stand emotionally in gratitude to toast their maternal saviour, the windows are flung open in a terrifying blast and the howling rage of the invisible Captain Hook disrupts the self-congratulatory equilibrium. Back at the London house, the children have been snatched and a kidnapper's note is stabbed with a knife to the nursery door.

Wendy now tells Peter that he must return to Neverland and make himself remember. The quest is not just to recapture his children, but to recapture his own childhood. The whole premise of Barrie's play has been turned around. Initially, *Peter Pan* is concerned with a child's defiance of the real world of domestic security in favour of imaginary escapism and the excitement of a brush with the forces of pantomime evil; but even there, Wendy becomes for Peter a potential surrogate mother figure.

The fantasy island and the huge dry-docked *Jolly Roger* in the film were the creations of John Napier, who was the RSC designer on all the great Nunn/Caird collaborations, including *Peter Pan* in 1982. His movie Neverland is a cluttered theme park with skateboard circuits, food-pelting competitions, secret caves, a lagoon populated by seductive mermaids, and a general air of a Duke of Edinburgh's Award assault course; Tom Sawyer's island as an outpost Disney World. The tribal hairstyles, costumes and smart rap patois – Williams asks if this is a *Lord of the Flies* pre-school – also relate to another influential Nunn/Napier stage production, *Starlight Express*. This is a way of Spielberg cutting into the youth culture. But it is also a means of taking the make-believe not towards the dreamy, timeless inconsequentiality of Barrie's escapism, but to the tougher, stage-bound pantomime conventions of the play itself. Julia Roberts's seven-inch Tinkerbell, a leggy, gamine sex object in a ball of light, gives Peter a tough old time, knocking him out, urging him on, before briefly emerging in full womanly dimensions to plant a lascivious kiss on his lips. This pricks the sides of Pan's intent – the Happy Thought which Tinkerbell has bullied him to rekindle is one which ironically defeats her and renders her devotion tragic: Peter wanted to be a father.

His paternity suit is further spruced up by the sight of his son hitting a home run in a baseball game supervised by Hook, who has decided to defer the death sentence in favour of assuming the father role himself. 'That's my boy,' Hook sighs contentedly as the child biffs the ball into the stratosphere. And the staginess of these central episodes is certainly reinforced by Dustin Hoffman's magnificent bravura performance as Hook. Variously likened by the critics to Charles II, Terry-Thomas, William F. Buckley Jr, Basil Rathbone, Captain Morgan on the rum bottle, and every King Louis, Hoffman's gap-toothed, laboriously posh-vowelled rollicking swordsman with a gleaming silver mitt is the ultimate cultural revenge on generations of English actors both flaunting their educated manners in Hollywood and adopting phoney American accents on the stage. Bob Hoskins, delightful as Smee, is Hook's sidekick, waxing his master's twirly moustaches with the contents of his own eardrums. The grotesque, Herod-like obscenity of Hook's campaign – Barrie's 1928 rewrite included the chilling line 'A holocaust of children, there is something grand in the idea!' – is missing, perhaps, but Hoffman has never been funnier. He may not actually cry out 'Floreat Etona' but he is certainly blooming eaten when time runs out and a concealed crocodile finally swallows him up.

The ultimate, reinforcing message of the film, and a slightly depressing one, is that families are better off staying together because the alternative really is less desirable. More fun, but inadequate to our emotional needs. Wendy's home in London may be cosy and reassuring but Neverland, threatened by the gruff nastiness of Hook and his crew, is not only dangerous, but depressingly artificial. The film is also concerned about how you live with family and friends, and the need for maintaining those ties. Maggie herself is not promiscuous in friendship, nor does she worry all that much about 'keeping up appearances' – except on stage and screen, of course. And it's been fascinating to see how she adapts those demands to the ageing process. She is fiercely and unshakably loyal to those friends and colleagues – and the closest colleagues become friends, too – who make her professional life tick over as time goes by.

Michael Blakemore believes that she really does organise the world in terms of friends and foes. 'I love her, but she's a killer,' says Patricia Millbourn, the hairdresser Maggie has used regularly since the late 1950s. Millbourn bleached Maggie's hair blonde for her first television role, and went backstage in tears after *What Every Woman Knows* at the Old Vic. 'Oh God, you're 'opeless,' Maggie said. She has collected an Oscar with Maggie and been on holiday several times with her to Barbados. Their routine is to swim miles out to sea, swim back, play Scrabble, read and relax, and enjoy a glass or two of bubbly. But the hair is really what keeps them together: 'She does have one of the most wonderful heads of hair as an actress that I've known. It can be so versatile, short or long, off the face, and she has a great profile. She knows instantly what the hair should be for each part. Other actors study the period, read history books. She gets it in one.'

On the first night of *Mary, Mary*, Millbourn sat in front of the *Times* critic, who said to his companion what a marvellous wig Maggie was wearing. It was her own hair. And every night during *Private Lives*, Maggie would affix her eyelashes and put her hair in Carmen rollers to achieve the Marcel-wave style; similar routines have been undertaken on many plays. Maggie always takes advice from Millbourn before going abroad in a play, or unofficially during film shoots. They usually decide on a wig, in order, as Maggie says, to avoid 'funny 'airdressers in Atlanta'. At which point the wig and make-up specialist, Kenneth Lintott, is invariably contacted. Lintott, who started his career in 'Wig Cremations' (Coral Browne's term for Wig Creations), was for many years associated with the RSC and did not work with Maggie until she needed wigs for the American tour of *Private Lives* in 1974. Lintott was introduced to Maggie by the designer Anthony Powell. He took an instant shine to Maggie having at first been apprehensive. 'I was knocked out by how beautiful she was. She used to wear horrendous make-up in those days and I'd only ever seen her with all that stuff on. It never suited her at all. But she was divine. And everything about her was tiny: tiny hands, tiny feet, tiny head.'

They got on well. And that, Lintott thought, was that. But then he was asked to Stratford, Ontario, by Maggie and Robin Phillips, to work on her wigs and general 'look'. He regards her stay there as 'her cleansing-out period'. Her previous 'look' had been compounded by all the make-up. Now she had some skin removed from her eyelids – she used to call these pouches her 'shopping bags' – and her make-up was simpler, although Lintott wooed her into a false, built-up nose as Titania. There was nothing 'stuck on' for her Rosalind, and the freckles for Ganymede were based on her son's, little Toby's. Lintott worked on the films *Quartet*, *The Missionary* and *Evil Under the Sun*, *The Lonely Passion of Judith Hearne*. On the latter, he says that a lot of the crew found her 'in the role' depressions disconcerting. She was given a blue dress to wear one day. She was not pleased. 'I can't wear this. I look like a sofa in Maples,' she said, and it was changed.

Lintott thinks she has a thing about blue. Similarly, in Canada, she referred to a dress provided by Daphne Dare for *The Way of the World* as 'Daphne's revenge'. That was brown. Watching her in the fitting room, a friend told her that she had a February face. 'So would you in this, dear,' she said. 'I can't do comedy in brown!'

Even closer than Lintott is Anthony Powell, who first worked with Maggie as costume designer on *Travels with My Aunt*. Many colleagues declare that they love Maggie. One or two, including Powell, possibly the film director Jack Clayton and certainly the veterans Joe Mankiewicz and George Cukor, were all palpably in love with her. Powell even landed her the role of Wendy in *Hook*. The late Peggy Ashcroft had been cast originally and one of Spielberg's co-producers rang Powell when he (Powell) was in New York to see Dustin Hoffman for fittings. He said, not knowing that Powell was a friend of Maggie's, that Ashcroft had withdrawn with illness and back trouble, and that he had always loved Maggie's work. How old was she now, he enquired? 'Ooh, I dunno,' bluffed Powell, 'she must be in her early nineties by now... ninety-one – ninety-two...' Maggie was cast. Although she worked only once each with the great film directors Joe Mankiewicz and George Cukor, both men figured as large as anyone in her private life.

Maggie's obsessive attention to detail carries over into the photography sessions. She will not sit for photographs if she does not feel that everything is absolutely right. And if she could choose her snapper in the theatre, it would usually have been Zoë Dominic, who remembers Maggie cancelling a photo-call because she was dissatisfied with her earrings. 'With any other actor,' said Dominic, 'I would have forced the issue. But with Maggie I would never argue.' She finds her a great subject and a great actress, who is primarily physically funny: 'She is the only actress I know who can walk in one direction and be acting with her head in the reverse direction. I've always found that hysterically funny. She has immense physical grace, which is why I like to catch her on the move. On a bad day – and I try not to photograph her if she's unhappy, or not ready – she shrinks, in face and body. But when she feels good, and that's the ideal time to photograph anyone, she positively blossoms. She looks like a wonderful peach. Whether she's conscious of that or not I don't know. I wouldn't dream of discussing it with her. She's tremendously subtle.'

Maggie, says Dominic, commands loyalty, but never demands it. She probably feels a lot closer to some people than she is capable of indicating. During the time of the boys' growing up, she was very close to her brother Alistair and his wife. But she drifted out of touch with the other brother, Ian, when he moved to New York. Letters were exchanged across the Atlantic, but not very many. Ian thinks the difficulty arose because he had not achieved anything as an architect comparable to what she had achieved as an actress. In other words, he was not Robert Venturi or Michael Graves. It is almost certain that such a thought never occurred to Maggie. But Ian, for years, felt slightly hurt by the distance she maintained between them. He tried to ring every day during *Private Lives* but never got through. During the entire New York run of *Lettice and Lovage*, he saw her once. Not until their father died peacefully in April 1991, and Ian came over to stay with Maggie and Beverley in Sussex for ten days, spending more time with her in that week than he had in the previous twenty years, did he realise that his paranoia was only partly justified. He had profoundly misunderstood his own sister. 'I had been very upset all this time, but now I realised I need not have been. What I had been interpreting as a sort of rejection was in fact just this obsessive reclusiveness which had nothing to do with me. I was shocked when she told me that she found it virtually impossible to eat lunch, that to do so would make her physically ill.'

Maggie pops up again halfway through *Hook* in the flashback sequence of Peter's marriage into the family. She is too old to fly herself any more. And she glimmers effectively at the end, taking on the semblance of a softer version of Wendy Hiller, as the family is reunited and Peter Banning throws away his telephone with a sign-off rewrite of Pan's most famous line: 'To live will be an awfully big adventure.' By living, we now mean spending time with the kids. The frank emotional vulgarity of the film is one of its greatest strengths, and the class of Maggie's acting is an important factor. But you could hardly say she was anything like extended. She is far less strenuously made up than she was for Aunt Augusta in *Travels*. She adopts a slight lisp for the older voice, but otherwise understates the whole process of elderly impersonation, leaving her eyes to do the talking.

In *Memento Mori*, although playing an aged character in Muriel Spark's vigorous and black 1959 mystery comedy of senility and gerontology, Maggie did not have to obliterate herself so much. Mabel Pettigrew is old, but she is less old than most of the other characters dotted around London and tucked up in the Maud Long Medical Ward for female last-gaspers. Mabel has a good figure and good legs still, luxuriant and well-cut hair, a well-dressed and confident manner, and the constitution of a horse. To these attributes Maggie adds a deadly appropriate cutting edge and twinkle as the manipulative blackmailer in a world of ancient and festering liaisons thrown into confusion by the telephone calls of an anonymous agent of mortality. She keeps her own red hair, swept up, and presents Mabel as a woman much nearer her own age, a sexy sixty-year-old, conveying only hints of senescence in the pinching of her mouth, the acquisition of reading spectacles and the sour, grim demeanour of the terminally disappointed. Cut out of a former employer's will when she expected to inherit the lot, she is told there is £50 in her name: 'Fifty pounds? I spent about that much on her sodding wreath!'

Renewing her professional liaison with director Jack Clayton (this was Clayton's last film before he died in 1995), Maggie leads a magnificent cast in a buoyant festival of mortality which the BBC had the unexpected wit to broadcast to the nation on Easter Sunday, the Feast of the Resurrection. In fact, Clayton and his fellow screenplay writers, Alan Kelley and Jeanie Sims, perpetrate some crucial adjustments to Spark in the name of narrative coherence, and lead to a point of positive conclusion that is their own. Clayton wished to acknowledge what the retired detective inspector Henry Mortimer (John Wood) calls the 'stubborn gallantry' of this extraordinary collection of confused Edwardian relics. The community of oldsters is rocked by the calls ('Remember you must die') and summons the inspector to investigate. The first, and most spooked, recipient is Dame Lettie Colston (Stephanie Cole) whose brother Godfrey (Michael Hordern) is married to the novelist Charmian (Renée Asherson). Dame Lettie seeks solace and clues from Charmian's old housekeeper, Jean Taylor

(Thora Hird), now serenely domiciled in the Maud Long Medical Ward.

The catalyst of anxiety and exploitation is Mabel, who tightens a tyrannical grip on Godfrey not only because she knows about his past affairs but also because she knows that a glimpse of stocking is, in his case, an effective method of subjugation. Clayton's film relishes the black humour of senility – the precarious motorcar-driving of Godfrey, the tea-time mayhem caused by Cyril Cusack's enraged and doddery old poet, the amnesia, narcolepsy and general decrepitude – but also celebrates the poetry of survival, the flickering spark of sensual appetite. By overcoming the interference of Mabel, and of Godfrey's sponging son, Eric (Peter Eyre), a homosexual and second-rate novelist, and by finally refusing to answer the sinister telephone calls, Charmian and Godfrey are indeed renewed in loving partnership. And the defiance of old age is complete when Jean Taylor comes out of hospital to visit Charmian as a friend, not as a dependent employee.

Memento Mori is a richly macabre, stunningly well acted and beautifully crafted film (the lighting, costumes and overall pace are evidence of a governing technical perfection) in which Maggie's Mabel Pettigrew is a captious, lurid villainess, deeply disturbing because her performance goes deliberately against the film's grain of generosity and humour. She epitomises all those who take advantage of the old and weak, perhaps the most despicable of all sinners. Her vowels are mean and common and her campaign one of undiluted viciousness and spite. Whereas the old poet's granddaughter (Zoë Wanamaker) shows Godfrey her stocking tops in a spirit of pity and understanding, Maggie's Mabel traps the old boy like a fly in her web, leading him downstairs with a look of vindictive and petrifying triumph.

It is one of Maggie's tautest and funniest performances, but it thrives especially because of the company it keeps. At the start of her career, Maggie was a comedienne who surprised people by wandering into the murkier tragic waters of Desdemona, Hilde Wangel and Hedda Gabler. In Canada, she had synthesised her comic and tragic elements in a buoyant and idiosyncratic style of high-tension performance flecked with emotional truth and perception. She had matured into a great all-round actress. And she could now play extravagant boulevard comedy and concentrated tragedy with equal fervour and panache.

One of Ilford's other performing progeny, Ken Campbell, extrapolated in his monodrama *Pigspurt* the two sides of his acting persona in the Jungian sense of conflicting archetypes: the kindly housewife and the spanking squire. Maggie, too, has a soft side and a brutal side, and throughout her career she has brought the one into play against the other. This tension characterises her performances in tragedy as much as in comedy. William Gaskill admired her lightness and effervescence, John Dexter her steely backbone; the clown of Oxford revue and *Black Comedy* endured the fire of the classical disciplines, as well as the emotional upheavals of her own private life, to find the sad heartbeat of Judith Hearne and the plaintive resilience of Alan Bennett's alcoholic vicar's wife. She could blaze in glittering merriment as Congreve's Millamant, in fierce splendour as Cocteau's Jocasta, in a cascade of sparkling eccentricity as Shaffer's Lettice Douffet. John Wood, working with Maggie on *Memento Mori* for the first time since their salad days in the OUDS *Twelfth Night* in an Oxford college garden, said that she had not changed at all. She was recognisably the same talented, funny and attractive girl who broke hearts and burrowed conscientiously into the centre of each role she played. Whatever satisfaction Maggie Smith gains from her acting, the spiritual rewards are transitory and rarely savoured.

The cast and production team of *Memento Mori* gathered at the British Academy of Film and Television Arts in Piccadilly in March 1992 to see the first screening of their work with Jack Clayton and the producer Louis Marks. There were drinks beforehand, drinks afterwards and a high decibel-level of animated conversation, greeting and reunion. The film, another long-cherished project of Jack Clayton, had been an exceptionally happy one for all concerned. Lady Antonia Fraser, the Oxford aristocrat who rode her bicycle while Margaret swept up and made tea in the Playhouse, sat between Michael Hordern and her husband Harold Pinter. Clayton's film-maker best friend Karel Reisz was there, so were most of the actors, and an impressive array of leading film bigwigs and technicians.

By not attending the BAFTA screening, Maggie was not preserving her top-billing status but merely being true to form. She could not even contemplate the torture of sitting through the film and her own performance. It was bad enough having to while away the time between dawn and dusk at home. As the country prepared for a General Election and as various leading entertainers ludicrously followed the American example of declaring their allegiances, Maggie sat back and disparagingly contemplated the whole sorry spectacle. Acting, she knew, though she would never say such a thing, was more interesting and mysterious than the self-deluding vanities of politicians. To describe it, discuss it, or use the reputation won by it to promote a cause or a politician, is, to her, the biggest betrayal of all. Her personal style, however, though critical, has never been censorious. Her amusement at the follies of others was ever a trick to compensate for the inflexible standards and recurring sense of disappointment with which she has been afflicted from the start.

Sure enough, she did eventually get round to Lady Bracknell – the role for which she was long destined, despite the looming memory of Edith Evans in the famous film version – in a production of *The Importance of Being Earnest* at the Aldwych in London in March 1993 produced by Robert Fox, directed by Nicholas Hytner and designed by Bob Crowley. She was no haughty old dowager guarding a bank of magisterial put-downs, but a scheming whirlwind, body askance in dove grey silk, flyaway hat and perfect coiffure, a figure of frightening elegance, not to be tampered with. She combined powerhouse presence with a grim but glorious glamour and a blazing eye for the demands of etiquette. And she found a fresh underbelly to the role in conveying a sense of the arriviste, of someone whose right to assume authority on matters of social decorum is deeply suspect and defensively fanatical; in effect, she played Lady Bracknell as someone of whom she was critically disapproving.

She inspected the young people – Richard E. Grant and Alex Jennings as Algernon and Jack, Susannah Harker and Claire Skinner as Gwendolen and Cecily – like a beaky adjutant on parade, running her eyes up and down the hapless Jack Worthing, her nephew Algernon's co-conspirator in romantic adventurism, with the alacrity of those zip fasteners evoked in her disdain for Archer in *The Beaux' Stratagem*. But this was not one of Maggie's frantic, signalling performances; her body language was as tightly corseted as her physical frame. In Act One, she was a silver shark, bustled with fins. In Act Three, she assumed a more dry-land, squirrely appearance, trading grey for brown, a colour more suited to the country.

And the handbag? That Becher's Brook of a line was no more, for she careered straight through it, staggering slightly on the sofa at the accumulation of news concerning Jack's foundling status. The portrayal was fired by the assault on her dignity and the energy with which she defended herself. In ticking off her list of maternal requirements, she was outfoxed by unwanted information ('the line is immaterial' could have killed at five paces), gathering laughs as she went before exploding at the climactic prospect of her daughter marrying into a cloakroom and forming an alliance with a parcel. 'Parcel' was indeed a special delivery, hissed venomously through splayed lips.

Cecily's 'profeel' was applauded in an affected giveaway. For the carapace would crumble, revealing both girlishness and a curious vulnerability beneath, something entirely original in this perform-ance of the role. When the General's true name was discovered in the military records, this final deflation was answered with a simple, almost weak, admission that she knew what it was all along. This was the most dangerous, and the most delicate, moment in a production that otherwise divided the critics. The amazing designs comprised a louche red and green clubland flat dominated by a stage-high portrait of Algernon; a monumental topiary peacock in the country garden shadowing a tilted model of the Georgian house and a view of five counties; and a creamy morning room, launched on its side like a skew-whiff Heartbreak House. With Maggie on stage, all this witty, emphatic angularity seemed superfluous; at least, this was what she thought. Would she take this production to Broadway? she was asked. She wouldn't take it to Woking, she replied.

Maggie's movies around this time were startlingly contrasted, and laid down a pattern for the ensuing two decades. A new look at a children's classic, Frances Hodgson Burnett's *The Secret Garden*, directed by Agnieszka Holland, heads what I would call a category of high-quality historical movies, all quite modestly conceived and budgeted. A BBC television film of Tennessee Williams's *Suddenly, Last Summer*, the first

time Maggie played an American heroine, presaged a trio of remarkable stage performances in the plays of Edward Albee, and also a run
of notable, human-scale UK independent movies starting with *Ladies
in Lavender* in 2004 right up to the filmed version of another blistering
theatrical performance in the title role of Alan Bennett's *The Lady in
the Van* in 2015. Finally, a pair of flat-out funny movies in Hollywood
with Whoopi Goldberg, *Sister Act* and *Sister Act 2: Back in the Habit*,
prefaced just three more Hollywood comedies before Harry Potter took
over the world, with Maggie on board, becoming the biggest grossing
movie franchise of all time, the eight films netting a global gross box
office of US$7.7 billion.

Taking these three loosely defined categories in reverse order, *Sister
Act* turned out much better than Maggie had feared; she was none
too confident about a hit-and-run comedy in the gambling dens of
Nevada, where Whoopi Goldberg as a nightclub singer called Doloris
Van Cartier has witnessed her married lover wipe out a hoodlum
before taking refuge, and the veil, in a San Francisco convent – where
Maggie is the Mother Superior – with the guarantee of police protection so she can help pin down the lover (Harvey Keitel) and his gang.
Once in the nun's habit, Whoopi transforms the holy choir into a
hot-gospelling big attraction in the local community, to the initial
horror of Maggie's top nun ('I am a relic, and I have misplaced my
tambourine,' she irately protests in one of several beautifully played
head-on collisions). But Maggie is won round by the impact the
choir makes in the parish community, where the Irish Monsignor
was played by her old friend from *Night and Day*, Joseph Maher. The
crooks eventually capture Doloris, and Maggie leads the salvation
assault in the Reno casino, bleakly encouraging her squadron of
singing nuns to 'try and blend in' as they dash among the blinking
fruit machines.

In the slightly less enjoyable sequel, Doloris, back in the habit,
takes on the lower-risk task of reforming a bad-attitude class in a
run-down neighbourhood through her music. In both films, playing
opposite Whoopi's brazen, no-holds-barred celebratory effusiveness,
Maggie could exercise the full range of her understated English sense
of propriety breaking out in expressions of wincing distaste and sour
disapproval. But in Richard Eyre's BBC film of *Suddenly, Last Summer*

she rises magnificently to the renewed task of following one of the two great iconic performers her own career tracks and challenges, Katharine Hepburn (the other is Edith Evans), whose over-the-top Mrs Venable in Gore Vidal's screenplay of 1959 (directed by Maggie's adored Joseph Mankiewicz) was a juddering, almost scary, compilation of roars and misgivings. In contrast, Maggie is stern, bewitching but recognisably human as a still beautiful bereaved mother in her pearls and elegant mauve silks. And, as with Lady Bracknell, this portrait is primarily one of self-justifying defensiveness, the source of its tragic power.

Eyre's film faithfully adheres to the play's one-act structure and restricts the horror of what befell Mrs Venable's poet son Sebastian – eaten alive by young boys – to the lines, and to the brilliant performance of Natasha Richardson (so tragically killed in a skiing accident in 2009) as the infatuated cousin who procured for him. The writing, poised on the disputable border of genuine poetry and gothic self-parody, had assumed a new metaphorical resonance in the wake of the first AIDS-blighted age. Eyre and the designer Bob Crowley created a stifling botanical environment in those same Shepperton Studios where Hepburn, Montgomery Clift and Elizabeth Taylor made their freer, more hysterical, version. So stifling was the atmosphere, says the producer Simon Curtis, that when Eyre had to re-shoot an entire scene due to an error of over-recording on the tape, he was dreading Maggie's response to his request to start over. Her response, however, was characteristic: 'Good. I can do it better.'

The thankless Clift role of the prompting doctor who needs money for his research is very well taken by Rob Lowe. The tension finally erupts as Maggie rises in rage and lays about her with a stick, shouting at Lowe that he should cut the hideous story out of the sick girl's brain with nothing less than a full frontal lobotomy. Maggie instinctively finds the exact tone of Williams's idiosyncratic music, revelling in the careful structure of the sentences just as she revelled in the antithetic shape and coloration of Oscar Wilde's prose and would do soon in the arch exactitude of Edward Albee's rancorous and meticulously phrased high style. She brought a world of sighs and Southern gentility to bear on the life she knew, and the life as she chose to remember it: 'I was actually the only one in his life.

We were a famous couple. Sebastian and Violet are at the Ritz in Venice ... Sebastian and Violet have taken a house for the season at Biarritz ... We constructed our days. We would carve out each day of our lives like a piece of sculpture.'

17

Secrets and Lies in Yorkshire and Italy

Maggie's status in her industry was confirmed with two major honours in the early 1990s, a fellowship from the British Film Institute and a lifetime achievement award from BAFTA. Exhausted by the filming of *Suddenly, Last Summer* in a swamp-hot studio, she was unable to attend the first ceremony. But at the BAFTA shindig, a couple of weeks after she had opened in *The Importance of Being Earnest*, she acknowledged her ovation with words – written by Beverley – that touched on a recently reactivated public debate on sex and violence in the movies: 'If it's possible to be in films without taking your clothes off or killing people with machine-guns, I seem to have managed to do it.'

There was quite a lot of pent-up sex and emotional violence at least in *The Secret Garden* and its companion piece, *Washington Square*, both directed by Agnieszka Holland, both remakes of 1949 movie classics and each based on a canonical work of literature – the first a 1911 children's book by Frances Hodgson Burnett, the second a novella by Henry James that had been converted by Ruth and Augustus Goetz into a Broadway hit drama called *The Heiress*. Maggie's roles were major supporting, rather than leads: a beastly Yorkshire housekeeper, Mrs Medlock, in *The Secret Garden*; and a spinsterish, desiccated aunt, Lavinia Penniman, in *Washington Square* ('I feel one of my headaches coming on').

The Secret Garden is a tale of awakening and recovery in a dour and emotionally dilapidated big house, Misselthwaite Manor, on the Yorkshire moors – the chief location was Allerton Park, near Harrogate, a fine example of the nineteenth-century gothic revival stately home – where a sickly young crippled boy, Colin, is shut away in a darkened bedroom by his grieving, widowed father, Lord Craven, and one particular garden on the estate shut up since his mother died ten years ago. This garden is studded with overgrown bracken, tangled vegetation and frozen statuary, but there is a leaf-strewn swing, a few green shoots and a lone visiting robin. The catalyst for renewal is the return to the house of Colin's ten-year-old cousin, Mary Lennox, who has been orphaned after an earthquake in India and collected at the docks off the ship by Maggie's Mrs Medlock, who wastes no time in reminding Mary that her mother was a real beauty, adding, half under her breath, that she obviously didn't hand much of that commodity down to her daughter.

The MGM movie starred Margaret O'Brien as Mary and Gladys Cooper as a fearsomely tyrannical Mrs Medlock, and memorably followed the example of *The Wizard of Oz* in going from black-and-white (or sepia) into colour, the garden of course being the corresponding symbol of blooming efflorescence, though it's infinitely more beautifully shot in Holland's later version. And whereas Gladys Cooper is grotesquely Grand Guignol, Maggie makes Mrs Medlock's nastiness more explicable than despicable in the character's notion of doing what she feels to be right in terms of propriety and discipline. Maggie gives her performance a good dose of Jean Brodie and her own mother, and yet she is still decidedly feminine, still lustrous, her hair up, her blue eyes occasionally sparkling, her brutal shenanigans – as when she dons a mask to 'treat' Colin's palsied legs, or sticks him in an iced bath to encourage his blood to flow ('You could be clotting') – borderline hilarious.

The healing process, physical and spiritual, has nothing to do with medicine, Burnett's story thus reflecting the growth in interest at the time in Christian Science, which eschews all treatments. Colin's condition is 'all in the mind', and made worse by Mrs Medlock's pandering to it in the form of cossetting overreaction, while John Lynch's glowering, sorry-for-himself long-haired nobleman is redeemed through Mary's agency of love, good works and the summoning of an angelic choir on the soundtrack singing a ghastly but effective song by Linda Ronstadt. Maggie's Mrs Medlock, having broken down inconsolably in tears at Colin's recovery and the dissolution of her repressive purpose in life, offers to resign on the spot. But she softens, and is last seen, radiant and smiling, at a window overlooking the garden, the green shoots of her own incipient late spring thaw and redemption pushing up.

Ten-year-old Kate Maberly as Mary Lennox made an auspicious début before developing a successful career, playing her scenes with adults and children alike with exceptional poise and authority. It helps that Maggie Smith is never soft or gloopy playing with children (not that she could be, really, as Mrs Medlock), but she allows young Kate to give as good as she gets because that is precisely her own modus operandi.

Maggie's second collaboration with Holland, *Washington Square*, has many qualities of the first – generous narrative detail, superb cinematography and some fine performances, notably from Jennifer Jason Leigh as the 'ugly duckling' heiress, Catherine Sloper, and Ben Chaplin as her calculating (is he genuine or just gold-digging?) suitor, Morris Townsend, roles taken in the superb William Wyler 1949 black-and-white movie (retaining the title of the play it was adapted from and follows closely, *The Heiress*) by the excessively glamorous Olivia de Havilland and the watery-eyed golden boy, Montgomery Clift. Miriam Hopkins (an arch enemy of Bette Davis who had appeared in the film of *Design for Living* with Gary Cooper and Fredric March) was in the Maggie role of the aunt, and Ralph Richardson, giving one of his greatest screen performances, was Catherine's autocratic father, Dr Sloper; that role was now somewhat curiously taken by Albert Finney, one of Maggie's oldest friends and favourite co-stars from her earliest days at the National Theatre.

Finney is fine, but doesn't really seem austere and frightening enough in the role, his outbursts sounding like those of someone in a bad temper after too good a lunch. The dislocation between the modernity of the acting and the period accuracy of the settings is probably deliberate, and there's a touching modern anxiety about Maggie's auntie-like advice to Jason Leigh's susceptible Catherine to be warm, but pure, amorous but chaste, in her response to Townsend's overtures, which are launched by Ben Chaplin on a crest of bovine lust; the ambiguity surrounding his intentions is artfully maintained almost to the very end, and it's interesting that Maggie has a similar unravelling to that at the end of *The Secret Garden*, as she tries her best to save the situation. But Catherine has been hurt once too often, and hurt too badly, and Jason Leigh settles tragically into a life of determined, barren spinsterhood, though without the great exit line in the stage play (and first film), 'Yes, I can be very cruel. I have been taught by masters.'

In between these two page-to-screen classics, Maggie appeared as a furious Duchess of York in an outrageous, highly enjoyable 1930s movie version of Shakespeare's *Richard III* starring Ian McKellen (whom she had not worked with since the NT *Much Ado About Nothing* in which he played Claudio) and directed by the *Missionary* director, Richard Loncraine, very much based on, but opened out from, the performance directed at the National (and on a subsequent world tour) by Richard Eyre in 1990. McKellen edited and published his own screenplay of the film, a brilliant and scholarly text full of perceptive and juicy insights and annotations. On screen, the play – oddly decked out with Third Reich insignia while checking into such ultra-British locations as St Pancras Station, the Brighton Pavilion and the Senate House of the University of London – rushes by in just 100 minutes, heavily cut, with McKellen as a jack-booted, wheedling, cigarette-smoking fascist dictator dashing about from one microphone to another, screeching for a horse, a horse, his kingdom for a horse when his jeep jams in the mud on the battlefield – which is an encampment at Battersea Power Station – and falling backwards off the top of that evocative industrial ruin into the blazing inferno beneath, grimly accompanied by Al Jolson warbling on the soundtrack that he is sitting on top of the world, just rolling along, just singing a song.

Maggie's role of the Duchess of York was craftily combined with that of Richard's mother, the old Queen Margaret, and she grabbed a maternal curse or two from the famous incantatory trio that was now missing. This would be the first of four films she would make with Kristin Scott Thomas – a striking, beautiful, drug-addled Queen Anne who was only too sure to be sick 'and like to die' after a few weeks in the sack with the maniac king – and a reunion with Jim Carter (Carson the butler in *Downton Abbey*) from *A Private Function*. A great cast also included Jim Broadbent as Buckingham, Annette Bening as Queen Elizabeth, John Wood as the old King Edward IV, Nigel Hawthorne as Clarence (his throat cut in a bathtub, not drowned in a butt of malmsey in the Tower) and Robert Downey Jr conflating four minor characters into the less minor one of Rivers, and coming to a gruesome demise from a spike thrust through the underside of a mattress (and his guts) while *in flagrante delicto*.

Beverley died in March 1998, following treatment for a series of aneurysms. This was a terrible blow. Maggie lost not only her husband, but her rock, her protector, her best friend. 'Everybody says it gets better,' she told me a few years later, 'but I don't think it does. It gets different.' Her eyes filled with tears and reddened. 'Jane Birkin's mother, Judy Campbell, once said an extraordinary thing to me when her husband died; that it was strange feeling you were not number one with anybody. I have many good friends. But I tend to keep to myself anyway. It's odd, doing things and having no one to share them with.'

Maggie simply set to and carried on working as normal. Her elder son, Chris Larkin, reckons the double blow of losing the two men who meant most to her within three years (Robert had died in November 1995) hit her pretty hard, though she hadn't seen much of Robert, or had anything to do with him, really, until towards the end of his life. She now had to fly solo. She has managed, to this day, with the close-knit support network of her agent, Paul Lyon-Maris (who succeeded Duncan Heath); her secretary, Janet Macklam; her hairdresser, Patricia Millbourn (known as 'Passion Flower'); and her accountant, Helen, who has lately talked her into buying a new Mercedes even though she still pines for the old one, gathering moss, in a garage at home. And the impetus is always the work, the next job. It was some comfort to her, too, that the first film she worked on after losing Beverley was *Tea with Mussolini* in which she co-starred with her friends Judi Dench and Joan Plowright, under the direction of Franco Zeffirelli, who had directed the joyous *Much Ado About Nothing*.

Within this cluster of period costume drama movies, *Tea with Mussolini* is the first of a European trilogy – the others are *The Last September* and *My House in Umbria* – set in Italy and Ireland, all of some literary pedigree (with screenplays by John Mortimer, John Banville and Hugh Whitemore), all enacted against a backdrop of political upheaval and personal tragedy. It is Maggie, as Lady Hester Random, widow of the former British ambassador to Italy, who really does take tea with Mussolini (seizing the teapot she enquires of the dictator,

'Shall I be mother?') in Rome, where she has gone, on behalf of her group of lady ex-pats, the Scorpioni, living in Florence, to protest about his Blackshirts rioting on the streets and disrupting their café afternoons. But, like Jean Brodie, Lady Hester is a big fan of Mussolini, and is convinced she can talk him round. Instead, she and her Florentine friends face disillusion, even though they stay put throughout the subsequent war, right up to their liberation by the allied forces among the Tuscan towers of San Gimignano. One of those liberating Scots officers was played by Chris Larkin (just slightly more than that cough and a spit in his first film appearance as a swaddled baby in *Hot Millions*); another was given very short shrift when encouraging Lady Hester to move right along: 'Do be quiet, Major, whoever you are...' By now, the plot has diverged into a thriller of sorts as the grown-up boy (a stand-in for Zeffirelli himself, whose autobiography is the source of Mortimer's screenplay) is caught up in a side-story of embezzlement, romance and betrayal with one of the other Scorpioni, a wealthy American socialite, Elsa, played by the singer Cher.

The Zeffirelli surrogate, Luca Innocente, the illegitimate son of an Italian businessman and his deceased dressmaker mother, has been virtually adopted by another of the Scorpioni, Joan Plowright's Mary Wallace, while another of the group, Judi Dench's Arabella, a dabbling painter and a singer, tells the young lad he should live as an artist and share in the divine plan. The boy is sent away by his father to learn German in Austria, while the storm clouds gather, Italy joins the war against Britain and France, and Lady Hester and Arabella find themselves imprisoned in San Gimignano, where Maggie sets about teaching the guards how to say 'good night'. The Jews are proscribed, the other ladies – including a surprisingly subdued Lily Tomlin's lesbian archaeologist – are moved to a hotel, thanks to Elsa's money. This causes a moment of seismic shock to Maggie's Lady Hester, as she thought that old Benito himself was footing the bill: 'We're creatures from two different worlds,' she exclaims to Elsa, 'and we both trusted men who turned out to be bastards.'

Elsa's been shafted, literally and metaphorically, by her lawyer lover, while the trust fund she started for Luca (she was fond of his mother) has found its way into the pockets of the Italian resistance because of his jealousy – he's fallen in love with his benefactor – and Elsa's art collection has been commandeered as a putative pawn in her escape plan to Switzerland which, again, Luca knows about. The film is now piling up far too much story for a structure built on anecdote and reminiscence; then again, you could say that Zeffirelli is telling some sort of truth about himself and detonating the film's first half into a confusion of destiny and infraction in the second. Still, moment by moment, it's highly entertaining, especially with that curious *galère* of leading ladies (three Brit dames, two American oddballs). It also marked, poignantly, the last screen appearance of Judi Dench's late husband, Michael Williams, as the British consul.

That screenplay alliance between Zeffirelli and Mortimer was immediately trumped by John Banville adapting a beautiful 1929 novel by Elizabeth Bowen, *The Last September*, about the last days of the Anglo-Irish gentry, the Protestant Ascendancy, in County Cork in 1920. This was a tense time, between the Easter Rising and the civil war, and Maggie presided over the proceedings in a large country house, Danielstown, as the scheming Lady Myra Naylor, impervious to change and to the tensions, trimming her roses in a wide-brimmed hat and a high-class accent, as if life were going to continue as one long garden fête through an unending summer. Hers is in some ways a glittering Restoration comedy performance, busying herself with the marital arrangements or prospects of anyone who crosses her bows, family or friends; in others, a satirical last hurrah for one kind of socialite dowager before she regressed historically into the source material, the unflinching Edwardian corsetry of Lady Violet in *Downton Abbey*.

Bowen's novel, her second and her own personal favourite, was in part a memory of her own childhood in Cork, and the mansion of Lord and Lady Naylor (Michael Gambon is the bluffly accommodating milord) a direct equivalent of her family home, Bowen's Court, in the north-east of the county. Banville's adaptation catches exactly that restlessness in the area, as trouble – and the Troubles – brew between the British soldiers, known as the Black and Tans, who are house guests of the Naylors at social functions, joining their visiting friends the Montmorencys (played by the classically handsome Lambert Wilson – formerly in love with Lois's mother – and the deliciously flaky Jane Birkin) and the local revolutionaries who will one day set fire to the large properties, symbols of oppression.

This sense of life going on, but hanging by a thread, is beauti-fully suggested in what was, incredibly, theatre director Deborah Warner's début movie (and she hasn't made another one since). She and Banville made one major character innovation, supplying the heroine, Lois Farquar (Lady Hester's orphaned niece, tremulously played by a doe-eyed Keeley Hawes), with a romantic alternative to her dalliance with a British subaltern from Surrey, Gerald Lesworth (David Tennant); this new character, Peter Connolly, a smouldering, resentful terrorist in the performance of Gary Lydon, lurks in a dilapidated mill on the Danielstown estate when he's not causing havoc elsewhere, luring Lois to a dangerous sexual initiation and creating a conflict in her political and carnal allegiances.

When the film, produced by Neil Jordan and others, came out, Hermione Lee, the eminent scholar and Elizabeth Bowen biographer, challenged some of the decisions made by Banville and Warner, including this creation of the IRA gunman named Connolly. 'He's what's out there in the landscape,' said Warner (in a piece Lee wrote for the *Guardian*), 'you've got to make it more tangible if you're making a film; you've got to make passion visible.' Banville, terrified that the film might have come across (heaven forbid!) as a Merchant Ivory costume drama, wanted the violence, deeply buried in the novel, to be hardened up. The ending departs radically from Bowen, too: the Naylors remain in the house, which doesn't burn. Warner and Banville told Lee that the burning of the house might have been a cinematic cliché, like the conflagration of Manderley at the end of Daphne du Maurier's *Rebecca*. 'As it is,' said Warner, 'the film leaves us with the right level of ambivalence. We feel compassion for these people and we also see their absurdity and their displacement by a more democratic future. They are victims of history; there's no revolu-tion without casualties.'

Warner rehearsed for a week, before filming started, in an old house in County Meath, to reinforce this tribal bonding, and the four main female actors in particular – Maggie, Keeley Hawes, Jane Birkin and Fiona Shaw (who, with Gambon and Maggie, was a future cast member of the Harry Potter series) – struck up a good understanding and interplay. There was even talk, much later on, that the director might one day produce a *Waiting for Godot* with Fiona and Maggie as the tramps, an idea that, had it come to anything, might have displeased the notoriously pernickety Beckett Estate almost as much as Warner's collaboration with Shaw in the Beckett monologue of *Footfalls*, which ignored all the stage directions and liberated the actress from a minimal pedestrian plank to an exploratory ambulation around the entire interior of the theatre. Still, Maggie Smith in Beckett might have spiced up the West End box office returns for a few months.

A few years later, and again with Richard Loncraine as director, Maggie made *My House in Umbria* as an HBO made-for-television movie, though it has the scale and 'feel' of a proper cinematic adventure, and takes place in the aftermath of a terrorist bomb on the railway track between the Italian countryside and Milan in the summer of 1987. Although a bomb on a train between Florence and Rome had killed 16 people (and wounded 200) in 1984, the Irish novelist William Trevor always insisted that his story was not triggered by that event, or any other ('It's all from the head, I'm afraid,' he told the *New York Times*). This was Maggie's second brush with one of her favourite writers (the first was on the televised version of his short story, 'Mrs Silly'), who had published this novella together with another, *Reading Turgenev*, under the generic title of *Two Lives* in 1991. Maggie's role, that of Emily Delahunty, a romance novelist with a history of romantic misfortune despite being a woman of the world ('I will not deny that men have offered me gifts, probably all of which I have accepted'), was one of the best of her career: we come to learn that Emily was the unloved child of travelling entertainers who had no use for a child, and a retired prostitute and madam complete with the alcoholic tendencies that had marked Judith Hearne and Susan in *Bed Among the Lentils*.

Emily was on the fateful train on a shopping expedition and, in an act of instinctive, redemptive charity, and after a short stay in hospital, she invites a few of her surviving fellow-travellers back to her idyllic villa for a period of recuperation. She is the controlling narrator of the story, confessing that 'I was the only one not to have lost a loved one, having had no one to lose'. She and her attentive, kind-hearted Irish gardener/chauffeur (a lovely, understated performance by Timothy Spall, who is keen on relaying bits of the house's architectural history to the visitors) gradually embrace other lifestyles and stories within their own. The three new residents are Werner, a young German photographer who, it transpires, may have been involved in planning the attack; a retired British army veteran and widower, the General (touchingly played by the comedian Ronnie Barker, who had been at the Oxford Playhouse with Maggie in the mid-1950s, and at architectural college with her brothers), who has lost his daughter in the explosion; and a young American girl, Aimee, who has lost both parents and is now traumatised and mute. Emily's writer's block – she has decided to make her visitors' lives the subject of her writing – has resulted in a second explosion, that of her own walled-up interior life and, in the retelling of it, she says, she sort of dreams what happened.

This heart-breaking performance deservedly won Maggie an Emmy in the American television awards, although you can't help feeling that Hugh Whitemore's otherwise exemplary adaptation collapses in a soft belly-flop of a climax as the credits roll on a light-footed, white-garbed Maggie cavorting radiantly in her garden with her adoptive daughter and the genial old gardener, who's also decided to stay on.

18

Onstage with Albee, Bennett and Hare

Stage appearances over the past twenty years since *The Importance of Being Earnest* have become scarcer, perhaps more precious, as the two major franchises of the Harry Potter films (2001–11) and *Downton Abbey* (since 2010, sixth and final series in the can for release in the autumn of 2015) invaded Maggie's life and saved her from the retirement home. Still, the catalogue of theatre work in this period contains some of her most enthralling performances: three definitive, high-wire interpretations of *Who's Afraid of Virginia Woolf?* author Edward Albee (having played Virginia Woolf herself on the stage, Maggie presumably felt no urge to answer the question by playing Martha); a reunion with Alan Bennett not only on the 1996 stage version of *Bed Among the Lentils* but also as filthy old Miss Shepherd in *The Lady in the Van* in 1999; and then, three years later, her first stage appearance with Judi Dench since their Old Vic days in David Hare's *Breath of Life* at the Theatre Royal, Haymarket, jewel of the West End.

All three of her Albee performances have been directed in London by Anthony Page, a notable artistic director of the Royal Court in the mid-1960s who embarked on a series of American drama productions (Tennessee Williams and Eugene O'Neill as well as Albee) with the British première of Albee's *Three Tall Women* in November 1994. Albee's reputation and critical standing had been in decline on both sides of the Atlantic until the first New York production of this play at the off-Broadway Promenade Theatre (where I saw it in July 1994), though this had never dented his own confidence or self-esteem.

Maggie's participation in his 'come-back' play cannot be underestimated as part of a great upswing in his critical fortunes. As someone who had a difficult relationship with her own mother, she was surely responsive to Albee's lacerating portrait of his own adoptive mother in *Three Tall Women* – a senile, wealthy bigot who threw him out when he was eighteen and parlays, in the play at least, a healthy youthful interest in erections of the male member into a pronounced reluctance and distaste for fellating her own husband. Maggie's quite a stickler for propriety on the stage, but she wouldn't have blanched too much at these outpourings after some of the confessional demands already made on her by Alan Bennett. Bennett had a curious, but not unusual, relationship with his own 'Mam', of course, conjuring her spirit, with a lovely affection only slightly tainted by sarcasm, in several of his later plays, not least *The Lady in the Van*, where, having turned foul-mouthed and incontinent in a nursing home, she becomes a parallel, complementary object of his disaffection and guilt while dealing with the long-term tramp-like squatter parked in the van in his own front garden.

The social mix in Albee and Bennett are worlds apart. Albee's privileged advantages didn't make his life any easier, though; as in Bennett's conflicted background of respectable lower-middle-class expectations and Oxford opportunities for a clever boy, Albee's rebellion against what was foisted on him as a child of luxury was the making of him as a writer. The gay outsiderism, more marked in Albee than in Bennett, was an extra ingredient: he was armed for conflict on two fronts. At the end of his adoptive mother's life, Albee discovered that his natural father had abandoned his natural mother; he was born Edward Harvey and adopted, in upstate New York, by a childless couple, Reed and Frances Albee (this all-around barrenness – the lack of a child, the missing child, the dead child – is a tragic theme in his plays). Reed owned a chain of vaudeville theatres, while Frances (one foot taller and twenty-three years younger than her husband) was a well-heeled product of the White Anglo-Saxon Protestant hegemony – the WASP factory, racist and snobbish. They lived in the suburb of Larchmont, twenty miles from New York, where little Ed enjoyed (or endured) a pampered childhood of electric train sets, private schools, nannies and tennis lessons with national hero and Grand Slam legend Donald Budge. *Three Tall Women* is a moving and funny resolution of his own domestic statelessness, and a scathing character study – as a dramatic diptych – of Frances. In the first act she's in bed, attended by a lawyer and a nurse. In the second, those two have been translated into younger versions of herself in middle age and youth.

There's a way in which you can view Albee as the Big Daddy of the modern dysfunctional family play – what other plays are there, you often feel these days? – and this disfigurement of the American Dream dates from Eugene O'Neill, running right through Arthur Miller and Albee to Sam Shepard. Sounds grim, but from the minute he saw the play in New York, Anthony Page thought of it as a Restoration comedy about death. 'A good cry lets it all out,' says the nurse. 'And what does a bad one do?' asks the old lady with a reflex lash of the tongue. As Paul Taylor said of Maggie's performance in his *Independent* review, this was a stunning portrayal of querulous, hapless senility refusing to go gentle into that good night: 'Making expert use of those pained, lightly poached eyes, a chin that can rebuff from any angle, and a voice that can swoop from an imperious neigh to a hard-bitten, undeceived bass, she miraculously never turns the role into a caricature.' She also, noted Taylor, brilliantly hinted at the younger selves who appear in person after the interval, 'like layers in a shifting palimpsest'.

The characters in the play are simply named A, B and C (yes, that is slightly off-putting). B and C were Frances de la Tour and Anastasia Hille and, a year later, in the same play, and at the same theatre, Maggie returned with Sara Kestelman and Samantha Bond (John Ireland was still the mute boy) in support. It was, says Anthony Page, a new production:

> Maggie really felt she hadn't got to the bottom of it. She wanted to change a few things, including her position on the stage in the second half. She felt that sitting on the right of the stage didn't help her, I don't know why. So we put the chair on the left, and she said yes, that made things a lot easier. She was still working on the part right through to the end of the second run.

The casting of Kestelman and Bond as, respectively, the caustically cynical mid-lifer and the hopeful, idealistic twenty-six-year-old who still sees herself as an ingénue, made the work feel, opined Paul Taylor, 'both tighter and more humanely balanced than it did previously'. And the *Daily Mail*'s Jack Tinker, who had previously thought of the

play as a two-act trick for a one-woman bravura turn, now hailed 'a
searing search into the process of ageing . . . an achingly splendid
account of how a long life and all its attendant trials and chances
can shipwreck even the strongest of wills'.

Looking back on both New York and London productions, it's
the audacious formal structure as well as the actual performance I
remember as much as anything. The nonagenarian termagant of the
first act lies dead (after a stroke) on her bed in the second while her
divided selves recapitulate, at different stages of her life, in reverse conditions of resignation, fancy and hope. This is something worked out,
in a different style, by Stephen Sondheim in his equally ambitious,
part autobiographical 1981 musical, *Merrily We Roll Along*, and, for
me, the piece exudes a similar poignancy, stripped of its sentiment, to
that of Thornton Wilder's photo-shutter study of a small community
in *Our Town*. But whereas both those seminal American works started
outwards then worked inwards to the human story, Albee goes the
other way around. This is a study of extreme old age, more worldly
than in Beckett, and how we (or she) got there. With a light, dramatic
irony, said Michael Billington, Albee shows how the blind optimism
of youth gives way to the shrugging resignation of old age. Although
in a way it was a revenge play, Albee always denied this. He realised
that he and his adoptive mother had made each other very unhappy
over the years but he tried, and I think succeeded, to write an objective
play about a fictional character 'who resembled, in every way, and in
every event, someone I had known very, very well'.

In a *Times* interview with Matt Wolf, Page was asked about working
with Maggie on this play, and on their subsequent Albee collaboration
on a 1997 Theatre Royal, Haymarket, revival of *A Delicate Balance*, in
which she played Claire, an alcoholic, don't-give-a-damn live-in sister
of Agnes, played by Eileen Atkins, in a Connecticut country house:
'She's like a blowtorch; her mind, in trying to get to the reality of something, how to give it comic edge and energy. She's just got an amazing
theatrical imagination. I don't think she's interested in mannerism
at all. She wants to be totally convincing.' This is interesting, as if
the director is getting his defence in first, perhaps because of what
Frank Rich had said about Maggie: that, while her screen career was
one of paring down to the truth and the bone, the acting on stage

retained its exterior, almost baroque, efflorescence, its gestural beauty and extravagance. There's something in this: Maggie's old-fashioned enough to still believe you have to 'give' something to the audience on stage that you don't on film. It's a bigger, more exposing, medium in that respect, and I think she's right.

A Delicate Balance is a sort of long night's journey into day of recrimination, booze, terror and vindictive occupation and displacement. A couple of neighbours seek sanctuary and stake out the room of Agnes's thrice-married daughter, Julia. The latter returns home, all guns blazing, after a fourth relationship débâcle, to reclaim her territory. The play was critically overshadowed on Broadway in 1966, ironically, by a triple-headed British threat of Harold Pinter's *The Homecoming* (arguably his best play), Frank Marcus's *The Killing of Sister George* (fun, games and crypto-lesbianism at the BBC) and Peter Shaffer's riotously funny *Black Comedy*, in which Maggie had first appeared at the National. But it did win Albee his first Pulitzer Prize, and shared with *The Homecoming* an atmosphere of unnamed, unnerving terror; it ends with Agnes resuming a conversation that was interrupted as the play began.

Albee said that the play was about people turning their backs on each other. With Maggie, Atkins and Sian Thomas as Julia firing on all cylinders, it struck me more as a magnificent piece of theatrical hokum about the magnet of the drinks cabinet, the need to fuel small talk with large measures and the collapse of civilised pretence in domestic matters. And why all that bitterness about the child who died, Julia's brother? All those refreshingly long words and finely formed sentences had made a Gothic, rarefied impression on a very young me at the Royal Shakespeare Company's monumental British première at the Aldwych, where it had been directed with tragic, hieratic overtones by Peter Hall and featured three great actresses – Peggy Ashcroft as Agnes, Elizabeth Spriggs as Claire and Sheila Hancock as Julia. Maggie and Eileen Atkins somehow humanised the domestic catastrophe, while retaining its significant outline. And Maggie did what she does best, while reaching for an accordion to dampen everyone's spirits: she sniped venomously and triumphantly from the sidelines. Her empty glass dangled like an inquisitive appendage from an expressive left wrist as she claimed small victories in each exchange she entered.

I questioned Albee about this deliberate conflict in his plays between naturalism and style; he is much nearer to Tennessee Williams
as a poetic writer than he is to either Arthur Miller or David Mamet,
in that he doesn't necessarily want his characters to sound like 'real'
people. 'There is no such thing as naturalism in the theatre,' he said
emphatically, 'merely degrees of stylisation. The wonderful thing
about theatre is the total suspension of disbelief. Are we supposed
to think that the actors are the people they say they are, or that all
that papier mâché is *real*?' Apparently not. It's all smoke and mirrors,
all theatre. And what an intelligent actor like Maggie Smith does is
investigate that discrepancy between real and pretend, between feeling
and gesture, and give it the full attention of a theatrically convincing
truth. Out of this, in some magical way, emerges the truth itself. Or
so we kid ourselves.

Critical writing about Maggie was affected by these performances
in Albee, so that when she returned to Alan Bennett, in between the
two, with a stage performance of *Bed Among the Lentils*, one of the six
Talking Heads studies for BBC TV, at the Chichester Festival Theatre's
Minerva studio in 1996 (transferring for a season to the Comedy,
now the Harold Pinter, in town), she was praised for both her tragic
intensity and her technical skill; there had always been a tendency to
separate these virtues out. Alastair Macaulay, a dance critic who was
for a time the *Financial Times* theatre critic, praised her exceptional
economy of expression as Susan on the stage and opined that she
was the ideal Alan Bennett actor because she combined his charity
and malice. Her skill, he said, was that of a surgeon laying bare the
crucial details of a character's mental anatomy; Judi Dench and
Vanessa Redgrave, he added, were not Bennett 'types' because their
shared largeness of soul and vitality of temper were alien to his spirit,
meaning, I think, that spirit's appetite for detail, sarcasm, inflection
and nuance.

Bennett's six studies of resilient victims on the suburban margins
had won the artistic right of reply after life had treated them badly.
There had been many revivals in the theatre of these television pieces,
but not of Maggie's monodrama, as if in deference to her supremacy
as Susan. Even she wavered, but now took the plunge into these five
mordant, plangent, elegiac riffs, with a skill and virtuosity unequalled

in our theatre. You could see more clearly how Bennett compressed the present tense of confession into the catch-up info of parish life among the vicar's (Susan's husband's) 'fan club', as viewed in a vivid critical aspic: those furtive visits to the off-licence; the escape to Leeds for sex in the afternoon with twenty-six-year-old Mr Ramesh, the grocer betrothed to a fourteen-year-old girl, who finally crosses the Pennines to set up a business in Preston; and the living hell of Alcoholics Anonymous. On television, Maggie's Susan seemed dowdier and sadder. On stage, with the warmth of an audience, she crumbled with both joy and grief at the character, presenting a more mythical figure, partly because we knew what we were expecting. In addition, there was a 'warm-up' or curtain-raiser in the form of Margaret Tyzack, Maggie's cohort in *Lettice and Lovage*, in *Soldiering On* – the Stephanie Cole role in the original *Talking Heads* – the tale of a middle-class, well-connected widow in decline, with glimpses of a wastrel son and mentally ill daughter who was sexually abused by her father, a pillar of society once 'second-in-command of meals-on-wheels for the whole of Sudbury'.

Edward Albee might have put himself onstage in the mute figure of the young boy in *Three Tall Women*, but that's it; Alan Bennett is less retiring, often appearing as an actor and performer, though always modestly and discreetly, and usually in his own work. And always as someone very much like himself. He certainly always writes and talks like someone conceived by Alan Bennett, and the schizophrenic nature of an artist feeding on his own character to the extent that he does was perfectly expressed in *The Lady in the Van*, a vehicle as much for his own creative ego as it was for the extraordinary woman he wrote about, Miss Shepherd, who camped in his small front garden in Gloucester Crescent, Camden Town, in 1974, and stayed there until her death fifteen years later.

Bennett not only memorialised Miss Shepherd in his diaries, on radio and in this stage play (and later, film), but meditated on his own role as her conduit, placing himself in the story, and on the stage, alongside her. With Maggie having a field day as this niggardly, sparrow-like eccentric – a bundle of dun-coloured fun – Bennett was duplicated in the flesh by the actors Nicholas Farrell and Kevin McNally, the first as her flustered, beseeching, often frankly irritated host and neighbour, an irately reluctant Good Samaritan; the second as a steely, seated onlooker, not immune to the opportunities the old bird presented to him as a beady-eyed observer looting material from his own front garden.

It was a delicious set-up, and ten years after Miss Shepherd's death, Bennett confessed in the play's printed introduction that he is transported back to the time of her garden residency whenever he hears a van door slide shut.

> With Marcel, the narrator in Proust's *Remembrance of Things Past*, the sound that took him back was that of the gate of his aunt's idyllic garden; with me, it's the door of a broken down Bedford van. The discrepancy is depressing but then most writers discover quite early on that they're not going to be Proust. Besides, I couldn't have heard my own garden gate because in order to deaden the (to her) irritating noise Miss Shepherd had insisted on me putting a piece of chewing gum on the latch.

And he must have cowered in both delight and dismay when Maggie drove the white van on to the stage (twice) at each performance, even treating us to a turn in her 'second home', a comical three-wheeler Reliant Robin. The van became her cathedral when the back doors opened to reveal her wrapped in prayer or lost in her musical memories. Miss Shepherd was a former nun who had driven ambulances during black-outs in the war. She had also trained as a pianist in Paris and might have gone mad because she had once fled the scene of a fatal accident. The spiritual centre of Nicholas Hytner's production was expressed in an overlapping of Beethoven on the turntable in Bennett's study with news of the cruel truncation of her own musical career. Despite the interference of various doctors and one representative, over-earnest social worker, and despite the author's own exasperation, the play becomes an exercise in biographical retrieval, and a moving one.

Maggie didn't allow a scintilla of sentimentality to creep in. She was, in the best possible way, absolutely frightful: arms permanently akimbo, those witty elbows now dangerous weapons, her large watery eyes at once beseeching tolerance and beatification, her darting tongue flicking like a lizard's on a rock. She emanated a strange amphibian quality, graced in grime and grimace, a madcap Everywoman. In some ways she was a seedy political shadow of Mrs Thatcher, in others a premonition of Nigel Farage and his UKIP party of disaffected Little Englanders, with plans for a new Fidelis party and a cabinet office where Bennett imagined disconsolate colleagues lining up for orders and abuse on a daily basis. In between entertaining visions of the Virgin Mary (often decked out as Queen Victoria, or in a sari), Miss Shepherd would badger Bennett for the private addresses of major politicians – Harold Wilson, Mr Heath, Enoch Powell, or 'Enoch' as she called him – so that she could send them copies of her cranky pamphlets. She assumed a sort of spurious celebrity while clearly living as a recluse, and Bennett wryly observed that she would con-sider her elevation (thanks to his efforts) to a secondary plateau of genuine celebrity after her death no less than she fully deserved. So it is a lovely twist that Bennett allows Miss Shepherd to rewrite her own funeral, rising imperiously from the grave in a scene of celestial ascension and not-too-tacky a transfiguration.

The play was presented at the Queen's by Robert Fox, continuing the association with Maggie and Nicholas Hytner that he'd started with *The Importance of Being Earnest.* Three years after *The Lady in the Van*, Fox initiated another West End play for Maggie, reuniting her on stage with Judi Dench. David Hare's *The Breath of Life*, directed by Howard Davies, took £2 million at the box office before it even opened at the Haymarket (a huge advance in 2002), but despite polite reviews and great public interest – the show was a hit, selling out for its limited run of eighteen weeks – the play proved earthbound, and even tempted one or two critics to suggest it was singularly lacking in the degree of animation implicit in the title. Fox maintains the critics were wrong, suggesting that their reaction would have been different had the play been presented at a less glamorous venue than the Haymarket and not as a 'commercial shoo-in', which riled them.

David Hare has written some stonking roles for actresses in a long and distinguished career, but this, even Fox admits, was not his finest hour. And it was hard to see, or say, exactly why. This is the downside of theatre magic and mystery. Why didn't it happen? Everything about it sounded so promising. Hare himself said he wanted to describe two women with a long past behind them but the expectation of a considerable future ahead. As the Maggie character said, in a sentiment she herself would whole-heartedly approve, 'It's boring living in the past; you always know what's going to happen.' The playwright insisted that he hadn't written the play with Dench and Smith in mind but, as it turned out, this was the biggest conjunction of home-grown stars in a new play since Ralph Richardson and John Gielgud teamed up on Harold Pinter's *No Man's Land* in 1976 at the National.

Maggie played Madeleine Palmer, a retired museum curator specialising in Islamic art, visited at her Isle of Wight hideaway by the novelist Frances Beale (Judi Dench), whose husband, a radical lawyer and Queen's Counsel, was Madeleine's lover; he's now decamped to Seattle with a younger model. The action of the play was continuous over twenty-four hours, a new alliance forged between the two women though there wasn't all that much in the way of head-to-head collision, as if Hare had somehow mislaid the ignition key to his own dramatic engine. And stuttering away in the background was an idea that the strained friendship implied a similar tension in Anglo-American relations, the waning of a transatlantic love affair. Frances has arrived in the first place because she is researching her memoirs and, as both women have been abandoned by the unseen cad, she is seeking closure and an end to the pain. Dench spent most of the evening sitting and writhing on the edge of tears, while Maggie fired off the odd squib. Her remark that all people did on the Isle of Wight was gardening and expiring reminded me that Alan Ayckbourn's unfriendly epitaph for his adopted home town of Scarborough was that there was nothing to do there except buy shoes and get drunk. Maggie's Madeleine recounted how she had met Martin Beale in Alabama during the civil rights campaigns of the 1960s and that he took her to orgies and, later, a Test Match. She hadn't destroyed Frances's marriage, exactly, she averred, but retrospectively undermined it during her twenty-five-year affair.

The play was no better received when revived in 2011 at the Lyceum in Sheffield, with Isla Blair as Frances and Patricia Hodge as Madeleine. Critics lamented the lack of show in the showdown, and were again surprised at the absence of rancour or recrimination in the proceedings. An exasperated Lyn Gardner in the *Guardian* went even further, attacking the whole premise of the play which, she said, 'showed complete disdain for the quiet, valuable lives of women across the world who make such a wonderful contribution in bringing up the next generation, and who live lives just as rich as those who strut and shout on public stages'.

Hare did write one terrific role for Judi Dench in *Amy's View*, one of the seventeen plays he has had performed at the National so far, and he has written roles that have been brilliantly occupied by the likes of Penelope Wilton, Kate Nelligan, Cate Blanchett, Helen Mirren, Irene Worth, Nicole Kidman and Carey Mulligan. In marked contrast to, say, John Osborne, he has been conspicuously successful in writing for women. It just didn't happen this time out. Maggie hasn't had any luck with Harold Pinter, either, having only ever performed a few of his lines in the screenplay he provided for the film of *The Pumpkin Eater*. And when Deborah Warner suggested to her, across the table at her (Maggie's) seventieth birthday party, that she might like to consider playing in Beckett's *Waiting for Godot* with Fiona Shaw, she roared with laughter, thinking this was the funniest idea anyone had ever come up with. She's nothing if not modern as an actress, but literary or theatrical modernism was never her bag.

So instead of taking *The Breath of Life* to Broadway, she happily concurred in a plan Robert Fox hatched with co-producer Duncan Weldon to take *Bed Among the Lentils* to Australia and New Zealand (Auckland and Wellington) on a three-month tour in 2004, reprising her double-act, too, with Margaret Tyzack in *Soldiering On*, and hiring Anthony Page to direct the tour. They opened in Sydney, moving on to Melbourne, Brisbane, Perth and Adelaide (Fox says Maggie was very funny about Adelaide; partly because there were so many dead bodies around after a plethora of murders).

Maggie thought she'd never go to Australia if she didn't go now. She thoroughly enjoyed the experience, and struck up a great new friendship with the painter Margaret Olley. She received the most incredible response, says Page, the minute she opened her mouth on the stage, 'and Margaret Tyzack was brilliant, too'. She was lionised at dinners and parties and Page remembers one particular occasion when everyone wanted to sit next to her after the Sydney opening. 'She wouldn't have any of that,' recalls Page, 'and insisted that I sat on one side of her at the table and Ken [Page's partner] on the other side, so we could sort of act as a buffer, fending everyone else off. The Australian producer's wife wouldn't give up so easily and asked if she'd like, one day, to do a harbour bridge climb, clamped to the structure with all the equipment, and so on. "No, I don't think so," Maggie said. But the woman persisted saying, "Oh you really should. It's so wonderful; my husband and I went up there on our honeymoon." "Well," replied Maggie, "I'm surprised the marriage lasted." And that shut her up, very quickly.'

Back on the London stage: (*top*) Maggie as Millamant in a new production of *The Way of the World* by William Gaskill at the Haymarket in 1984, with Joan Plowright as Lady Wishfort; (*above left*) as Cocteau's glittering, incestuous Jocasta in *The Infernal Machine* at the Lyric, Hammersmith, in 1986, directed by Simon Callow; (*above right*) and triumphant (with a Tony award on Broadway) at the Globe in Peter Shaffer's *Lettice and Lovage* (1987), with Margaret Tyzack

Above and right Two stage collaborations with
director Nicholas Hytner: as Lady Bracknell in
The Importance of Being Earnest at the Aldwych in
1993 with (left to right) Alex Jennings, Susannah
Harker, Richard E. Grant and Claire Skinner;
and as the titular tramp in Alan Bennett's *The
Lady in the Van* at the Queen's in 1999

Opposite page As a part-time Dublin
piano teacher with a crisis of confidence
in religion, Maggie gave an emotionally
raw and despairing screen performance in
The Lonely Passion of Judith Hearne (1987)

Maggie has specialised in the high-style plays of American dramatist Edward Albee: (*top left*) flanked by Anastasia Hille and Frances de la Tour in *Three Tall Women* at Wyndham's in 1994; (*top right*) with Eileen Atkins in *A Delicate Balance* at the Haymarket in 1997; (*above*) and as an angel of death in *The Lady from Dubuque* at the Haymarket in 2007, with Robert Sella (foreground), Jennifer Regan, Maggie's own son Chris Larkin, and Vivienne Benesch

Betsy Trotwood in *David Copperfield* was a long-coveted role, and Maggie played her for BBC TV in 1999, with a ten-year-old Daniel Radcliffe (in the bath) making his professional debut as the young David. Maggie later recommended him as Harry Potter

Wizard line-up in *Harry Potter and the Chamber of Secrets* (2002): Maggie as Minerva McGonagall, Miriam Margolyes as Pomona Sprout, Richard Harris as Albus Dumbledore and Alan Rickman as Severus Snape

Maggie and Judi Dench have been friends since their early days at the Old Vic in 1959. Their first film together was Merchant and Ivory's *A Room with a View* (1985), alongside Helena Bonham-Carter (*top left*), and they teamed again onstage as wife and mistress in David Hare's *Breath of Life* (2002) at the Haymarket (*top right*). In Charles Dance's *Ladies in Lavender* (2004), Maggie dubbed the two of them 'the lavender bags' (*above*)

Maggie as the acerbic Lady Violet, Dowager Countess of Grantham, with Shirley MacLaine as Martha Levinson, in *Downton Abbey* (2010–15), the biggest drama series export in ITV television history

At the annual flower show, Lady Violet – with Hugh Bonneville as Lord Grantham and Penelope Wilton as Isobel Crawley – upsets tradition by awarding her own customary first prize to the gardener

Two very different popular movies in 2015: John Madden's *The Second Best Exotic Marigold Hotel* with (left to right) Celia Imrie, Ronald Pickup, Diana Hardcastle, Judi Dench and Bill Nighy joining in the wedding party; and Nicholas Hytner's *The Lady in the Van*, with Alex Jennings as Alan Bennett pushing Maggie's defiant old crone around Camden Town . . . downhill all the way?

19

TV Specials for the Lady from Dubuque

There was another three-year lull before Maggie's third and final bout with Edward Albee, *The Lady from Dubuque*, which would prove her last West End appearance in 2007, not by design, necessarily, but by the demands of filming and the continuation of *Downton Abbey*. Until *Downton*, television appearances were comparatively rare, but worth the wait. *Suddenly, Last Summer* was followed by just three major television films for the BBC: Julian Jarrold's *All the King's Men* (1999), Simon Curtis's *David Copperfield* (also in 1999), and Stephen Poliakoff's *Capturing Mary* (2007), one of her most distinctive performances which also reunited her with a playwright whose *Coming in to Land* at the National had been a rewarding experience.

The first two were co-productions with WGBH, the Boston-based non-commercial television station, thus guaranteeing exposure on the American networks. In the case of *All the King's Men*, in which Maggie played a radiant, red-haired Queen Alexandra in glittering costumes, audiences were reacquainted with one of the most unusual Great War stories, that of the 5th battalion of the Norfolk regiment (drawn from workers on the Queen's Sandringham estate) who simply disappeared in the mist at Gallipoli. The producer was Gareth Neame, the future executive producer of *Downton Abbey*, and the battalion was led by David Jason as Captain Frank Beck, married to Phyllis Logan, *Downton*'s Mrs Hughes. It's a fine film, and Maggie does her stuff, but she does no more than meets the requirements of a routine study in beadily observant and emotionally generous old-style royalty, although there's always something satisfactorily 'askance' about her brushes with the privileged élite; and there's a lovely moment when Captain Beck's watch, a royal gift, is found, still ticking, on the battlefield, as though confirming the unbreakable link between Queen and subjects across the globe.

Julian Jarrold, who made his name with the feisty Brit-com movie *Kinky Boots*, cast Maggie in another 'lost' story, *Becoming Jane* (2007), as an imperious dowager – social mobility was becoming a 'little Smith girl' (as Edith Evans called her) speciality – Lady Gresham, a wealthy acquaintance of Jane Austen's family whose nephew Wisley (Laurence Fox) was a prime suitor to Anne Hathaway's budding novelist. This was a backstory 'making of a novelist' contribution to the thriving Jane Austen heritage industry, with beautiful locations (the movie was shot in Ireland, rather than Austen's home county of Hampshire), correct period costumes and a clever elaboration by scriptwriters Kevin Hood and Sarah Williams on the well-documented early friendship of Jane Austen with a young lawyer, Tom Lefroy.

James McAvoy translated Tom into a wild Byronic figure and possible template for Mr Darcy in *Pride and Prejudice*, the novel Jane sits down to write (and read from) as the credits loom. She's already started on a manuscript then titled 'First Impressions' and after accepting Wisley she falls back under Tom's spell, only to 'sensibly' dampen her ardour when she realises that his first duty is to support his family and dependants. Thus the spinster artist, who knew something of passion, thanks to Tom, is born. It's a clever construct, not without foundation, and Maggie plays her part in it vividly, in a few scenes, conjuring the harsh society world Jane Austen relished and simultaneously flinched from. 'It was fun doing the film,' Maggie told me. 'It was in Ireland, of course, on a shoe-string, no time, the usual...'

She exhibited what Jarrold viewed as 'similarities to Lady Catherine de Bourgh in *Pride and Prejudice*' but with hidden vulnerabilities, which stemmed from the pain of never having had children and her controlling power over Wisley. In *Pride and Prejudice*, Lady Catherine haughtily tells Elizabeth Bennet: 'Your father's estate is entailed on Mr Collins, I think. For your sake, I am glad of it; but otherwise I see no occasion for entailing estates from the female line. It was not thought necessary in Sir Lewis de Bourgh's family.' By the time Maggie came to her other great dowager in *Downton Abbey* she had changed her tune to a more flexible Edwardian view of lineage and inheritance.

The second BBC/WGBH movie for television took a more traditional line on another great English novelist, Charles Dickens, in resisting any speculation on the author's evolution beyond the simple and indisputable fact that the ever popular *David Copperfield* is semi-autobiographical – and that Betsey Trotwood, whom Maggie makes the beating heart of Simon Curtis's affectionate and highly enjoyable film, is one of the great characters of English literature. It's a three-hour production, and was originally shown in two parts over the Christmas holiday weekend in 1999. The cast includes such popular character actors as Bob Hoskins as a genial Mr Micawber, Nicholas Lyndhurst as a carrot-headed, mean-mouthed Uriah Heep, Trevor Eve as a wonderfully despicable Mr Murdstone and Ian McKellen as the sadistic schoolmaster Mr Creakle, voice as dry and husky as a sandpaper parchment, mouth as slobbery as an eel. McKellen had himself played the older David Copperfield in a 1966 BBC serialisation (the second of the corporation's three adaptations to date) with Flora Robson as Betsey; now Maggie's Betsey formed an alliance with a showbiz first-timer as the young Davy – Daniel Radcliffe.

This was ten-year-old Radcliffe's first professional role and I don't mean it as a major insult to say that he exhibits all the still, phlegmatic, almost anonymous 'ordinariness' that makes Harry Potter such an appealing hero; Harry's wizard powers are always seen as something over which he has no real control and which come alive in circumstances demanding the uncomplicated exercise of his instinct for decency, fortitude and bravery. Young Copperfield – who is sonorously informed by Murdstone that life's struggles lie ahead and that it is time to begin – endures not dissimilar trials to Harry's at the abusive, bullying hands of his stepfather, the sadistic regime of the schoolmaster, his apprenticeship in the blacking factory in London and the journey on foot, penniless and alone, to Dover. There, he finds his one surviving relative, his great-aunt Betsey, who greets him with a frantic dismissal ('Go away! No boys here . . .') before collapsing into one of her own garden bushes and rising to chase some unattended donkeys from her sloping lawn.

The comedy of Betsey's initial unfriendliness is based, Maggie makes clear, on her disillusion with men of all sorts since her bitter experience of them, though Adrian Hodges' script has deleted the errant husband who, in the novel, turns up at odd moments to demand money. From the first reel, when Maggie enters like a whirlwind in expectation of a young baby girl – 'She must be called Betsey Trotwood Copperfield,' she instructs a bemused and uncomfortable Emilia Fox as Clara Copperfield – to her fearsome attack on the exposed Heep, grabbing Lyndhurst by the lapels of his jacket and shaking him like a rag doll, and her unconditional generosity towards the emigrating Micawber family, she is a moral weathervane, undergoing an improving transformation herself.

Dickens's Copperfield narrates his own story (this version uses neither Radcliffe's voice nor a fresh-faced older David's, Ciaran McMenamin's, but Tom Wilkinson's) and comments on Betsey's handsome, though facially inflexible, features, noting in particular her very quick, bright eye. Maggie's Betsey suggests this brittleness, but develops her performance as one of progressive unbending of her unbending side, especially in her guardianship of David and the hospitality she has always shown towards the touchingly simple-minded Mr Dick (beatifically played by RSC veteran Ian McNeice, who had popped up in *Judith Hearne*). While she bathes David, she recalls how her husband treated her cruelly – 'that's what men do, as far as I can see' – and when he falls asleep, she's won over completely. So won over, that she recommended young Radcliffe for Harry Potter two years later; you do note, in the Harry Potter series, how Professor McGonagall will often brush Harry with the slightest of affectionate gestures, something that might date from this first work experience together. But no one flares up like Maggie can, and her attack on Trevor Eve's murky Murdstone is a high point of ferocity, accusing him of breaking Clara's heart and breaking the boy, too, as an instrument for his own guilt. And she has another donkey-related broadside for Murdstone's metallic sister, Jane (Zoë Wanamaker, as righteously prim as a picky parson), as they leave her premises: 'Let me see you ride a donkey over my green again, and I'll knock your bonnet off. And tread on it, for good measure.'

There was a time when our leading dramatists were regularly represented on television, but that has all changed with the incursion of American drama series – *Mad Men* and *Breaking Bad* are both cited by Julian Fellowes as a direct influence on *Downton Abbey* in terms of pace and narrative propulsion – and the collapse of the idea of a televised 'single play' or film unless it's the ponderously evoked life of a celebrity, preferably a comedian with flaws – Kenneth Williams, Tony Hancock, Frankie Howerd have all been memorialised in this way – or a politician or a celebrity such as a Great Train robber, pop singer Cilla Black or a mass murderer. It seems a lifetime ago – well it is; it was 1983 – when Alan Bennett's *An Englishman Abroad* (with Alan Bates and Coral Browne, directed by John Schlesinger), William Trevor's *The Blue Dress* (starring Denholm Elliott, Virginia McKenna and Susan Fleetwood) and David Hare's *Saigon – Year of the Cat* (Stephen Frears directing Judi Dench and Frederic Forrest) were all aired on different channels on the same November night; and that was just three days after a Channel 4 screening of Mike Leigh's *Meantime* with Gary Oldman and Tim Roth. Discussing the work of the great television dramatist Dennis Potter (best known for *Nigel Barton*, *Pennies from Heaven* and *The Singing Detective*), Melvyn Bragg said that his was the representative talent 'which made television the true national theatre and the place where this country talked to itself'.

So when the BBC commissioned an interrelated tripartite drama from the experienced dramatist (and filmmaker) Stephen Poliakoff, it was both a major event and an ideological aberration, a throwback, almost. *Capturing Mary* was set in the same luxurious Georgian town house as the first drama, *Joe's Place*, and they were both shown within a week of each other, with the middle, much shorter monologue, *A Real Summer*, as a link, or bridge passage. This link featured Ruth Wilson as Mary Gilbert, a journalist and witness to the 'Swinging Sixties'. Mary's story, in full, is told by Maggie in *Capturing Mary*, recalling her life, and tragic exploitation and decline, when she revisits the old house and is shown around by the still resident young caretaker Joe, played by Danny Lee Wynter. As she sits with a cup of tea, she hears the sounds elsewhere in the house of ping-pong, opera, drawing room conversation. And she revisits in her mind's eye the glamorous soirées once held here for the rich and famous – Alfred Hitchcock, Ava Gardner, E. M. Forster – which she attended as a shooting star of Fleet Street, a journalist hailing from Manchester tempered in the postwar hothouse of Oxford University, and already notorious for demanding more sex, and more reality, in the movies. She sees her younger self, played by Ruth Wilson, intrigued by a mystery man,

Greville White, at one such gathering. Greville, played by David Walliams, the star of the scatological, satirical sketch show *Little Britain*, knows everyone and doesn't do anything. He's one of those cultural and social power-brokers who have nothing to exchange except their own limpid vanity, self-importance and creepy, deferential manner, making themselves indispensable to the movers and shakers they both aspire to become and wish to undermine. And Mary is soon firmly in his sights. Inveigling her down to the wine cellar, away from the throng, Greville exercises a controlling grip on Mary by telling her the terrible truth about the establishment: its orgies, forays into sexual abuse and degradation, anti-Semitism, cruelty and lies, the whole disgusting underbelly of the upper classes and their high society hangers-on.

She promises never to spill the beans although, ever since the Profumo affair in 1963, right through to the rituals surrounding the public disgrace of countless politicians and media figures which multiply by the year, it seems unlikely a journalist such as Mary would have remained quiet for all this time, even though she loses her job as 'the voice of youth' thanks to Greville (she believes). But Maggie presents a forlorn character cast adrift from her own past. She's managed to lead a reasonably successful life in magazine journalism, but she's missed her chance, and the boat, and is now a sad-eyed giraffe mourning the loss of her talent.

Maggie sympathised to a degree with Mary Gilbert: 'She started at the same time as I did,' she said in a rare promotional interview. 'It can happen. Something horrid that will change your life. Something that won't go out of your mind.' Ruth Wilson, who had lately made a television film of *Jane Eyre* (opposite Maggie's son, Toby Stephens, as a memorable Rochester) scripted by Poliakoff's wife, Sandy Welch, responded to the sexual dynamic in the piece as it dealt with the great wave of change, and also power, between men and women in the 1950s and 1960s. And there was something uncannily and convincingly similar in the coloration and flayed intensity of younger and older actresses in the same role, a story of corrupted innocence and bad experience lived by one and recollected in tragic tranquillity by the other. There's a great scene at the end when Maggie goes for a walk in Kensington Gardens, near the house, with Joe, hoping she might by chance see Greville after all this time. And she does. But unlike her, he hasn't aged. She's laid the ghost, but she's become one herself, drinking on a park bench, crying for her youth, alone.

For what may prove to be her last major stage performance, she came full circle to Edward Albee, in the 2007 Haymarket première of *The Lady from Dubuque*, a play that had closed on Broadway in 1980 with Irene Worth in the lead after eighteen previews and only twelve performances. And, despite Maggie's presence in the cast as the mysterious Elizabeth, the lady from Dubuque who appears like an angel of death right at the end of the first act, it was not all that more successful in the West End. Why did the play not take off? All sorts of reasons have been submitted. The star doesn't appear until too late, somebody's actually dying of cancer on the stage, the writing is too severe and minimal – the script lacked 'tangible flesh and blood', said Walter Kerr of the first New York production – and has always been ahead of its time. Producer Robert Fox says he was in two minds about the play's commercial prospects and was surprised when Maggie told him she wanted to do it. He suggested a smaller West End venue, but she insisted on the Haymarket. He also thinks it might have been received differently, by critics and public alike, if it had been put on in the Donmar Warehouse or the National's third and smallest auditorium. 'Maggie's always very clear about what she doesn't want to do,' says Fox, 'very straightforward in her choices. Once her mind is made up, that's it.'

Anthony Page thinks of the play as a Greek tragedy and likens the sinister appearance of the Lady and her black chauffeur, Oscar, to that of the two strangers who turn up from nowhere in Harold Pinter's *The Birthday Party*. They arrive in the middle of a neighbourly alcoholic shindig in the Albee land of Connecticut Yankees which, at the Haymarket, was an all-white, split-level modernist suburban palazzo, magnificently designed by Hildegard Bechtler. The four guests were, à la *Virginia Woolf*, deep into drink, badinage and insults while the dying hostess, Jo, and her fraught husband, Sam, ramp up the hostility quotient. The meekest guest, played by Chris Larkin, Maggie's son, is grateful, as he leaves, for yet another average, desperate sort of evening. When he returns because his wife, Lucinda, Jo's old college friend, is suffering a crisis on the lawn, he is asked what has he forgotten: his youth, or his dignity? No one but Albee would write such a line, and there immediately follows a macabre dialogue between Sam and Jo about his life after her death from cancer. As Sam carries her upstairs in throes of agony, Jo remarks that it had been a lot easier to get her into bed before this happened.

You could feel a chill descend on the theatre. This was going to be the very opposite of a feel-good entertainment. But then Albee's always been like this. In the introduction to his first volume of collected plays he summed up his attitude: 'I do not plan out my plays to fit in with either critical bias or commercial safety: nor do I worry that my themes may be difficult or dangerous and my techniques unconventional. I go with what my mind tells me and I take my chances.' And fifty years later, he was still an ageing enfant terrible. 'Every play I write,' he told me, 'is the first play I've written. And yes, I'd like to think I'm still one or two steps ahead of the game. When I first showed *The Goat* [the play in which a married, middle-aged architect falls in love with a goat] to two close friends, they said, "Oh, Edward, don't let this be done – it will destroy your career." "Really?" I said. "Wow, then I'd better go straight ahead!" And of course I did. And I always shall.'

So what did Maggie do? With a delayed entrance that, had it not been totally unannounced and unexpected, might have been similar to Agamemnon returning from the Trojan War to face the music at Thebes, or Dolly Levi sashaying defiantly down the steps of the Harmonia Gardens feted by a dancing chorus of waiters ('Well, hello, Dolly!'), Maggie went to the opposite extreme of making a big hoo-ha. She simply stepped on the stage in a navy Jean Muir three-piece suit and double row of pearls, speaking naturalistically and restrainedly, insisting that she is Jo's mother (she's not) and resisting all temptation to play the lines, as she might easily have done, with a Coral Browne-like grandeur, humanising the dialogue to the point of naturalistic comedy. Jo accepts her offer of a comforting embrace, and her great speech about dying on a beach is suddenly moving; you realise that if this lady is indeed an angel of death, she is also the figure of comfort and succour we should all hope to find once the physical terrors and psychological fears have been endured.

But who was she, really, this bizarre uninvited guest? Easier to say who she's not. Albee had taken a prompt from the *New Yorker* magazine whose founding editor Harold Ross was asked who might be the average reader of his new publication: 'One thing I know, the magazine is not going to be written for the little old lady from Dubuque.' Dubuque is a town in Iowa, so named after one of the first European settlers, Julien Dubuque, a lead miner. Albee's view was that, as nothing else the character in the play says is true, she might as well say that she's the Lady from Dubuque who, as she exists in the popular imagination, is much more like the New Jersey woman (Jo's mother) described in the play as overweight and homely, balding with pink straggles of hair.

Albee had begun thinking about a play called *The Substitute Speaker* as far back as 1960, but the success of *Who's Afraid of Virginia Woolf?*, which opened soon after the Cuban missile crisis of 1961, and touched a national nerve during the Kennedy years, had led him elsewhere. By the time he returned to the play in the mid-1970s, he was starting to write in a much more compressed and daring manner. He had been much taken by a book published in 1969, *On Death and Dying*, by the Swiss-born psychiatrist Elisabeth Kübler-Ross. Widely credited with inspiring the hospice movement, Kübler-Ross expounded in her book her 'five stages of dying', in which a person diagnosed with terminal illness goes through denial, anger, bargaining, depression and acceptance. In *The Substitute Speaker*, Jo dies early in the play and Sam dresses up in her clothes and assumes her identity; that is, he becomes the substitute voice of his lost and loved one.

In 2007, Albee lost his partner of over thirty-five years, the Canadian artist and sculptor Jonathan Thomas, who died of cancer. Had this compelled him to reconsider the retitled play as first performed in 1980? 'I wrote the play before I experienced personal tragedy or loss,' he says. 'I was astonished, after going through my lifetime partner's death, how on target I was, having intuited what the response would be. I think with this play, as with all my plays, the idea had been floating around for years.' Not only was the subject unsettling, so was the format, in which characters regularly broke down the fourth wall and addressed the audience as if they were in a theatre, performing a play. Elizabeth, though, did not, declaring to the other characters, not the audience, at the start of the second act (invariably following an interval full of muttering and speculation),

'I have come home for my daughter's dying.' It's just not the sort of thing a Haymarket audience wanted to hear from their favourite star. But that didn't bother Maggie, her son confirms; she retained, he says, complete faith in both Albee and the director Anthony Page.

And she taught Chris a lesson or two, as well. He'd never been on a stage with her before (except as a walk-on in *Interpreters*), not that they ever really interacted in this play. 'We had no eye contact on the stage,' says Chris,

I don't think she ever even looked at me, and if she did, it was completely disparagingly – within the context of the play, of course! The nature of the piece helped in that as we were a bunch of anal, detached Connecticut types. I did learn a lot from her, and I think it was harder for her being in a rehearsal room with me than it was for me being with her. Changing my name has helped distance me from her professionally. And so she could put me right, as she might any younger actor. One day we were discussing the refusal of one of the other actors to play the stage direction as written, something I felt was impacting massively on this particular moment in the play. I fought my corner vociferously to get it changed with Antony Page; and mum told me never, ever, to do that – he was the director, and if it was fine by him, we should all live with that. We must do as he says. Of course, she would have got her own way on such a point because of her seniority, but I wasn't in that place, and she was right to pull me up. Normally, actors are never really told how they are perceived. She did. I was a prat!

Was the comparative failure of *The Lady from Dubuque* the reason why Maggie has not been on the stage since?

Not at all. She was very proud of it though obviously disappointed that it didn't do better. There was the health scare with breast cancer around this time, but that's all fine now. Of course she's not getting any younger, and eight performances a week, even if you don't come on till just before the interval, is pretty tiring. But it was such fun being on stage with her because she's always very twinkly.

There's no chance of her ever going into a home. She's one of those who says, 'Take me to Switzerland if anything starts going south and I can't remember your names . . .' She's almost terrifyingly sanguine about critics, success, failure. She doesn't worry at all and simply says you can only do what you do. She's still a great reader and listener to the radio, and she's still got all those green-backed Virago books on her shelves, rows and rows of them. Tobes and I used to call them the green girlie books. And she's not wanting not to be doing anything; that would be, for her, just as destructive as working too hard. When she's not working she gets bored very quickly. She's happiest working and being with other actors. And this is doubly important now that she's on her own, although the paradox is that she loves being on her own. As a granny she's absolutely fantastic with our children – I have two, Tobes and Anna-Louise have three – but she does need her own space after a while . . .

Maggie has grown closer to her sons as they have grown older. Toby says that she retains a good deal of unnecessary guilt about their childhood, but both he and Chris agree that she set standards in the house. These are the legacy of her own childhood regimens in Ilford and Oxford. Chris would not describe her in any way as a disciplinarian. 'But she certainly wasn't a freethinker. And she was very hot on articulation. We were not allowed to slur our words. And every Canadian colloquialism was drilled out of us within three months of coming back here. Above all, I remember this very piercing voice from my childhood: "It's pardon, not what!" And she was fairly rigorous about table manners.'

Chris and his wife Suki, a drama teacher, live in Kemp Town, Brighton, and inhabit the very opposite of a *Downton Abbey* existence, so it amuses him no end to recount a couple of stories related to the executive directors, Neame and Fellowes. He was at school with Gareth Neame, and good friends, though they were very different types:

He was always going to be on the other side of the camera, and we had a convivial dinner ten years ago when he was moaning about how much he had to pay the actors. I countered with the argument that he wasn't paying them, but buying them off and then selling the series – at the time it was *Rosemary and Thyme* starring Felicity Kendal and Pam Ferris – worldwide. After we left the restaurant, I was fumbling around with my bicycle lights to cycle home to Hammersmith when I heard a beep-beep behind me and he drove smoothly past in a £40,000 Mercedes!

Unlike Maggie and, to a lesser extent, his brother Toby, Chris has had to make progress the hard way. Ten years after catching the chandelier every night in *Phantom*, he found himself playing a small role in Franco Zeffirelli's 1996 film of *Jane Eyre* starring Charlotte Gainsbourg, and William Hurt as Rochester, alongside another small-part player, Julian Fellowes.

Fellowes and I came in every day, and every day our parts got smaller and smaller until, one day, his was gone! He got on to Harvey Weinstein and was told that he was contracted to the film and was now an extra! We were filming in Derbyshire and staying in a hotel that was part of Gulliver's Theme Park; outside, there were little chalets, and a thirty-foot boot, and lots of knitting needles. I found Julian one morning at breakfast in his Viyella shirt, cravat and waistcoat, disconsolately tapping at his boiled egg while reading the *Telegraph* in a room full of muppets. And he was repeating, under his breath, and over and over again, 'I am in hell, I am in hell...'

No wonder he was beginning to concentrate on the writing with a view to creating a country-house working environment rather more congenial to his taste, social status and personal wardrobe.

20

Goodbye Hollywood,
Hello British Comedy

There was a pattern early in her career of Maggie flying the coop to Broadway, Hollywood and Canada before returning 'home' to the London stage and the Shepperton or Ealing film studios, but this internationalism has been revoked as she grows older, and you feel it would take something very special now to lure her back to work in New York or Los Angeles. The last phase, or late flowering, of 'Maggiepanthus Smithsoniensis' begins ten years ago with the low-key, charming British movie *Ladies in Lavender* in which she starred with Judi Dench ('the lavender bags', Maggie dubbed the pair of them) and marks the start of a more wistful, melancholic and perhaps surprising investigation into the attributes, and occasional disadvantages, of growing older and wiser with a modicum of grace and good will.

This caught something in the zeitgeist about old age as, waking up to the fact that the ageing population was growing, and that the grey pound was at least as potent as the pink one, all the media over the past ten years have pandered more consistently to this new target audience, with over-age choirs, pensioner rewrites of *Romeo and Juliet* and *Much Ado About Nothing* (Siân Phillips played Juliet aged seventy-nine at the Bristol Old Vic, and Vanessa Redgrave played Beatrice aged seventy-six at the Old Vic), property-porn television programmes about where to go and live when you retire, and senior citizen sitcoms. This all reflected a much deeper understanding of, and sympathy for, the ageing process. As Alan Bennett said in his annual 'Diary' published in the *London Review of Books* at the start of 2015, there was a time when one saw an old couple walking along holding hands and the thought was of Darby and Joan; nowadays, one just wonders which of them has Alzheimer's.

And for Maggie and Judi Dench, this was a bonus development in their film careers, taking them from elderly spinster sisters in *Ladies in Lavender* through to the two wildly successful *Best Exotic Marigold* movies without any suggestion that being old was a side effect of being wilfully eccentric or tragically over the hill. Put more brutally by the cynical alcoholic actress played by Goldie Hawn in the first of Maggie's last batch of Hollywood movies, *The First Wives Club*, while Shakespeare may have said there were seven ages of man, there are only three ages for women in Tinsel Town: babe, district attorney and *Driving Miss Daisy*. The point she didn't make was that these three phases now carry an equal weight. Still, after the two *Sister Act* movies, Maggie bade a not too sorry farewell to Hollywood, signing off with three fairly hard-boiled romantic comedies, none of which stretched or challenged her. Two were hits, while the middle one, *It All Came True* (1998), first released with the title *Curtain Call*, went, in most markets, straight to TV or home video, even though it was distinguished director Peter Yates's last movie for cinema and reunited Maggie with her *Californian Suite* co-star Michael Caine.

It was as though, having discovered a favourite star and blessed her with a pair of Oscars, Hollywood had now just about run out of ideas on how best to keep her grazing on those Beverly Hills. The roles simply didn't present themselves as fruitfully as they did back home. Well, they did for a short while, but in the exuberant feminist comedy *The First Wives Club* (1996), produced by Scott Rudin and directed by Hugh (*Police Academy*) Wilson, Maggie has only three scenes as Gunilla Garson Goldberg, 'queen of New York society', and does little more than dispense advice and encouragement to the disgruntled ex-wives, a wonderful trio of Diane Keaton, Goldie Hawn and Bette Midler. The ex-wives' campaign of revenge – one of hitting the guys where it hurts most, in the pocket – is kick-started by their college friend (Stockard Channing) jumping off her penthouse roof in a fur coat, drink in hand, on learning that her ex-husband has married his mistress the day before. The film struck a chord and became a box-office smash, but Maggie's there for the ride as the bolshie trio vie with each other in one-liner paradise. As Goldie Hawn's ageing alcoholic film starlet pouts into view at the funeral, someone says to the brassed-off, bimbo-bamboozled Midler, 'She looks fabulous; do you think she's had any work done?' 'Honey, she's a quilt.' Hawn's cosmetic surgeon is more worried: 'If I give you one more facelift, you're going to be able to blink your lips.' The satirical honesty behind these exchanges makes the film enjoyable. It's both witty and funny, and the triumphant (of course) trio dance down the street at the end, all in white, singing Lesley Gore's 1963 hit 'You Don't Own Me'. No accident, then, that this comes after a cocktail party attended, in real-life person, by Ivana Trump ('Don't get mad, get everything!' is her advice to the girls), feminist icon Gloria Steinem and the Mayor of New York, Ed Koch, no doubt delighted that the film's sixty tourist-baiting city locations included the Chrysler Building, Central Park, Christie's auction house and a suite at the Waldorf-Astoria.

It All Came True pandered more obviously to what people had come to expect from Maggie Smith, referencing her performance in *Private Lives* in the quarrelsome, glamorous ghost of Lily Marlowe, an actress of the 1930s who haunts an empty townhouse along with Max Gale, her husband and onstage sparring partner, her Elyot Chase, laconically played by Michael Caine. It was followed by *Divine Secrets of the Ya-Ya Sisterhood*, another tribal feminist comedy with the dark underside of an historic abusive childhood for Sandra Bullock as Siddalee Walker, a Broadway playwright, at the hands of Ellen Burstyn as her mother Viviane, who it turns out was mentally unstable and suffering the consequences of haywire medication. The sisterhood, formed with a blood oath of undying loyalty in the woods of Louisiana in 1937, is led by Viviane, and includes Maggie as Eliza, Shirley Knight as Denise and Fionnula Flanagan as Aimee. Now middle-aged Southern belles, they rally to the rescue of Siddalee's relationship with her mother and her marriage to a solid fiancé. Callie Khouri's direction (and screenplay) doesn't break the bonds of the time slips in the novel by Rebecca Wells and seems both over-mawkish and over-shoehorned into just under two hours, though there are some notable performances by James Garner as Siddalee's father and Ashley Judd as the younger, troubled Viviane. Maggie is afflicted with a cough (and an oxygen mask) for much of the action, which doesn't make much sense in either the movie itself or in her character, who clings to the odd piercing line – 'the only disease that could survive in our bloodstream is alcoholism' – like a shipwreck victim clinging to a raft.

The First Wives Club at least has an innate vivacity and perky contemporary application, whereas these last two films seem contrived
and effortful. So it must have been with some relief that Maggie seized
on an invitation from actor Charles Dance to stay at home – in Britain,
at least – and headline his first movie as a director, *Ladies in Lavender*,
with Judi Dench. She followed through with Niall Johnson's *Keeping
Mum* (2005), with Rowan Atkinson and Kristin Scott Thomas – 'the
first time I've been required to kill people,' Maggie chuckled, delightedly, of her role as an Ealing Comedy-style gruesome granny – and
Emma Thompson's second *Nanny McPhee* film in 2010, the one where
she (Maggie) sits in a cow pat and wisely informs the children, 'You
want her [Nanny McPhee] when you don't need her, and need her
when you don't want her.' These three British movies, all shot in
beautiful locations – the first two in Cornwall, coincidentally, and
within a few miles of each other, the third in the picture-book Buckinghamshire village of Hambleden, also used in the filming of *Chitty
Chitty Bang Bang* – took her back to her own culture and background.
When filming *Keeping Mum*, she said that she caught sight of herself
in a mirror and saw that she looked just like her own mother... 'an
odd feeling'.

Charles Dance, a former lead actor at the Royal Shakespeare Company and later one of the stars of the hit television series *Game of
Thrones*, had tried his hand at script writing without success until,
reading a book of short stories by the Edwardian writer William J.
Locke, he thought that one of them would make a good film and that
the two spinster sisters, Ursula and Janet Widdington, whose lives are
turned upside down by the unexplained arrival of a castaway Polish
musician on the beach at the bottom of their cliff garden, would
make an ideal movie for Judi Dench and Maggie. He visited them in
their dressing rooms at the Haymarket during the run of *The Breath
of Life*, and they agreed in principle on the spot. By now, Maggie was
embroiled in the Harry Potter series, but she managed a holiday in
Venice before joining the shoot in various Cornish coves and beauty
spots (including Helston and St Ives) in September 2003. Raising the
finance proved a problem, even with the stars committed, but a crisis
was averted when the UK Film Council decided at the last minute to
double their investment and facilitate an acceptable financial structure.

The story was updated from 1908 to 1936, which gave it a sense of pre-war idyll in which the washed-up Polish survivor, Andrea, is perhaps a doomy premonition of the persecution and migration to come. The sisters nurse the violinist – played by the fine young German actor, Daniel Brühl – back to rude health, Ursula (Dench) developing quite a crush on him while a beautiful Russian artist, Olga Danilof (Natascha McElhone), on holiday in the vicinity, becomes romantically and professionally involved, too. Olga happens to be the sister of a famous musician, and she kick-starts Andrea's career. Maggie watches beadily from the sidelines ('I know it's not very Christian of me, but I dislike that woman intensely'), as indeed does the village doctor, played with a suppressed carnal yearning for Olga by David Warner, the definitive RSC Hamlet of the mid-1960s. There's a barn dance in the village hall where Andrea gets recklessly drunk, playing wild gypsy music, and a more sedate concert in London where he makes a professional début, playing an extravagant, lyrical romance, proudly attended by his two devoted nurses. Some of the plot points are frankly implausible, but the acting is wonderful, not just from Dench and Smith – one dewy-eyed, deluded and tragically romantic, the other stoical and practical (she's had nearly two decades to recover from losing her loved one in the Great War) – but also from a gallery of British character actors: Warner, turning up like Uncle Vanya with a bunch of flowers, only to see Olga waltzing off with Andrea; the great Freddie Jones as a robust, rubicund fisherman; his son Toby (who 'voiced' Dobby the house elf in the Harry Potter films) as the village postman; Finty Williams (Judi's daughter) as a buxom village girl; and Miriam Margolyes (also doffing her *Harry Potter* wizard's hat) as the sisters' fussing housekeeper.

After the sedate propriety of *Ladies in Lavender* – one American critic, not unreasonably, described it as 'innocuous as a nosegay' while another, Stephen Holden of the *New York Times*, heralded the return of the 'Comfy Movie', 'the cinematic equivalent of a visit from a cherished but increasingly dithery maiden aunt' – Maggie went on the front foot in *Keeping Mum*, described as a 'black comedy' but nothing like as black, or as barbed, as Joe Orton. Again, it's an English idyll of a kind, but there's poison round the edging. For the second time in a film with Maggie, Emilia Fox is pregnant in the opening scenes, travelling on a train with a large trunk which seeps blood; the bodies inside are those of her husband and his mistress, and before long she's packed off to a secure unit for the criminally insane. That's in 1962. Cut to Maggie as Grace Hawkins, forty-three years later, taking a job as the housekeeper of a country vicar, Walter Goodfellow (Rowan Atkinson), and his wife Gloria (Kristin Scott Thomas) in the village of Little Wallop. She clocks in with that same trunk which contains, she says, a lifetime of memories and a few clothes. Little Wallop soon echoes to the sound of some quite big wallops as Grace, hilariously impervious to the immorality of her actions, disposes of a neighbour's troublesome dog, then the neighbour himself, and bashes Patrick Swayze over the head with an iron when she catches him spying on Gloria's naked daughter.

For while she's obviously a lunatic, Grace is a good-hearted catalyst of change for the better: Gloria's marriage is on the rocks, and she's on the brink of an affair with her golf instructor (a self-regarding Swayze, launching a seduction scene in a ludicrous thong), Walter's bound up with God and his parishioners (like the unseen Geoffrey in *Bed Among the Lentils*), and the nymphomaniac daughter's taken up with a spikey-haired Goth ('Oh, is it Halloween?' is Grace's reaction). Gloria's son is a 'good' boy so naturally he's targeted by a gang of bullies, but Grace does for them by cutting the brakes on their bikes before they head off to hunt down their prey. She also reanimates Gloria's marriage by pointing out to Walter that God is best taken with a pinch of salt and a dollop of humour, and that the Book of Solomon is all about sex, liberating his hormonal instincts and undermining, by proxy, his tedious funny-vicar sermon (an Atkinson speciality) at a convention of Anglican clergy.

Niall Johnson rewrote the American author Richard Russo's story to accommodate these (literally) parochial deviations, and Maggie sustains a level of outrageous gusto right to the end. There's no chance of this subsiding into a simple 'mother and daughter' scenario when, after Grace has gone, a pair of drainage men surprise Gloria by turning up to investigate the pond full of algae. That's where the bodies are buried, and the credits roll over an underwater shot of the drainage men down there, too.

Another, far less dangerously mad, character, the village shopkeeper

Mrs Doherty, presented itself to Maggie in Emma Thompson's *Nanny McPhee and the Big Bang* (released in the US and Canada as *Nanny McPhee Returns*). It's a wartime family film, with Maggie Gyllenhaal trying to keep the family, and their initially loathsome wealthy young cousins, in order while guarding the farm from the clutches of a wastrel uncle (Rhys Ifans) who's in effect gambled it away in a casino and is being hunted down for his debts by two wildly eccentric women who resemble refugees from an alternative circus. Everyone's eccentric to a degree, Maggie's oddness established in a scene in the shop where she's forgotten everything (amnesia) and can't find anything (stupidity) because she's filled all her cupboard drawers with loose treacle. The farm's in chaos – kids falling into grunge and poo all the time, wicked uncle trying to get rid of the pigs, an unexploded bomb in the fields – because dad's away at the war, reported missing in action, even though one of the children knows 'in his bones' that he's not dead.

Thompson had based her script on several of Christianna Brand's *Nurse Matilda* books which were illustrated by her cousin, Edward Ardizzone. They had heard the stories about the hideously ugly nursemaid from their grandfather, and it's interesting that Thompson makes no bones about making her grotesquely repellent, with a face full of warts and a straggly single tooth that hangs down over her lower lip like a stalactite.

It all makes for an unusual addition to the literature of children's films, Nanny McPhee an obvious antidote to the saccharine ministrations of Mary Poppins, say, or Deborah Kerr in *The King and I*, and there's no chance of a romantic entanglement. She's got her good heart, her magic bike and powers, and her trusty raven, Edelweiss (and that name conjures another Rodgers and Hammerstein child-minder, Maria in *The Sound of Music*). Maggie's Mrs Doherty is married to Sam Kelly's air-raid warden, a likeable refugee from *Dad's Army*, and there are nice cameos from Ralph Fiennes as an austere 'high up' in the Foreign Office, from Daniel Mays as a flustered chauffeur, comedian Bill Bailey as a neighbouring farmer and Sinead Matthews and Katy Brand as the henchwomen from hell.

It's interesting that Maggie, like Judi Dench, often decides what to do on the basis of who else is doing it. Considerations of the script itself (that can be worked on) as well as the congeniality of the conditions, locations and general set-up come a little later. In *Nanny McPhee* she has far less to do than she has in either *Ladies in Lavender* or *Keeping Mum* but she adds a little sheen of class to the proceedings and confirms her place at the heart of new British comedy films. They may not have been all-time classics, these three, but they gave a lot of pleasure to an awful of people. And, she did sit on a cow pat ('Very comfy!') in the picnic scene.

21

Harry Potter and Downton Abbey

'Cast children you like,' was Richard Eyre's advice to his colleague Simon Curtis when the latter was casting *David Copperfield*. The Dickens television film happened in the first place because of Maggie's desire to play Betsey Trotwood. And both Curtis and Maggie liked Daniel Radcliffe very much indeed. One day on filming at a country house, Curtis recalls, ten-year-old Daniel wandered off on his own down to the fish pond and he thought it a good opportunity to dash after him and have one of those 'arms round shoulder' moments every actor needs now and again. Although he is the son of a literary agent and a casting director, Daniel had no definite intention, at that stage, of becoming a fully fledged professional actor. After *David Copperfield* he planned to resume his schooling. 'Whatever happens,' Curtis told him, 'even if you do become an actor, you will never again play the title role in a famous novel with Maggie Smith in the cast, as well as so many other great British actors.' Years later, amused at his own lack of wizard-like prophetic powers, Curtis says that it was Maggie's advocacy of his talent and likeability with the Potter producers that led to Daniel making the move that changed his life.

Maggie donned her wizard's hat for the Harry Potter movies in the very first of the series without knowing where she would end up. She was an instant hit, but Professor Minerva McGonagall – deputy headmistress of Hogwarts, head of Gryffindor House and Professor of Transfiguration – was never going to be one of her greatest roles, even though her association with the franchise gave it an initial credibility that its own runaway success soon transcended. There was no great story for her character and she herself said (and we could see) that she had less and less to do as the movies went on. She was less essential to the narrative than she was in *Downton Abbey*, which started filming as the Harry Potter series drew to a conclusion. These two mega-mythical blockbusters – boy beats monsters and bad wizards; monster madam rules the roost as queen of the country house castle – have dominated the last fifteen years of her professional life, and it's a testament to her insatiable appetite and professional desire that she's continued doing a whole lot of other decent, perhaps lower profile but more demanding, work in this period while investing both the *Harry Potter* high-jinks and the high-class soap suds of *Downton* with such wit, class and energy.

The appeal of Potter is partly to do with the reappropriation of ancient myths, from Beowulf defeating the dreaded Grendel (and Grendel's mother) in the great hall – not dissimilar to the great hall at Hogwarts – to such other quest adventures as in Arthurian legend, the *Lord of the Rings*, *Oedipus Rex*, *Jason and the Argonauts* and the Famous Five of Enid Blyton. The saga taps every sort of childhood folkloric fantasy, with tragic undertones in the films, inflating them to a new level of cinematic weirdness and, in online quasi-academic circles, bulging critical perspectives. But over the eight films, what stays with you most is the roster of great performances, from Ralph Fiennes's noseless Lord Voldemort (he looks at first like a head-stockinged bank robber with a voice problem, the ultimate baddie who's responsible for wasting Harry's parents), to Robbie Coltrane's screen-filling, good old hirsute Hagrid, Kenneth Branagh's narcissistic, hilarious, scene-stealing Gilderoy Lockhart, David Bradley's embittered, scrawny ancient caretaker, Filch, Helena Bonham Carter's horrid Bellatrix Lestrange, Miranda Richardson's outlandish squeaky journalist, Rita Skeeter, Jim Broadbent's carefully observed Horace Slughorn, a donnish eccentric and semi-retired Potions master, and, especially, Alan Rickman's sinister Snape, stalking the corridors and back passages like Hamlet's ghostly dad, smelling a rat and realising that smell is under his own nose all the time because it can't go away.

Michael Gambon's benign, Irish-inflected head of Hogwarts, Albus Dumbledore, was a turn that developed unexpectedly, and beautifully, after the static, wispy dignity of Richard Harris in the role in the first two films. Bill Nighy was delighted to be cast, albeit belatedly, in *Harry Potter and the Deathly Hallows: Part One*, because that meant he was no longer, he said, the only English actor not appearing at all in the series. He made up for his late entry by scarily filling the screen in his first shot as Rufus Scrimgeour, the new Minister for Magic, reassuring the nation that in dark times his ministry remained strong. There did indeed come a point when the nation of actors divided into those who had been in a Harry Potter film and those who hadn't. And those who had, as in the case of, say, David Ryall (now dead, but a stalwart of the Laurence Olivier years at the National Theatre) or Frances de la Tour (a brilliantly distinctive artist with a long record of appearances at the RSC and the National), would always be tagged as *Harry Potter* actors; no harm done in de la Tour's case as she's a hilarious bonus in the *Goblet of Fire* episode as Olympe Maxime, head of the French girls' school of wizards competing in the tournament, before she gets down and foxy with Hagrid at the Yule Ball.

The fans will have worked out where exactly Maggie's Professor McGonagall fits into all this, and into the evolving friendship of Harry (Daniel Radcliffe), Ron Weasley (Rupert Grint) and their dependable, clever friend Hermione Granger (the entrancing Emma Watson). But from the start she's a benign presence in her glimmering visage and curly high wizard's hat. Her surname is that of the nineteenth-century Scottish bard of low-grade doggerel, William McGonagall, while Minerva, in ancient history, is the Roman goddess of wisdom. It's she who welcomes the new pupils to the four houses of Gryffindor, Slytherin, Hufflepuff and Ravenclaw (enunciating those names with a deadly precision that makes them sound funny), and she who tries continuously to keep Harry from danger and on the straight and narrow. She does a brilliant cat transformation in class in the first film (reminding us where she came from at the start) and orders the pupils back to their dormitories when told of their attempt to steal the Philosopher's Stone. But she's a helpful, transgressing presence, too, mixing her disciplinarian tartness with a softer, more positive side – this trait is repeated in Maggie's portrait of the Downton dowager – for instance, sending Harry his first broom, a privilege not normally open to first-year students, and recommending him as the Seeker on the Gryffindor Quidditch team.

In the second movie, *Harry Potter and the Chamber of Secrets*, she teaches, in a lovely Miss Brodie-like scene, how to change animals into water goblets, and later on warns that Hogwarts will close if a stop is not put (come on, Harry!) to all these Petrification attacks. But with the incursion of Gambon's Dumbledore, she recedes in the third film, Alfonso Cuarón's *Harry Potter and the Prisoner of Azkaban*, to a tame role *in loco parentis*. In a hazily filmed sequence in a pub with veteran Old Vic alumnus Robert Hardy as Cornelius Fudge, the Minister of Magic whom Nighy succeeded, she merely fills in a bit of back story about Sirius Black (Gary Oldman, another supporting star, when allowed to crackle through the fiery furnace), Harry's godfather, who supposedly betrayed his parents. Despite minimising Maggie, this is my own personal favourite of the series, followed by the next one, Mike Newell's *Harry Potter and the Goblet of Fire*.

Both these movies, in different ways, especially the Cuarón film, guard against repetitive production tropes and explore a new language of film and lighting. *Goblet of Fire* is particularly good, too, because the narrative outlines are so classic and clear. Harry – who is a boy, not a piece of meat, Maggie sternly reminds Dumbledore – is embroiled in a tri-wizard tourney of three Herculean tasks: the collection of an egg from a dragon, the underwater rescue of stolen treasure, and the recovery of the trophy in a dangerous maze. En route, Maggie's Professor berates Brendan Gleeson's eye-swivelling colleague, Alastor Moody, expert in Defence Against the Dark Arts, informing him that 'we never use transfiguration as a punishment' after he's transformed the bully-boy Malfoy – the young actor playing this blond and nasty piece of work, Tom Felton, is like an embryonic Christoph Waltz – and announces the Yule Ball on Christmas Eve as a night of well-mannered frivolity. This is the scene where Jonny Greenwood (of Radiohead) and Jarvis Cocker make an appearance, so Minerva's worst fears for the evening are probably justified, though not shared by anyone else; it's a real blast, as opposed to a fictional one.

There's even less for Maggie to do in the fifth film, *Harry Potter and the Order of the Phoenix*, though she does it quite well, even buttoning her lip in longshot during a new-term welcome. But she does spring back to life in a tasty face-off with Imelda Staunton as Dolores Umbridge, the new Defence Against the Dark Arts teacher and, eventually, reforming headmistress, questioning her 'medieval methods' as though she was the new media-unfriendly Mary Whitehouse. It's a key moment in the running, subordinate fear that Hogwarts is going off the rails. And this is the film where Harry, Ron and Hermione edge towards their new pubescent relationships, Harry kissing Cho Chang under the mistletoe – the love of his life, Ron's sister Ginny (the excellent Bonnie Wright), is warming up in the background – while Ron and Hermione form a new kind of submerged alliance that is sweetly approved of by their mutual friend Harry. It's because of this development, and also because of Harry's growing attachment to his dead parents, that Harry can announce confidently to Voldemort – their battle to the death coming into focus – that he, Voldemort, is the weak one: 'You'll never know love or friendship.' There's no answer to that. Ron and Hermione know, too, that they have something Voldemort doesn't have, something worth fighting for. Increasingly, that something is each other.

'Why is it,' Maggie asks in the sixth film, *Harry Potter and the Half-Blood Prince*, 'when something happens, it's always you three?' And she's lost her hat, too. But it's back on later as she mourns Dumbledore, everyone raising their wands as the sky rumbles overhead. Snape has killed Dumbledore with the time-honoured curse of 'Avada Kedavra' (which sounds suspiciously like the panto imprecation in *Aladdin*, 'Abracadabra') and Harry is now in hot pursuit of the Horcruxes. The last two films of the series are increasingly dark and violent, as Voldemort and his band of Death Eaters call the shots, Snape takes over (with a Voldemort agenda) as head of Hogwarts, and Harry goes in pursuit of his Excalibur, the sword of Gryffindor bequeathed to him by Dumbledore. Maggie's not in the first *Deathly Hallows*, but turns up in the second one (at the point of its release, the third-highest grossing film of all time) to bolster Harry's resolution. As all hell breaks loose, she promises to secure the castle and give Harry all the time he needs to do the necessary. She also mobilises the Gothic armed statuary around the place, with a wicked gurgle of 'I've always wanted to use that spell!'

The key twist in the plot is the killing of Snape by Voldemort, which leads to the passing of the Elder Wand (which Snape took hold of when he killed Dumbledore) and of his memories (in a magic vial) to Harry. There follows the devastation and ruin of Hogwarts, with Maggie moving mournfully through the chaos like Clytemnestra in the palace at Thebes. Before the final battle, and the scenes of resistance, she stands alone, hair straggled down her right cheek, not involved. It's one of the weaknesses of the series that she's not given a story, and she fades away completely as Harry faces his near-nemesis. Michael Gambon's Dumbledore, on the other hand, has grown in paternal stature through the films, even after his death, and there's no end to the twists and turns of fate and fortune in the tales of Snape, Hagrid, Sirius – even Harry's mum, who is so touchingly sketched in by Geraldine Somerville. Pottermania has taken over the world, the cinematic equivalent of the (to me) mysteriously long-running wizard musical *Wicked*. In that show, the best song is about defying gravity. In *Harry Potter*, the age-old trials of heroism are re-imagined in a school environment. That's what's so clever, and appealing, about the stories.

And on film we see the growing up and maturation of Harry, Ron and Hermione in a way we simply can't, really, from the books. Daniel Radcliffe remains gawky and geeky throughout, but with a stillness and modesty that make his journey utterly enthralling. His post-Potter portfolio, already considerable, includes London and Broadway stage appearances in Peter Shaffer's *Equus* (with the late Richard Griffiths, his loathsome suburban Uncle Vernon in the movies) as well as such unexpected film diversions as the atmospheric horror movie of *The Woman in Black* (2012) and as the beat poet Allen Ginsberg in *Kill Your Darlings* (2013). Rupert Grint manages to ring all sorts of changes to his fixed expression of horrified disbelief (his mouth is like a large, hyperactive oyster) and would prove himself a fine stage actor, too, in a West End revival of Jez Butterworth's *Mojo* in 2013. And Emma Watson puts down her marker for future stardom in every move she makes, mixing a continuous career with taking an English literature degree, conquering the fashion and modelling world, training to teach meditation and yoga, and launching a United Nations campaign for women's rights and gender equality. I guess after what these kids went through with *Harry Potter* the sky's the limit, and perhaps not even that.

While these films were adapted from novels, what she really liked about *Downton Abbey*, said Maggie, was that it wasn't an adaptation of anything at all and gave her 'proper things to say'. The series launched in 2010 and was an instant hit, touching a television-watching nerve that hadn't been tickled since the 1970s series of *Upstairs, Downstairs*, which attracted 300 million viewers internationally and won numerous Emmy awards in the United States. Whatever pious politicians say about the benefits of a 'classless society' we Brits remain absolutely obsessed with rank and hierarchy. What's so funny about Maggie Smith's dowager of Downton is that it's basically a piss-take; but so good a piss-take that everyone takes it for real, because that's how we'd like to view our decaying aristocracy.

One distinguished director not associated with the show said it was disappointing that Maggie hadn't been stretched, or asked to do anything new, in the role. My response is that she does something unique with Lady Violet, as she did, really, with Lady Bracknell; she presents someone she, personally, probably doesn't much like, while gaining the maximum purchase on what's funny or not very nice about her. Which is why her performance is so compelling. When each scene starts, you really don't know where it's going, because her temperament is always going to get in the way. 'I'm a woman,' she says early on, 'I can be as contrary as I choose,' and she's always chivvying along Penelope Wilton as her neighbour, Isobel Crawley, a few rungs down the ladder, with killer lines like 'Just because you're an old widow, I see no reason why you should eat off a tray.' There's a great moment in the fifth series when she looks down on the party people and acridly remarks, 'They've cast the net wide tonight.' She has a tricky relationship, too, with her manservant Spratt (a lovely picture of muted malevolence by Jeremy Swift), who tries to undermine her with his long-running objection to the new housemaid, Denker, played by Sue Johnston: 'You're testing me, Spratt, and I warn you, testing me does not bring out the best in me.' This conflict comes to the boil, literally, in the surrogate soup episode, when Denker's recipe (produced under cover by Sophia McShera's delightful, self-improving Daisy in the Downton kitchens) is savagely exposed by Spratt as not her own at all, and then brutally discarded; it's a high point of Maggie's performance that she turns on Spratt with such an undiluted venom.

There's always something ticking away with her, you feel, waiting to explode. 'No one wants to kiss a girl in black,' she ominously tells fellow Essex girl Michelle Dockery (she's from Romford) as Lady Mary, the earl's first daughter, in the first episode of the first series, and she's equally frank when Penelope Wilton raises the issue of what to call each other: 'We could start with Mrs Crawley and Lady Grantham,' she suggests, just this side of satirical oleaginousness. But her first big moment of revelation is when she cedes her habitual triumph at the village flower show – she's been recipient of the best bloom in the village prize since time immemorial – to footman Moseley's (Kevin Doyle) elderly father. And her reaction to Lady Mary's bedroom romp with a well-connected Turk is to suggest that, were she to go abroad for a while, 'You can normally find an Italian who isn't too picky.'

There's a constant, clever undermining of her own character, as others perceive her, which makes her fascinating. She also, quite shockingly, sees across class boundaries, with foreboding: 'God knows who the next heir will be,' she says. 'Probably a chimney sweep from Solihull.' The modern world, generally, is a problem, and Maggie's dowager sums up all *Daily Telegraph* leaders on the subject with pin-point and terrifying accuracy: 'give power to these little people' – and she's talking about the transparently decent Scottish doctor (David Robb) who keeps his flame flickering for Isobel Crawley all the way through – 'and it goes to their heads like strong drink'. In the next minute, she's asking if the telephone (a new contraption) is a means of communication or a means of torture, and she's expressing in a phrase the fears of an older generation today about social media. But she also goes quickly from harsh gorgon to melting gorgonzola, skewering the vicar who's dithering over whether or not to marry the village girl to a war hero on his death bed ('I've got a cold,' she says, unexpectedly dabbing her eyes); and it's she who knows that the war may be at an end, but the upheaval's only beginning.

No British actress today has a larger global reach than Maggie Smith, thanks to this programme. By the end of the fifth series in 2014, the show was distributed in 250 territories, including North America and China, and was established as the biggest ever British television drama series export. There's no doubt, either, in anyone's mind, least of all the *Downton Abbey* producers', that Maggie is the star of the show, and for two reasons: she is the biggest name on the marquee (as she has been for most of her career) and is therefore a magnet for other big names, and notably fine young actors, to appear alongside her; and she plays a role which has enormous appeal. She is, says *Downton* writer Julian Fellowes – who writes every episode, sharing the load only briefly, twice, in the first series – touching 'something diurnal about people's values, even though she is old-fashioned in one sense, and she never, or at least very rarely, does anything you could think of as mean. Lady Violet is judgmental and absolutist, but not mean. She usually takes the audience with her in the positions she occupies.'

The position is similar to that of Lady Bracknell, stern but compassionate under the steely façade, utterly representative of the background she comes from – country house aristocracy – and horrified at the very idea of something called 'the weekend'. Shooting parties, house parties, dinner parties and similar social functions are simply not bound, where she comes from, by the concept of professional work, or that of a daily routine having any kind of competitive function. The crisis in the future of the great house is the dramatic springboard of the series, precipitated by the distant disaster of the sinking of the *Titanic* in 1912 on which perished the Earl of Grantham's two nephews, heirs apparent to the estate. The earl (Hugh Bonneville) has three daughters, none of whom can inherit the title or the estate or indeed the fortune of the earl's American wife, Lady Cora (Elizabeth McGovern), whose money has been 'contractually incorporated into the comital entail in perpetuity'; and it's that American money Maggie's Lady Violet wants, in the first place, disengaged from the entail (that is, the succession and the estate).

Her steeliness and disapproval characterise the performance from the get-go, and she makes her presence felt every time the issue arises. And from this stems her hawkish, slyly confrontational attitude towards everything that ensues: the arrival of her cousin Isobel's son, the lawyer Matthew Crawley (Dan Stevens), who might be a suitable match for the earl's first daughter, Lady Mary; the do-gooding conciliatory outlook of Isobel herself – 'I wonder your halo doesn't grow heavy, it must be like wearing a tiara round the clock,' Maggie says with the expression of someone sucking on a lemon; and then, after the catastrophe of Matthew's death in a car crash immediately after the birth of a male heir to Downton (this thunderbolt was unleashed in the Christmas Day special at the end of the third series), her struggle to countenance Lady Mary's confession to a trial by dirty weekend in Liverpool of a prospective replacement husband's suitability within the sheets: 'Can we be confident there will be no unwanted epilogue? ... In my day, a lady was incapable of feeling physical attraction until instructed to by her mama.'

She is the gauge, and sometimes the moral compass, for all melo-dramatic developments: the revelation that the visiting Turkish dip-lomat has died during an undercover bedroom tryst with Lady Mary, as if being in her bedroom at all wasn't bad enough ('No Englishman would dream of dying in someone else's house'); the furore over Lady Edith's (Laura Carmichael) love child, Marigold, being taken in by pig farmers on the estate; or the earl's unwillingness to share a recovered letter from the deceased Matthew stating that he wanted his wife to be his sole heir, not their son ('When you talk like that I'm tempted to call for your nanny and put you to bed without any supper').

Downton Abbey is filmed mostly on location at Highclere Castle in Hampshire, a privately owned Jacobethan edifice with a park designed by Capability Brown that represents the height of baronial splendour and privilege in the late Victorian and Edwardian ages. In 1922, the fifth Earl of Carnavon, Highclere's owner, discovered, with Howard Carter, the tomb of Tutankhamun, often described as the first 'global world media event'. It is neatly ironic, then, that the present Earl and Lady Carnavon, who still, as it were, live above the shop, should preside over another 'global world media event', as the mummies and daddies of Downton are disembalmed among their own hallways, bedrooms, library and reception rooms. The below-stairs kitchen scenes are filmed in Ealing Studios, the village and church scenes in Bampton, in Oxfordshire, while Lady Violet's Wren cottage on the Downton estate is Byfleet Manor in Surrey, built in the seventeenth century on the site of a hunting lodge given by Edward II to his reputed lover Piers Gaveston.

The anxieties over the future of Downton, the slow acceptance by the earl of his daughter's and son-in-law's farming and modernisa-tion plans, the status of the house in the community, the running costs, the adaptability – Highclere Castle really was transformed into a hospital for wounded soldiers on the front in the First World War, just as it is again (for officers only) in the television series – all act as metaphors in the ongoing struggle to preserve these great country houses in the twenty-first century. The earl talks a lot about what he's duty bound to preserve and fight for, but it's his mother, Lady Violet, who represents the innate dignity and values of the tradition, the authentic historical line which weathers the storm of the passing times and changing mores while sticking up for the old ones. Surveying the impromptu convalescent ward of the injured and mutilated she mutters, 'It's like living in a second-rate hotel where the guests keep arriving and nobody seems to leave.'

In 2012, Alan Bennett's play *People* at the National Theatre, directed by Nicholas Hytner, came across not only as a satire on the preservation and survival theme of *Downton Abbey* but as a commentary on the real-life wheezes and money-raising ruses most of the major stately homes and grand country houses now adopt to keep going. Highclere Castle has *Downton Abbey* filming there for six months each year. The bedraggled, cash-strapped female companions in the run-down fifteenth-century Yorkshire house in *People* – and 'Downton Abbey' is in Yorkshire, not far from Ripon and Thirsk – are wooed by representatives of the National Trust and a consortium of camel-coated auctioneers but decide instead that first dibs should be given to a low-rent film company making pornography. Julian Fellowes enjoyed the play but felt it was a little out of date. 'That was much more how it was in the 1960s and 1970s. Now the younger generation have moved in and taken over, transforming the land into home farms, outlets and factories. Families that managed to hold on to their estates are now, on the whole, in much better shape.' Lady Violet, no doubt, would be very glad to hear it, though one can't help feeling that the whole process down the years would send her into the sort of instant apoplexy followed by serene scorn and dutiful acceptance that Maggie manages to convey in almost every other line of the *Downton* script.

Downton Abbey, says chief executive producer Graham Neame, is a precinct drama; except that it's set in a castle, not a police station. By series three, we'd advanced to the spring of 1920 and Maggie's function as a tart, unforgiving observer of the changing social scene was underlined in such remarks as 'an aristocrat with no servants is as much use to the county as a glass hammer'. Time is moving on, and the Irish chauffeur, young Tom Branson (very well played by new star Allen Leech), who had married the earl's second daughter, Sybil, and become 'family', is now dressed, in her eyes, 'as the man from the

Prudential'. Inspecting a new downstairs recruit, she says he resembles a footman in a musical revue. On the other hand, and there's always that with Violet, she remarks on the earl's third daughter Lady Edith's (Laura Carmichael) journey into journalism with a quasi-feminist reflection that a woman's place is in the home, 'but I don't see the harm in having fun before she gets there'.

It's this mixture of what should by rights and tradition happen, and what actually does, that gives the series its sense of flux and development. The marriage of Lady Mary and Matthew Crawley was the plot prompt for the first three series, while Violet charts the changing social landscape (in which she wants no part) by remarking that, as the family has already absorbed a solicitor (Matthew) and a car mechanic (Branson), they might as well put up with a journalist (Lady Edith) in their ranks. Much of this disapproval about the changing world is inflected through social gatherings that, in her view, have gone downhill anyway, judging by the looks she dispatches from a full quiver – occasions such as the ghillies' ball (and she first went to one at the royal residence in Balmoral, where 'all the men were as tight as ticks'), the cricket match, even a routine house party: 'I'm afraid Tom's small talk is very small indeed,' she says. 'Everyone can't be Oscar Wilde.' 'That's a relief!' And that last riposte carries with it a shudder of disapproval of, and dismay over, the whole Oscar Wilde story, not to mention his plays.

The Maggie dowager construct had begun with Julian Fellowes's Oscar-winning script for Robert Altman's *Gosford Park* in 2001. Maggie, Fellowes says, had always been a haunting presence in his life, someone who, as an actor, developed into a strange persona who could flip between emotional states without changing gear. He saw her play Desdemona opposite Olivier as Othello – 'Shakespeare usually bores me to death' – and he's never forgotten that night at the Old Vic. 'I could see then that she could play tragedy one minute, comedy the next, and you do know, as a writer, that she can put "funny" and "moving" together like nobody else.' *Gosford Park*, he says, was a surreal adventure, with me 'determined to put some of my old boys in it – I always write parts for older actors – and Bob was convinced that he couldn't get great actors to do tiny parts for no money unless they could sleep in their own beds at night'. The key compromise was that they would film at Wrotham Park in North London, a Palladian mansion previously used for Kenneth Branagh's *Peter's Friends*, ITV's *Jeeves and Wooster* series with Hugh Laurie and Stephen Fry, various 'costume' movies (*Vanity Fair, Sense and Sensibility, Jane Eyre*) and Simon Cowell's fiftieth birthday party. The finance was minimal, so the 'overnight' budget was contained. And Fellowes's baptism of fire, as he calls it, with Maggie, happened when she asked him a question about the marmalade; she didn't understand what it was about the importance of it. 'So I told her that a great aunt of mine had said that every house that's properly run has its own jams and jellies; if they've run out, it's not properly run.' Instantly, she said, 'I've got it.'

Gosford Park was a flashpoint movie in Maggie's career in so many ways: she was surrounded by a magnificent cast of old colleagues and new friends – Alan Bates, Derek Jacobi, Richard E. Grant, Helen Mirren and Eileen Atkins were all below stairs; Tom Hollander, Kristin Scott Thomas and Charles Dance all languidly above – while playing the grand dame among them and responding instinctively to Altman's casual, improvisatory method. 'No great things happen in my films,' he said, 'except as mistakes—that's where you hit the truth button; this one's not a whodunnit, but a why-was-it-done.' He further, self-deprecatingly, referred to his role as a director at the Oscars ceremony as someone who stands in the same place as the best actors. But he undermined his own low estimation of his role in brilliantly freezing the action, and studying it with a moving camera, as the staff all huddle in corridors, and on the stairs, listening to an Ivor Novello song. The film stops and soars at the same time in a moment of imaginative cinematic statement that you never get, for all its virtues, in *Downton Abbey*. Soon afterwards, we see Maggie putting cucumber slices on her eyes before getting dressed – Michael Gambon's house party host has been murdered at his desk, pushed down on to his own paper knife – and telling Stephen Fry's ostentatiously useless detective that 'we must all pull our weight ... but I won't be any help!'

There's a sense in which *Gosford Park* does the job of *Downton Abbey* in just two hours plus, and it's set in 1932, eight years further on from where we've got to after five series of the TV drama. And, like *Downton*, it frames the period, expresses a view of it, rather than indulging merely in a high-class nostalgia wallow. It also, incidentally, rediscovers, or revisits critically, not only the music of Ivor Novello as played by Jeremy Northam, but also the lyrics (by Edward Moore) of one of his most beautiful compositions, 'The Land of Might-Have-Been', which plays over the final credits: 'Somewhere there's another land / different from this world below, / far more mercifully planned than the cruel place we know. / Innocence and peace are there – / all is good that is desired. / Faces there are always fair; / love grows never old nor tired.' Still, Altman's take on the period is anything but wistful or even sympathetic.

Alan Bates's tricky, comically self-important head butler is an entirely different sort of customer to Jim Carter's cuddly old curmudgeon Carson in *Downton*. *Downton Abbey* is altogether less edgy and unsettling, maybe. It revels in its own historicity. It's a deliberate exercise in evocation, preservation in aspic, because the franchise dictates an eternity for its characters. It is a chilling fact about *Downton Abbey* that whenever Maggie chooses not to do it any more, the show will not be the same. Producer Gareth Neame, whom I spoke to before the sixth series was announced to be the last, never envisaged more than ten years. Fellowes diplomatically says that he does what he's told, reminding me that when *Mad Men* wanted to pull the plug, NBC offered each top member of the cast $2 million to continue. Yet while everyone else in the *Downton* cast is out there beating the drum for it – playing the red-carpet game of film premières, race meetings, fashion shows, celebrity junkets – Maggie is nowhere to be seen, reading a book or just staying home.

Whereas the death of Matthew – Dan Stevens decided he wanted out and made a beeline for Broadway and Hollywood – was a blow to the watching millions, it was, says Fellowes, rocket fuel to the writing and helped develop Lady Mary, for a start, into a more interesting and more tortured character:

Dan was marvellous – I remember how he was so delighted that the actor who dubbed him in Spain was the guy who always does Tom Cruise – and we all missed him, but we could use the loss in a way we couldn't with Maggie. Her all-seeing, all-knowing, deus ex machina character with both a sense of humour and an iron will would be much harder to replace; you can't just wheel someone on to do that.

One of the key clues to Maggie's personality as an actor is nailed by Fellowes:

> She's not without ego, obviously, but she is totally unconcerned about playing a dislikeable character. That of course puts a sharp edge on all her comedy, and is also very liberating. Most actors want to be liked in their characters, all the time. She's not bothered with that at all. And it affects everyone else. Michelle Dockery as Lady Mary has certainly been influenced by this and now simply does not bother about being liked or disliked in her role.

Which is just as well, you feel, as she gets stupider with every passing episode; what she hasn't yet fully mastered is Maggie's knack of retaining your interest while challenging your patience. She has started to become annoying. 'The other thing,' Fellowes says, apropos of her dislike of publicity, 'is that Maggie doesn't talk about what she does because she knows there's always a danger with anything creative that whatever it is you are going to do, you can talk it away; like those people who talk all the time about writing a book you know they never will, because they talked about it too much.'

Gareth Neame concurs, saying that you could not read the first draft of the first *Downton Abbey* script without knowing that Violet was Maggie Smith.

> Although in some ways, *Downton Abbey* is an update of *Gosford Park*, and a continuation of Lady Trentham, I would also say, as an outsider on this process, that there is an extraordinary connection between the way Julian writes and the way Maggie acts. It's quite uncanny. We often find an actor on the show who doesn't quite get the moment, or the nuance, or something, and we redo it, and so on, but in all of Maggie's scenes, dramatic or comic, she always gets it, and finds the rhythm, and the scene always sounds as it should. Actors often regard themselves, rightly, as the custodians of their characters, which sometimes leads them to say, 'I don't want to say that line.' Maggie does not subscribe to that at all. She finds a way. And all she's concerned about is the truth of what she's playing, likeable or not.

And it's not an easy life. You're never at home, always in a ghastly
trailer somewhere. The car comes for you at five in the morning,
and you're home late.

Neame adds that, because she's never stopped as an actor, those ath-
letic muscles you need – remembering lines, repeating scenes, waiting
around for three hours, and then suddenly popping up in front of the
camera again – are all very toned; 'in that respect, her technique for a
person of her age is extraordinary.'

Each episode of *Downton Abbey* (usually of about forty-seven minutes' playing time) is shot in thirteen days, each series over six months
starting in February. 'Maggie's utter professionalism is exemplary,'
says Fellowes, 'she always delivers. In television, it's two scenes in the
morning, three in the afternoon. You can't hang about for hours,
weeks even, waiting for the sun to go down or whatever. It's not a
David Lean movie. So actors like Maggie who are always on the bulls-
eye are very important to you.' On the social front, I ask Fellowes
– than whom you could not really imagine anyone more different
from Maggie – how they get on: 'Very well professionally, but we never
meet to tear a pheasant. Like most people, I'm slightly in awe of her
and respect her need to keep a distance.'

One of my favourite dinner scenes is when the socialist school-
teacher Sarah Bunting (Daisy Lewis) – 'that tin-pot Rosa Luxembourg,'
Lord Grantham calls her – who's going out with the embedded chauffeur, crassly disrupts a dinner party with a left-wing political rant
against the village war memorial. There's utter silence, broken only
by Maggie's acerbic aside to the effect that principles are like prayers,
'noble of course, but awkward at a party'. Manners maketh man, and
no philosophy or conviction can be more improving. 'All this thinking,' she says, brusquely, 'is so overrated. Before 1914, nobody thought
about anything at all!' The thing about Violet, though, is that she does
think, quite a lot, and she's intensely vulnerable to the soft option, in
manners or anything else, when it's presented in the right way. The
meanness is a sort of carapace.

This fragility is further exposed when Lily James as young Lady Rose,
Violet's grand-niece, who is staying at Downton while her parents are
in India, throws a tea party for a group of Russian refugees including,

it transpires, the handsome Prince Kuragin who once danced with the dowager at a ball in the Winter Palace in St Petersburg (when she was travelling through with her husband); the very fan he gave her is among Lady Cora's proudly displayed relics. As Maggie squirms defiantly, then relaxes into a transfusion of romantic memories, Lady Mary exclaims, delightedly, 'Granny has a past!' When Violet and Isobel visit the refugees again, in the crypt of York Cathedral, she confesses that the prince asked her to run away with him. And he presses his case one last time – 'Our last chance!' – when he arrives at her house while she's still breakfasting in bed, which is slightly presumptuous of him. The matter is not resolved until the Christmas Day two-hour special (actually ninety-four minutes of playing time plus loads of adverts) of the fifth series, when the upstairs faction at Downton have removed to Brancaster Castle for a shooting party (the location is Alnwick Castle in Northumberland, one of the exterior locations for *Harry Potter*, but Maggie resists the temptation to whip off her tiara and cast a spell or two). Having flirtatiously reminded Kuragin at a drinks reception that 'the presence of strangers is our only guarantee of good behaviour', she defends her girlishness with a piercing afterthought: 'I will never again receive an immoral proposition from a man – was I wrong to savour it?'

Before that Christmas 2014 edition – what Polly Toynbee in the *Guardian* disapprovingly called 'a two-hour wallow in heritage visions of our feudal yesteryear, as glimpsed through rose-tinted decanters' – the fifth series ended with a broadcast of the eighth episode on Remembrance Sunday, 11 November, in the centenary year of the Great War. Pace Polly, the conflict was the tidal wave event behind the whole of the series so far, and cleverly woven in through clear storylines and close observation without any hint of roseate tinting, starting with the earl pronouncing gravely, as news of the Archduke's assassination arrived at the end of the first series: 'I'm afraid we haven't heard the last about that,' a line that could easily be turned right around in a funny voice but of course wasn't. The second series took us directly into the muck and bullets of trench warfare (again, cleverly linked to the corresponding upheavals at home) while the earl – forcibly restrained from joining up – has to be satisfied with ceremonial dinners and making speeches. Downton was transformed into a convalescent home for officers only ('What next,' wondered Maggie, 'amputations in the dining room, resuscitation in the pantry?'). It was interesting to see, in the summer of 2014, the Royal Shakespeare Company 'do a *Downton*' on an Edwardian-style double-header of *Love's Labour's Lost* and *Much Ado About Nothing*, tragically tinged comedies reinterpreted in pre- and postwar scenarios, with a hospital for soldiers set up in the country house common to both plays.

So, after all the convulsions, and the local fall-out, it was a doubly poignant scene when the business of the cook Mrs Patmore's nephew not being mentioned on the stone war memorial in the village was finally resolved. Other matters, though, remain spectacularly unresolved even after the shooting party: Lady Mary has not remarried, and the truth about the murdered valet remains unrevealed as the guilt shifts uneasily between Brendan Coyle's limping Bates and the demure, lip-trembling confusion of his wife, Anna, whom award-winning Joanne Froggatt has turned into a compelling, long-running whine of looking down in the dumps. Anna's problem of trying to decode, and then deal with, Bates's marital and criminal past, is seriously compounded when she's raped by a visiting valet while the nobs downstairs are being titivated by Dame Kiri Te Kanawa letting rip with 'O mio babbino caro'. 'What a relief,' whispers Violet to Isobel, 'I thought we were in for some dreadful German lieder. You can always rely on Puccini.' 'I prefer Bartók,' counters Isobel. 'You would!' This sequence is one of the best examples of parallel plot writing for dramatic effect. Some of the other ironies are more long range, such as the earl's sporty and secretive dalliance with a housemaid (in whose son he has taken a benevolent, paternal interest) in the second series, which lodges in the background to Lady Cora's less furtive friendship with Richard E. Grant's serpentine art expert in the fifth series; the earl's weakness is biological, Cora's the result only of a man's charm and intellectual flattery.

One of Polly Toynbee's main objections to the show – apart from its way of controlling history by rewriting the past, in her view, rendering class divisions anodyne and cosy – is that there's no sense of real drudgery and pain below stairs, no filth or slopping out of chamber pots, no scrubbing of floors or scouring of grease. She's right to a degree, but this sort of thing would be the province of a completely different project and not one, like this, that is never likely to promote a Marxist view of that history. Within its own compass of interest and expression, there is anyway quite a lot of friction, bad blood and tension between the kitchen and the high table, though most of these problems are mollified by the avuncular Carson before they suppurate into outright hooliganism. No one ever actually pees in the soup, or spits in the blancmange (which must have happened all the time), though there is one very funny scene of menu vengeance, and the targets are the repellent sons of Isobel's suitor, Lord Merton, who don't want their father to remarry beneath him. It's just as easy to see the sense of entitlement that characterises the Grantham clan, and their associates in privilege, as something unfair and nauseating without rubbing our noses in it. The ongoing relationship of adjustment between Tom Branson and the earl is subtly done on both sides of the argument of class background, for instance. And the anti-Semitism experienced by Lord Sinderby is real and unpleasant enough when his son, Rose's fiancé, Atticus Aldridge (charmingly played by Matt Barber), is 'entrapped' in a drunken party on his stag night with some paid whores. It's one of my favourite plot twists when, as Lord Sinderby's mistress makes an unscheduled entrance, the resourceful Rose – who's already been bounced by the family out of an 'unsuitable' affair with a black nightclub singer – saves the situation, and the thunderous Sinderby's bacon (well, his fish balls at least).

The entire series is a minefield of hierarchical faux pas and pretensions, muted bigotry and thinly veiled tolerance, as much upstairs as downstairs, and that ripple effect expresses something deep and true about our island race. One of the most sinister characters is the Iago-like Thomas Barrow of Robert James-Collier, a repressed homosexual who bends colleagues to his nasty will, creates divisions and unhappiness and is himself susceptible to a disastrous gambling and drug culture; some of this is melodramatic, but some of it tells you a lot about the misery and resentment that Polly Toynbee claims is missing.

And then, of course, there are the visiting Americans or, specifically, Shirley MacLaine and George Clooney. The first, playing Lady Cora's mother, Martha Levinson, represents the outlook on the future, as opposed to Violet's attachment to the past. She storms into the third series for the wedding of Matthew to her granddaughter and immediately locks horns with her opposite number, who is quickly aghast: 'She finds our underbelly every time, like a homing pigeon – dreadful!' Violet later describes her as a relentless nonentity, like a runaway train. The visit is all to do with money, of which Martha, the widow of a wealthy dry goods merchant in Cincinnati, has a good deal; but, unfortunately for the Downton clan, who are concerned about Matthew not bringing much of his own to the table, none of it is to be set aside for the sake of the future of the house. The wedding of Matthew and Mary still goes off with all the panoply, even in a small village church, of what the television-watching nation treated, in effect, as the next royal wedding. In an interview at the time, Julian Fellowes discussed the character, and fortunes, of Matthew Crawley who, in Dan Stevens's performance, became Downton's poster boy: 'There's a modern illusion that if you're rich and privileged you're on a glissando of good fortune. Of course, that's nonsense. I do believe that, whoever you are, you must be pro-active, bang the drum a little, make things happen. We must get behind the wheels of our own lives.' Matthew, alas, gets behind the wheel of his own car, too, and ends up dead in a ditch just as his son is born: 'We've done our duty,' he tells Mary. 'Downton is safe.' Whether it is or not is the major outstanding, unresolved issue of the saga. 'My world is coming nearer,' Martha tells Violet, 'and your world – it's slipping further and further away.'

George Clooney doesn't appear in the show proper, but in a ten-minute comedy sketch, broadcast in two snippets on 19 December 2014 during ITV's three-hour charity fund-raiser, *Text Santa* – a total of over £5.5 million was raised for six major charities. This is *Downton Abbey* sending itself up, in costume, and in Highclere Castle, and it is very funny. The future of Downton is still insecure (of course) and Lady Mary has worked out – we're still in 1924 – that they would save £40,000 a year if they started dressing themselves. There's a picture in the newspaper of Maggie's dowager breaking the ski jump world record. And Jeremy Spiven, popping in from another long-running television series, *Mr Selfridge*, delivers some of his famous store's lingerie for Penelope Wilton. Meanwhile, below stairs, there's drinking, gambling and strip poker, and Moseley covered in tattoos.

So, what's going on? Thanks to the intervention of a Christmas Fairy, played by Joanna Lumley, Lord Grantham is given an out-of-body experience (after he's taken the car for a spin, always a dangerous Downton occupation at Christmastime) and, subsequently, a chaotic vision of the future in which he's lost all the money – again – and Lady Cora has married George Clooney. Actually, the new doge of Downton is the Most Honourable George Oceans Gravity, the Marquis of Hollywood, and he is seen embracing and dancing with Lady Cora, big time. Maggie summons Clooney to the chaise longue and enquires if his family has a coat of arms or, indeed, a coat. He declares that he finds her charming and kisses her extended hand. She faints backwards, and falls from the chaise longue to the floor, still holding on to her hat. It's a comedy fall, straight out of revue; and George goes round the room kissing every lady who's interested. They all are, and so is the sadly conflicted Thomas Barrow, trying to land a smackeroo on Cooney's chops himself, while loitering with malicious intent, as usual, in the doorway.

Lord Grantham finds Julian Fellowes sitting at his desk and berates him with the complaint that none of this makes any sense. Nobody cares, says Fellowes. 'But you go mad if anyone eats a grapefruit with the wrong spoon!' To which Fellowes sanguinely replies, 'Ah, yes, but that's cutlery.' This was a sly dig at all the people who have pointed out anachronisms in manners, speech and occasionally what's laid on the tables or served in the kitchens. Downton Abbey, in short, has gone to rack and ruin but, after a group selfie with the marquis, Hugh Bonneville is hit on the head with a silver tray by Joanna Lumley and returns to what he is pleased to think are his senses. All the staff downstairs have clubbed together and saved the day, and the Abbey!

22

Late Flowering of Marigolds around the Van

Even with a dream British cast, as in a fantasy football team, certain of success, there was no expectation that John Madden's delightful *The Best Exotic Marigold Hotel*, which opened as the second series of *Downton Abbey* went to air, and which featured a disparate group of middle-class British white folk in late middle age coming to rest in a rackety hotel 'for the elderly and the beautiful' on the outskirts of Jaipur, would become such a runaway hit. The combined box office take in Britain and Australia was greater than in the US, where it was also a success; that is very unusual, in fact it never happens, says Madden.

The story of people taking a second chance on life, as the first one ebbs away, in challenging and exotic surroundings, clearly hit a nerve with that generation who were staying at home. But there's a double perspective, too, in the story of the young hotel manager, Sonny – played with irresistible cheek and brio by Dev Patel, the star of Danny Boyle's *Slumdog Millionaire* – in his entrepreneurial and amorous adventures, all of which are tagged by his overweening mother. This meant that the children of that older generation, now in their thirties and forties, wanted to see it, too; they were on the brink of middle age themselves and were curious about what might happen to them. 'If one thing was okay about the film,' says Madden modestly, 'it was that it treated old people as if they weren't old people.'

The magnificent seven ex-pats were all clearly defined, not least Maggie's housekeeper, Muriel Donnelly, first seen in a British hospital demanding to see a British doctor (she needs a new hip) before taking the plunge on the flight, declaring that she can't hang about for an operation because she can't plan ahead – 'I don't even buy green bananas.' The others on the plane are Judi Dench's newly widowed housewife, Evelyn Greenslade (who keeps a blog as a narrative throughout the film); Bill Nighy and Penelope Wilton as a bickering married couple, Douglas and Jean Ainslie, who have lost their savings, he keen to escape the prospect of a beige bungalow fitted with a panic button and hand rails, she a bitterly reluctant accomplice in their change of scene; Celia Imrie as Madge Hardcastle, a much-married, rebellious granny, fed up with baby-sitting; Ronald Pickup as her sort of soulmate, Norman Cousins, an ageing Lothario with hopes of pill-enhanced further activity; and Tom Wilkinson as Graham Dashwood, a retired High Court judge who, having lived in India earlier in his life, is returning to find the Indian youth he was forced to abandon as a lover, and does find him, though he's now long-married.

Film critic Philip French was quick to point out that this was no *Jewel in the Crown*, any more than it was an updated *Passage to India*, but the movie still has a sense of the tidal wave impact India makes on new arrivals, even those as apparently thick-skinned as Maggie's Muriel, who declares confidently on the airport bus, when offered a local snack, 'If I can't pronounce it, I don't want to eat it.' Later in the film, she's taken to an ordinary family dinner where she shows to what extent her resistance is crumbling, at the same time revealing that her prickliness, even the incipient racism, is a cover for her own fear and loneliness.

Most of the filming was in the state of Rajasthan, in and around Jaipur, some in Udaipur, with an 80 per cent local crew. The film is based on a novel by Deborah Moggach called *These Foolish Things* and the first script, hers, Madden says, was sent to him some years before the movie was actually made. While the film preserves the spirit and the dynamic of the novel, the end result, written by Ol Parker, is quite a long way distant in significant detail – in the novel, Norman is the prime evacuee, dispatched to India by his medical son-in-law whose cousin, Sonny, has the brainwave of sending older people to a country that doesn't treat its senior citizens like dirt – and more specifically tailored for the actors they knew were going to be in it. Judi Dench was always 'the target' for Evelyn, while Maggie had been involved, and had then withdrawn. Matching the availability of actors you want on a film like this is always tricky, Madden says, and Fox Searchlight, the major source of finance, had 'very strong views' about who those actors would be. It's probable that Ronald Pickup as Norman wasn't one of them, but it's not the least of the film's appeal that so skilled and experienced an actor – with a great career in classical theatre but only a sporadic one in movies – should be cast, and so prominently.

Judi Dench's film career, unlike Maggie's, is quite low key until she starts making the Bond movies as M in *Goldeneye* in 1995 – she made seven, before being killed off in *Skyfall* – and then, in 1996, *Mrs Brown* directed by John Madden. That won her a first Oscar nomination, and she snared the top prize in *Shakespeare in Love* two years later, again directed by Madden, even though she only appeared for eight minutes as Elizabeth I (perhaps she made up for this by playing the fairy queen Titania as a stately Gloriana in *A Midsummer Night's Dream* at the Rose Theatre, Kingston, in 2010). Despite this, Madden says that 'Judi is still convinced she doesn't have the full skill set for movies, doesn't know where all the knobs are. But this is common when people come to film from theatre, and she was over-mystifying the process.' Once initial reassurances have been given, everything falls into place after a few days.

Madden recalls a bizarre day – 'a dame sandwich' – when he drove from Judi's house to Maggie's, pitching the film and, at last, Maggie committed.

We sent her the script two weeks before we went to India and of course she threw it back at me, saying, 'You can't say this sort of stuff – "He can wash all he likes and the colour's not coming out" – you can't say that!' But I explained that that was exactly who Muriel is, and she can, it's how she speaks. She resists tremendously, but that's all to do with perfectionism, and she's never convinced she's achieved anything. She erects a scaffold of scepticism, saying things like, 'Why would anyone want to do this ... or see it?' This isn't to do with any idea of power, or control. It's testing the assumptions, and she needs to feel, as all actors do, that she's standing on firm ground.

At first, for instance, Maggie 'auditioned herself' as Muriel for a couple of days in an Irish accent. But it wasn't working, and she switched to that exaggerated Cockney accent that she hadn't used since *Black Comedy*, when she assumed the voice of Mrs Punnet, the cleaning woman. Muriel, too, was a housekeeper, but for forty years, not a few seconds when fuming half-naked at Derek Jacobi's irate ex-mistress in a black-out.

At the end of the movie, Judi rides off into town on the back of Bill Nighy's moped, while Maggie, having at last got to her feet out of the wheelchair, and having discovered a way of sorting out the chaotic accounts at the hotel, is starting over as the assistant manager. The other stories are mostly resolved, and it certainly feels like the end... unless you're curious enough to want to know what happens next and how the hotel might fare as a reconstituted business; and that's what *The Second Best Exotic Marigold Hotel*, again written by Ol Parker, sets out to tell. Madden had to fight for the title, which works on three fronts (the second movie, the second hotel, and the hint of hand-me-down shoddiness), but of course the American producers wanted to know why anyone would want to see anything that's second best. It's not really a sequel, but a second chapter (it doesn't have the legs to become a franchise), in which Sonny expands his dream, and the hotel, into taking over the Viceroy Club, a possibility suggested when the first hotel has only one room left and two new separate arrivals – Tamsin Greig and Richard Gere – contesting it. Meanwhile, Dench's Evelyn and Nighy's Douglas have joined the Jaipur workforce, Norman is developing his live-in relationship with the impetuous, good-living Carol of Diana Hardcastle, and Imrie's Madge is weighing up the romantic options, which are further disrupted by her first sight of Richard Gere's smooth operator Guy Chambers ('Lord have mercy on my ovaries'). There is a way in which you can look at the first film as Judi's, the second as Maggie's: Muriel spots that moving into the new hotel is a good idea and she wants to help, but at great personal cost to herself.

The follow-up is as enjoyable as the set-up, with the added intricacies of the business operation, a Bollywood-style dance sequence at the wedding party after romantic complications, and a big all-round hear-hear to Bill Nighy's tortuously expressed avowal to Ronald Pickup that the thing about life is that 'it's got so much bloody potential', though he does accompany the sentiment with the start of a frown and a cloudy contemplation of the future. His wife, Penelope Wilton, returns to drive through her divorce; she also wants to revisit the old crumbling ruins – and see how the hotel is doing, as well. It's been doing fine for eight months, though Sonny does take a morning roll call to make sure no one has died in the night. We see this routine with the various parties shouting back 'here' as he calls their names, except for Maggie who, on hearing 'Muriel Donnelly', manages a husky 'what's left'. It's revealing, technically, that she gets that laugh by virtue of being on the move, the others all sedentary. There's a wonderful 'in joke' for the dames, too, when Judi – who's been musing in Muriel's company that, sometimes, the difference between what we want and what we fear is the width of an eyelash – complains to a distracted, half-listening Maggie: 'I don't know why I tell you anything'; 'Because I'm older and wiser'; 'Only nineteen days older'; 'That's the entire lifespan of a wasp.' In real life, the age gap is the other way round, Judi older than Maggie, the difference still nineteen days.

The ending is decidedly downbeat and melancholic, the moped of the first movie joining a moped motorcade climbing up the screen like a swarm of flies. Maggie is alone, raw and wrung out, summing up a life in a sentence with no idea of whether or not history is to blame: 'I spent forty years scrubbing floors and the last months of my life as the co-manager of a hotel halfway round the world.' *Daily Telegraph* critic Robbie Collin said that watching this monologue 'feels like you are watching a Ferrari reach the end of an average speed-check zone and whistle off into the distance'.

In between the two *Marigold* movies, Maggie completed, apart from three more series of *Downton Abbey*, two other films – Dustin Hoffman's *Quartet* and, attracted by the prospect of working with Kevin Kline, and filming in Paris, Israel Horovitz's *My Old Lady* – both of them adapted by the experienced, septuagenarian authors, Ronald Harwood and Horovitz, from their own stage plays, both occupying the limbo, transitional world of old age not so much in decline as in a late flowering.

Maggie had not worked with Harwood since their time in the West End on *Interpreters*, and in the interim he had not only written the play on which *Quartet* is based but also won a best adaptation screenplay Oscar for *The Pianist* (2002) and received a knighthood. He was now, in fact, a grand old man, but he added a commentary in the *Daily Mail* to coincide with the film's opening to the effect that all of his success had come to him later in life and that we, as a society, were not endowing the elderly with appropriate dignity. Around this time there were many instances of maltreatment of residents in care homes around the country, and the deeper-lying problem was that people in such homes, he felt, had no common cause or passion, no shared experiences or relationships. They were just dumped there.

This downside of the ageing experience was addressed with a kind of solution in *Quartet* – not to be confused with Maggie's 1981 Jean Rhys film of the same title – which is set in a home for elderly musicians and singers called Beecham House, so named after the celebrated conductor, Sir Thomas Beecham. It doesn't take Maggie long to note the appropriate irony of a house like this being named after a man whose grandfather made a fortune in laxatives. The film, said Harwood, owed much of its genesis to the composer Verdi and the house in Milan, where he lived and is buried, which he bequeathed as a care home for aged opera singers. Harwood's home in *Quartet* is under financial pressure and threat of closure, but proceeds from an annual gala offer hope. The crux of the film is whether or not the latest arrival, Maggie's famous old soprano Jean Horton, will join her colleagues in a recreation of a renowned recording of the great quartet from Verdi's *Rigoletto* and save the day. The other three old singers – Tom Courtenay's Reggie, one of her former husbands, Pauline Collins's quivering, bright-eyed Cissy, and Billy Connolly's dirty-minded old Wilf – are already there, committed, and raring to go. But she skulks in her room, like Achilles in his tent, becoming angry and upset when the subject is broached over dinner. Her life seems to swim before her as she listens to the old recording, but she's on the warpath again at breakfast, silencing the whole room with another outburst: 'It's not an honour, it's insanity!'

In his début as a director, Hoffman improves on the play in many ways, not least in scenes like that one. On stage, the home seemed vastly underpopulated; here the place heaves with real musicians,

many of them retired orchestral players and singers, one a famous
ENO Rigoletto, John Rawnsley, another the great soprano Gwyneth
Jones ('It's not make-up she needs,' snipes Maggie as show-time
approaches, 'it's a paper-hanging job'), though you do still wonder
why there are never any visitors at any time before the concert begins.
The other great improvement on the stilted, old-fashioned 1999 stage
presentation (led by Donald Sinden in typically fruity, roaring form
as Wilf, with Alec McCowen as Reggie, Angela Thorne as Jean and
Stephanie Cole as Cissy) is the intimacy and heat not just of the
music we hear throughout the film but of the quartet's realignment
and emotional card play. There's a real musicality in the acting: Tom
Courtenay is deliciously nervous and tentative, a twinkling Connolly
controls Wilf's vulgarity just this side of oafishness, and Collins's
Cissy – again, the casting of Collins had been suggested to Hoffman
by Maggie – is just so beautiful, touching, slightly drifting away on
a cloud of dementia; when Maggie assaults Collins in a fury when
she's brought her some peace-token flowers, you can hardly bear to
watch the screen. From this moment, Maggie is in retreat from her
own awkwardness. She digs deep, finds remorse and kindness at last.
When told that Gwyneth Jones will be singing 'Vissi d'arte' from
Tosca, Maggie bridles with 'Over my dead body'. 'Is that a yes?' She's
softened!

The 'performance' of the quartet in the stage play was deeply em-
barrassing. Hoffman's masterstroke in circumventing the real possibility of the sounds not looking as though they are emanating from the
actors' mouths is to wheel away to an exterior shot of the illuminated
house – Hedsor House in Buckinghamshire, yet another handsome
Georgian mansion to feature in Maggie's country house guide – as
the music begins and the credits roll. In this way the music becomes
a powerful underpinning of the romantic resolution of the film, which
is the renewed love affair of Maggie's Jean and Tom Courtenay's Reggie.
She had confessed to him a brief post-marital affair at La Scala and
he'd run away in a self-pitying huff, 'the biggest mistake of my life,'
he now calls it. And he has now heard her whispering to Cissy about
the bust-up, which she has always regretted. Hoffman regards the film
as 'an homage to Maggie', and for her it was the first time of being
directed by a director who was also a movie star – 'so he knows all

the problems!' Not only that, Michael Gambon, Albus Dumbledore in *Harry Potter*, was also on the set, playing the eccentric director of the musical activities and reminding interviewers off it that he had first worked with Maggie in 1964 and Tom Courtenay in 1965. They probably all felt they should have stayed where they were when the film was over.

But bedpans and carpet slippers are not what these late, autumnal films are about. They're much more about adapting to new circumstances and renewing possibilities. In that regard, Maggie met a fellow-traveller in Israel Horovitz, an evergreen off-Broadway playwright, partly living in Paris, whose 2002 play *My Old Lady* became the basis of his first film as a director. And just to keep open the possibility of being accused of being too young for the role, Maggie's character Madame Girard, Mathilde, is ninety-two years old, and in robust health, though she tries to kid Kevin Kline that she's only ninety. The slightly unenticing title instantly evokes Marie Lloyd's music hall song 'My Old Man Said Follow the Van' (and don't dilly-dally on the way . . .). Kline plays Mathias Gold, a twice-divorced, penniless, recovering alcoholic and failed writer who comes to Paris to claim the apartment bequeathed to him by his father. A quick sale will solve his financial problems. But Mathilde is a sitting tenant in what is known in French property law as a *viager* – she stays put until she dies and is paid a monthly fee by the new owner, who takes full possession only when she snuffs it. As she hasn't, and shows no immediate signs of doing so, Mathias is stuck with debts on top of despair. Mathilde advises him not to jump in the Seine as he'd probably fail at that, too, and end up with a bad cold. Instead, she invites him to stay and then startles him further by introducing her daughter, Chloé, in the shape of a hacked-off, resentful Kristin Scott Thomas, who also lives in the apartment. Chloé teaches English – at a school her mother has owned and sold on – and is having an affair with a married man.

It emerges that Mathias's father bought the apartment for reasons not unconnected with his previous association with Mathilde, a woman who counts the great jazzman Django Reinhardt among her lovers. The plot not so much thickens as tangles as Mathias uncovers more family history and becomes closer to the slowly melting Chloé; will they be lovers – or are they in fact brother and sister? The film has an old-fashioned charm, though you can't help feeling that Horovitz has both sacrificed a crucial strand from his own story and missed a trick in deleting the Jewishness from his own play, which included numerous references to the Nazi occupation of Paris and clearly invokes the country's history of anti-Semitism. Still, the performances are superb, and there's a strong atmosphere of the city and in particular the Marais district around Notre Dame. Maggie plays the role simply and straightforwardly, inviting Mathias into her spider's web of routine, memories and mealtimes – dinner is always at 8 p.m., breakfast at 8 a.m.: 'Precision is the key to a long life; precision, and wine' – but is hit by a bombshell when Mathias tells her his mother committed suicide.

This issue of property and rights of occupation is raised again in Alan Bennett's *The Lady in the Van*, Maggie's latest film in which she returns to the role she played on the stage in 1999, all guns blazing as Mary Shepherd, the Camden Town squatter in the playwright's front garden. Over the fifteen years she stayed there, Miss Shepherd managed to requisition Bennett's porch as her bedroom so that the van became her living quarters and study. In his 'Diary' of 2014, published in the *London Review of Books*, Bennett says that his house is currently inhabited by a photographer (he has moved out to an address in nearby Primrose Hill) but that the premises are being used for the film, and he's clearing out all his papers and books which are still there, revisiting more intimately the paintwork and plasterwork, some of which he applied himself when he first moved into 23 Gloucester Crescent in 1968. Filming started in October 2014 and Bennett describes popping round one morning to find them preparing the scene where manure is being delivered and Miss Shepherd (Maggie) comes hurrying over to Alan Bennett (played by an uncannily lookalike Alex Jennings; even Bennett thinks he looks more like him than he himself does) to complain about the stench and to ask him 'to put a notice up to tell passers-by that the smell was from the manure not her'. Bennett reminds the crew that the manure, if fresh, would probably be steaming. They can't find a way of doing this, dry ice and kettles of hot water proving too laborious. 'So in the end we go with it unsteaming,' says a crestfallen author, 'the net result of my intervention being that whereas previously everybody was happy with the shot now thanks to me it doesn't seem quite satisfactory.'

Working again with Bennett and Nicholas Hytner as the director, Maggie is enmeshed in a company with many overlaps of experience: Jim Broadbent and Frances de la Tour were both in the Harry Potter series, and both have theatre 'form' with Bennett (the first in *Kafka's Dick* at the Royal Court, the latter in *The History Boys*, *The Habit of Art* and *People* at the National Theatre); and Bennett is happily reunited with three of his 'History Boys' – James Corden (playing a local greengrocer in Inverness Street market, on the brink of his new career as a late-night chat show host on the American network CBS), Dominic Cooper and Samuel Adamson. It's a crucially significant fact that the film is relatively small-budget, and a co-production between the BBC and TriStar Productions, an offshoot of the much larger Sony Corporation with a track record in off-beat, unusual and 'high-quality' projects. Nicholas Hytner says that the film gives Maggie much wider scope to explore Miss Shepherd's past, to acknowledge her wasted opportunities, to expose her vulnerability – 'as well as giving full rein to all the nightmarish comedy that comes out of thrusting her into the middle of Gloucester Crescent. And of course the fact that she really *is* on Gloucester Crescent makes for a different experience.'

Given that the role is such a transforming one for an actor, I wondered if Maggie's somewhat surprising early career participation in Method-style workshops with Anthony Page and Lindsay Anderson had led to a kind of permanent immersion in the role for as long as she was dealing with it. Hytner's reply gives a final, vivid picture of this great artist at work:

She's still Maggie between takes. But she brings all Miss Shepherd's vast and crazy energy to the set, and works off that. She's fiercely analytical about what she's doing, and she's in tune not just with her own part but with what the world around her must be. If she's given an unconvincing prop, she's on to it immediately. She knew exactly what the interior of the van should look like, scene by scene. She's unusual in having the complete picture in her mind – and, at the same time, unusually trusting of colleagues who have won her respect. She never worried about how she was being shot, always worked with whatever the shot was, always wanted to be told what she'd done had worked, and of course responded with glee to her fellow actors.

The lady in the van was in the can.

In Old Glory and New Celebrity

Maggie was referenced in three major public events in 2013 while continuing at full spate with her work on *Downton Abbey* as well as *My Old Lady* and *The Second Best Exotic Marigold Hotel*. In the previous autumn, her second son Toby Stephens had appeared at the Chichester Minerva Theatre in a revival of *Private Lives*, the play that both marked and summarised the break-up of his parents' relationship thirty years previously. Toby, like his father Robert, played Elyot Chase, opposite his off-stage wife. But Anna-Louise Plowman, a very tall and willowy Canadian, and the mother of his children, played not Amanda (Maggie's role) but Sibyl Chase, Elyot's new nit-picking wife ('Don't quibble, Sibyl!'), while Anna Chancellor steamed around as Elyot's first wife, and true love.

When the production moved into the Gielgud – the former Globe Theatre, renamed for the director of Maggie's *Private Lives* – it came to rest on the same block as his parents had occupied, a few yards along from the Queen's. Toby was reported as saying that Mum had popped along to Chichester to see Jonathan Kent's production and was mildly approving, which means that it must have been absolutely terrific. And so it was, Toby getting along just fine with both of the Annas – Plowman and Chancellor – he was married to. Toby Stephens and Anna Chancellor played their quarrelsome past to perfection, most impressively, in the vivid and immediate present. They were creatures of appalling impulse, driven to displays of irritation and affection on some primal, rhythmic surge of fear and loathing in a Jazz Age junket of manic self-indulgence. More so than his dad, Toby's haughty Elyot was a slightly ridiculous and hearty poseur in a barathea blazer on his balcony, clearly bored with Plowman's vacuous Sibyl, while Chancellor's Amanda, all bony shoulders and beaky bravura, was a jagged and rhapsodic bohemian, far more muscular and free-thinking than Maggie's hilariously stylised mannequin. She could have stepped down from her own wall in the grand Paris apartment, a riot of gold leaf and paintings in the abstract, cubist and colourful style of Juan Gris, Fernand Léger and Picasso; she retaliated to Elyot's elision of the Waldstein sonata and 'Some Day I'll Find You' on the piano with a savage dance routine to her vinyl recording of *The Rite of Spring*.

This same year marked the fiftieth anniversary of the National Theatre, and Maggie featured large. The two parts of the BBC's celebratory television history were called 'The Dream' and 'War and Peace', the second revisiting the industrial action by backstage staff that added considerably to Peter Hall's woes as he took charge of the new building on the South Bank in 1976 in succession to Laurence Olivier and compounded his own bad press by moonlighting on a television arts programme and producing at Glyndebourne, which idyllic opera house he also ended up running. There are two theories about Hall's behaviour in this period. Either, the National could only have survived and thrived, as it did, if run by such an energetic, driven and dedicated obsessive (Olivier, clearly, could not have begun to make the new place work); or, as Olivier's former associates Michael Blakemore and Jonathan Miller believed, the entire operation became an exercise in vanity and self-aggrandisement. This accusation is partly true, as it would be of any great artistic director, but as the film made clear – despite opening with Hall's confession that he always got his own way as an only child as he studied scripts by a swimming pool in his back garden – his vanity was the lever to the wider success, and by the time he left, and was succeeded by Richard Eyre in 1987, the NT was truly up and running.

The brilliant appointment after Hall was not so much that of Eyre as that of Mary Soames, daughter of Winston Churchill, as chairman of the NT board. Appointed by Mrs Thatcher's government, this was clearly intended as a move to close establishment ranks against the 'liberal insurgency' Hall had instigated by putting on plays like Howard Brenton's *The Romans in Britain* (an allegory of the contemporary Irish troubles in the historical occupation of Britain, with some simulated buggering of Druids) and becoming such a fierce spokesman for subsidy in the arts. Instead, Soames and Eyre sort of fell in love with each other, and she in turn left the programming entirely to him, as was right and proper, while concentrating on the first forays into sponsorship and convincing the 'pinkos on the South Bank' she had been appointed to demonstrate that commercial patronage could be as valuable, and innovative, as the state kind.

And so it remains today, with the natural inclination of the National to be radical and subversive where possible, underpinned by city financiers and moguls such as Lloyd Dorfman, sole supplier of the Travelex cheap ticket scheme. This used to be called repressive tolerance in the 1960s, but I think nowadays it's more like disinterested enthusiasm, though it surprised many that, after an extensive refurbishment of the National costing £80 million, to which Lloyd Dorfman had contributed a cool £10 million, the NT's third auditorium, the Cottesloe, reopened in 2014 under a new name, the Dorfman. Such a place is not the kind of corporate-style development Maggie recognised as concomitant with the glorious rough and tumble of her own NT days in the Old Vic; her one appearance in the new building – in Stephen Poliakoff's *Coming in to Land* – never loomed large in her admittedly thin portfolio of undiluted happy memories.

Still, the National under the successive regimes of Hall, Eyre and Hytner has always been in awe of, if not in thrall to, its illustrious early days. The two films, smartly and rather beautifully made by Adam Low, and narrated by Penelope Wilton, contained a mine of treasurable contributions. In 'The Dream', Maggie described the nimbus of untouchability that surrounded Olivier on stage ('I was petrified – I'd come from revue!'); Peter Shaffer claimed, not unreasonably, to have invented total theatre in *The Royal Hunt of the Sun* (in which, said Derek Jacobi, he wore a wig that made him look like Cilla Black); and Jonathan Miller said that literary manager Kenneth Tynan – with his war cry of 'let's not be national, let's be international' – was a necessary irritant and an essential guide to Olivier through the sort of repertoire with which he was unfamiliar.

In the second film, 'War and Peace', Miller poured scorn on the expansionism of the NT – hard to see how that could have been avoided with the new building – and Hall's claim to be head of a 'centre of excellence'; once you start using phrases like that, said Miller, you really are just revelling in your own self-importance.

Maggie has never entered the lists in these disputes, never been seen as belonging to any particular regime, not even necessarily Olivier's, on account of her battle of wills with him in performance. One of the side-narratives in the NT story was the ideological split between two old friends (and close neighbours) from *Beyond the Fringe*, Miller and Alan Bennett. While Miller moaned and faded from the London theatre into the international opera whirligig, Bennett moved centre stage, backing into the limelight: he launched Eyre's regime at the newly dubbed Royal National Theatre with the first ever stage representation of the Queen in *A Question of Attribution* (1987), himself playing the art historian and traitor Anthony Blunt. It was startling to learn that the board – who had wanted the adjectival 'Royal' against the wishes of the artistic executive – tried to stop the play and Eyre threatened to resign if they did. And of course Maggie had been one of the key interpretative artists instrumental in Bennett's rising stock outside the National.

Maggie's association with the latest NT director, Nicholas Hytner (who was succeeded in 2015 by Rufus Norris), was forged in *The Importance of Being Earnest* and cemented in their second West End collaboration on Bennett's *The Lady in the Van*. Bennett's NT work was an inherited thread from Richard Eyre's time there, but just how vibrantly radical Hytner's regime has been was underlined by his opening-season statement of linking *Henry V* (with a black monarch in the field in Iraq, shortly after the invasion) – brilliantly contrasted with Olivier's wartime triumphal oratory in the 1944 film – to Kwame Kwei-Armah's *Elmina's Kitchen*, unforgettably set in a drugs-and-violence milieu on Hackney's Murder Mile. Peter Brook found the experience of visiting Hytner's National, with its buzzing foyers and street theatre and circus acts on the doorstep outside, akin to going to the rough-house Elizabethan Globe through a market-place.

The overall mood at the National Theatre gala on 2 November 2013 was one of unanimity and mutual recognition. At the end, a phalanx of black-garbed stage management personnel marched to the front of the stage to the biggest cheer of the night, the applause led by Maggie Smith, Judi Dench, Michael Gambon, Simon Russell Beale, Alex Jennings and the whole cast of ninety-nine actors. I know I shouldn't have been, but I was at first taken aback, and then overwhelmed, by this show of feeling and deep affection for the place and its unlovely concrete manifestation. At the amazing party in the Lyttelton foyers afterwards, well after midnight, I found myself in a remote corner with Maggie, William Gaskill and two remarkable stalwarts from the Olivier and Hall eras – David Ryall (who did a music-hall turn in the second *Quartet* and died on Christmas Day, 2014) and James Hayes. I found it impossible to order my memories or my thoughts, so, like everyone else, simply indulged in a burble of happiness and good will, with random shafts of remembered production details. I felt as if my whole life in the National – queuing for Old Vic standing places and gallery slips along the Waterloo Road in 1964, attending the opening week of South Bank performances with my friend Helen Dawson, John Osborne's fifth wife, in 1976, and the gala first-night disaster of Goldoni's *Il campiello* – was flashing before me. And there was Maggie, gracious and glowing, at its absolute centre.

In his introductory remarks, before the live television broadcast began at 9 p.m., Nicholas Hytner name-checked his predecessors, drew applause for the seventy-five employees who had received twenty-five-year service medals and even welcomed 'the small band of critics and arts correspondents – who have sometimes been right' (meaning, not often). For one night only, he said, we were comrades. Peter Hall, very ill now, was watching at home on television, but his son Edward (who directed two episodes in the fourth series of *Downton Abbey*) was there, as were several members of the Olivier family led by Joan Plowright, who waved seigneurially from the stalls in dark glasses (her sight now bordering on blindness); her recording of a great speech of Saint Joan was made only a few days previously, a stunning contribution. Ironically, this Shavian Joan said she could do 'without my war horse', even if the NT itself couldn't: *War Horse* has been the biggest money-spinner for the theatre since *Amadeus*, and Joey, the larger than life-size puppet equine manipulated by three handlers, duly cantered to the front of the stage in docile triumph. I was seated between Joan Plowright's carer and Benedict Nightingale, former critic of *The Times*, who reprised a few heavy sighs for old time's sake and encored his touching performance of muddled confusion over not knowing who anyone was or what on earth the plays were. Everyone I know who saw the broadcast said how pungently the extract from

Peter Nichols's *The National Health* came across. And there was the original cast member Charles Kay, forty-four years on, still lying in a hospital bed surrounded by flustered and overworked medical staff.

Key NT playwrights loomed – Tom Stoppard, Michael Frayn (Roger Allam was absolutely riveting in a speech from *Copenhagen*), David Hare – but only Alan Bennett took to the stage himself, hilarious as Hector in the naughty French lesson scene from *The History Boys*, re-united not only with Clive Merrison as the headmaster and Stephen Campbell Moore as Irwin, but also with James Corden, Jamie Parker, Sacha Dhawan and Dominic Cooper in his underpants. The other comedy highlight was Nicholas le Prevost and Penelope Wilton snuggling up in bed with pilchards on toast in Alan Ayckbourn's *Bedroom Farce* and channelling the original performances of Michael Gough and Joan Hickson. Turbo-charged turns there were, from Ralph Fiennes, sensational as a predatory, fearsome Lambert Le Roux in Hare and Brenton's *Pravda*; Judi Dench as Cleopatra and (though I never cared for her performance, or the production, of *A Little Night Music*) sending in Stephen Sondheim's clowns; Helen Mirren, with Tim Pigott-Smith, vengefully post-coital in Eugene O'Neill's *Mourning Becomes Electra*. As a show, overall, the gala was simply breathtaking. The Olivier stage had never looked so good, or changed so smoothly, or been so effectively populated, the linking film and scene changes done to perfection, not a false note, nor any obvious omission. And, all the time, the sense of continuity, passing it on (as Hector says in *The History Boys*), something else coming... I didn't find my taxi home till well into the small hours, but I'd already resolved to stay alive for the next fifty years. Though I wasn't expecting ever to hear again a difficult, intriguing Restoration comedy speech delivered so gracefully, wisely and skilfully as did Maggie discharge Mrs Sullen's serpentine catalogue of celebratory wedlock caveats in *The Beaux' Stratagem*.

Two weeks after the gala, Maggie was back 'on show' at the *Evening Standard* awards ceremony, a black-tie dinner event at the Savoy Hotel instead of the traditional lunchtime party and ceremony at the same address in the early days of January, levered into reluctant participation by her own good manners on being invited to accept yet another gong. I think she feels more keenly than most that awards are really about the people giving them rather than about those who say grace and thank God for what they are about to receive. Richard Eyre once said that the right people often receive awards, but usually for the wrong reasons (though he might have retracted that under his breath as he gleefully accepted the best director award for his gloriously symphonic production of Ibsen's *Ghosts* starring Lesley Manville). Whereas these awards were once a prestigious adjunct of the *Standard*'s arts coverage, they're now an extension of the proprietor's curiously do-gooding and highly developed sense of vanity; but the Russian oligarch Evgeny Lebedev's salvation of the title in a collapsing newspaper market has been as spectacular as his editorial campaigns against poverty, illiteracy and gangland culture. The arts for Lebedev really are an expression of London's metropolitan identity, hence the award-giving podium speeches of the Mayor, Boris Johnson, and Deputy Prime Minister Nick Clegg.

When called to the stage as a guest presenter by host Damian Lewis, basking in the first flush of his *Homeland* fame, the absurdly over-dressed Dame Edna Everage, aka Barry Humphries, kept things simple in giving the oddly named award for comedy to David Walliams for his Bottom in a fairly modest West End revival of *A Midsummer Night's Dream* and by clarifying why Lord Fellowes wasn't to be lured away from writing *Downton Abbey*: 'Maggie needs the work.' Maggie managed a wry, self-deprecatory smile before taking the stage herself to modestly accept the even more oddly titled Theatre Icon award, yet another discretionary gong, one of several that now seem to be an add-on to the core judicial procedure. But how touchingly she accepted it: 'I've done nothing in the theatre to justify this,' she said, astonishingly, adding that the pleasure of appearing in the National Theatre's gala had made her want to do more. But what? she wondered. Did anyone have any suggestions? Would someone write something for her to do on the stage? She recalled that when she received her first *Evening Standard* award as best actress in Peter Shaffer's *The Private Ear* and *The Public Eye* (in 1961, starring with Kenneth Williams), she promised 'to do better next term'. Perhaps this was the moment to reflect that the one thing lacking from her CV in the past twenty years is any sign of classic roles on the stage. What could she have done, what might she still do? The Countess of Roussillon in *All's Well That Ends Well*, perhaps, or Constance in *King John*, Lady Wishfort, that old peeled wall, in *The Way of the World*? One can hardly see her scurrying off to Stratford-upon-Avon, at this late stage, to play, as Eileen Atkins did in 2014, the wonderful and not too demanding title role of the Jacobean tragedy *The Witch of Edmonton*.

A year later she went as high as she could go (barring the Order of Merit) when, on 17 October 2014, she was made a Companion of Honour by the Queen at Windsor Castle, joining her select contemporaries Peter Brook, Judi Dench and Ian McKellen, who were inducted, respectively, in 1998, 2005 and 2007. It's a discretionary honour, numbers limited to sixty-five, including the Queen, but standing today at about four dozen. The Order of Merit, restricted to twenty-four members, includes Tom Stoppard as sole theatrical representative (painters and composers do better among all the Tory grandees), but Maggie should feel reasonably at home on a list of past CHs who include such pioneering forebears as Lilian Baylis (who founded the Old Vic), Annie Horniman (who founded the Abbey in Dublin and the first regional theatre in Great Britain, the Gaiety in Manchester), Sybil Thorndike, Alec Guinness, Paul Scofield and Harold Pinter. Lady Violet, Dowager Countess of Grantham, would never countenance such company, nor approve so rackety and bohemian an upstart mob. But this, insofar as awards mean anything at all, was the pinnacle.

Maggie's older brother, Ian, the surviving twin, is long retired and settled in France, with his wife. Toby and his family live in a newly fashionable *quartier* in the East End of London, and they all spend half the year, at the moment, on location in South Africa, where Toby is filming a cable channel series *Black Sails*, a kind of prequel to *Treasure Island*; Toby plays Captain Flint, and Long John Silver is still a biped. Chris says he 'chugs along', having opened at Hampstead Theatre in March 2015 in a charming revival of Hugh Whitemore's *Stevie*, alongside Zoë Wanamaker as the poet Stevie Smith, author of 'Not Waving but Drowning'.

For Maggie, the recent television fame has been a mixed blessing. When filming in Paris on *My Old Lady* she was mobbed by *Downton Abbey* fans, something that has never happened to her. She found the experience as disturbing as being told, two or three years ago, that there were seven million worldwide tweets on her birthday. She is not new-media, or social-media, savvy and is one of that generation, says Chris, who will have no truck with any of it. She is distressed by the fact that she now feels she cannot go out without being accosted by tourists, but her natural instinct for camouflage is not completely defunct. She still shops in the local Waitrose. One day, she was looking at prawns and a child said, 'I've seen you somewhere before.' His mother said, 'Don't be rude, she's just a lady in the supermarket.' She couldn't have been more pleased. A lady in the supermarket. A lady in the van. A lady in lavender.

EPILOGUE

My quest – 'pursuit' sounds far too dramatic and slightly perverse – for Maggie Smith began in November 1990, in preparation for an earlier edition of this book, when she was coming towards the end of the Broadway run of Peter Shaffer's *Lettice and Lovage* at the Ethel Barrymore Theatre. I wrote to her, saying that I was coming to New York and asking if, although we had never met, she could spare me a few minutes to discuss something that had arisen, the matter of a biography. There was none. I had been asked by a publisher to see if I could supply one. I added that I had been raised in the place of her birth, Ilford in Essex, before removing, like her, but as an undergraduate, to the more amenable environment of Oxford, though why I should have thought that would have any bearing on the matter I've no idea.

When I arrived in New York on a Wednesday, I checked into the Algonquin Hotel and, on an impulse, before I had even unpacked, wrote her a note announcing my arrival and apologising for pestering her. I remembered to add that if by any chance she had not received my first letter this second communication would appear both puzzling and impertinent. I walked three or four blocks across the theatre district to the Ethel Barrymore and left the note at the stage door. I returned to the Algonquin and was deep in that strange process of acclimatisation to a new hotel bedroom, slowly unpacking my suitcase, when the telephone rang. Alarmingly, it was Maggie Smith. She must have literally just come off the stage. My heart was in my mouth, my underpants in my hands.

I stumbled out something grotesquely crass about writing a book. 'Ooh, how absolutely ghastly. How absolutely awful. I can't think of anything worse.' The voice twanged and gurgled, rich with the strain of a demanding performance. I thought of a glass of madeira. 'Ooh, but there's nothing to write about.' Your career. 'But I haven't done anything. I don't know what it is I do.' I was flummoxed. I said something to the effect that she must be relieved she was coming to the end of an exhausting run, during which she had suffered the aftermath of a painful back injury and other assorted physical misfortunes. 'Six hundred performances is quite enough. I've told them I can't do the American tour next year. Vanessa's going to do it.' Vanessa? 'Vanessa Redgrave.' Of course; as opposed to all the other Vanessas, dumbo. (Vanessa never did do the tour of *Lettice and Lovage*; she fell out with the management after remarks she made about America's involvement in the Gulf War of 1991.) The conversation suddenly, and still alarmingly, became relaxed. 'How do you like the Algonquin?' Very much, I said, except that I didn't think they had dusted much since the last time I was here. 'Yes, Michael Blakemore [the director of *Lettice and Lovage*] said something like that.' How is your hotel? 'Ooh, it's just like a glorified bed and breakfast really.' It wasn't. 'I can't wait to get home.' Was there any chance I could call backstage to see her between the shows on Saturday? 'No, I can't do that. Ring me on Friday morning at about eleven o'clock.' Fine, but I had a ticket for the Saturday matinée. 'Ooh, no, you mustn't do that. It'll be awful at the matinée. Well, do come back. I only said not to because Joe Mankiewicz's maid – do you know Joe?' I didn't, but knew that this distinguished Hollywood writer and director, creator of the best backstage movie ever, *All About Eve*, had directed her with Rex Harrison in the 1967 remake of Ben Jonson's *Volpone*, *The Honeypot*, and was now very, very old. '. . . I spend the weekends here with Joe and his wife – their maid, Dolores, is coming to see the matinée. Do you mind sharing with a Spanish maid?'

Almost capriciously, she then added, 'But ring me anyway on Friday morning. I'd better go now because they're all giving me funny looks here.' I put down the receiver, intrigued by the pictorial notion of Maggie Smith in her dressing room surrounded by a seething mass of disgruntled backstage staff pulling faces at her, wanting to go home. I rang at the appointed time on Friday morning and she answered instantly. If anything, she sounded even huskier than on Wednesday night. The glass of madeira would no longer suffice. It had to be port, or a fine old cognac. She had been thinking about my suggestion. 'I really don't think it's a very good idea. I still can't think of anything worse. But please come back after the matinée.' I was now convinced she would have nothing to do with me, but the more she protested, the more I was determined not to be too downcast. We had another, though necessarily shorter, fairly buoyant telephone conversation. As its temperature rose, I emitted several involuntary cackles of laughter; as I was sitting in a crowded newspaper office at the time, it was my turn to feel funny looks in the back of my neck. I now realised that you could not have a half-cocked, tentative conversation with Maggie Smith. It was all or nothing: usually, nothing.

I anticipated the matinée with relish. These were the best sort of days in New York: bright and sharp, sunny and cold. But on Saturday the weather turned foul and the heavens opened. The Ethel Barrymore was heaving with damp mink and fur. A well-heeled, vulgar quartet from Texas pondered the forthcoming entertainment in the bar, one of the men drooling over a semi-clad model in the *Playbill* pro- gramme's advertising pages: 'Too darned bad she's not in the show,' he cracked, pleased with himself. The performance was a riot, better than in London. I went backstage as bidden, but when I was ushered into the dressing room, there was no sign of Dolores the Spanish maid. Dame Maggie was wrapped in a grey dressing gown, shaking out her luxuriant ginger mane, having given it a quick wash, and sipping half a glass of something red. Perhaps, after all, it was madeira. I stood about awkwardly, blurting out a few comments which she received graciously, curtsying deeply in a very Lettice-like mock-Elizabethan style, one hand clasping both woolly lapels over her chest. She was ticking off each performance and dying to get home. I said she was certain to need a rest before the evening show as I backed towards the door. This tiny, frail and bird-like creature had to be popped back in its cage for a couple of hours. Had she thought any further on the book? She really did think it was a very bad idea.

Before she finally closed the door on me, should I not speak to her husband, the film and theatre writer Beverley Cross? She immediately wrote out the home telephone number in Sussex and told me to ring him. She said that she would 'warn' him of my approaches. That was it, as far as she was concerned and probably as far as I was concerned, too. On returning to London, I immediately rang Beverley Cross. He was keen that I should proceed. He confirmed the existence of the archive kept by Maggie's father in Oxford and promised that it would be made available to me. Other proposed studies of the actress – a *New Yorker* profile by Kenneth Tynan and authorised books by critics Penelope Gilliatt (one of John Osborne's wives) and B. A. Young (my mentor and first arts editor on the *Financial Times*) – had all come to naught. It was high time a book was written, he said, and both he and Dame Maggie would extend their cooperation to me as far as was reasonably possible.

A few months later, I accompanied Maggie and Beverley to Hamburg, where she was to receive one of Europe's most prestigious awards, the Shakespeare Prize. At dinner, on the night before the ceremony, she disconsolately pushed a piece of fish around her plate and sipped modestly from a glass of mineral water. She was tense almost to snapping point: 'You get involved in these things and wonder why on earth you did.' At the adjoining table, a couple were eating their way doggedly through one course after another as if their lives depended on it. Maggie shot them an acid glance and wondered, sotto voce, if they, too, had won a prize for something.

She opened her address in Hamburg with an almost stuttering disclaimer: 'It might be a relief to us all today if I were to be as brief as the evil Don John in *Much Ado About Nothing* . . . "I thank you. I am not of many words, but I thank you!" ' We were sitting in the great Gothic town hall, the Hamburg Rathaus ('Where the rats come from,' Maggie had whispered), bright May sunshine streaming through the windows. Suddenly, with that opening shot, it appeared to be all over. But Maggie, simply dressed yet again in black with a single rope of pearls, pushed her reading glasses further up her nose and glided smoothly into a résumé of her life among the Shakespearean comic heroines and 'any number of queens'. After the academic encomium intoned by a local professor, Maggie's aperçus had the merit of both practicality and concision. Beatrice, she said, was 'a very pleasant evening' because the lady doesn't have all that much to say and most of it is in prose: 'The secret is that everybody else is always talking about her.' Rosalind, on the other hand, had a very great deal to say, and to do. 'Where a sentence will serve for Beatrice, Rosalind prefers paragraphs. If Beatrice has something of Noël Coward's Amanda, then Rosalind shares Mr Stoppard's or Mr Shaffer's enthusiasm for verbosity.'

This identification of the witty, independent heroine in English drama from Shakespeare, through the Restoration to modern theatre, was as much a point worth making as a revelation of her character. As teasingly playful as Beatrice, as wilful, androgynous and enigmatic as Viola – 'I am all the daughters of my father's house; and all the brothers, too' – Maggie's comic, romantic stage persona embraces the trenchant, dignified wit of Millamant and the melting, resourceful passion of Rosalind. She pinned us to our seats with Millamant's great proviso speech – 'These articles subscribed, if I continue to endure you a little longer, I may by degrees dwindle into a wife' – and moved us to tears with Rosalind's adieu: 'If I were a woman, I would kiss as many of you as had beards that pleased me, complexions that liked me and breaths that I defied not. And I am sure as many as have good beards, or good faces, or sweet breaths, will for my kind offer, when I make curtsy, bid me farewell.'

We met up again soon afterwards in Sussex. She had just given up smoking, for the second time in her life. I asked if there was any chance of her going back to the National Theatre: 'I just wish the building wasn't such an unfriendly place to work.' No more Cleopatras? 'Oooh, no. I'm glad I had a go.' Do you wish someone would write a new play for you? 'Yes, but I never know what to wear in new plays. I spend most of my time on stage and on film, come to that, dressed in costumes, I'm baffled by what to wear in modern dress on stage.' You have done so many different things in your career. 'That's because people didn't know where to put me. They thought of me in revue, but I did want to act. And the age thing was easier then. Nobody minded if you were too old for a part. I'm too old for most things now.'

As we leave for lunch in a nearby pub, we spy a man we take to be acting suspiciously standing by the next field. A mile or so down the road, the general feeling is that we should return. As we re-enter the drive, the man is still standing by the field, looking at another man who is shooting at birds. 'Won't he think we're a bit odd, going out and coming back straight away?' asks Maggie. Undaunted, Beverley strides manfully over to the potential felon, hands on his hips, putting on his best jolly country manner. He comes back to the car, appeased. 'Got the password,' he says, relieved and beaming. The two chaps have been given permission by a neighbouring farmer they all know to feel free in the field and take a few pot shots. 'Well, he definitely must have thought we were a bit odd,' concludes Maggie, finally.

Two hours later, driving me back to the station, Maggie acknowledges for the first time in my hearing that I am writing this book and thanks me for bothering, as though it were the most unbearable drudgery. I say that all her friends and colleagues have taken pleasure in talking about her. Silence. 'I can't imagine what anyone would say. I wouldn't say anything.' She drives very fast and very securely. I remember that she once berated Simon Callow for not driving. How could he not drive? she wanted to know. Having a car was like having an extra cupboard. Another place to hide. She is playing a soothing baroque motet as we speed through the leafy lanes.

When the BFI asked me to curate a season of Maggie's films in December 2014 to celebrate her eightieth birthday, they asked if they could sell the biography in their shop. I said it was out of print and out of date, and this was the spur to revisit, rewrite and replenish the original. In the intervening years I'd met Maggie briefly on several occasions, but not for much of a chat, or another lunch. But when she was rehearsing *The Lady from Dubuque* in a church hall on the Tottenham Court Road in 2007, the *Evening Standard* asked if I could arrange an interview with her. When reluctantly dragged into such parlous and (for her) unwanted situations, she's resigned to operate on the principle that the devil you know is preferable to the devil you don't. I booked a table in Heal's, right across the road from the church.

Once inside the department store, we manage somehow to get lost in the bedding department. 'You have booked a table, haven't you,' she mutters loudly, 'or is it a room?' We pass through several other departments – glassware, kitchen utensils, and so on. 'Where exactly are we going?' she cries, her voice rising, and my sense of direction (non-existent) shrivelling. And why Heal's, anyway? Maggie had not been in the place for decades but suddenly recognises an old wooden staircase as we try our luck round another corner. 'Oh, I remember that,' she exclaims. 'I had no idea about the rest of it, though. Are you sure there's a restaurant here?' After asking ten members of staff for contradictory directions, we find the restaurant and hide in a corner. Maggie orders a glass of water. That's it. I go mad and call up a coffee. The dame does not do interviews, on the whole, and she certainly doesn't do them to have fun at a lunch table.

As usual, she is fraught with anxiety. And she has been ill with 'flu. 'I think they all think I'm going to die. And I might. I'm very scared about the stage at the moment. I've always been scared, actually, but I didn't know I'd be this scared. Perhaps it will be all right on the night. Well, it won't be on the first night, but afterwards, perhaps, I don't know . . .' I think it's being so cheerful that keeps her going. She trails off, suddenly noticing my tiny Olympus tape-recorder. 'What's that?' she snaps, recoiling into her scarf and coat as if surprised by a slug on a lettuce leaf. The horror of talking about herself is fully alive. She reacts sharply to my reporting of Edward Albee's view that there is no such thing as naturalism in the theatre, merely degrees of stylisation. 'Did he really say that? How odd. I suppose he's right, only you try and make everything natural, like Gerald du Maurier.' Du Maurier (father of Daphne) was the godfather of light comic acting, school of Wilfrid Hyde-White and Rex Harrison. We're not really allowed to talk about dead people any more in arts journalism, I remind her. 'Aren't we? Well, I'm sorry, then I've got no conversation. I do find I'm talking about the dead most of the time.'

Another low moan of despair. She perks up at the mention of Helen Mirren winning an Oscar for her performance as the Queen in *The Queen*. 'Yes, isn't that great? Her and Jude [Judi Dench] really have cornered the market in queens, haven't they? I only get the odd duchess, and a wizard, of course.' This is uttered not with acid so much as a splash of vinegar. Which of the Harry Potter films does she like most? More low moaning. 'Is it five, now? I seem to be doing less and less. I liked the first one when I changed from a cat.' That's the end of the 'in-depth' on that subject.

She's more forthcoming on Albee: 'He gives you a wonderful text, but he also gives you explicit stage directions. You might just have a name, but you know about this woman by the end of the play. His plays are fiendish to learn, but they do play like music, it's sort of like a roundelay.' As we leave the restaurant to get lost in Heal's once again, she dares me not to leave a tip on the silver salver. The tip I leave is larger than the bill for the two meagre drinks. 'Isn't that Ian Richardson?' she whispers, identifying a solo diner at a far table as the great voice of middle-period RSC and the television star of *House of Cards*. 'He's dead,' I say. 'Oh well, we can't talk about him then.' 'And anyway,' I persist, 'he looks more like Sydney Tafler...' 'Don't you start,' she says, pushing me unceremoniously towards the exit. And she skips between cars and buses back to the rehearsal hall.

ACKNOWLEDGEMENTS

It strikes me that, from the moment I first saw her on the Old Vic stage in 1964, Maggie's career has been rushing through my life like a sparkling river, and it was thanks in the first place to Beverley Cross, who provided information, contacts and encouragement, and to Nathaniel Smith, that I was able to get going. Ian Smith, Maggie's brother in New York, now retired and living in France, was crucially informative, as were Maggie's sons with Robert Stephens, Chris Larkin and Toby Stephens.

Documents, recordings and viewing facilities were loaned or provided by the BBC, the Stratford Festival, Ontario, Julie Pearce and Marcus Prince at the British Film Institute, Alastair Macaulay, the Oxford High School for Girls, Kathleen Tynan, Sandy Wilson and B. A. Young. I acknowledge the *Evening Standard* for permission to reproduce part of an interview published in 2007.

I am grateful to David Pelizzari of the Citadel Theatre in Edmonton, Alberta, who conducted an interview on my behalf with Robin Phillips, and to Robin Phillips himself. The following spared time to be interviewed: Edward Albee, Dorothy Bartholomew, Brian Bedford, Alan Bennett, Michael Blakemore, Diana Boddington, Margaret Bonfiglioli (née Slater), Ronald Bryden, Simon Callow, Jack Clayton, Sir Michael Codron, Bridget Davidson (née Senior), Dame Judi Dench, Zoë Dominic, Christopher Downes, Patrick Dromgoole, Veryl and Peter Dunlop, Lord Fellowes, Angela Fox, William Gaskill, Sir Peter Hall, Sir Derek Jacobi, Bernard Levin, Kenneth Lintott, Alec McCowen, Janet Macklam, John Madden, Joseph Maher, Miriam Margolyes, Patricia Millbourn, John Moffatt, Richard Monette, Gareth Neame, Riggs O'Hara, Anthony Page, Michael Palin, Nicholas Pennell, Stephen Poliakoff, Anthony Powell, Lynn Redgrave, Kate Reid, Sir Peter Shaffer,

Ned Sherrin, Shân Smith, Robert Stephens, Christine Stotesbury (née Miller), Judith Stott, Margaret Tyzack, Isabel van Beers and Peter Wood.

I enjoyed correspondence and telephone conversations with John Beary, Sir Michael Caine, Ruth Clarke (née Ayers), Simon Curtis, Robert Fox, Bamber Gascoigne, Jeremy Geidt, Alice Ghostley, Sir John Gielgud, Shirley Halstead (née Jenkins), Sir Nicholas Hytner, Verena Johnston (née Hunt), Lady Olivier and Sir Tom Stoppard. Special thanks are due to Paul Lyon-Maris, Maggie's agent; Caradoc King, Mildred Yuan and Millie Hoskins at United Agents; Alan Samson, Simon Wright and the team at Orion; and my wife, Sue Hyman.

INDEX

For literary discussion, author insight,
book news, exclusive content,
recipes and giveaways, visit the
Weidenfeld & Nicolson blog and
sign up for the newsletter at:

www.wnblog.co.uk

For breaking news, reviews and exclusive competitions
Follow us @wnbooks